THE VOICE
AND
VOICE THERAPY

Third Edition

DANIEL R. BOONE
The University of Arizona

PRENTICE-HALL, INC., Englewood Cliffs, N.J. 07632

Library of Congress Cataloging in Publication Data

BOONE, DANIEL R.
   The voice and voice therapy.

   Bibliography
   Includes index.
   1. Voice—Care and hygiene. 2. Larynx—Diseases.
   3. Speech therapy. I. Title. [DNLM: 1. Speech therapy.
2. Voice training. 3. Voice. WV 500 B724v]
RF540.B66–1983   616.85′5   82–13139
ISBN 0–13–943118–7

Editorial/production supervision by Joyce Turner
Cover design by Jeannette Jacobs
Manufacturing buyer: Ron Chapman

© 1983, 1977, 1971 by Prentice-Hall, Inc.,
Englewood Cliffs, N.J. 07632

Printed in the United States of America
10 9 8 7 6

ISBN 0-13-943118-7

Prentice-Hall International, Inc., *London*
Prentice-Hall of Australia Pty. Limited, *Sydney*
Editora Prentice-Hall do Brazil, Ltda, *Rio de Janeiro*
Prentice-Hall Canada Inc., *Toronto*
Prentice-Hall of India Private Limited, *New Delhi*
Prentice-Hall of Japan, Inc., *Tokyo*
Prentice-Hall of Southeast Asia Pte. Ltd., *Singapore*
Whitehall Books Limited, *Wellington, New Zealand*

To Mary and our four

Contents

Preface

In this third edition of *The Voice and Voice Therapy,* continued focus is given to problems of phonation as they may relate to vocal abuse and misuse. The majority of voice patients who want to improve their voices must learn to use voice in an easy, optimal manner. It is hoped that this book will provide clinical guidelines to follow while helping the patient develop better use of the larynx with a resulting better sounding and more efficient voice. As stated in the preface to the second edition of *The Voice and Voice Therapy,* "sometimes medical-surgical management is required. Sometimes voice therapy is needed. Sometimes both are required."

The success of the first two editions of this text dictates that we again follow the same basic format. We have attempted to update our literature, change some old ideas, and perhaps say things more clearly, which required a major rewrite of the previous text. In Chapter 1, we continue to present the overview of the need to use the larynx optimally, avoiding the excesses of effort and strain. In response to the urgings of teachers who have used the text, we have expanded Chapter 2 to include more information on the normal processes of respiration, phonation, and resonance. However, by design the text is a clinical book, requiring that the student of voice disorders have additional lectures and readings specific to the normal aspects of pulmonary function, laryngeal anatomy and physiology, and upper airway structure and function. Chapter 3 continues to describe various vocal pathologies and their management with an expanded section on the voicing parameters of dysarthria. An increased description of instrumentation in evaluation and of evaluation forms and rating scales may be found in the current Chapter 4. Chapter 5 continues to be the most important chapter of the book, presenting twenty-five facilitating approaches that the clinician can use with the patient in the search for the most easily produced voice. For each facilitating approach presented, a rationale is given for its use as well as the specific procedures of application. Special problems, such as voices of the deaf, dysarthria, or spastic dysphonia, are considered in Chapter 6; in this chapter we also present a twelve-step vocal hygiene program that can aid any of us, including our patients, in developing optimal utilization of voice. Many problems of voice related to faulty resonance are presented in Chapter 7 with specific management strategies, including medical-surgical-dental intervention as well as the procedural steps of voice therapy. No area of clinical treatment has changed more than the overall management of the patient with laryngeal cancer, as reflected in the new Chapter 8 in this third edition.

It is my hope that this new edition of *The Voice and Voice Therapy* continues to offer a message of hope for clinician and voice patient alike. For most voice problems can be improved. We must individualize our therapy approaches to match the understanding and competency levels of the individual patient, using our instrumentation, evaluation data, and therapy methodologies to help the patient in his or her quest for a more efficient, better-sounding voice. The quality of the patient's vocal response in effect dictates what we do in voice therapy.

My thanks is given to the hundreds of friends, colleagues, and students who have freely given to me their views on my views. I am grateful for the wonderful professional setting in which I work at the University of Arizona, a setting of inquiry, scholarship, daring, freedom, and camaraderie. Once again this edition would not have been possible without Mary's understanding, Barbara's typing, my tennis buddies, and the pure luck I have had specific to having a few great friends, good health, and often being at the right place to feel needed.

Remember, when we begin to study voice therapy and begin actual voice remediation with our patients, there is no clinical group in speech-language pathology more responsive to what we have to offer. Our patients indeed "make us look good."

Daniel R. Boone
Tucson, Arizona

1

The Voice and Voice Therapy

This book is about voice disorders, their management and habilitation. Voice therapy has been found to be effective for correcting functional voice disorders, particularly voice problems related to vocal hyperfunction (excessive effort and force while speaking and voicing). Organic problems of voice generally require the medical-surgical intervention of the physician as well as symptomatic voice therapy by the speech-language pathologist. The focus of symptomatic voice therapy for both functional and organic voice problems is searching with the patient for the best voice possible with the least amount of patient effort.

Every now and then we hear a beautiful voice. About as often, we hear a poor sounding one. Most of the time, we hear average, normal voices around us, voices that continually change according to the status and role of the speaker, the demands of the listener, and the noise in the speaker-listener background. One component of normal voice is adequacy of pitch. That is, the speaker's voice has a pitch level that sounds like the voices of his or her peers. The loudness of the voice should also be appropriate for the situation. The quality of the normal voice sounds pleasant, free of strain, and similar to the voices around us. The resonance of the normal voice is free of excesses of nasal resonance or inappropriate oral resonance. We shall discuss the aspects of pitch, loudness, quality, and resonance of the normal voice in Chapter 2. The voice when singing or speaking demands a combination and interaction of the mechanisms of respiration, phonation, resonance, and speech articulation. The best speakers and singers are often those persons who by natural gift or training, or by a fortunate blend of both, have mastered the art of using optimally these vocal mechanisms.

The focus of this book is on voice disorders and what can be done about them. Most voice disorders can be corrected. Despite the relative ease in correcting voice disorders, whether they show themselves in disorders of phonation or alterations in resonance, the prevalence of voice problems makes them one of the largest handicapping conditions among communication disorders. For example, a recent national incidence study among school-age children found the prevalence of voice disorders to be at 3 percent (Hull and others, 1976). In a study of 32,500 children in the schools, Senturia and Wilson (1968) found that 1,962 (or about 6 percent) of them had voice deviations; it should be mentioned that their definition of voice deviation included disorders in both phonation and in resonance. The incidence of voice disorders varies according to the criteria used for determining whether the voice is normal or sounds pathological. If prevalence of voice disorders is based solely on phonation (frequency-intensity-quality) impairment, the prevalence will be lower than when resonance deviation is also included. Boone wrote in 1980 that for phonation disorders the "prevalence is probably in the neighborhood of three percent. If resonance-based voice disorders are included then we would expect that a reasonable figure might be a percentage point or two higher" (1980c, p. 313).

The patient with a voice disorder may use his or her vocal mechanisms in a faulty manner, often using too much effort or force. Sometimes, however, the disordered voice is a symptom of a physical disorder. Let us consider separately functional disorders of voice and organic problems that can produce voice disorders.

FUNCTIONAL VOICE DISORDERS

The majority of phonation disorders are related to faulty use of the larynx, known as *functional voice disorders*. A common problem is vocal abuse, which involves using the laryngeal mechanisms excessively for such behaviors as continual throat clearing, yelling, or crying. Examples of vocal misuse include excessive voicing at inappropriate frequencies (low or high pitch), loud intensity levels, or initiating voice with hard glottal attack. These types of excessive vocal efforts were first described in 1943 by Froeschels as hyperfunctional voice behaviors characterized by too much muscular force in the wrong places. In the many voice problems related to vocal hyperfunction, the patient over a period of time may use the vocal mechanisms (respiration, phonation, resonation) in a forceful, tense manner, eventually producing some form of dysphonia (phonation problem). This dysphonia may be wholly related to functional misuse with no structural change of the mechanism, or perhaps after prolonged functional misuse, actual tissue change will occur with the patient developing vocal fold thickening, or vocal nodules, or polyps.

An example of a hyperfunctional voice disorder may be seen in this description of a young boy with vocal nodules.

Eli B., age 7, was described by his parents as a boy "who was always talking, yelling, and letting the family know that he was around." For the past year it was noticed that Eli often demonstrated a low pitched, hoarse voice, particularly toward the end of the day after many hours of noisy play. His hoarseness was noticed by his pediatrician who subsequently referred him to an ear-nose-throat specialist, an otolaryngologist. Initial attempts by the otolaryngologist at indirect laryngoscopy were not successful because of the boy's intolerance for the laryngeal mirror. After a second visit, however, the physician was able to visualize his vocal folds and found small bilateral vocal nodules. He was then referred to the speech-language pathologist in the same hospital who took a thorough case history from both the parents and the boy. A number of abusive noises which the boy produced were heard and a gross determination was made of how often these abuses occurred. The speech-language pathologist saw Eli for several sessions, presenting him graphic materials which showed him in language he could understand how abusing his voice had produced the "little bumps he now had on his vocal folds." The counseling was coupled with requests that he make serious attempts to curb his yelling and funny noises. Each time he found himself making a noise he was asked to chart it on a time graph which the clinician gave him to take home. After several weeks of monitoring his yelling behavior with the help of his parents, he returned for another visit with the otolaryngologist. This time it was observed on laryngoscopy that his nodules were much smaller. It appeared that curbing his vocal abuses had a direct influence on lessening the laryngeal strain he was experiencing, resulting in a reduction in the size of his vocal nodules.

The management of the voice problem for the boy just described primarily utilized a few sessions of counseling specific to his vocal abuses. If he had needed voice therapy over a longer period of time, the focus of his therapy would have been searching to discover what kind of abuse or misuse was present and then designing a program to reduce that abuse. We also would search with him for the best voice he could produce. The voice clinician must continually search for the patient's best and most appropriate voice production. This searching is necessary because so much of our vocal behavior is highly automatic, particularly the dimensions of pitch and quality. The patient cannot volitionally break down vocalization into various components and then hope to combine them into some ideal phonation. Voice therapy techniques are primarily vehicles of facilitation; that is, we try a particular therapy approach and see if it facilitates the production of a better voice. If it does, then we utilize it as therapy practice material. If it does not, we quickly abandon it. As part of every clinical session, we must probe and search for the patient's best voice. When an acceptable production is achieved, we use it as the patient's target model in therapy. The patient's own best voice becomes his or her goal.

Some patients develop for wholly functional reasons no voice at all (aphonia). Aronson defines aphonia as "the absence of a definable laryngeal tone. The voice is either severely breathy or whispered" (1980, p. 5). On laryngoscopic examination the vocal folds appear normal in function, but they remain apart when the patient attempts to phonate. Such a finding today is usually called *functional dysphonia*. Not long ago patients who demonstrated functional aphonia were described as having a hysterical or conversion symptom (the voice problem was but a symptom of an underlying psychiatric problem), and they were usually referred for psychiatric consultation. Actually, we now know that by using a symptomatic voice therapy approach, such as searching for vegetative phonation and shaping it into communication, we can usually be successful with the functional aphonic patient and help him or her restore normal voice. As a group, such aphonic patients present a favorable prognosis, usually recovering normal voice. While the aphonic patient has no voice, most patients with functional voice disorders employ voice with too much force and effort at the various sites of the vocal tract. Although they have a voice, it is not normal.

THE SITES OF VOCAL HYPERFUNCTION

Excessive muscular contraction and force of movement in respiration, phonation, or resonance can be labeled as vocal hyperfunction. An identification and description of the specific anatomical sites and physiological functions associated with vocal hyperfunction will provide the reader with a beginning look at the problem.

Respiration

The larynx is primarily a valvelike "guardian," watching over the airway and preventing the entrance of foreign bodies into the respiratory system. Yet, beyond this primitive capacity, humans have developed the further ability to prolong their exhalation while the true vocal folds are gently approximated to produce phonation. Phonation as part of speaking or singing requires a continuous closing and opening of the vocal folds, with shortenings and elongations of the folds as needed for continuous variations in frequency. Variations in intensity require continuous and subtle fluctuations of air pressure with corresponding changes in vocal fold resistance. The regulation of this outflow of air is basically involuntary and highly automatic in ordinary speech, but the public speaker or singer learns to rely heavily on a partial control of his or her breathing mechanism. Singers, for example, require an additional supply of air in excess of that obtained in normal inhalation and are able to replenish their air supply quickly and efficiently. Singers must be able to sustain a prolonged exhalation. The trained speaking voice (a voice that does not tire easily) and the accomplished singing voice (a voice that is aesthetically pleasant and musically competent) require adequate control of expiration. Although it is possible to develop some control over respiration, particularly over the expiratory phase of breathing, this control must be within the limits of the individual's oxygen needs. While an actor or singer may require respiration training, the typical voice patient rarely needs special training in breathing.

Unusual force or muscle tension (hyperfunction) can be observed in various phases of respiration among both normal persons and clinical voice patients. While the normal speaker without vocal pathology can tolerate vocal stresses related to inadequate and inefficient respiration, the patient with vocal pathology usually cannot tolerate such respiratory inefficiency. Perhaps the most common problem of respiration observed among voice patients is the attempt to speak on an inadequate expiration. The inspiratory phase may be inadequate for the phonatory task. The untrained singer may be observed to elevate his or her shoulders, using the neck accessory muscles for inhalation. Or the lecturer or the singer, in his or her need to get in a "big" breath, in taking a maximum inhalation, displays an obviously distended abdomen, a fixed thorax, elevated shoulders with the associated neck accessory muscles in a hypertonic state, and possibly a head thrust forward. Although such "deep breathers" may have increased their air volume, they are in no position to parcel out their exhalations for a controlled sustained phonation. More commonly, perhaps, we see the patient who suffers not from too little or too much of an inhalation, but from improper utilization of his or her expiration. The speaker may let out so much expiration early in a verbal passage that by the time the end of the sentence is reached, he or she is short of breath. Studies of the normal speaker by Otis and Clark (1968) and Bless and Miller (1972) have found that a subject will closely match the prolonged timing of his or her expiration to the length of verbalization he or she wishes to say. The patient with vocal hyperfunction often does not demonstrate this normal timing of expiration to match his spoken utterances, displaying symptoms of struggle with breathing as he attempts to voice. We shall discuss normal respiration and its role in supplying the expiratory air volumes and pressures needed for normal phonation in Chapter 2, considering at that time some of the excesses in respiration often demonstrated by the patient with a voice disorder.

Phonation

Anyone who hears a great singing voice like that of Pavarotti or the collective voices in a chorus singing Beethoven's Ninth Symphony can fully appreciate that the larynx can produce great tonal beauty. From a physiological point of view, however, the primary function of the larynx in the human and other mammals is to serve as a valve to protect the airway.

While most mammals are physically capable of using the laryngeal valving folds for phonation, a few species, such as rabbits and deer, are usually silent. At the other extreme is man, whose control over phonation has resulted in the fantastic achievement of human speech, with its requirements of sustained phonation, abrupt cessation of phonation, frequency variation, and changes in intensity. The vegetative, life-sustaining role of the laryngeal mechanism stands in sharp contrast to the role the laryngeal apparatus is called upon to play for purposes of human speech. Optimal phonation for speaking and singing requires continuous abduction-adduction of the vocal folds, with subtle changes in fold length and mass. The subglottal and transglottal air pressures force the gently approximated vocal folds apart, setting them into vibration. It is at the anatomical site of the glottal opening where many hyperfunctional voice problems begin, because of inappropriate (inadequate or excessive) vocal fold approximation.

While the symptoms of vocal hyperfunction are often produced by the excessive force and contraction of muscles concerned with respiration and supraglottal resonance, there are specific types of hyperfunctional behavior at the site of the larynx. Sometimes the vocal folds are approximated too tightly together. The membranes that cover the vocal folds are placed so firmly together that the larynx acts as a valve, preventing the flow of air which normally sets the vocal folds into vibration. The resulting voice is tight, sounding at times almost like the strained voice of the laryngeal "stutter" or spastic dysphonia. An opposite problem may be observed when the vocal folds are brought together in such a lax manner that far too much breath escapes between them, producing the whispered or very breathy voice. How the vocal folds are approximated has much to do with the quality of our voices.

There is much disagreement among voice authorities about the influence of inappropriate pitch level or fundamental frequency on the development of various vocal pathologies. While for some patients it might appear that an inappropriately low or high pitch level is a primary etiological factor in a vocal disorder, there are other patients whose faulty pitch levels have developed secondarily from the increase of vocal fold mass due to early polypoid or nodule growth. That is, sometimes the inappropriate pitch level produces the dysphonia, and sometimes the prolonged dysphonia produces vocal fold tissue changes with a resulting alteration in pitch. It is important for any speaker or singer to use the vocal mechanism optimally with regard to fundamental frequency. Speaking or singing at an inappropriate pitch level requires excessive force and contraction of the intrinsic muscles of the larynx, leading to vocal fatigue or the hoarseness related to a tired vocal mechanism.

A common pitch deviation may be the inappropriately low pitch of the young professional male, such as the teacher or preacher, who speaks at the bottom of his pitch range in an attempt to convey some extra authority through his voice. Or there is the young professional woman who speaks at a fundamental frequency value well below the normative values of the average adult female. An inappropriate pitch level, whether it be too low or too high, requires unnecessary muscle energy to maintain the necessary vocal fold adjustments of length and mass to produce the "artificial" voice. Of the many variables we often identify as hyperfunctional voiie behaviors, inappropriate pitch level is one of the easiest of the disorders to remedy. Sometimes just by raising or lowering the fundamental frequency slightly, the patient will experience a lessening of the energy one employs to speak, which will result in a noticeable decrease in one's dysphonia.

Abruptness of voice initiation, known as hard glottal attack, is another symptom of unnecessary vocal effort. The patient speaks with unnecessary precision, sounding as if he is biting off each word as a separate entity. This abrupt glottal attack, as heard in the voices of TV-movie personalities such as Bette Davis, or Don Adams as Maxwell Smart, represents an unnecessary effort in talking and may over a period of time lead to dysphonia. The opposite kind of glottal attack is heard in the easy, almost slurred speech of some southerners in the United States, such as in the voice of Jimmy Carter. Easy glottal attack or easy voice onset does not appear to have aversive effects on the laryngeal mechanism. In fact, in voice therapy we often deliberately teach the patient with hard glottal attack to soften his or her attack in an attempt to reduce or eliminate unnecessary effort in phonation.

Vocal abuse and misuse are among the most common causes of vocal dysfunction. Continuous talking, excessive laughing or crying, talking loudly over loud background noises, and screaming and yelling can all take a toll on laryngeal efficiency. The vocal fold edema or vascular engorgement that may result from excessive phonation, such as in screaming or yelling, produces by its additive nature an enlargement of the vocal folds, which may produce an alteration in phonation; the patient may further add to his or her difficulty by attempting to compensate for this change in his or her voice by making new adjustments and contractions of the intrinsic and extrinsic laryngeal muscles. Coughing and excessive throat clearing frequently contribute to the problem of dysphonia and laryngeal pathology, perhaps adding edema and irritation to an already pathological condition. True infection of the larynx is often the primary etiological factor in dysphonia, with the patient experiencing acute or chronic laryngitis; instead of imposing upon himself a temporary period of voice rest during the infectious stage of the disease, the patient may continue to phonate, compounding vocal fold irritation. Lecturing or serious singing "on top" of an existing laryngeal infection can have disastrous aftereffects and perhaps damage the vocal mechanism permanently. External irritants, particularly once laryngeal pathology has been established, may have an exacerbating effect on certain vocal pathologies; smoking, excessive alcohol consumption, smog, and dust have all been identified as culprits that help maintain various laryngeal disorders. It would appear that once any kind of vocal abuse has been identified, intelligent efforts by the patient to reduce future such abusive behavior might well result in a noticeable lessening of vocal symptoms.

Resonance

The voice, originating by the air stream vibrating the vocal folds, is amplified in the upper airway cavities of the neck and head. This amplification is called resonance. In normal voicing, the vocal fold vibrations produce the source of sound that flows into the resonating tubes of the vocal tract (the hypopharynx, the oral pharynx, and the nasal cavities, all described in Chapter 2). The vocal tract is much like an extended tube starting immediately within the larynx and extending up the throat into the oral cavity, which is in turn coupled with the nasal cavity. Certain sounds or frequencies of the voice are amplified selectively, depending on the surface, shape, and restrictions of the resonating cavities. The resonating cavities have particular compatible natural vibrations that respond optimally to certain frequencies of the sound spectrum, known as *resonance frequencies*. If the sound wave frequencies in the upper airway are compatible with the natural resonances, natural amplification and resonance will occur. Many cavity resonators, however, are altered by changes in surface and shape so that natural resonant frequencies are changed, perhaps altering natural frequency of vibration, resulting in a dull voice often lacking amplification and resonance. Some speakers alter or diminish their natural resonance potential by using various hyperfunctional behaviors. Where the individual places the voice, according to Perkins (1981), low or high in the resonating tract has much to do with ease of phonation and how the voice sounds to the listener.

The bottom of the resonance tube is the hypopharynx. An occasional patient may contract the lower pharyngeal constrictors and retract the tongue posteriorly, almost filling the hypopharyngeal opening. This posterior tongue retraction, coupled with pharyngeal constriction, produces an acoustical bottleneck that may result in a change of oral resonance. This filling of the hypopharynx may occur only during particular anxiety states of the patient or be conditioned to occur only during particular speaking events; at these times, however, the patient experiences extreme difficulty in "getting out" his or her voice. Posterior tongue retraction also occurs in the oral pharynx, producing a *cul de sac resonance* (this phenomenon is discussed in some detail in Chapter 6 with regard to the voices of the deaf). This posterior arching of the tongue is sometimes a predisposing factor to such resonance deviations as hypernasality or denasality. Although hyperfunctional carriage of the tongue may create many acoustical variations of voice, it is often erroneously not identified as a contributing cause of an existing dysphonia.

One of the most commonly observed types of hyperfunctional behavior in the vocal tract is speaking with mandibular constriction, or talking "through one's teeth." The patient makes most of the muscle adjustments required for continuous speech almost wholly with the tongue, with the mandible locked in a passive role. For the various adjustments required for producing vowels, the patient changes the dimensions of his or her oral cavity by flattening or elevating the tongue, with little or no size change contributed by the movement of the mandible. Many patients with mandibular restriction complain of symptoms of vocal fatigue, pain, or fullness in the hyoid area after prolonged speaking or singing. The entire burden of articulation is on the tongue. Mandibular restriction is a commonly observed diagnostic entity in many patients with hyperfunctional voice disorders. Recognizing this, Froeschels (1952) developed the *chewing approach* in voice therapy. Voice clinicians using the chewing approach for selected voice patients generally report that it not only promotes greater mobility of the mandible, but also reduces other oral hyperfunctional postures.

Hyperfunction is sometimes observed in the patient's overuse of the tongue tip and lips in speech articulation. Such a patient overarticulates, frequently accompanying his or her overarticulations with a hard and abrupt glottal attack. This patient maintains a posture of articulatory precision with excessive constriction and force, and consequently one's speech and voice lack ease and naturalness of production. At another extreme is the patient who speaks with a masked expression and dullness of articulation. The voice quality may be muffled and his or her overall speech-voice production lacking full normal resonance.

Some patients display problems in nasal resonance related to variations in coupling the oral and nasal cavities together. In normal voice, only the nasal consonants (*m, n, ng*) are given nasal resonance by relaxing the velum and allowing the velopharyngeal port to be open. The sound waves then pass into the nasal cavity for further resonance. While most symptoms of excessive nasalization are related to structural causes (cleft palate, short velum, severe head cold, and so on), there are occasional voice patients who keep the velum and pharyngeal wall separated for wholly functional reasons.

Most hyperfunctional behaviors affecting resonance alter the size, shape, and surface of the resonating cavities, altering their preferential response to certain frequencies. The best sounding voice is often the voice that was given the most amplification because of compatibility between the frequency of vibration of the vocal folds and the resonant frequencies of the supraglottal (above the vocal folds) resonators. Voice therapy is often effective in identifying unnecessary force and tension at the various sites of the upper airway. Once such a hyperfunctional behavior is identified, such as speaking through clenched teeth, the patient should be made aware of the forceful behavior and its noticeable effect on the voice. The clinician asks the patient to produce the hyperfunctional behavior and then contrast it with an easy behavior (such as using voice while the teeth are clenched and then voicing with a wide-open mouth). He or she then is asked to hear the difference in the sound of the voice between the two contrasted behaviors, effort versus ease. When natural resonance is uncovered, often by using a more natural opening of the mouth, the improvement in the sound of the voice is usually markedly improved.

VOICE DISORDERS RELATED TO ORGANIC PROBLEMS

While the majority of voice problems appear to be related to functional factors, many disorders of voice are caused by various organic problems. The voice can be altered in frequency, intensity, quality, or resonance primarily because of physical factors. That is not to say that there won't be a functional overlay or reaction to the organic disorder that may give the patient a greater voice problem than he or she needs to have. Organic problems of voice can be caused by impairment in the active movement of the folds, by mass-size changes of the folds, by severe sensory loss (such as deafness), by physical problems in respiration, and by structural and functional alterations of the resonance cavities.

Any voice problem that lasts more than a week should be medically investigated for possible physical causation. Sometimes the required treatment will be medical-surgical, with voice therapy only helping to find and maintain the best possible voice. Some organic voice problems are static, relatively fixed, and not responsive to medical treatment; for these problems, voice therapy becomes the only remediation possible. Although specific disorders of voice related to organic problems and their management will be presented in Chapter 6, let us consider a voice problem related to a physical cause.

Mary Jane C., a fifty-five-year-old interior decorator, began to experience increasing symptoms of hoarseness. Since she was a heavy smoker, smoking almost three packs of cigarettes daily, she attributed her deteriorating voice to her inability to curb her smoking. Eventually she consulted an otolaryngologist, who on mirror laryngoscopy found that both her vocal folds had heavy amounts of "leukoplakia." He explained to the patient, "Your vocal cords are covered with white patches or plagues. In my opinion the patches are directly related to your heavy smoking." He went on to tell the woman that the type of lesion she had, the leukoplakia, was a precancerous-type lesion directly related to smoking and would have to be watched closely. He recommended that the plagues be removed surgically, that she stop smoking and eventually get "some voice therapy to improve the sound of your voice." Mary Jane immediately went to a smoker's clinic, stopped smoking, and within a month had surgery to remove the many plaques from her larynx. She subsequently was seen for a voice evaluation and therapy. Her pitch was found to be excessively low and the quality of her voice characterized by "breathiness and moderate hoarseness." Therapy efforts were directed toward slight elevation of her voice pitch and learning to use her vocal mechanism in as easy and optimal manner as possible. After twenty-eight individual voice therapy sessions, twice weekly for about fourteen weeks, the patient was discharged with a normal sounding voice. She continued to be followed by the ENT physician for a period of several years; she remained free from further leukoplakia and maintained the voice gains she had experienced after voice therapy.

The case of Mary Jane is a good one to illustrate how a purely organic problem can cause severe voice symptoms. While medical-surgical treatment was primarily used to correct her problem, the subsequent voice therapy helped her to develop a more normal-sounding voice.

Impairment in the Movement of the Folds

There are several physical ways that the movement of the vocal folds may be impaired. The vocal folds normally move toward one another (adduct) for phonation by the active contraction of the intrinsic laryngeal muscles. The folds are held together by active muscle contraction during phonation, working against the tendency to be blown apart by the airflow beneath and between them. The adduction of the folds is sometimes compromised by destruction of the nerves that innervate these laryngeal muscles, as described in Chapter 4. This produces weakness or paralysis of the laryngeal muscles, resulting in vocal fold paralysis. There may be other neuromuscular problems that prevent normal vocal fold approximation as a result of some kind of destruction within the cerebrum, perhaps as a result of a stroke or some form of degenerative disease. When phonation is impaired because of a problem in the central nervous system (CNS), it is usually part of a dysarthria (speech-voice-fluency impairment secondary to CNS involvement). We will discuss the problem of dysarthria and its voice symptoms in greater detail in Chapter 6. Overall management of voice problems related to problems of neural innervation requires medical management as well as the short-range and long-range participation of the speech-language pathologist.

Mass-Size Changes in the Vocal Folds

When someone has a severe cold with an accompanying laryngitis, this is a good example of a voice problem related to a mass-size change of the vocal folds. In laryngitis, for example, the patient experiences severe swelling and redness of the membrane that covers the vocal folds; this irregular thickening along the total anterior-to-posterior border of the folds contributes to the lowering of pitch and the hoarseness we commonly hear in laryngitis. Most of the mass-size changes that lead to dysphonia are clearly observable growths, such as the warty-like papilloma seen in the larynges of children or the leukoplakia-type lesion described in the foregoing case illustration. The mass added to the vocal fold will drastically change the vibratory characteristic of that fold, usually resulting in a lowering of fundamental frequency. The added mass is often on the margin of the vocal fold, preventing the two folds from optimally approximating one another. Occasionally patients may have endocrine or metabolic dysfunction of some kind that causes alterations in the structures of the larynx, resulting in voice changes that set the patient's voice apart from his or her peers. Most additive lesions, unilateral or bilateral, to the vocal folds will have a profound influence on the frequency of the voice (usually lower), on the intensity of the voice (usually softer), and on voice quality (usually breathy and hoarse).

Other Organic Factors
Influencing Phonation

Phonation may be adversely affected by a variety of other organic factors. For example, the influence on the voice of severe hearing loss or deafness has been well documented in a number of studies that we will describe in Chapter 6. It appears that the typical deaf person will demonstrate in the voice severe fluctuations in pitch, a tendency to use a higher speaking pitch, and a back-in-the-throat sounding resonance. For the deaf patient who is attempting to use oral speech with hearing people in the hearing world, these abnormalities of pitch and resonance often interfere with the intelligibility of what he or she attempts to say. Ling (1976) has suggested that working directly on voice is as important and as helpful to the deaf child as is working on articulation and language. Direct trauma to the external larynx from an accident, such as getting hit on the larynx by a swinging baseball bat, can cause devastating symptoms on phonation as well as a direct threat to the open airway. Many patients who experience laryngeal trauma must first experience a lifesaving opening in their trachea (tracheotomy) to give them an open airway, free of any obstruction. Eventually, most patients with a traumatized larynx require surgical reconstruction, so that the larynx will once again function as an airway protection-valve, no longer requiring the tracheotomy. Eventually the patient will require extensive voice therapy to help develop the best voice possible with the reconstructed larynx. More and more we see voice problems related to faulty respiration, often related to allergies, infection, and increasingly to a disease called emphysema (a loss of elasticity of lung tissue, usually secondary to a long history of heavy smoking). The patient experiences severe shortness of breath, which prevents normal voicing. Voice therapy, sometimes coupled with respiration therapy of some kind, can give the patient a more functional voice, a voice loud and strong enough to be heard. In the ensuing chapters of this book we will consider other physical causes of phonation disorders, how we evaluate them, and what kind of voice therapy may be indicated.

Organic Factors Influencing Resonance

Much of the early literature on therapy for resonance disorders had its origins from writings that described problems of excessive nasal resonance (hypernasality) secondary to poliomyelitis. Some forms of polio caused weakness or paralysis to muscles of the velum and pharynx. The form of voice therapy needed, therefore, was to strengthen weakened muscles so that the patient would experience better velopharyngeal closure and less hypernasality. Although some patients with central nevous system disorders causing dysarthria experience symptoms of hypernasality and require strengthening therapy, most excesses in nasal resonance require some kind of structural intervention. For example, the patient with a cleft palate may have a large opening between the oral and nasal cavities that permits a massive flow of air and soundwave to travel through the nasal cavities. Problems of cleft palate today are managed by a combination of surgery, dental prosthetics, orthodontia, and extended speech and voice therapy. For the voice therapy to be effective in correcting excessive nasal resonance, the patient must first have a structural correction, permitting good velopharyngeal closure, usually the result of combined surgical-dental efforts. Some soft palates are too short or do not rise adequately to produce closure between the oral and nasal cavities; the management approaches here are about the same as if the patient experienced a cleft palate. In most cases, excessive nasal resonance is the result of inadequate velopharyngeal closure; there are only occasional cases where excessive nasal resonance is strictly the result of functional causes, that is, the patient is hypernasal with a perfectly normal mechanism.

Lack of nasal resonance (denasality), heard in the voice of someone with a very severe head cold, is most always related to some kind of nasopharyngeal blockage. Denasality is characterized by insufficient nasal resonance of the three nasal consonants, *m, n,* and *ng.* Children with severely enlarged adenoids, for example, sometimes lack normal nasal resonance; the adenoidal tissue is so large that it blocks the normal passage of airflow and soundwave through the nasal cavities. In some cases the surgical or dental treatment for hypernasality has been seemingly too successful, not only correcting excessive nasal resonance, but also blocking even normal nasal resonance. We may observe a child who has experienced too broad a pharyngeal flap, so broad that normal nasal resonance is blocked. In summary, most problems of denasality are related to structural blockage of the nasopharynx whether it be from infection, allergy, large adenoids, or the result of excessive surgical-dental correction. Voice therapy is seldom effective in correcting this lack of nasal resonance until after the physical obstruction blocking the normal coupling of the oral and nasal cavities has been corrected.

SUMMARY

The majority of voice disorders are related to abusing and misusing the laryngeal mechanism. This vocal abuse and misuse is known as vocal hyperfunction. Symptomatic voice therapy programs have been found to be highly effective with such functional voice problems. The focus of this symptomatic therapy is fourfold: (1) search with the patient to identify abuse and misuse; (2) reduce the occurrence of the abuse-misuse; (3) search by using various therapy approaches for the best voice possible; and

(4) use the therapy approach that works as a therapy focus. Problems of voice related to various organic conditions require a close interface between physician and the speech-language pathologist. There are few organic voice disorders, however, that can be wholly corrected by a medical-surgical approach alone; once physical causation has been corrected or treated, symptomatic voice therapy has been found to be effective in developing the best voice possible. Such a symptom-oriented approach requires that the voice clinician has a thorough understanding of the mechanisms of voice production, and that he or she be flexible and eclectic enough to adjust the therapy approach to fit the needs of the particular patient. The outcome hoped for is that the voice patient will eventually experience a better-sounding voice.

2
The Normal Voice

The effective voice clinician must have some knowledge of the basic structures and functions necessary for the production of normal voice. We shall look separately at the three primary components of voice—respiration, phonation, and resonance. For each of these components we shall describe the body structures that are involved and the current view of how they function.

Although it is convenient to separate the normal speaking voice into three separate parts (respiration, phonation, and resonance) for purposes of study, it must be remembered that the three components of voice are highly interdependent on one another. For example, without the expiratory phase of respiration there would be no normal voice in either its phonation or resonance components. Let us first consider the structures and function of respiration, particularly as they relate to production of voice.

RESPIRATION

Humans have learned to use respiration for speech, sustaining their exhalations for purposes of phonation. Both speaking and singing require an outgoing air stream capable of activating vocal fold vibration. When "training" his or her voice, the speaker or singer frequently focuses on developing conscious control of the breathing mechanism. This conscious control, however, must always be consistent with the physiological air requirements of the individual. It is often the conflict between the physiological needs and the speaking-singing demands for air that causes faulty usage of the vocal mechanism. Our dependence upon the constant renewal of our oxygen supply imposes certain limitations upon how many words we can say, or how many phrases we can sing, on one expiration.

Respiration Structures

In Figure 2-1, The Respiratory Tract, we see that inspired air begins through the nostrils and passes into the nasal cavities. For an individual breathing through the nose, the air would pass from the nasal cavities into the nasopharynx through the open velopharyngeal port into the oropharynx. For mouth breathers, the air would enter through the open mouth, pass through the oral cavity over the surface of the tongue and into the oropharynx. The air would then flow through the hypopharynx. From the hypopharynx, the inspiration would flow into the larynx, pass between the ventricular or false vocal folds and between the true vocal folds down into the trachea or windpipe. At the bottom end of the trachea, the airway divides into the two bronchial tubes shown in the photograph of the lungs and tracheal bifurcation in Figure 2-2. The bronchial tubes further branch into branches known as the bronchioles, eventually terminating in the lungs in little air sacs, known as the alveoli. While some of the bronchioli can be seen in Figure 2-2, most of the bronchioli and all the alveoli are covered by the pleural membrane covering the lungs.

The ribs connected to the twelve thoracic vertebrae and their connecting muscles play an active role in respiration, as we will see when we discuss respiratory function. The thorax can move in several ways. For example, the rib cage wall expands to produce inspiration of air and collapses for expiration. Sometimes the accessory muscles in the neck assist in inspiration when they contract, elevating the shoulders, increasing the vertical dimension of the thorax. At the base of the thorax is the important diaphragm, a composite of muscle, tendon, and membrane that separates the thoracic cavity from the abdominal cavity. As the diaphragm contracts, it descends, increasing the vertical dimension of the thorax; as the diaphragm relaxes, it ascends back to its higher position. As we see in the photograph of the lungs in Figure 2-2, the diaphragm has direct contact

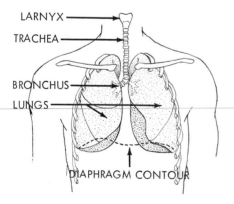

LARNYX

TRACHEA

BRONCHUS

LUNGS

DIAPHRAGM CONTOUR

FIGURE 2-1.
A line drawing of the respiratory tract. Note the resting level of the diaphragm as outlined is the diaphragm contour.

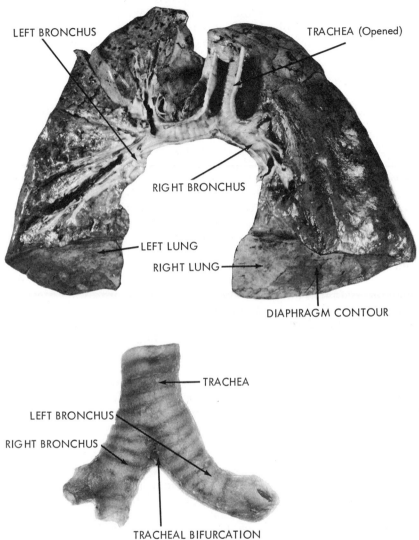

RESPIRATORY TRACT

LEFT BRONCHUS

TRACHEA (Opened)

RIGHT BRONCHUS

LEFT LUNG

RIGHT LUNG

DIAPHRAGM CONTOUR

TRACHEA

LEFT BRONCHUS

RIGHT BRONCHUS

TRACHEAL BIFURCATION

FIGURE 2-2. Lungs and tracheal bifurcation. Photograph above well illustrates the tracheal bifurcation that introduces air into the lungs by way of the left and right bronchi.

with the lungs, with only the pleural space between the lungs and the
diaphragm; the shape of the diaphragm, its superior contour, can be seen
on the lower surface of the cadaver lung shown in the photograph. The
relaxed diaphragm is high in the chest behind the rib cage with the stomach
and liver lying directly below it. As the diaphragm contracts and descends,
it pushes from above on the abdomen below, often displacing the ab-

dominal wall, pushing it outward on inspiration. The abdominal wall is composed primarily of the abdominal muscles that also may play an active role in expiration. We will identify those muscles of the thorax and the abdomen that relate to respiration as we discuss respiration function.

Respiration Function

The respiratory tract functions much like a bellows. When we move the handles on the bellows apart, the bellows become larger, the air within it becomes less dense than the outside air, and the outside air rushes in. The inspiration of air into the bellows is achieved by active enlargement of the bellows' body. Similarly in human respiration, the inspiration of air is achieved by active movement of muscles that enlarge the thoracic cavity. When the thorax enlarges, the lungs within the thorax enlarge. The air within the lungs becomes less dense than atmospheric air, and inspiration of air begins. The air is expired from the bellows by bringing the handles together, decreasing the size of the bellows' cavity, forcing the air within it to rush out. In human respiration, however, much of expiration is achieved by passive collapse of thoracic size and not by active muscle contraction. Hixon, Goldman, and Mead (1973) have described the forces of human respiration as having two types of forces that are always present in respiration, passive forces that are always there (such as the elastic lungs) and active, volitional forces (such as contraction of muscles of inspiration). The pleural membrane that covers the lungs clings (almost adhesively) to the inner wall of the thorax. As the thorax expands by muscular contraction, the lungs within it expand. The inherent elastic force of the lungs is always there. Their elastic recoil will be as fast as thoracic collapse allows. In fact, in at-rest expiration (the expiration during the quiet breathing of sleep, for example), the expiratory phase of respiration is wholly accomplished by the elasticity of the inherent or passive forces.

We need now to consider the muscles of respiration that contribute active, volitional force in inspiration as seen in Figure 2-3. The primary muscle of inspiration is the *diaphragm*, as already noted. Perhaps the *external intercostals* play the next most important role in inspiration; because of their oblique angulation, when they contract, they lift the rib below, enlarging the rib cage on a somewhat horizontal plane. Slight elevation of the thorax is achieved with contraction of the *pectoralis major* and *minor*, the *costal elevators*, and the *serratus posterior*, and the *neck accessory muscles* (primarily the *sternocleidomastoid*). While the primary inherent elasticity and recoil of thoracic structures come into play when the active muscles of inspiration cease contracting and relax, there are some muscles of expiration that can assist in expiration. These expiration muscles may contract in some conditions of talking, singing, and forced expiration such as we use in playing wind instruments. The primary muscles of expiration are the four abdominal muscles, the *internal oblique abdominal, external oblique abdominal, transverse abdominal,* and the *rectus abdominal*. Some thoracic decrease can also be achieved by active contraction of the *internal intercostals* (they slant

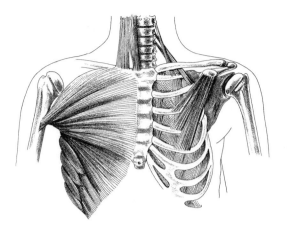

FIGURE 2-3. The thoracic surface muscles of respiration, including the pectoralis major, the external and internal intercostals, the scalene, pectoralis minor, and the sternocleidomastoid muscles. Bones readily identified include the clavical, sternum, scapula, and ribs 1–8. Used with permission, J. M. Palmer, *Anatomy for Speech and Hearing.* New York: Harper & Row (1972), p. 149.

upward in the opposite direction of the external intercostals) and the *posterior inferior serratus.*

In passive respiration, the kind of breathing we do when sleeping, the active contraction of inspiratory muscles produces the inspiration with the expiration phase of the respiratory cycle wholly related to the passive (non-muscular) collapse properties of the thorax. When we add the function of expiratory muscles to the passive expiration, we alter the duration and force of the expiration; for example, while speaking a long passage, we may well begin with a passive expiration with active contraction of expiratory muscles coming in after the passive expiration has begun. Anytime we prolong the expiration beyond a simple tidal volume (see definitions in next paragraph), we have added some active muscle contraction of the expiratory muscles. In Figure 2–4 we see the simple tracings of a pneumotachometer, showing the relative time for inspiration-expiration for a passive, tidal breath, for saying the numbers "one-two-three-four-five," and for singing the musical passage, "I don't want to walk without you, baby" from the old song by that title. Note that the inspiratory time during normal tidal breathing is much longer than the quick inspiration for speech and singing. While the tidal expiratory time is longer than inspiration, the expiratory times for speech and singing are remarkably longer.

In subsequent discussions we will use terms describing aspects of respiration, which we need to define at this point:

Lung volumes and capacities
Tidal volume (TV) is the amount of air inspired and expired during a respiratory cycle, determined by the oxygen needs (not the speaking or singing needs) of the individual.

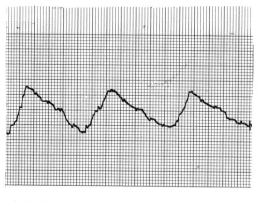

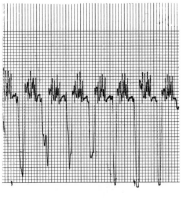

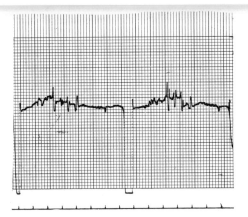

FIGURE 2-4
Pneumotachometer tracings measure air flow over time. One can see the relative time for inspiration as opposed to expiration for three conditions: Tracing A (three tidal breaths) produces an inspiration-expiration time ratio of about 1 to 2; Tracing B (counting 1–5 on eight trials) produces a ratio of about 1 to 3; Tracing C (singing twice, "I don't want to walk without you, baby") yielded an inspiration-expiration ratio of approximately 1 to 10.

Inspiratory reserve volume (IRV), sometimes known as *complemental air* (Comroe, 1956), is the maximum amount of air that can be inspired after the peak of the tidal inspiration.

Expiratory reserve volume (ERV), known also as *supplemental air,* is the maximum volume of air that can be expired beyond the end of a tidal expiration.

Residual volume (RV) is the volume of air that remains in the lungs after a maximum expiration. No matter how forceful the expiration, the residual volume cannot be forced from the lungs.

Vital capacity (VC) is the total amount of air that can be expired from the lungs and air passages from a maximum expiration, representing the total volumes listed above, with the exception of residual volume (which cannot be expired).

Total lung capacity (TLC) represents the total volume of air that can be held in the lungs and airways after a maximum inspiration and can only be measured by special volume displacement tests (not by measuring the total expiratory volume).

Methods for evaluating respiratory volumes and capacities will be discussed in Chapter 4, The Voice Evaluation. In the normal inspiratory-expiratory cycle of tidal volume, the relative timing of inspiration-expiration, as shown in Figure 2-4, is slightly longer for expiration. The human being appears to have a slight bias toward longer expirations, apparently quite compatible with the need for extending expiration for purposes of communication. It should be remembered by the reader that the respiratory system supplies the activating part of phonation, as described in the myoelastic theory of phonation later in this chapter. Influencing our type of respiration will be the interactions and pragmatics between the speaker and the listener, the type of utterance being produced, the background noise in the setting, the relative arousal level of the autonomic nervous system, the comfort of the speaker, and so forth. Therefore, some of the ensuing descriptions of the physiology of respiration, when lifted out of speaking or singing context, often read deceptively simple. For example, when one begins to speak or sing, the inspiration time unit is often shortened (by employing more vigor to the muscles of inspiration) and the expiration time is obviously extended. Hixon, Mead, and Goldman (1976) have studied the dynamics and function of the thorax, rib cage, diaphragm, and abdomen during speech and have concluded that there are marked differences in respiratory function according to body position and type of speech task. For example, utterances that required near total use of one's vital capacity activated different activity zones, depending on whether the patient was in the upright or supine body position; the inspiratory activity ''was governed predominately by the rib cage and the abdomen in the upright body position and by the diaphragm in the supine position'' (Hixon, Mead, and Goldman, 1976, p. 297). It appears that during the inspiratory phase preceding speech, we shorten our inspiration and then use the chest wall and the abdomen in different ways for the expiratory phase (when we are actually speaking). We find that we renew inspiration and ''catch up'' on inspiration during our conversational passages, tucking in the abdomen with a slight elevation of the rib cage. Hixon has written that the ''importance of this shape is that it forces the diaphragm—our major expiratory muscle—into a highly domed position where its action results in the development of great amounts of inspiratory force very rapidly'' (1980, p. 63).

Bless and Miller (1972) and Otis and Clark (1968) have written that the normal speaker adjusts inspiration-expiration to match the linguistic utterance he or she wishes to say. Inspiration during conversation, public speaking, and even singing happens quickly, usually masked from the view of all but the searching eye. After the quick inspiration, we then begin the passive expiration, quickly using the tidal volume and adding the sustained expiration of the expiratory reserve. Fluctuations of expiratory air flow, to meet the speaker's demand for stress and changes in vocal intensity, are apparently made by slight chest wall adjustments. Increases in air flow and subglottal pressure are made quickly and with little visible effort to match the linguistic or artistic needs of the speaker or singer. The gifted talker or singer also learns to take little, quick ''catch up'' inhalations sandwiched within what appears to the listener to be a continuous inspiratory flow.

PHONATION

The airway requires various kinds of protective structures to prevent the infiltration of liquids, the aspiration of food particles and fluids during deglutition (swallowing), and the inhalation of foreign bodies during respiration. In most higher mammals, particularly man, the larynx serves as the basic valvelike entryway to the respiratory tract. All incoming and outgoing pulmonary air must pass through the valving, glottal opening of the larynx. Negus (1957) wrote that the primary biological role of the larynx is to prevent foreign bodies from moving into the airway, and also to fixate the thorax by stopping the air flow at the glottal level, which permits the arms to perform heavy lifting and extensive weight-supporting feats. This primitive, valvelike action appears to be the primary function of the larynx in man. Using the laryngeal valving mechanism for phonation is undoubtedly an evolved, secondary function, which has required the development of intricate neural controls that permit man to use the approximating valvelike vocal folds for the precise phonations required in speaking and singing. The valving action of the larynx functions because, first, we have a fixed framework (the laryngeal cartilages); second, we are able to open (abduct) and close (adduct) the valve, primarily by using the intrinsic muscles of the larynx; and third, the valving mechanism receives external support from the extrinsic muscles of the larynx.

Laryngeal Structures

Prominent above the trachea is the larynx with its large, protective thyroid cartilage covering the individual cartilages, muscles, and ligaments that compose the total laryngeal body. In some people, particularly in adult males, the thyroid cartilage (called the ''Adam's Apple'') is so prominent that it can easily be seen rising high in the neck during swallowing, dropping low during conversational speech, and rising slightly on high notes while singing. Photographs of the five primary laryngeal cartilages (thyroid, cricoid, paired arytenoids, and epiglottis) may be seen in Figures 2–5 through 2–9. Two other small paired cartilages, the corniculates (small cone-shaped bodies that sit on the apex of the arytenoids extending into the aryepiglottic folds) and the cuneiforms (tiny cartilage pieces under the mucous membrane covering the aryepiglottic folds), apparently play only a minimal role in the phonatory functions of the larynx. The reader should read thoroughly the legends under each of the cartilage photographs, observing some of the other structures that are also identified. The three major cartilages seem to play separate roles, each one dependent on the other primarily by muscle and ligament action. The cricoid appears almost as an enlarged tracheal ring and forms the solid base of the larynx. It is circular in shape and the two triangular-shaped arytenoids sit on its high posterior (signet-shaped) wall. We shall see that the arytenoids rock and rotate on their articular facets on the cricoid by action of the intrinsic laryngeal muscles. Surrounding the cricoid and arytenoids is the U-shaped thyroid cartilage, which has several articula-

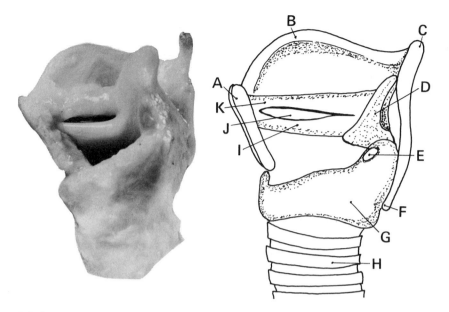

FIGURE 2-5. A lateral left view of the larynx is shown with the left thyroid cartilage removed. The untouched photograph is remarkable in its view of the ventricle opening between the true folds and the false folds. Structures may be identified by viewing the line drawing letter identifications: (A) cut edge at lamina of thyroid cartilage; (B) arch of the thyroid cartilage; (C) superior horn of the thyroid cartilage; (D) arytenoid cartilage, right; (E) articular facet of the cricoid and arytenoid cartilage; (F) inferior horn of the thyroid cartilage; (G) cricoid cartilage; (H) tracheal ring; (I) vocal fold, right; (J) ventricle; (K) ventricular fold or false fold.

tions with the cricoid cartilage below. All the laryngeal cartilages (similar to cartilage throughout the skeletal system) are coated with a tough, leathery covering (the perichondrium), which gives the lateral view of the larynx in Figure 2–5 such a waxy look. This perichondrium covering has been removed in the subsequent photographs of the separate cartilages.

There are two main groups of muscles of the larynx, the extrinsic and the intrinsic. The extrinsic muscles usually have one attachment to the larynx with the other attachment to some structure external to the larynx. The extrinsic muscles give the larynx fixed support and elevate or lower its position in the neck. Functionally, the extrinsic muscles (all but the cricopharyngeus) may be divided into two groups, elevators and depressors:

elevators	depressors
digastrics	omohyoids
geniohyoids	sternohyoids
mylohyoids	sternothyroids
stylohyoids	thyrohyoids

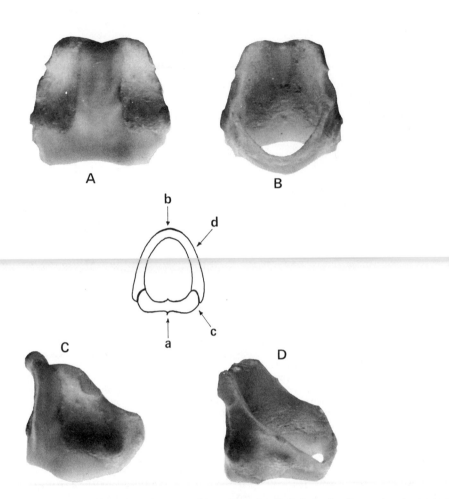

FIGURE 2-6. Four views of the cricoid cartilage. In all photographs, ligament and muscle attachments and the membranous covering have been removed, showing the bare cartilage. The line drawing shows the overall superior contour of the cricoid and the anatomical site of the cricoid photograph [(a) indicated that photograph A was taken from that view]. Photograph A shows the posterior surface of the cricoid; the difference in texture (smooth and rough) is related to ossification; the smooth portions represent the ossification. Photograph B shows an anterior view. (C) shows the right lateral view of the cricoid ring with the cartilage tipped upward, exposing the superior rim of the signet portion of the cartilage; upon this clearly defined rim rotate the two arytenoid cartilages. (D) shows a right lateral view of the cricoid; note the contrast in thickness between the thin anterior portion of the ring and the high signet posterior portion.

The extrinsic elevators lift the larynx high during swallowing and slightly during production of high singing notes. The depressors lower the larynx after deglutition and high-note singing as well as lower the larynx a bit for production of the low singing notes. Actually, the normal speaker should experience only minimal vertical excursion of the larynx. The other extrin-

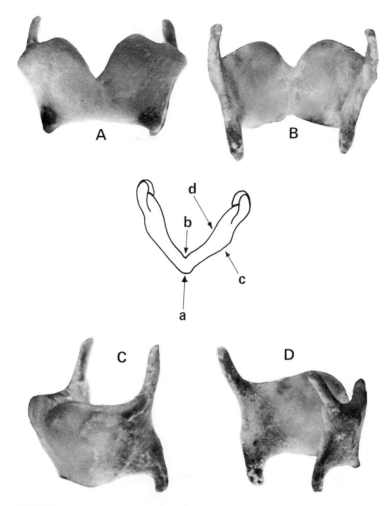

FIGURE 2-7. Four views of the laryngeal thyroid cartilage. The line drawing of the superior view of the thyroid cartilage indicates the side of the cartilage photographed. A-a shows a direct frontal view of the thyroid. B-b shows a posterior view of the cartilage; note the clear extension of the inferior and superior horns on each side. C-c shows primarily the thyroid cartilage wall. D-d shows the thyroid posteriorly from a three-quarter view.

sic laryngeal muscle is the cricopharyngeus, which fuses with the lower portion of the inferior pharyngeal constrictor. The sphincterlike fibers of the cricopharyngeus, originating from the posterior wall of the cricoid cartilage, help anchor the larynx in the fixed position where it usually lies. Greene (1980), in her fourth edition of *The Voice and Its Disorders*, feels that "the steadying influence of the cricopharyngeus on the larynx during phonation is of importance" and that the cricopharyngeus "is in fact an antagonist to the cricothyroid muscle" (pp. 36 and 38). In the production of the singing voice, the distance between the larynx and the hyoid bone

A

C

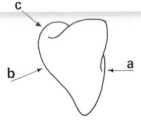

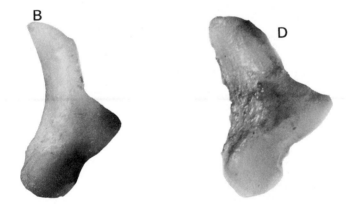

B

D

FIGURE 2-8. Four views of an arytenoid cartilage after removal of ligament, muscle, and membrane attachments. Photograph A shows a lateral view of the indentation (fovea) toward the base, which receives the attachment of the thyroarytenoid muscle (vocal fold), and the higher indentation on the left margin receives the fibers of the ventricular fold; the muscular process to which the posterior and lateral cricoarytenoids are attached may be seen at the right base. (B) shows a medial view of an arytenoid that has been tilted up slightly to the left; the right angular corner is the vocal process. (C) shows a posterior-lateral view of the muscular process at the base; note toward the right base the cricoarytenoid articular facet (point of joint articulation). In D, a view similar to B, the camera lens picks up the base of the cartilage as well as its medial wall; the curving base of the arytenoid allows it to rotate upon the cricoid rim below.

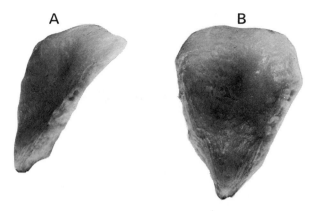

A   B

FIGURE 2-9. In these two views of the epiglottis, the epiglottis has been removed from its attachment on the lower, internal surface of the thyroid cartilage. For the purposes of photography, the cartilage has been denuded, excising away its ligament and muscle attachments and its membranous covering. (A) shows the epiglottis from a frontal-lateral view; the rotation of the cartilage permits us to see the concave epiglottal contour. (B) shows the epiglottis in its whole anterior dimension, which represents the lingual surface.

above, as determined by the function of the extrinsic muscles, is often the focus of singing teachers in the production of a good-sounding singing voice. It does not appear that the good-sounding speaking voice, however, requires much active muscle movement from either elevators or depressors.

The sphincteric action of the larynx and its phonatory capabilities appear to be the function of the intrinsic muscles of the larynx, which we will consider in a bit more detail than we did the laryngeal extrinsic muscles. There are six intrinsic muscles of the larynx. Four of them are clearly identifiable in the photographs and drawings in Figure 2–10, and two pairs of them can be seen in some detail in Figure 2–11. One pair of muscles, the posterior cricoarytenoids, is known as the lone vocal fold abductors (they open the glottis by separating the folds). The other five intrinsic muscles can be classified as adductors (close the glottis by bringing the folds together), although they have other functions. A brief description of each muscle will aid the reader in identifying them in Figures 2–10 and 2–11:

Posterior cricoarytenoids. This lone abductor muscle is the largest of the laryngeal intrinsic muscles, as seen in the designation E in Figure 2–10. The fibers originate from a middle depression on the posterior surface of the cricoid and angle up, inserting in the muscular process of the arytenoid on that side (right-sided fibers go to the right muscular process, and so on). This paired muscle is innervated by the recurrent laryngeal nerve. Its primary function is to abduct the folds by rotating the arytenoids.

Lateral cricoarytenoids. This paired muscle (F in Figure 2–10) functions as a direct antagonist to the posterior cricoarytenoid as it plays its ad-

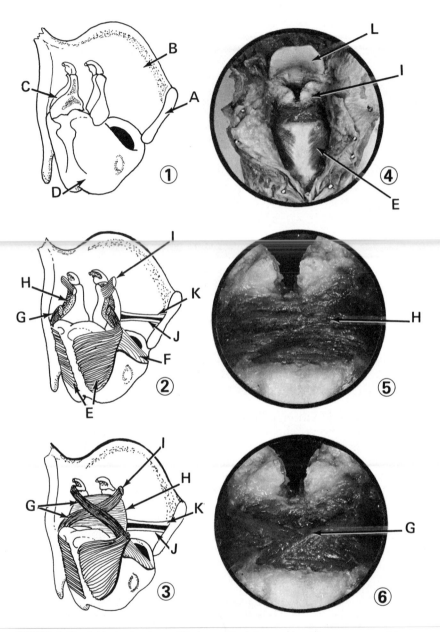

FIGURE 2-10. Intrinsic structures of the larynx. Basic laryngeal cartilage structures: (A) cut away of right thyroid wing; (B) left thyroid cartilage wall; (C) left arytenoid cartilage; (D) posterior cricoid cartilage. The other sketches and photographs identify the following intrinsic muscles by letter: (E) posterior cricoarytenoid; (F) lateral cricoarytenoid; (G) oblique arytenoid; (H) transverse arytenoid; (I) aryepiglottic; (J) thyroarytenoid (vocal fold); (K) ventricular fold. (L) identifies the epiglottis.

ACTION OF
CRICOTHYROID
MUSCLE

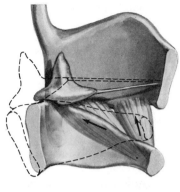

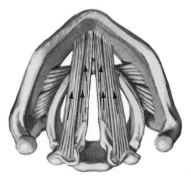

ACTION OF VOCALIS AND THYRO–ARYTENOID MUSCLES

FIGURE 2-11. The cricothyroid muscles can be seen in the drawing on the left, obliquing from the inner-superior surface of the cricoid cartilage up to the thyroid cartilage. The medial fibers of the vocalis section and the lateral section of the thyroarytenoids are seen clearly in the drawing on the right. © Copyright 1964, CIBA Pharmaceutical Company, Division of CIBA-GEIGY Corporation. Reprinted with permission from THE CIBA COLLECTION OF MEDICAL ILLUSTRATIONS, illustrated by Frank H. Netter, M.D. All rights reserved.

ductor role. The lateral cricoarytenoid originates from the upper border of the arch of the cricoid cartilage and inserts into the muscular process of the arytenoid on the same side. Innervation is also the recurrent laryngeal nerve. When this muscle contracts, it rotates the muscular process forward.

Transverse arytenoids. These muscle fibers (H in Figure 2-10) originate from the lateral margin and posterior surface of one arytenoid and insert on the same sites on the opposite arytenoid. As such, the transverse arytenoids are not paired muscles per se. They transverse the distance between the two arytenoids. Innervated bilaterally by the recurrent laryngeal nerves, when these muscles contract, they approximate the arytenoid cartilages together, functioning as adductor intrinsics as well as having the function of compressing the folds together.

Oblique arytenoids. The obliques are clearly labeled as G in Figure 2-10. The muscle originates from the muscular process of one arytenoid and obliques upward and across to the apex of the opposite cartilage. The fibers actually continue obliquely to the lateral border of the epiglottis and are known as the aryepiglottic muscles after they leave the arytenoid apex. The aryepiglottics become part of the aryepiglottic folds, which also include some cuneiform cartilage and membrane; these folds are active in the swallowing mechanism. The oblique arytenoid muscles are innervated bilaterally by the recurrent nerves and active in bringing the vocal folds closer together.

Thyroarytenoids. The paired thyroarytenoids are best seen in Figure 2-11 and form the muscular portion of the vocal folds. The inner section of the thyroarytenoid is known as the vocalis section and the larger, more lateral fibers are known as the thyromuscularis or external thyroarytenoid (Zemlin, 1981). As seen in Figure 2-11, the fibers originate on the inner surface of the thyroid cartilage and extend posteriorly to where they insert in the vocal process (vocalis fibers) and the lateral surface (external thyroarytenoid) of the arytenoid cartilages. The inner border of the vocal fold contains the vocal ligament that originates at the anterior commissure and extends to the vocal process end of the arytenoids. In summary, the vocal folds include both sections of the thyroarytenoids, the inner surface of the arytenoid cartilage, and the vocal ligament, with the whole apparatus covered with a tough, white membrane known as the conus elasticus. The drawing in Figure 2-11 shows the individual components of the vocal folds, while the photograph, Figure 2-16, shows the white membranous covering of the vocal folds (as they appear to the eye), with the folds in an open abducted position. The muscular aspect of the folds, the thyroarytenoids, are also innervated by the recurrent laryngeal nerve and they seem to have a dual function: they shorten themselves as required for producing lower phonation frequencies, and by their own muscular tension and elasticity function as glottal adducting structures.

Cricothyroids. In Figure 2-11 we see the anteriorly placed cricothyroid muscles that lie external to the larynx. The fibers originate from the anterior-lateral arch of the cricoid cartilage and end in two distinctly different insertions: The lower fibers insert near the lower horn of the thyroid cartilage while the more superior fibers oblique to the lower margin of the lateral thyroid cartilage wall. This pair of muscles is innervated by the superior laryngeal nerve. When they contract, they increase the distance between the thyroid and arytenoid cartilages (thus, contributing to pitch elevation), and the tensing of the vocal folds (by elongating them) is an adducting action.

Phonation Function

As the reader has seen, it is difficult to describe the cartilages and the muscles of the larynx without some description of laryngeal function. At this point, we should review in our minds the various laryngeal structures that have been presented, as a prelude to describing function and laryngeal physiology. We shall subscribe to the aerodynamic-myoelastic theory of phonation, which basically begins with the beginning of an expiration (air volume and air pressure) setting the approximated vocal folds in vibration as the air flow passes between the folds (transglottal pressure). In the prephonation period, the vocal folds may well be abducted in the inspiration position as seen in Figure 2-12. The folds begin to approximate one another as the expiration phase of the breath cycle begins. The five laryngeal adductor muscles contract to bring the vocal folds together. Two of the adductors, for example, the lateral cricoarytenoid and the

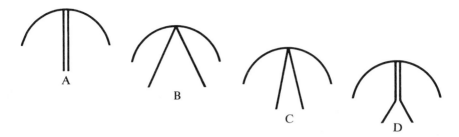

FIGURE 2-12. Various glottal configurations. (A) The vocal folds are approximated for phonation. (B) The folds are widely abducted for forced inspiration. (C) The folds are in the typical expiratory (nonphonatory) position. (D) shows the typical inverted Y glottis for whisper with anterior 2/3 (vocal folds) laxly approximated and the posterior 1/3 (arytenoids) rotated in an abducted, open position. In drawings B and C, inspiration and expiration, the glottal surfaces were drawn deliberately longer to represent the increased length of the vocal folds during inspiration-expiration, as contrasted with their shortened length during phonation and whisper.

thyroarytenoids, have been found to have very rapid contraction times, sometimes as fast and fifteen msec which Martensson (1968) has written is "exceedingly fast and . . . surpassed only by the extrinsic eye muscles" for speed. It would appear that vocal fold adduction is achieved in milliseconds, prior to the onset of voicing. As the folds approximate, they begin to obstruct the air flow passing through the glottal level of the airway. Zemlin (1968) wrote:

> It is extremely important to note that complete obstruction of the air passageway is not necessary to initiate phonation. If the glottal chink is narrowed to about 3 mm, a minimal amount of air flow will set the folds into vibration. (p. 175)

The subglottal pressure builds up when the folds are approximated. The volume of expired air leaving the lungs is impeded at the level of the glottis, resulting in an increased velocity of air flow through the glottis. Subglottal pressure increases and the vocal folds are blown apart reducing subglottal pressure (the opening phase of one cycle of vibration). Because of the mass of the folds (their muscle and ligament covered with a membrane) and the *Bernoulli effect,* they come back together again to their previous approximation line (the closed phase of the phonatory cycle). The Bernoulli effect is the sucking attraction of the vocal folds toward one another, caused by the increased velocity of air passing between them. This results in a suction that draws the folds together. To repeat, the vibratory cycle of the vocal folds can be summarized as follows: The intrinsic adductors approximate the folds as expiration begins. Subglottal pressure increases. The air flow passes through the glottal opening and blows the folds apart. The static mass of the folds and the Bernoulli suction bring them back together again. The vibratory cycle then repeats itself.

During normal phonation, the vocal folds approximate one another in their total anterior-posterior dimension. In Figure 2–13, line drawings

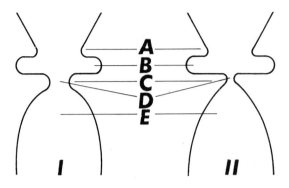

FIGURE 2-13
A line tracing of a tomogram that presents an X-ray frontal view of the vocal folds, showing vocal fold approximation contours for I, chest register; and II, falsetto register. (A) ventricular fold; (B) open ventricle; (C) vocal fold; (D) glottis, opening between folds; (E) trachea. Note the thicker fold approximation for the chest register as opposed to the thinner, superior approximation of the two folds during the production of the falsetto register.

show the relative approximation contours of the vocal folds during normal phonation, and also during normal inspiration, normal expiration, and whispering. The vocal folds appear slightly shorter during phonation and whispering in the line drawings, as they do in the normal larynx; that is, the vocal folds will always be longer in the open abducted position than in the closed adducted one (Hollien and Moore, 1960). The configuration of the glottis for whispering is characterized by an open, posterior chink, with the arytenoid cartilages and their vocal processes angled in an open, inverted V position. Although the vocal folds are parallel to one another during whispering, they do not firmly approximate. This lack of adduction, particularly in the posterior chink, produces frictional sounds when the outgoing air stream passes through, producing what we perceive as whispering.

The vocal folds appear to be maximally long during at-rest breathing and shortened somewhat during phonation. In fact, at the lower end of one's pitch range, at the level where conversational phonation is generally found, the vocal folds are considerably shortened. When we begin to speak about the length thickness of the folds, we begin to talk about fundamental frequency, or the pitch of the voice that we hear. Fundamental frequency is directly related to how many vibratory closings-openings (cycles) the vocal folds make in one second. The rate of vibration is related to their thickness-length-elasticity. A short, thick, somewhat lax fold vibrates at a much slower rate than a long, thin, tense fold. Hollien and his colleagues (1960a, 1960b, 1962, 1970), Hixon, Klatt, and Mead (1970), and Sonninen (1968) have found that the length of the vocal folds increases almost in a "stair-step" fashion, corresponding to increases in frequency. By using X-ray laminagraphy, which permits cross-sectional, coronal viewing of the vocal folds, Hollien found that the mean thickness, or mass, of the folds systematically decreased as voice pitch increased. It appears, then, from the multiple studies conducted on vocal fold length and thickness by the Hollien group, that fundamental frequency, or voice pitch level, is directly related to the length and thickness of the individual's vocal folds. The relative differences between men and women in vocal fold length (approximately 20mm for men and 15mm for women) and vocal fold thickness appear to be the primary determinants of differences in voice pitch between

32

the adults of the two sexes (the typical fundamental frequency for men is around 125 cps; for women, around 200 cps). Examples of normal pitch values, including pitch range and fundamental frequency, are given in Table 2-1. When an individual phonates at increasingly higher pitch levels, he or she must lengthen his or her vocal folds to decrease their relative mass. Increases of pitch, therefore, appear to be related to a lengthening of the vocal folds, with a corresponding decrease of tissue mass and an increase of fold elasticity. Lowering the pitch is directly related to relaxation and shortening of the folds. It would appear that both the cricothyroids and the cricopharyngeus play an active role in elongating the vocal folds, which in turn increases their elasticity. The vocal folds are stretched by the action of the cricothyroids, which increase the distance of the arytenoids from the thyroid cartilage by drawing the cricoid cartilage up toward the thyroid, which in effect lowers the posterior cricoid rim. The cricopharyngeus, when contracted, can pull the cricoid slightly posterior, adding to vocal fold elasticity. For a detailed description with accompany-

TABLE 2-1.   Normal Fundamental Frequency (F_0) and Pitch Ranges for Four Voices (Bass, Tenor, Alto, and Soprano)

NOTE ON PIANO	PHYSICAL (CPS)	TYPICAL F_0 AND PITCH RANGE			
		(BASS)	(TENOR)	(ALTO)	(SOPRANO)
C_6	1,024				1,040
B	960				
A	853				
G_5	768				
F	682			700	
E	640				
D	576				
C_5	512		550		
B	480				
A	426				
G_4	384				
F	341	340			
E	320				
D	288				
C_4	256				F_0 256
B	240				
A	213			F_0 200	
G_3	192				
F	170				170
E	160				
D	144		F_0 135	140	
C_3	128				
B	120				
A	106	F_0 100			
G_2	96			95	
F	85	80			

ing drawings of the elongation functions of the cricothyroid muscles, the reader may find helpful the description of Broad in his phonation chapter in *Normal Aspects of Speech, Hearing, and Language* (1973). Relaxation of the cricothyroids with the simultaneous contraction of the thyroarytenoids appears to be essential for shortening and thickening the folds, which lowers the pitch of the voice. Greene (1980) has suggested that the cricopharyngeus may play an antagonist (shortening) role to the cricothyroids.

It appears that at the upper end of the natural pitch range, increased elasticity of the vocal folds results in increased glottal resistance, requiring increased air pressure to produce higher-frequency phonations. Increased tension of the vocal folds requires greater air pressure to set the folds into vibration. Van den Berg (1968) has written that the average person must slightly increase subglottal pressure in order to increase voice pitch; however, because increasing subglottal pressure has an abducting effect on the vocal folds, the folds must continue to increase in tension to maintain their approximated position. While the primary determinant of pitch appears to be the length, mass, and tension of the vocal folds, increases in pitch level are usually characterized by increasing subglottal pressures.

The vocal folds can elongate and stretch only so far. If the singer wants to extend his or her pitch range beyond what normal vocal fold stretching can do, he or she is forced to produce a *falsetto* voice. We might describe the production of the falsetto voice in this manner: the folds approximate with tight, posterior vocal-process adduction; the posterior cartilaginous portion is so tightly adducted that there is little or no posterior vibration; the lateral portions of the thyroarytenoid are not actively vibrating in the falsetto voice. The inner vocalis segment of the muscle is extremely contracted along the vocal ligament; as the membrane wraps the ligament, the membrane itself becomes the primary vibrating structure during falsetto. Judson and Weaver (1965), Rubin and Hirt (1960), and Hollien and his colleagues (1962) have all described the falsetto (called the "loft" register by Hollien) as a production of the vibrating membrane on the anterior two-thirds surface of the glottal margin.

The kind of pitch opposite from the falsetto is the low glottal fry. Greene (1980) described the *fry* as the pulse register, the "lowest range of notes and synonymous with vocal fry, glottal fry, creak and strohbass" (p. 81). The glottal fry sounds something like the sputter of a low-powered outboard motor. Zemlin (1981) wrote that fry is produced when the folds are approximated tightly with a flaccid appearance along the glottal margin. Moore and von Leden (1958) found that during fry there is a double vibration of the folds followed by a prolonged period of approximation (almost two-thirds of the vibratory cycle). Vocal fry may well be the normal vibratory cycle one uses near the bottom of one's normal pitch range. Some speakers may add fry to their phonation, adding in their minds an authoritative quality to what they are saying. While fry does not appear to be a vocal abnormality, some voice patients successfully work to eliminate it by slightly elevating their pitch levels.

Related to the production of voice pitch and the pitch range of any individual is *voice register*. It appears that a particular register characterizes a certain pattern of vocal fold vibration, with the vocal folds approximated in a similar way throughout a particular pitch range. Once this pitch range reaches its maximum limit, the folds adjust to a new approximation contour, which produces an abrupt change in vocal quality. Van den Berg (1964) describes three primary forms of voice register: chest, mid-voice, and falsetto. Hollien and his colleagues (1962), in their laminagraphic X-ray studies of vocal fold movement, describe two vocal registers: normal and falsetto. In the frontal, coronal view of the folds sketched in Figure 2–13, one can identify the thickened folds of the chest or normal register contrasted with the thin folds of the falsetto register. From the perceptual viewpoint, voice register is confined to the similar sound of the individual's voice at various pitches. While this similar quality is undoubtedly related to the similarity in vocal fold approximation and vibration characteristics, teachers of voice are desirous of blending together the various registers, so that the difference in quality of voice becomes almost imperceptible as the singer goes from one register to the next. Some singers seem to have only one register; no matter how they change their pitch, their voices always seem to have the same quality, with no discernible break toward the upper part of the pitch range. Such persons' frontal X-rays would probably show a relatively stable contour in the approximations of the vocal folds. An excellent review of the literature and detailed description of voice register may be found in Luchsinger and Arnold's *Voice-Speech-Language* (1965).

The intensity of the voice, perceived as the loudness of the voice, is directly related to changes in subglottal and transglottal air pressures. Hixon and Abbs (1980) have written, "Sound pressure level, the primary factor contributing to our perception of the *loudness* of the voice, is governed mainly by the pressure supplied to the larynx by the respiratory pump" (p. 68). It appears that the trained voice of the actor or singer increases intensity by increasing both subglottal pressure and air flow rate, with only minimal increase of glottal tension (Bouhuys and others, 1966). The untrained voice at very loud levels often increases in pitch as part of the loudness. It is difficult for the untrained voice to produce loud voice at very low pitch levels.

As voice intensity is increased, the vocal folds tend to remain closed for a longer period of time during each vibratory cycle, and the greater intensity of voice is characterized by greater excursion of the vibrating folds. It would appear that as intensity increases, increased glottal tension impedes the rate of airflow, increasing subglottal pressure. At lower pitch levels this tension during intense phonations is minimal, causing the singer, for example, to "run out of air" sooner when producing varying intensities at low pitches than at high ones. It appears that the speaker or singer who continually requires a loud voice could use his or her vocal mechanism more optimally by developing his or her expiratory skills, relying more on increased subglottal air pressure and increased airflow rates, and less on increased glottal elasticity, to achieve louder intensities.

Besides pitch, loudness, quality, and register as measurable dimensions of voice, Perkins (1978) has added constriction and vertical focus to the production of voice. He describes the feeling of constriction on a continuum of open (the yawn) to closed (the swallow). Imagery or feeling is used for determining the vertical focus of the voice, "the perception associated with the placement of the focal point of the tone in the head" (Perkins, 1978, p. 113). At the low end of the vertical focus, the speaker or singer feels voice is being squeezed out of the throat, while at the high end the focus seems to be high in the head. Vocal efficiency seems to occur best at the higher end of the vertical placement. It has been our experience using the Visi-Pitch that subjects given these instructions relative to the imagery of constriction and verticality, produce voices with greater aperiodicity (hoarseness) at the low end of the vertical scale with greater vocal clarity at the higher end. In time, the Perkins's construct of constriction and vertical focus may well have greater measurement potential and utilization.

While vocal quality may well be primarily related to supraglottal resonance, important components of the spectrum of the laryngeal tone have its origins at the level of the glottis. How the vocal folds are approximated together, laxly or tightly, will in part determine the quality of the voice. Many individuals can produce several "different voices," all at the same pitch level, by varying the approximation characteristics of the vocal folds. A breathy voice is often produced by adding phonation to the ongoing expiration with the folds only laxly approximating one another. Spectrographic analysis of the breathy voice shows us that noise and aperiodicity produced by the air flow typifies the first part of the utterance with phonation (greater periodicity) coming in after some delay. The three spectrograms shown in Figure 2-14 contrast the breathy voice (with much aperiodicity and noise) with a harsh voice (with hard glottal attack), and with a normal voice. Each of the spectrograms was produced by the same normal speaker prolonging an /i/. In hard glottal attack, the opposite kind of vocal onset is observed; here the first voicing patterns begin abruptly with the onset of expiration. It appears as if the glottis is held tightly until there is a sudden release of air that sets the folds into vibration. Another example of a faulty positioning of the vocal folds can be seen in the patient with spastic dysphonia. Here the patient brings the folds so tightly together that they act like a valve, almost totally preventing the flow of air from traveling through the glottis. The patient's voice is strained with a stranglelike quality. How the folds are approximated has much to do with how our voices sound. Our study of the vocal fold "set" aspect of phonation limits us to use such methods as high-speed film, viewing the larynx through indirect laryngoscopy, or by spectrograms displaying visually the voice that we hear. While we know something about the extremes of breathiness and hard glottal attack, our knowledge of vocal fold physiology for most of the voices we hear is relatively lacking specific to vocal fold approximation and its effect on quality.

RESONANCE

The fundamental frequency that is produced by the vocal folds would be a weak-sounding voice without the additional component of resonance. This writer observed a patient years ago who had been cut from ear to ear with a

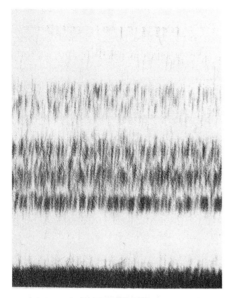

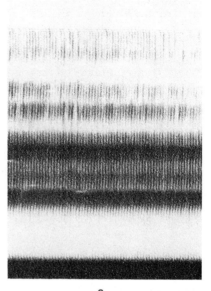

1
Breathy

2
Normal

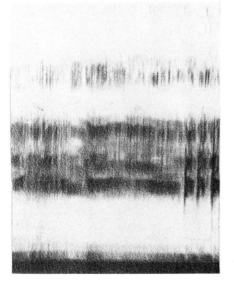

3
Harsh

FIGURE 2-14
Three spectrograms of the same speaker producing the vowel /i/ under three conditions: breathy, normal, harsh. The relative spacing of the formants stays the same as the signal source changes.

massive wound opening immediately superior to his thyroid cartilage. Before the wound was sutured, we heard the patient's feeble attempts at phonation. Much of his air flow and soundwave escaped through the wound opening, producing a voice that no one had ever heard before. Someone likened it to the thin bleat of a baby lamb. It would appear that what is perceived as the quality, timbre, and loudness of the voice is produced by the supraglottal resonators. While the structures of the chest and trachea may play some role in resonance, their role is not as clearly defined as the supraglottal resonators.

Structures of Resonance

The vocal tract begins for all practical purposes at the level of the glottis. The air flow and soundwaves probably have some beginning passage in the ventricular space (B) between the true folds (A) and the ventricular folds (C). As we see in Figure 2–15, the cavities of the vocal tract have been shaded in black. The epiglottis (D) by its concavity probably serves as a

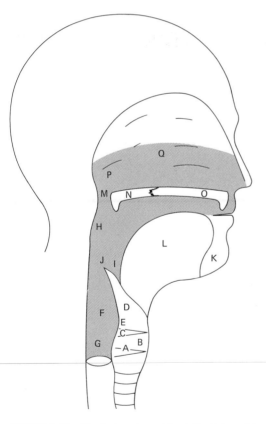

FIGURE 2-15. The F-shaped vocal tract. The letters A through O identify various structures of the vocal tract as identified in the text that follows.

deflector as soundwaves travel between the aryepiglottic folds (E) into the hypopharynx (F). The hypopharynx is the cavity directly above the esophagus (G) with its anterior border the structures and opening of the larynx (G), its sides and back wall composed of the lower pharyngeal constrictors (G).

Just before we near the tip of the epiglottis, we see the oropharynx (J). The small angular space between the front of the epiglottis and the back of the tongue (L) is called the vacula (I). Cutting away the mandible (K) in our lateral view, we see the great body of the tongue occupying most of the oral cavity, forming the constantly changing floor of that cavity. The hard palate is designated (O) in the drawing with the soft palate or velum (N) forming the roof of the oral cavity. The lips, teeth, and cheeks play obvious front and lateral roles in shaping the oral cavity. The middle and superior pharyngeal constrictors form the lateral and posterior muscular wall of the oropharynx (H). The site of the velopharyngeal closure, necessary for separation of the oral and nasal cavities required for oral resonance, is slightly enlarged in our drawing to represent the Passavant's pad (M) area of the superior pharyngeal constrictor; most subjects do not have such Passavant area enlargement. Superior to the velopharyngeal contact point, the posterior pharyngeal wall, as observed in Figure 2-15, makes a sharp angulation forward forming the superior wall of the nasopharynx (P) and continuing on as the superior wall of the nasal cavity. We will make no further structural breakdown of the nasal cavities (Q) as a prelude to our discussion of resonance. The reader should also be advised that our use of the gross line drawing of the sagittal head limits any drawings of lateral walls, pillars of fauces, muscles of the palate, pharynx, and tongue. If we look again at the overall lateral drawing of the vocal tract, we see that the total darkened areas look slightly like a large alphabet letter *F*. Our vocal tract in the drawing resembles an *F* because the velopharyngeal port is open, connecting the oral and nasal cavities together. If the port were closed at the velopharyngeal contact point (M), the vocal tract opening available for voice resonance would resemble a printed *r*, formed only by the pharynx and the oral cavity opening above the surface of the tongue.

Mechanism of Resonance

A vibrator, such as the string of a violin or the vocal folds, originates a fundamental vibration (or soundwaves), which by itself produces weak, barely audible sounds. This vibrating energy is usually amplified by a resonating body of some type. For example, a violin string, when plucked, will set up a fundamental vibration; this vibration becomes resonated by the bridge to which the strings are attached, which then sets into vibration the sounding board below and in turn the main resonating body of the violin (the chest), which provides open cavity resonance. When all the violin parts are working together in harmony, the fundamental tone of the involved string becomes louder and fuller in quality. The same string stripped out of its mount on the violin and then plucked (even with the same amount of tension to the string) will sound less intense and thinner in quality. The violin provides a ready example of the two main types of resonance, the *sounding board effect* and the *open cavity effect*. When a particular string of the violin is bowed, the airwaves that develop are low in amplitude and barely audible; however, since the vibrating string is stretched tightly over the bridge of the violin, it sets the bridge itself into vibration. The bridge functions as a sounding board. The sounding board then vibrates, setting into vibration the air over a much larger area, increasing the loudness of the tone. The sounding board vibration also introduces the soundwaves into the violin cavity itself.

The main body, or chest, of the violin provides cavity resonance to the source sound of the vibrating string. The string vibrating alone, which is similar to laryngeal vibration without supraglottal resonance, will produce a barely audible tone. The cavity resonance provided by the body of the violin increases the volume of the vibrating string. The size and overall shape of the resonating cavity has an obvious relationship to the resonance of a vibration. It appears that for every frequency of vibration there is an ideal resonating cavity size and shape. The ideal is represented by the cavity that seems to give the loudest tone and the tone with the fullest amount of amplification to its overtones. This observation can be easily tested by placing a tuning fork over a large glass, varying the amounts of water in the glass. At a particular level of water, the glass will provide optimum resonance, heard as the increase in loudness of sound. The lower the frequency of the vibrating wave, the larger the size of the resonating cavity. The thinner string of the violin requires a much smaller resonating body than the larger string of the bass viola, which requires a resonating body as tall as the person who plays the instrument.

At this point we must cease descriptions of relatively fixed resonating bodies if we are to understand the mechanisms of resonance as they apply to the human speaking voice. Our vocal tract is continually changing. As Minifie (1973) has written:

> During the production of vowels the vocal tract may be viewed as a tortuously shaped tube open at one end (the opening between the lips) and bounded at the other end by a vibrating valve which has the effect of closing off the tube at the larynx. The three-dimensional geometry of this tube may be altered through the contraction of muscles which regulate the movements of the tongue, velum, pharynx, mandible, lips, epiglottis, and larynx. These structures may be moved individually or in various combinations. The combination of structures which move during the production of a particular speech sound will determine the unique vocal tract configuration, and hence, the unique acoustical filter for that sound. (p. 243)

Some areas of the vocal tract, depending on their configuration, are compatible with the periodic vibration coming from the vocal folds and amplify the fundamental frequency and its harmonics. For example, a fundamental frequency of 125 cycles per second will resonate harmonic frequencies at 250, 375, 500 (each subsequent harmonic frequency is a multiple of the fundamental), and so on. The continuous vocal tract tube is continually interrupted at various sites from the intrusion and movement of various structures. Some of the interruptions or constrictions may be severe, such as carrying the tongue high and forward in the oral cavity. Any movement of mandible, tongue, or velum will, for example, greatly alter the opening of the oral cavity. Some of the movements have no effect on the fundamental or sound source; some of them filter or inhibit the fundamental. What finally emits from the mouth or the nasal cavity and is perceived as voice has become a complex periodic signal with the same fundamental frequency as the vocal fold source, but has become highly modified in its overall sound characteristics. We can hear, for example, several familiar female voices all saying the same few words at the same fundamental frequency, but we will still be able to differentiate each voice and assign it to each familiar person. The vocal characteristics related to the individualization of each person's vocal tract will have given each voice its own characteristics as the result of the amplification and filtering unique to each vocal tract.

The "F" configuration of the supraglottal vocal tract is always changing. What happens in any one portion of the tract has an influence on the total flow of air and soundwave through the total tract, influencing the sound that eventually emits from the mouth (or nose). By action of the pharyngeal constrictors and supraglottal muscles, the overall dimensions of the pharynx are always changing. The membranes of the pharynx and the degree of relaxation or tautness of the pharyngeal constrictors will have noticeable filtering effects. It would appear that higher frequency vocalizations receive their best resonating effects under a fairly high degree of pharyngeal wall tension. Lower frequencies appear to be better amplified by a pharynx that is somewhat relaxed.

The oral cavity, or mouth, is as essential for resonance as the pharynx. Of all our resonators, the mouth is capable of the most variation in size and shape. It is the constant size-shape adjustment of the mouth that permits us to speak. Our vowels and diphthongs, for example, are originated by a laryngeal vibration, but shaped and restricted by size-shape adjustments of the oral cavity. The mouth has fixed structures (teeth, alveolar processes, dental arch, and hard palate) and moving structures; in our study of voice resonance, it is the moving structures, primarily the tongue and velum, with which we are most concerned.

The tongue is the most mobile of the articulators, possessing both extrinsic and intrinsic muscles to move it. Each of the extrinsic muscles can, upon contraction, elevate or lower the tongue at its anterior, middle, or posterior points and extend it forward or backward. The intrinsic muscles control the shape of the tongue by narrowing, flattening, lengthening, or shortening the overall tongue body. The various combinations of intrinsic and extrinsic muscle contractions can produce an unlimited number of tongue positions with resulting size-shape variations of the oral cavity. These tongue positions and their relationship to the formation of specific vowels and vowel formants have been well described in several references such as the Peterson and Barney study (1952), and in chapters by Netsell and by Daniloff in the *Normal Aspects of Speech, Hearing and Language* (1973).

The structural adequacy and normal functioning of the velum are likewise important for the development of normal voice resonance. The

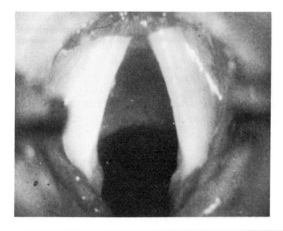

FIGURE 2-16
The normal vocal folds photographed using indirect mirror laryngoscopy, showing the open glottis during a normal expiration. The anterior portion of the two folds is at the top of the picture; the mirrored view of the right fold is to the left, the left fold to the right; the posterior, vocal process ends of the folds are at the bottom of the picture. The dark central inverted V area is the open glottis.

elevation and tensing of the velum are vital for achieving velopharyngeal closure. A lack of adequate palatal movement, despite adequacy of velar length, can cause serious problems of nasality. While the velum probably serves as a sounding board structure in resonance, it plays an obviously important part in separating the oral cavity from the nasal cavity. The movement and positioning of the velum changes the size and shape of three important resonating cavities: the pharynx, the oral cavity, and the nasal cavity. Therefore, any alteration of the velum (such as a soft palate cleft) may have profound influence on resonance. Velar movement is only one component contributing to velopharyngeal closure (Zwitman, Gyepes, and Ward, 1976). Closure patterns that separate the oral and nasal cavities from one another may include velar action coupled by posterior pharyngeal wall movement or velar action with active lateral and posterior pharyngeal wall movement. Regardless of the type of closure pattern (velar-posterior-lateral pharyngeal), the site of closure is generally in the Passavant's area, designated as M in Figure 2–15.

The fundamental frequency that comes from the vocal folds is amplified throughout the vocal tract. Movements and constrictions within the tract contribute to the overall amplifying or filtering of the voice. Faulty use of the structures of the vocal tract often leads to excesses in resonance.

SUMMARY

In our review of the respiratory aspects of phonation we found that the outgoing air stream is the primary activating force of the larynx. The good user of voice develops good expiratory control. A description of the physiology of phonation included a review of the structures and mechanisms of normal phonation including the aspects of frequency and intensity. Supraglottal structures and functions specific to resonance were reviewed, finding that the entire vocal tract contributes to the amplification and filtering of the fundamental frequency.

3
Disorders
of Vocal Fold Mass
and Approximation

A traditional view of voice disorders separates them into two etiologic categories, functional and organic. Functional voice problems are related to abuse and misuse of the larynx. Organic voice disorders are the result of some kind of physical change in the structure or function of the larynx. Categorizing voice disorders for purposes of voice therapy on the functional and organic dichotomy can be misleading and confusing. While the identification of organic laryngeal disease is obviously imperative in medical management, there are not separate voice therapy procedures for both functional or organically caused problems. Rather, in this chapter we will consider the various voice disorders according to whether they are related to changes in vocal fold mass or in vocal fold approximation. Additive lesions, such as nodules (functional) or papilloma (organic), weight the folds with added tissue, changing the mass of the folds, altering their vibratory characteristics. How the folds approximate is obviously affected both by mass additions on the glottal margin and by how well the folds come together. The kind of voice therapy required is often determined by the mass-size of the folds and how they approximate one another.

The term *dysphonia* includes many deviations in phonation. The listener may use various terms to describe the voice disorders one hears—*hoarseness, breathiness, harshness, huskiness, stridency,* to name only a few—but, unfortunately, there is little common agreement as to what these terms mean. What is *hoarseness* to speaker A may be *huskiness* to speaker B. Our own private vocabularies for voice defects hinder us in developing an understanding of voice problems. This lack of a common vocabulary for the various parameters of voice production and voice pathology is perhaps related to the number of different kinds of specialists who are concerned with voice—the laryngologist, the singing teacher, the speech-voice scientist, the speech pathologist, and the voice-and-diction teacher. The laryngologist is primarily interested in identifying the etiological and pathological aspects for purposes of treatment; the singing teacher uses imagery in an attempt to get the desired acoustical effect from the student; the speech-voice scientist has the laboratory interest of the physiologist or physicist; the speech pathologist often attempts to use the knowledge and vocabulary of all three of these disciplines; and the voice-and-diction teacher assesses the dynamics of voice production and uses whatever is necessary to "get" the best voice. It is no wonder that interdisciplinary communication among voice specialists breaks down.

The general public tolerance of and indifference to voice problems makes the early identification of voice pathologies difficult. Hoarseness that persists longer than several days is often identified by the laryngologist as a possible symptom of serious laryngeal disease. And it may be. Hoarseness is certainly the acoustic correlate of improper vocal fold functioning, with or without true laryngeal disease. The distinction between organic disease of the larynx and functional misuse has been a prominent dichotomy in the consideration of phonatory disorders. It is important for the laryngologists, in their need to rule out or identify true organic disease, to view the laryngeal mechanism by laryngoscopy in order to make a judgment with regard to organic-structural involvement. In the absence of structural deviation, the laryngologist describes the voice disorder as functional. This functional-organic dichotomy persists in the literature of voice therapy, despite warnings that "such a dichotomy is completely inadequate in describing any but the most primitive of human behaviors. Etiologies of vocal disorders always exist along a continuum" (Murphy, 1964, p. 2). It is usually impossible to separate the organic voice problem from the functional one. For example, continuous faulty abuse and misuse of the vocal cords may lead to the development of vocal nodules. The structural or organic problem results from the functional misuse, and to separate the functional from the organic in such cases makes little sense. Or, the child may experience dysphonia with relatively normal vocal folds, perhaps with only a slight edema or swelling. With little or no structural change of the vocal folds, the functional-organic dichotomy would have us identify such a disorder as a functional one. From the point of view of voice therapy, however, there would be little difference between our therapeutic approaches, which in either case would be to reduce the vocal abuse-misuse.

Rather than struggle with the functional-organic dichotomy, which really does not tell us much, we would understand our voice patients and their dysphonias better if we focused on the process of phonation, the size and mass of the vocal folds, and the degree of fold approximation. Normal phonation requires that the vocal folds have appropriate tension and vibration, and any alteration of cord size is likely to produce phonation changes.

Hollien and his colleagues (1960a, 1962) have demonstrated by their vocal fold measurements that there is a direct correlation between the size and mass of the vocal folds of an individual and his fundamental frequency. Lengthening of the folds causes an increase in their inherent elasticity, which increases their rate of vibration, elevating the voice pitch; decrease of fold length is essential for phonating at the bottom of one's pitch range. Another aspect of vocal fold size and mass is register. As we indicated in Chapter 2, the approximating edges of the vocal folds differ for chest-register phonation as opposed to falsetto-register phonation; the inferior approximating surface of the vocal fold is the primary point of contact for lower chest-register frequencies (with a broader surface of contact), while the falsetto-register fold contact is a thinner, more superior point of contact. Inconsistencies in register may well have their origins in inappropriate mass-size adjustments of the vocal folds. Vocal fold increases in size and mass are brought about also by such obvious factors as puberty, with its increase in the size of the laryngeal structures; virilizing drugs, with their enlargement of the vocal folds (Damste, 1967); laryngeal abuse-misuse, with its swelling of fold tissue; infection followed by edema; and many other causes that we shall consider separately.

Normal phonation requires that, in addition to proper mass-size adjustments, the two vocal folds approximate one another optimally along their entire length (from the anterior commissure up to, and including, the vocal process). The easy imitation of voices by some actors suggests that we are able to vary the strength of fold approximation. Consistent with this observation is the further one that most functionally caused dysphonias are related directly to under- or overadduction of the vocal folds and to alterations in air flow. In underadduction, the folds are too laxly approximated, resulting in a breathy type of phonation. Sometimes after prolonged hyperfunctional use of the voice, the folds will show an open chink posteriorly; actually, this posterior chink is the incomplete adduction of the vocal processes. Overadduction of the folds results in the tight valving of the glottal mechanism, so much so that the individual may be unable to phonate for speech. Spastic dysphonia is a clear example of a severe overadduction problem: The voice sounds strained, like the kind of phonation we hear from someone attempting to talk while lifting a heavy object; the valving action of the larynx (fixed, tight adduction) overrules the individual's desire to phonate, and phonation becomes almost impossible. Often such conditions that increase the mass-size of the vocal folds—that is, thickening, nodules, or polyps—will, by their size, make the optimum adduction of the vocal folds impossible. Glottal growths, such as nodules and polyps, interfere with the approximating edges of the vocal folds, often producing open chinks between the approximating folds on each side of the growth. Any structural interference between the approximating edges of the vocal folds will usually result in some degree of dysphonia. Occasionally unilateral or bilateral paralysis of intrinsic muscles of the larynx will result in paralysis of one or both of the vocal folds, producing obvious voice problems related to faulty approximation.

In Table 3-1 we have listed twenty-five laryngeal disorders that may

TABLE 3-1. Laryngeal Disorders Causing Changes in Mass-Size and/or Approximation Characteristics of the Vocal Folds

DISORDER	MASS–SIZE CHANGE	APPROXIMATION CHANGE
Carcinoma	X	X
Contact ulcers	X	
Diplophonia	X	X
Dysarthria	X	X
Endocrine changes	X	
Functional aphonia		X
Functional dysphonia		X
Granulomas	X	X
Hemangiomas	X	X
Hyperkeratosis	X	
Laryngectomy		X
Laryngitis	X	X
Laryngofissure		X
Leukoplakia	X	
Papilloma	X	X
Phonation breaks		X
Pitch breaks	X	
Pubertal changes	X	
Spastic dysphonia		X
Thickening (vocal fold)	X	X
Ventricular dysphonia		X
Vocal fold paralyses	X	X
Vocal nodules	X	X
Vocal polyps	X	X
Webbing	X	X

produce various phonation disorders. For each of the disorders, the table will specify if that disorder affects primarily the size-mass of the vocal folds, a change in their approximation, or a change in both mass-size and approximation. To facilitate using Table 3–1 as a reference when reading about specific laryngeal disorders, the various disorders have been listed alphabetically.

VOICE PROBLEMS RELATED TO MASS-SIZE DISORDERS

Any condition that adds to the mass-size of the vocal folds may alter their vibratory characteristics. We shall consider separately various mass-size alterations of the vocal folds, considering the possible etiology of the disorder and its probable management. Specific therapy procedures for the speech-language pathologist or voice clinician will be deferred until Chapters 5, 6, 7, and 8.

Laryngitis

Functional or infectious laryngitis is an inflammation of the laryngeal membrane covering the vocal folds, resulting in severe dysphonia and occasional aphonia. In functional laryngitis, the patient experiences a moderate amount of hoarseness secondary to phonatory trauma. Typical functional laryngitis may be heard in the voice of an excited spectator after a football or basketball game. In the excitement of the game, with his or her own voice masked by the noise of the crowd, the rooter screams at pitch levels and intensities he or she normally does not use. The inner glottal edges of the membrane become swollen (edematous) and thickened, an expected consequence of excessive approximation. The increased edema of the folds is accompanied by irritation and increased blood accumulation. The acute stage of functional laryngitis is at its peak during the actual yelling or traumatic vocal behavior, with the vocal folds much increased in size and mass. Brodnitz (1971b) wrote that functionally irritated vocal folds appear on laryngoscopic examination to be much like the thickened, reddened folds of acute infectious laryngitis. There is an important difference in treatment, however. For functional or *nonspecific laryngitis*—which is usually the result of continued irritation by such things as allergy, excessive smoking and alcohol drinking, and vocal abuse—the obvious treatment is to eliminate the vocal irritant whenever possible. In the case of functional laryngitis secondary to yelling or a similar form of vocal abuse, elimination of the abuse will usually permit the vocal mechanism to return to its natural state. The temporary laryngitis experienced toward the end of the basketball game is usually relieved by a return to normal vocal activity, with most of the edema and irritation vanishing after a night's sleep. Chronic laryngitis may typically produce more serious vocal problems if the speaker attempts to "speak above" the laryngitis: The temporary edema of the vocal folds alters the quality and loudness of the phonation; the speaker increases his or her vocal efforts; the increase in effort only increases the irritation of the folds, thereby compounding the problem; and finally, if such hyperfunctional behavior continues over time, what was once a temporary edema may become a more permanent polypoid thickening, sometimes developing into vocal polyps or nodules. For this reason, functional laryngitis should be promptly treated by eliminating the causative abuse and, if possible, by enforcing a short period of complete voice rest.

For the laryngitis that is a frequent symptom of upper-respiratory infection, the best voice therapy is a general systemic and topical treatment of the infection. While the focus of treatment is the medical elimination of the illness, the thickening and irritation of the vocal folds secondary to their infection makes it important that the patient do little or no talking during the acute stage of the laryngeal disease. Luchsinger and Arnold (1965) wrote of infectious laryngitis:

> If the patient tries to overcome the temporary hoarseness through increased vocal effort, such as in trying to sing with a cold, he may develop a localized hematoma, which may degenerate into an acute polyp. The wisdom of vocal silence when the throat hurts should be respected. (p. 178)

Acute, infectious laryngitis is not responsive to voice therapy. The patient should treat the infection and enforce upon himself or herself temporary voice rest until his or her phonation feels and sounds normal.

Fold Thickening

The same kind of vocal abuse that might lead to a temporary problem of laryngitis, if continued day after day, may lead to vocal fold thickening. Thickening occurs primarily at the anterior-middle third site of the vocal folds. The early nodules seen in Figure 3–1 are located at the anterior-middle third site, the same place where most thickening occurs. The anterior two-thirds of the folds is made up of muscle covered with membrane while the posterior third is the medial border of the arytenoids covered by membrane. The vocal folds seen in Figure 3–1 show the white membranous covering relatively free of irritation except the thickening and early nodule seen on the glottal edge. The anterior-middle third is actually the true midpoint of the vibrating muscular portion of the folds, the portion in which the folds have maximum excursion and contact with one another (Arnold, 1973). The free glottal edges become enlarged and slightly granular, changing often from their pearly white color to a more generalized pinkness caused by increased vascularization. Soft additive tissue begins to form followed by callous-like tissue developing to protect the

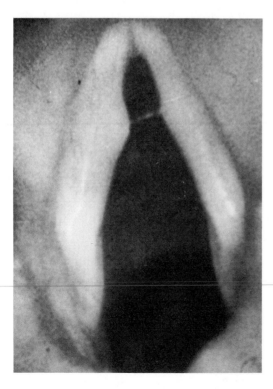

FIGURE 3-1
By mirror laryngoscopy a well-developed nodule may be seen on the patient's right vocal fold (at left of picture). Slight cord thickening may be observed on the corresponding site of the right fold. A typical mucous spittle thread is crossing the glottis between the right nodule and the left fold thickening.

membrane from further irritation. The resulting thickening is often the early formation of nodules and polyps with the nodules similar to callous formation and the polyps appearing more pliable and vascular. Fold thickening usually produces a dysphonia characterized by a lowering of pitch, increased noise in phonation (aperiodicity), and breathiness.

While some early thickening may be related to other factors than abuse-misuse, such as persistent allergies (Williams, 1972), the majority of such problems are related to the phonatory excesses frequently observed in hyperactive people. It does appear, however, that voice therapy directed toward reducing voice abuse-misuse is the best treatment for reducing and eliminating fold thickening. The efficacy of voice therapy for fold thickening is well illustrated by the following case:

A six-year-old girl was referred for a voice evaluation because of chronic hoarseness. On indirect laryngoscopy it was found that the child had bilateral cord thickening with no demonstrable history of allergy or infection. The parents were counseled to do what they could to help the child eliminate unnecessary crying and yelling, and the child was sent home. On a subsequent visit to the laryngologist, with no change in cords as observed by laryngoscopy, it was decided to "strip" the thickenings surgically. This was done with excellent results. Three weeks after surgery the child demonstrated clear cords bilaterally, free of thickening. After a postoperative period of approximately three months, the family returned to the laryngologist, complaining of the child's recurring hoarseness. Laryngoscopy found the child once again to have bilateral cord thickening, with the early formation of a vocal nodule on one fold. It was then decided to begin voice therapy. Special efforts were made to identify particular vocal abuses by the child, and a school playground situation was isolated as the cause of continuous vocal strain. Elimination of this and other adverse vocal behavior resulted in the gradual elimination of the vocal nodule and the near elimination of the bilateral thickening.

The preceding case illustrates that surgical treatment of cord thickening, without making attempts to remove the abusive causes of the problem, will not always lead to a permanent solution of the vocal problem. It would appear that reducing the source of the irritation (such as eliminating an allergy, reducing smoking, or curbing vocal abuse) is probably the best management of the problem.

Vocal Nodules

If the same vocal conditions that cause fold thickening continue over time, the patient may well develop vocal nodules. Nodules are usually bilateral. For example, the nodule on one fold in Figure 3–1 is larger than the nodule on the opposite fold; however, the callous, fibrotic nature of the lesion on the one fold will very likely produce a similar irritation on the same site of the opposite fold. Vocal nodules are the most common form of benign lesion of the larynx, commonly observed in prepubescent boys who do a lot of yelling (Toohill, 1975) and in postpubescent females who may be active in school cheerleading and dramatics (Case, 1981). As the nodules begin to form with continued abuse-misuse, they tend to get more fibrotic and larger. Identification and reduction of the identified abuse is generally an important prerequisite for voice therapy, which will reduce the nodules and in most cases eventually eliminate them. The typical voice of someone with nodules is heard to be low pitched, breathy, hoarse, and lacking sufficient loudness.

More often we see bilateral nodules, usually accompanied on each side by obvious open chinking of the glottis. The open glottal chink on each side—produced by the coming together of the bilateral nodules, which are in exact opposition to one another—results in a lack of firm approximation of the folds. This leads to a breathy, flat kind of voice (someday we will have a better and more exact terminology), lacking appropriate resonance. The patient complains of the need to clear his or her throat constantly, often feeling that there is excessive mucous or a foreign body on the vocal folds. The typical patient with a vocal nodule will say that his voice tires easily and that when he first starts to use it each day, it sounds much better. With prolonged singing or speaking, his phonation rapidly deteriorates. Small nodules and recently acquired ones can often be eliminated by voice therapy. Larger nodules and long-established ones are often optimally treated by surgery, followed by a brief period of complete voice rest and then voice therapy. It is not unusual clinically to see the surgical removal of nodules in both children and adults, only to have new nodules appear several weeks later. Unless the underlying hyperfunctional vocal behaviors are identified and reduced, vocal nodules have a stubborn way of reappearing.

Vocal nodules in children before puberty are more commonly observed in boys who generally are aggressive and noisy, busy controlling people with their voices. As boys get older, there is less evidence of nodules, with adolescent females showing a higher prevalence of additive lesions related to vocal abuse. The prevalence is also higher in those adult females who according to Aronson (1980) are "talkative, socially aggressive, and tense, and suffer from acute or chronic interpersonal problems that generate anxiety, anger, or depression" (p. 136). It has been this author's experience, however, that both children and adults with vocal nodules respond very well to symptomatic voice therapy, sometimes supplemented with strong psychological support and occasionally with psychological counseling. With less vocal abuse and misuse, their voices improve in quality and the nodules get smaller.

Vocal Polyps

Polyps of the vocal fold are usually unilateral, occurring at the same site (anterior-middle third junction) as vocal nodules. It appears that polyps are more likely to occur from a single traumatic vocal event.

Perhaps the patient indulges in excessive vocalization, such as screaming for much of an evening, producing some hemorrhaging on the membrane at the point of maximum glottal contact. The polyp forms out of the hemorrhagic irritation, eventually adding mass that becomes fluid filled. Once the small polyp begins, any continued vocal abuse or misuse will irritate the area, contributing to its continued growth. The typical polyp lies on the glottal margin, interfering with the approximation of the normal fold. Because it is a soft, pliable lesion, it does not irritate the same site on the opposite fold. Polyps may be broad based, as seen in the photograph in Figure 3-2, or narrow necked, attached to the glottal rim and hanging below or above the glottis. The most detailed descriptions of polyps, their formation, and their treatment, was developed by Kleinsasser (1979), who described the lesions as gelatinous, responding well to surgery. Unless the causative abuse is identified and reduced, however, polyps often recur after surgery.

Sometimes the entire glottal margin will break down on one or both folds, known as Reinke's polypoid edema. The space between the muscular portion of the vocal folds and the membrane surrounding it is known as *Reinke's space.* After excessive vocal abuse, this space sometimes becomes fluid filled, producing an irregularly shaped glottal margin that produces severe dysphonia. This type of polypoid degeneration is much more extensive than the well-defined unilateral polyp previously described. Patients with Reinke's polypoid degeneration often profit from a trial period of voice rest; if the membranous swelling reduces, continued voice rest is indicated. If the degenerative lesions remain, surgery is generally recommended, followed by voice therapy. Greene (1980), in reporting the work of Kleinsasser, reports that persistent polypoid degenerative lesions generally require surgery, followed by voice therapy postoperatively.

The voices of patients with unilateral polyps are characterized by severe dysphonia. The normal vocal fold vibrates at one frequency while the additive lesion seriously dampens the vibration of the involved fold,

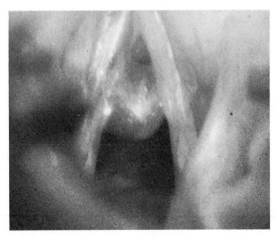

FIGURE 3-2
By mirror view a large broad-based vocal polyp may be seen attached to the right vocal fold. This polyp hangs below the glottis, actually below and unattached to the normal left vocal fold.

resulting in what is perceived as hoarseness and breathiness, often requiring (or so the patient thinks) continuous throat clearing. Voice therapy requires identifying and reducing vocal abuse-misuse and searching with the
patient for the best voice that can be produced by using various voice-
facilitating approaches (see Chapter 5). Voice therapy was successful in
eliminating a unilateral polyp from this woman:

> Jane F. was a twenty-nine-year-old teacher who was active in competitive
> sports. She admitted to doing a lot of yelling during her softball season,
> ending up with a hoarse voice that would not go away. Her teaching
> schedule required her to give six hours of lectures each day, supervise a
> study hall, and assist in girls' field hockey events. Finally, by noon each
> day she had no voice. Subsequent laryngoscopy found her to have a
> broad-based polyp (about 5mm in width) on one fold. Voice therapy ef-
> forts were initiated with focus given to reducing loudness, developing a
> soft glottal attack, and opening her mouth more as she spoke. An im-
> mediate consequence of the therapy was that when she spoke easily,
> without effort, her voice at first sounded "more hoarse." She kidded her
> students and colleagues that she would sound worse in the beginning as
> she learned to use her voice with less effort. In about twelve weeks, the
> unilateral polyp completely disappeared, and her voice became normal.
> She then made continuing efforts to avoid any kind of vocal abuse and
> misuse and has maintained a trouble-free larynx and normal voice.

Contact Ulcers

Contact ulcers form along the posterior third of the glottal margin.
The cartilaginous medial border of each arytenoid cartilage is believed to
slam together from excessive vocal fold approximation; this slamming
causes the membranous covering to ulcerate. Eventually, hard, crusty
granulated tissue develops around the ulcer craters. The classic cause of
contact ulcers was developed by Peacher (1961), who described the typical
patient with contact ulcers as a hard-driving person, who speaks with a
loud, controlling low-pitched voice, usually with excessive hard glottal
attack.
    The typical symptoms of contact ulcers are deterioration of voice after
prolonged vocalization accompanied by pain in the laryngeal area or pain
that sometimes lateralizes out to one ear. Laryngoscopy usually reveals
bilateral ulcerations with heavy buildup of granulation tissue along the approximating margins of the posterior glottis. Greene (1980) labeled the
toughened membranous tissue changes on the posterior glottis as
"pachydermia," citing the work of Kleinsasser (1979); Greene (1980)
wrote "that contact ulcers are not actually ulcers or granulomas but consist
of 'craters' with highly thickened squamous epithelium over connective
tissue with some inflammation (oedema)" (p. 147). The diffuse irritation
of the posterior glottis often associated with contact ulcers may be the result

of esophageal reflux, sometimes associated with diaphragmatic or hiatal hernia. The patient experiences esophageal reflux while sleeping, resulting in the pooling of acid secretions on the vocal process end of the glottis (Cherry and Margulies, 1968). In studying the sensitivity of the posterior larynx to gastric juices, Delahunty and Cherry (1968) were able to produce experimentally contact ulcers and granulation tissue in dogs by swabbing gastric juices on their vocal folds. It now appears that patients with contact ulcers who also demonstrate marked irritation of laryngeal-pharyngeal tissue should be candidates for a thorough examination of the gastrointestinal tract. If a hiatal hernia, for example, is found with contact ulcer, the patient is best treated with antiacids, elevation of the head of the bed, and voice therapy.

The focus of voice therapy for patients with contact ulcers is to take the effort out of phonation. The patient must learn to use a voice pitch level that can be produced with relatively little strain, speak with greater mouth and jaw relaxation, speak at a lower level of volume, and eliminate all traces of excessive glottal attack. We no longer see too many patients with contact ulcer. Those few who are seen, however, seem to respond well to voice therapy.

Papilloma

Papilloma are warty-like growths, viral in origin, that occur in the dark, moist caverns of the airway. Because they frequently occur in the larynx of young children, they can represent a serious threat to the airway, limiting the needed flow of air through the glottal opening. The majority of papilloma occur in children before the age of six; for this reason, hoarseness and shortness of breath in preschool children should be promptly evaluated specific to cause. While the majority of papilloma stop recurring about the time of puberty, Kleinsasser (1979) wrote that 20 percent persist beyond puberty. Papilloma of the airway in adolescents and young adults must be considered a serious laryngeal disease, primarily because of its recurrence and persistent threat to the airway.

When papilloma occur in the larynx, their additive mass often contributes to dysphonia. For this reason, the voice clinician should be particularly alert to any child who demonstrates dysphonia. Any child who demonstrates continued hoarseness for more than ten days, independent of a cold or allergy, should have the benefit of indirect laryngoscopy to identify the cause of the hoarseness. If papilloma are identified, the treatment is medical-surgical. The papilloma should only be removed when they impinge on the airway. Eventually, when the individual has developed the immunological state needed for him or her to resist the viral-inspired papilloma, they will no longer recur (Kleinsasser, 1979). The surgical management of papilloma may include laser-beam surgery, ultrasonic surgery, radiation therapy, and conventional excision surgery. After papilloma surgery, the patient is required to observe seven to ten days of voice rest to permit healing. Voice therapy is not recommended as a preventive therapy. Voice therapy can help some patients, however, to develop the best voice possible with the mechanism they have left for voicing. We recently saw a seven-year-old child who had a permanent opening in his neck (tracheostomy) to allow an open airway because of continuing papilloma growing in his trachea and larynx; at the time of our examination, he had received seventeen operations for removal of the recurring papilloma. The papilloma were never removed or surgically reduced until they were large enough to compromise his breathing. It was only possible for him to produce voice when he used his finger to cover his tracheostomy on expiration; his voice was very hoarse because of the papilloma mass and previous glottal scarring. Voice therapy was helpful to the child in phrasing his utterances, reducing his loudness attempts, and helping him develop better skills in occluding his stoma with his finger.

The treatment of papilloma is medical-surgical. Our voice therapy attempts are made to give the patient the best voice possible with whatever laryngeal function is available.

Granuloma and Hemangioma

Sometimes the laryngeal membrane is traumatized from disease or external trauma, producing granuloma or hemangioma. Any patient who is intubated during surgery or for airway preservation runs the risk of having a traumatized laryngeal membrane with the subsequent development of granuloma. The risk is particularly greater in children and women, who have smaller airways and thus are more often traumatized by large tubes (Whited, 1979). The physician places a tube down the pharynx into the airway, between the open (it is hoped) vocal folds, and on into the trachea. If the tube is larger than the glottal opening, the patient runs the risk of trauma. Ellis and Bennett (1977) have recommended that in order to prevent intubation granuloma or hemangioma, the patient should be intubated with a tube one size smaller than what would be needed "for a snug fit." Tomkin and Harrison (1971) reported that 4 percent of their patients developed some kind of laryngeal trauma from intubation, with less than 1 percent of the patients requiring corrective surgery.

Some patients demonstrate changed voices after general surgery. If the patient was intubated and shows a persistent hoarseness after surgery, he or she should have indirect laryngoscopy to identify any possible cause of the hoarseness. Granuloma and hemangioma, if present, have to be watched medically. Usually a brief period, about seven days, of voice rest will help the additive tissue disappear. Large granulomas and hemangiomas, and sometimes residual scarring, require surgery. After the physical condition has stabilized, voice therapy is sometimes helpful in developing the best voice possible with the mechanism that is left.

Other Growths on the Larynx

There are several kinds of benign growths that may be found on the vocal folds and contribute to dysphonia, but that are *not* the result of vocal abuse-misuse and are *not* responsive to vocal rehabilitation. Lesions of *leukoplakia,* which may also appear in other places, are caused primarily by chronic irritation, particularly from the tars of tobacco smoke. Leukoplakia is treated primarily by removing the cause of the irritation, that is, by eliminating the smoking. Severe cases of laryngeal leukoplakia require surgery and a close watch by the laryngologist. Another medical problem is laryngeal *hyperkeratosis,* a mass of accumulated keratin (a scleroproteinous-pigmented spot or covering) that may grow on the inner glottal margins, causing pronounced hoarseness. Hyperkeratosis requires the close supervision of a laryngologist, since it occasionally develops into a malignancy. It should not be treated by the speech-language pathologist.

Occasionally, growths in the larynx are found to be *cancerous.* When a malignancy is identified, the preservation of life requires its prompt removal. In the case of laryngeal malignancy, the earlier the diagnosis, the more effective the treatment will be. For those patients requiring the total removal of the larynx (*laryngectomy*), the need for developing a new pseudo-vibrator in place of the removed vocal folds requires extensive and highly specialized voice rehabilitation, which will be discussed in Chapter 8.

Laryngeal Web

Laryngeal web produces both a mass-size change of the vocal folds as well as a severe problem in fold approximation. The web seen in Figure 3-3 obviously occupies the major portion of the glottis, producing severe problems in air flow as well as in voice.

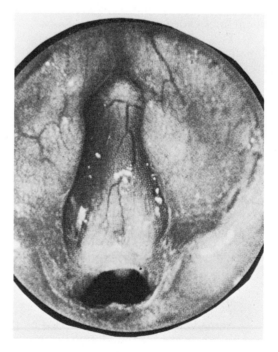

FIGURE 3-3
A laryngeal web occupies almost the entire glottis.

Anything that might serve as an irritant to the mucosal surface of the folds may serve as the initial cause of the webbing. Because the two vocal folds are so close together at the anterior commissure, any surface irritation due to prolonged infection or to trauma may cause the inner margins of the two fold surfaces to grow together. To explain further, one principle of plastic surgery is that offended tissue surfaces when approximated together will tend to grow and fuse together. This same principle is why webbing occurs. The offended surface of the two approximated folds will tend to grow together, in this case forming a thin membrane across the glottis. Webbing grows across the glottis in an anterior to posterior fashion, usually ceasing about one-third of the distance from the anterior commissure where the distance between the two folds becomes too great. Severe laryngeal infections sometimes cause enough glottal irritation to precipitate web formation. The more common cause, however, appears to be related to laryngeal trauma. For example, an individual may be seen who was wearing a lap seatbelt and was involved in a collision. His head lurches forward during the impact and his neck strikes a hard object like the dashboard or the seat in front of him. The larynx is traumatized and the thyroid cartilage may be fractured, driving the anterior protective cartilage back toward the vocal process ends of the arytenoids. During this trauma, the vocal folds may be lacerated anteriorly. Several weeks following the accident, the patient may require laryngeal repositioning surgically and, from this, may experience further vocal fold trauma. The vocal fold lesion that may occur anteriorly during laryngeal trauma is usually experienced by both folds. As part of healing, both folds may grow together anteriorly, forming a laryngeal web, sometimes called a *synechia*.

Laryngeal web may cause a severe dysphonia as well as shortness of breath, depending on how extensively the webbing crosses the glottis. The treatment for the formation of a web is surgery. The webbing is cut, freeing the two folds. To prevent the surgically removed web from growing again, a vertical *keel* is placed between the two folds and kept there until complete healing has been achieved. The laryngologist fixates the keel, which is shaped very much like a boat rudder and about the size of one's thumbnail, between the folds, preventing them from approximating together. The patient is then on voice rest as long as the keel is in place, as its presence inhibits normal fold vibration. When the keel is removed, often in six to eight weeks, the patient generally requires some voice therapy to restore normal phonation. If there was extensive damage to the larynx from the trauma, it may well be impossible after healing and voice therapy to ever develop the same kind of normal voice the patient had before the accident. The prognosis for voice recovery after webbing and its surgical treatment is highly individualized, depending on the extent of the trauma and the size of the resulting web.

Dysarthria

Some voice problems are caused by problems of the central nervous system, as observed in children with cerebral palsy or muscular dystrophy or in adults with multiple sclerosis and other degenerative diseases. Aronson (1980) wrote the "neurological voice disorders, technically, are dysar-thrias." Dysarthria is a disorder of speech caused by a central nervous system lesion that manifests itself in changes in respiration, phonation, articulation, and resonance. While we will discuss dysarthria and voice disorders in greater detail in Chapter 6, we include it here as a disorder of size-mass when central lesions affect the elasticity of the vocal folds. Flaccid weakness of the folds, which might be observed in a patient with myasthenia gravis, will increase the mass of the folds, lowering the pitch level of the voice; conversely, spasticity that might be observed in the folds of a patient with multiple sclerosis (Farmakides and Boone, 1960) may result in vocal fold tightening with a concomitant increase in fundamental frequency. Pitch changes related to changes in vocal fold mass secondary to some kind of nervous-system pathology are resistant to modification from any kind of voice therapy. We will see in Chapter 6 that voice therapy can often produce improvement in the overall communication of the dysarthric patient. Although specific manipulation of pitch in dysarthria as a therapeutic goal is seldom productive, gains often can be made in improving vocal prosody and quality.

Disorders of Voice Pitch

Aberrations in the pitch of the voice are generally produced by mass-size changes of the folds. The measured fundamental frequency is inappropriately high or too low. There are no greater dramatic changes in fundamental frequency that can be measured than following a child over time, from early childhood, through puberty, and on to adolescence. Such developmental changes in frequency of the voice for most children are normal and do not represent disorders of voice. As the larynx increases dramatically in size in all of its components (cartilage, muscle, tendon, nerves, membrane), so does fundamental frequency lower in both boys and girls. An excellent summary table of fundamental frequency changes in boys and girls may be found in D. K. Wilson's *Voice Problems of Children* (1979, pp. 72–73) where the author presents in summary form the fundamental frequency data of many different authors. We will also present a useful table of fundamental frequency data in the next chapter on evaluation. A disorder of pitch is diagnosed when an individual's voice is perceived as inappropriately low or high for his or her age. While some children experience delayed pubertal changes of the vocal mechanism, the majority of voice-pitch problems are functional in origin or related to additive lesions on the vocal folds, such as thickening or nodules.

These rapid changes in the size of the vocal folds and other laryngeal structures produce varying vocal effects during the pubertal years. Boys experience a lowering of their fundamental frequencies of about one octave; girls, a lowering of about two or three notes. This change does not happen in a day or two. For several years, as this laryngeal growth is taking place, the boy will experience temporary hoarseness and occasional pitch breaks. The wise parent or voice clinician witnesses these vocal changes with little comment or concern. The mass-size increases of puberty tend to thwart any serious attempts at singing or other vocal arts. Luchsinger and

Arnold (1965) point out that much of the European literature on singing makes a valid plea that the formal study of singing be deferred until well after puberty. Until the child experiences some stability of laryngeal growth, the demands of singing might be inappropriate for his rapidly changing mechanism.

The age and rate of pubertal development varies markedly. From the pediatric literature we find that the main thrust of puberty for any one child seems to take place in a total time period of about four years, six months (Marshall and Tanner, 1970); the most rapid and dramatic changes occur toward the last six months of puberty (this is when pitch breaks, if they occur, may be observed in some boys).

There is a different kind of pitch break that younger children and adults might experience, related to the voice breaking an octave (sometimes two octaves) up or an octave down when speaking at an inappropriate pitch level. When one speaks at an inappropriately low frequency, the voice tends to break one octave higher; speaking too high in the frequency range may cause the voice to break one octave down. The tracings seen in Figure 3–4 were recorded on a Visi-Pitch showing the inappropriately low fundamental frequency tracings of a fifty-three-year-old minister, suddenly breaking into abrupt upward shifts. His lower F_O value was 100 cycles and his higher (the pitch break F_O) was 300 cycles, about a two-octave shift. We will further discuss pitch breaks in the next chapter when we discuss finding a pitch level appropriate for the mass-size of the individual's vocal folds, thus avoiding or eliminating these sudden unwanted shifts in vocal frequency.

A double-pitched voice is known as *diplophonia* produced by laryngeal bodies vibrating at different frequencies. Any asymmetry or difference in size between the folds can contribute to the double voice. The most common cause of diplophonia is vocal fold paralysis, where one fold is normal and the other fold is paralyzed because of lack of innervation. The paralyzed fold generally loses much mass (atrophy) because of lack of innervation; final pathway or lower motor neuron lesions, such as from destruc-

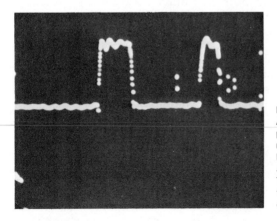

FIGURE 3-4
A Visi-Pitch tracing shows the voicing pitch breaks of a thirty-nine-year-old minister. The lower tracing is a prolonged /a/ at about 100 Kz breaking abruptly to the high tracing at 360 Hz. The pitch breaks occur when he sustains phonation at the lowest voice he can produce.

tion of the recurrent laryngeal nerve, cause atrophy of the muscles no longer innervated. In the next section we will consider in greater detail the problem of vocal fold paralysis. Diplophonia is caused by one paralyzed fold vibrating at a different rate than the normal fold, producing the double-pitched voice. Sometimes the voice clinician can search with a patient who has diplophonia in an attempt to find a single-pitched voice. In the few cases of diplophonia we have treated, we have eliminated the problem by elevating slightly the frequency of the normal fold. Other vibratory sites have been reported as the cause of diplophonia, such as one normal fold and one false fold vibrating, or the aryepiglottic folds producing voice while the true folds are phonating, or any other such combination. The voice therapy treatment is generally searching with the patient by trying various facilitating approaches (Chapter 5) in an attempt to produce a single voice.

Endocrine Changes of the Vocal Folds

Most of the inappropriate voice pitches we hear are not related to the structural changes of the vocal folds that result from endocrine problems. Occasionally, however, we see a patient whose voice is too low or too high for his or her sex and age, indicating endocrine imbalance. An extreme example of endocrine causation would be castration before puberty, which by preventing vocal mutation, maintains the boyish voice throughout life, as demonstrated by the castrato in early opera (Moses, 1960). We occasionally see men who do not experience voice mutation, as a direct result of poor gonadal, sexual development; such cases are rare and sometimes respond well to the glandular treatment of the endocrinologist. More commonly, the inappropriately high voice in the postpubertal male is functional in origin, related to the continuous overuse of the cricothyroid muscle as documented by Arnold (1973) in his myographic studies of falsetto. Sometimes the high pitch is the result of habit and personality-identity problems; this kind of voice problem is highly responsive to voice therapy, particularly in the absence of any endocrine causation. Specific therapy procedures for these functional mutational voice problems will be presented in Chapter 6.

In the Fourth Edition of Greene's *The Voice and Its Disorders* (1980), she develops a specific section of the text, describing various female disorders of pitch that may result from menstruation, the climacteric, and virilization of the voice. At premenstruation, when estrogen and progesterone levels are at their lowest, thickening of the vocal folds can cause the lowering of pitch and some hoarseness (Frable, 1972). Because of this, some professional singers avoid singing heavy operatic roles several days before and during menstruation. Flach, Schwickardi, and Simon (1969) examined 136 professional female singers and found that menstruation, particularly the few days before the menses, affected all of their voices slightly. For the typical woman with ordinary vocal demands, however, the effects of menstruation on the voice are rarely noticed.

The climacteric or menopause is another time of life when women may experience some vocal changes, particularly a lowering of fundamental frequency. Because of the secretion of excessive androgenic hormones, the glottal membrane becomes thicker, increasing the size-mass of the folds, producing a lowering of voice pitch (Gould, 1975). Some women have been administered virilizing drugs for various reasons, which produce a lowering of voice that is often irreversible. For example, testosterone is sometimes used for the successful treatment of uterine cancer (producing the side effect of lowering voice pitch). Some of the early oral contraceptives were found to have virilizing components that caused serious alterations (increasing size and mass) of the vocal folds of women, often found to be irreversible (Damste, 1967). Certain androgen drugs may cause considerable increase in the size and mass of the vocal folds, and if taken over time, may cause a lowering of fundamental frequency that resists attempts to change it with voice therapy. If androgen administration is stopped when voice symptoms are first observed, voice damage may be minimized (Vaughan, 1970). However, if certain androgens must be administered, such as in the treatment of cancer, the female patient should be counseled specific to possible voice changes occurring as a side effect of the therapy.

Occasional patients exhibit a lowering of voice pitch from other endocrinal disorders. Hypothyroidism, persisting over time, can cause a thickening of the vocal folds; Aronson (1980) described the lowering of voice pitch as the "typical effects of mass loading of the vocal folds by their infiltration with myxomatous material." Any endocrine imbalance, such as insufficient testosterone in the developing male, will inhibit growth of the larynx, producing a prepubertal, high-pitched voice. Abnormal growth of the vocal folds, such as seen in some forms of pituitary gland malfunction, may result in inappropriate low-pitched voices.

Changes in the overall size and mass of the vocal folds will produce some change in their vibrating characteristics. Some of these changes in size produce changes in fundamental frequency and create problems of dysphonia, some responsive to voice therapy and some for which voice therapy is inappropriate.

VOICE PROBLEMS RELATED TO PROBLEMS OF VOCAL FOLD APPROXIMATION

The quality and strength of phonation is highly related to the degree of vocal fold approximation. Any of the mass-size increases (such as nodules, polyps, or papilloma) may, if on the inner glottal surfaces, prevent the free glottal edges from optimally approximating. In this section we will consider other approximating problems related to functional underadduction (folds too loosely together) or functional overadduction (folds too tightly together); various paralyses of one or both vocal folds; and the use of the ventricular bands or false cords as a phonation source, with the true folds abducted apart.

Cord Thickening, Nodules, Polyps, and Papilloma as Obstructions to Approximation

Besides the additive effects of cord thickening, nodules, polyps, and papilloma, with their obvious consequences for vocal fold vibration, these mass structures sometimes extend into the glottis, preventing the folds from making their normal approximation. The larger the mass on the free margin of one or both cords, the greater its obstructive effects and the greater the dysphonia. In the illustrations of nodules and polyps in Figures 3-1 and 3-2, one can see that the mass of these vocal lesions could preclude optimal approximation of the folds. In cases of severe bilateral nodules, one will often observe open chinking of the folds on each side of the nodule. The outgoing air stream escapes through these openings quite audibly, so that what we hear is a breathy voice. The effects of obstructive masses that prevent cord approximation must be recognized by the voice clinician, since they may prevent the patient from achieving a "good-sounding" voice, no matter what he or she does.

Functional Dysphonia

Much of what is classified as functional dysphonia is the inability of the patient to approximate the vocal folds in an optimum manner, his or her approximation being either too lax or too tight. In addition, the patient complains of many vague disorders—throat "fullness," pain in the laryngeal area, dryness of mouth while talking, neck tightness, and so on—that are usually related to vocal fatigue. Those voice problems that are not the result of an organic pathology may be called *functional dysphonia*—a term that conveys very little to the voice clinician other than the important implication that there is no structural pathology present. In fact, the common usage of the term *functional dysphonia* is confined to those dysphonias where the problem persists independent of any kind of pathology observed on laryngoscopy. The typical patient has a history of continuing dysphonia. The patient is finally examined by laryngoscopy and found not to have any additive lesion, such as nodules or papilloma or granuloma (or whatever). A functionally caused dysphonia does not necessarily sound different from one that is organically caused. Some of the hoarsest voices heard are produced by people whose larynges demonstrate no pathology whatsoever; on the other hand, serious organic problems, such as beginning cancer, may produce no alteration of the voice. Anyone with persistent dysphonia (no longer than ten days) ought to have the benefit of indirect laryngoscopy to determine the possible cause of the problem. The identification of the possible lesion will indicate the type of management required. In general, however, voice therapy approaches do not distinguish between functional and organic problems. That is, for example, the patient with functional dysphonia, with or without the development of vocal nodules, will basically require the same general kind of voice therapy, a program designed to reduce abuse-misuse and to use the voice as easily as possible. One difference might be in the area of changing the fundamental frequency of the voice; obviously, for the patient with large bilateral nodules, a change of pitch level is not a realistic goal early in therapy.

Aronson (1980) objects to the term "functional" dysphonia on several grounds, feeling that such problems are generally psychogenic in nature:

> A psychogenic voice disorder is broadly synonymous with a functional one but has the advantage of stating positively, based on an exploration of its causes, that the voice disorder is a manifestation of one or more types of psychologic disequilibrium—such as anxiety, depression, conversion reaction, or personality disorder—which interfere with normal volitional control over phonation. (p. 131)

As developed in Chapter 1 in this text, it is this author's belief that most functional voice problems may be treated symptomatically, working on dimensions of voice directly to improve the sound of the voice. In most cases, however, the clinician should offer the patient much psychological support, attempting to minimize his or her anxieties and concern, and searching with the patient for the best voice he or she can produce. The first dimension of voice to be evaluated and worked on if necessary is fundamental frequency. If the patient has no organic problem contributing to this dysphonia but a faulty pitch is found to be a problem, the clinician uses various facilitating approaches (see Chapter 5) for developing an appropriate pitch. The vocal intensity of the voice is also measured; if the patient is found to have a loudness problem, direct attempts at changing the volume can be initiated. For the occasional patient whose voice loudness is directly related to feelings of shyness and insecurity, working on respiration and loudness per se would be less effective than attempting to improve his self-concept and interpersonal relationships. The majority of voice patients, however, with vocal intensity problems are quite responsive to symptomatic therapy attempts designed to increase their voice loudness. The clinician helps the patient change his or her pitch and loudness and evaluates how the patient views the changes. The clinician should observe how the patient responds to direct modification of pitch and loudness; for the occasional patient who is resistant to such direct approaches, we might employ a counseling approach or make a referral for concurrent psychotherapy.

Quality of voice is often the primary problem in functional dysphonia. The vocal folds approximate one another in a faulty manner, producing alterations in quality; such words as *hoarse, harsh, strident,* and *breathy* are applied to the quality dimensions of functional dysphonia. *Harshness* is often the product of overapproximation of the folds when they come sharply together, producing what is also perceived as hard glottal attack. Sometimes harshness is accompanied by inappropriate loudness, high pitch, possible tongue retraction, and contraction of the pharyngeal constrictors. Harshness to most people means a voice that requires a lot of effort and force to produce. The opposite problem may be *breathiness,* produced by folds that may approximate too loosely. Laxity of approximation generally produces an escape of air, perceived as breathiness. Sometimes, as Brodnitz (1971) suggests, the breathy, tired voice appears only after prolonged hyperfunctional voice use. It may emerge late in the day, after the patient has done a lot of phonating, particularly if such phonation has required a good deal of effort and force.

Functional dysphonia often becomes "the" voice of the person. This is the way he or she talks. This is him or her. For such persons, voice therapy is not often successful and in many cases should not be initiated, particularly if the patient wants his or her voice "that way." But for patients who are motivated to change the quality of their voices, and who are diagnosed as having functional dysphonia, voice therapy is remarkably successful.

Spastic Dysphonia

The most dramatic of all voice disorders related to faulty fold approximation is spastic dysphonia. Here the folds approximate so tightly together that the patient can hardly push out sufficient air flow to produce voice. The voice is characterized by a "strained, creaking, choked vocal attack and a tense, squeezed voice, accompanied by extreme tension of the entire phonatory system" (Luchsinger and Arnold, 1965, p. 328). The vocal symptoms are most severe when the patient attempts to speak to other people; he may have no problem in talking aloud to himself, in singing, in laughing, or in any other vocal action that does not involve interaction with people. The patient soon learns to expect phonation difficulties whenever he or she attempts to talk to someone, and in this sense the disorder is similar to the problem of stuttering. The patient overadducts the cords and attempts to force the air stream through the tight glottal closure, producing the "laryngeal stutter." While some authorities, for example, Heaver (1959) and Moses (1954), view spastic dysphonia as a functionally caused problem symptomatic of difficulties in interpersonal adjustment, Robe, Brumlich, and Moore (1960) conclude that its origin is in the central nervous system. The cause of the disorder is still unknown, although there have been some dramatic new surgical advances in the treatment of the disorder, which suggests that it is caused by faulty innervation of the laryngeal adductor muscles (Barton, 1979; Carpenter, and others, 1979; Dedo, and others, 1978). The surgical treatment, which we discuss in greater detail in Chapter 6, cuts the recurrent laryngeal nerve on one side, producing a unilateral fold paralysis. After the operation the patient experiences a breathy, easy voice, relatively free of tightness, somewhat typical of the patient with unilateral voice fold paralysis. The patient no longer has to push out air flow to phonate, and patient opinions are generally enthusiastic about the surgical results. This writer has followed a number of such patients, and all of them have shown a significant improvement in voice after the surgery, particularly when followed by several weeks of voice therapy.

Aronson (1980) has identified three types of spastic dysphonia: the adductor type (the most common and the type just described), the abductor type, and a relatively rare mixed adductor-abductor type. The voice of the patient with adductor-type spastic dysphonia is characterized by tight, strangle-like phonation. In cases of the abductor type, the patient will be exhibiting normal phonation and suddenly the vocal folds will have an abductor spasm, when the patient experiences a sudden opening of the glottis and a temporary phonation break. Zwitman (1979) has described abductor spastic dysphonia as having "intermittent moments of aphonia and breathiness," requiring a distinctively different treatment than the adductor type. It would appear that the adductor and abductor types are two distinctly different disorders, one characterized by sudden glottal tightness and one with sudden openness. Most patients with spastic dysphonia demonstrate some of the time a normal voice; suddenly, they experience their excessive tightness. The problem appears spasmodically and for this reason is more and more labeled by physicians as "spasmodic dysphonia" rather than as "spastic dysphonia" (Aminoff, and others, 1979; Levine, and others, 1979).

The onset of either type of spastic dysphonia is relatively abrupt and frequently follows an unpleasant, traumatic event. Often the patient will recount in detail the events surrounding the onset of the voice disorder, and in so doing will usually describe the relative consistency of the disorder. It has been my observation with several spastic dysphonic patients that such individuals give their vocal and personal histories with a rather fixed smile, and with a penchant for historical detail not ordinarily seen in the average patient. A typical history was given by a forty-two-year-old housewife whose voice problems appeared to be directly related to the death of her teen-aged son:

> The patient described what happened when her son was hospitalized with severe pneumonia: she and her husband went down to the hospital canteen for a cup of coffee. When they returned to the boy's room, they found that he had died during their absence. In the woman's shock, she was unable to speak for several days. Gradually, over a period of several weeks, her voice returned. Several years later a second child was hospitalized, also with pneumonia. While driving the boy to the hospital, the woman experienced severe difficulties in talking, similar to the sort she had suffered after the first boy's death. These voice difficulties persisted with no remission for several years. The patient would speak with a rather placid, smiling face, and at the same time would continuously push, or force out, her breath. She exhibited no normal phonation except when she laughed, which she would do frequently, using this relatively easy phonation as a "starter" for her verbal responses. Subsequent attempts at voice therapy, later combined with psychiatric therapy, were not successful in changing her spastic dysphonia.

If this patient were to be in treatment today, considering that she had the spastic dysphonia for several years, she would be a candidate for the surgical cutting of the recurrent laryngeal nerve followed by voice therapy.

Mild and recent onset problems of spastic dysphonia appear to be best treated by symptomatic voice therapy that couples relaxation with specific voice therapy approaches. The abductor form of the disorder is usually successfully treated by voice therapy designed to "take the work out" of phonation; the abductor spasms appear to reduce markedly in an overall milieu of relaxed phonation.

Functional Aphonia

In contrast to the overadducted vocal fold approximation of spastic dysphonia, the patient suffering from functional aphonia underadducts, keeping the folds apart. The patient has no speaking voice at all, managing a whisper for most social situations. On laryngoscopic examination the vocal folds appear to be normal; however, when the patient is asked to phonate, the folds generally abduct to a position farther apart than they were in before the command was given. Functional aphonia is frequently described as a *hysterical* or *conversion* symptom, according to Aronson, Peterson, and Litin (1966), who found these two terms used by various laryngologists for twenty functional dysphonic and aphonic patients they had observed. While functional aphonia may well be a form of conversion hysteria, Brodnitz (1971b, p. 65) recommends that we avoid using the term in the "presence of the patient because of the social stigma attached to it." Usually the patient has had several temporary losses of voice before the disorder becomes permanent. One might speculate that the temporarily aphonic patient may derive some reinforcing gains from his or her loss of voice, such as not having to give a speech or not being able to preside over a meeting. Aphonia may become permanent after moments of acute stress, maintaining itself for various reasons. Aronson, Peterson, and Litin (1966) report that the onset of functional dysphonia or aphonia in ten out of twenty-seven patients they studied was associated with an event of acute stress; in thirteen of the twenty-seven patients it was associated with stress over a longer period of time. The onset of functional aphonia is sometimes related to the patient's having experienced some laryngeal pathology or other disease. For example, Boone (1966) described the physical origin of functional aphonia in two patients, one who became aphonic after a meningitis attack, and the other after a laryngeal operation, when she could not end the voice rest imposed upon her by the laryngologist. Both these aphonic patients were highly responsive to voice therapy.

The patient with functional aphonia communicates well by gesture and whisper. The typical aphonic patient whispers with clarity and sharpness. Aphonic patients rarely avoid communication situations; conversely, they communicate effectively by facial expression, use of hands, and their highly intelligible whispered speech. What they lack in communication is voice. Embarrassed and frustrated by lack of voice, the aphonic patient generally refers himself or herself to a physician or speech-language pathologist. This typical case history of an aphonic patient was borrowed from this author's chapter in *Introduction to Communication Disorders* edited by Hixon, Shriberg, and Saxman (1980):

A thirty-nine-year-old computer programmer experienced functional aphonia for a period of five months. No matter how he tried, he could only whisper when he attempted to phonate. For four months, he received psychiatric therapy and it was the feeling of his psychiatrist that his "voice symptoms might be conversion symptoms reactive to his guilt feelings surrounding the break-up of his marriage." Despite psychotherapy, his aphonia continued. Symptomatic voice therapy was initiated and the patient was able to produce voice during the first therapy session. After three therapy sessions, he developed normal voice which he has maintained for the past ten years (p. 326).

The complete return of voice described in this illustrative case is not unusual. Most functional aphonic patients present an excellent prognosis. It is almost as if for whatever reason the patient has lost the "set" for phonation. The voice clinician's task is to help the patient "find" his or her voice, primarily by helping the patient use vegetative phonations, such as in coughing or in inhalation phonation. The patient then extends the vegetative phonation into the production of a vowel, then into single words, then phrases, and so on. Suggested methods of symptomatic voice therapy for aphonia are presented in Chapter 6. By using behavioral modification approaches, such as those suggested by Eysenck (1961), Sloane and MacAulay (1968), and Wolpe (1973), we have had excellent success in directly working on voice. The typical aphonic patient experiences a restoration of normal voice in but very few voice therapy sessions. Wilson (1979) described the "sudden and complete recovery" of several teen-age girls who responded well to symptomatic voice therapy. Suggested methods of symptomatic voice therapy for functional aphonia will be presented in Chapter 6.

Vocal Cord Paralysis

Most voice problems related to vocal fold paralysis result in dysphonias that are somewhere between normal functioning and no voice at all. By vocal cord paralysis we mean the inability of one or both cords to move because of lack of innervation to particular intrinsic muscles of the larynx. The interruption of the innervation of the larynx can be central or peripheral; it would appear that most cord paralyses are due to interruptions of the peripheral nerve fibers to the larynx, either the superior laryngeal nerve or the recurrent laryngeal nerve. Brodnitz wrote that the most frequent cause of vocal cord paralysis is "damage to the nerve during a thyroid operation" (1971b, p. 98). Among the causes he lists are damage during removal of a parathyroid tumor, traumatic damage, and compression of a nerve by tumors or enlarged glands (such as goiter) in the neck and chest.

Paralysis of the superior laryngeal nerve is rare, and if this nerve were damaged bilaterally, the patient would experience paralysis of the cricothyroid muscles and be unable to elevate his or her voice pitch. Unilateral damage to the superior laryngeal nerve would result in one fold elongating for pitch elevation and the other fold remaining relatively unchanged; the voice would be hoarse, lacking pitch variation and adequate loudness.

The most frequently observed laryngeal paralysis is a unilateral paralysis with the involved fold paralyzed in the paramedian position. The patient is unable to move the paralyzed fold into the midline for normal vocal fold approximation. This type of paralysis is traditionally called *unilateral adductor paralysis;* the patient is unable to adduct the fold to midline. (The name of the paralysis describes what the involved fold is unable to do.) The cause of unilateral adductor paralysis is usually trauma to the recurrent laryngeal nerve from such causes as neck (particularly thyroid) surgery and accidents. Much rarer is *bilateral adductor paralysis,* where both folds are paralyzed in the out, paramedian position; occasionally, the bilateral positioning is as wide as the glottis can open. Bilateral paralysis is usually caused by a central lesion in the brain stem and is, therefore, a form of dysarthria. The typical voice symptoms of adductor paralyses, particularly the bilateral form, is no voice at all, or *paralytic aphonia.* Unilateral fold paralysis is often temporary since the traumatized nerve can often regenerate. Regeneration is frequently observed within the first nine months after trauma. Surgical correction of vocal fold paralysis is usually deferred until at least nine months after onset, accompanied by hope for some nerve regeneration with a subsequent return of vocal function. In the interim period, however, voice therapy can be effective, helping the patient develop some functional voice. Respiration training, the pushing approach, ear training, and promoting hard glottal attack have all been found useful in helping the patient with unilateral adductor paralysis to develop some voice. If the paralysis is permanent, teflon injection of the paralyzed fold has been found helpful; a teflon paste is injected anteriorly into the atrophied fold, which fattens it sufficiently to permit the normal fold to make some contact, enabling the patient to produce some voice. Lewy (1976) has written that 96 percent of his patients experienced marked improvement in voice after teflon injection and that none of the patients experienced aspiration (inhalation of fluids) after surgery. Dedo, Urrea, and Lawson (1973) followed 135 patients after teflon, and they developed selection criteria to determine those patients with fold paralysis who would profit from injection and those who would not. A perceptual study of voice improvement after teflon (Reich and Lerman, 1978) found a general reduction of hoarseness with a marked increase in "pleasantness of phonation." Teflon does not guarantee good results for cases with a wide, glottal opening and for these cases, other surgical approaches have been successful. Isshiki, Tanade, and Sawada (1978) report using sutures in simulation of the lateral cricoarytenoid muscle, attached from the cricoid to the muscular process of the arytenoids; this has the effect of rotating the arytenoid to promote better fold approximation. Tucker (1977) has reported reinnervation of the paralyzed thyroarytenoid by modifying and applying the nerve-muscle pedicle from the omohyoid muscle and inserting it into the paralyzed vocal fold. Most surgical approaches require a followup with some voice therapy to enable the patient to fully utilize the altered laryngeal mechanism.

Abductor paralysis   is when the involved fold (or folds) stays in the midline position; this is a much rarer form of paralysis than the adductor type. The involved fold can in some cases abduct laterally to the intermediate position, but never to the full lateral position required for deep inspiration. The patient with abductor paralysis complains less about dysphonia and more about shortness of breath. Because of the decrease of the glottal opening, the patient experiences some actual decrease in inhaled air volume. While cord approximation may be sufficient for phonation and not cause any voice change, the heavy user of voice, such as the lecturer or singer, may develop dysphonia because of inadequate breath. The primary symptom of the disorder, however, is some impairment in respiration, often with little or no change in voice. The respiration problems become most dramatic if the patient experiences bilateral abductor paralysis (usually central in origin), with the cords relatively fixed in the adducted midline position. In this case, the compelling need for an adequate airway requires an immediate surgical operation, such as a *tracheostomy* (the creation of an opening into the trachea, just below the level of the larynx), with this emergency procedure perhaps followed by surgical repositioning of the folds to create an open glottal airway. After this primary treatment by corrective surgery, the laryngologist may prescribe voice therapy so that the patient can learn to use his or her reconstructed phonatory mechanism as efficiently as possible. The desired goal in abductor paralysis, whether unilateral or bilateral, is for the patient first to have an adequate airway, and then to reestablish optimum phonation.

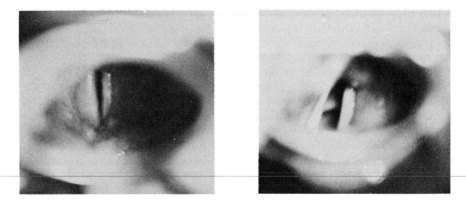

FIGURE 3-5.   Unilateral abductor paralysis. This is a mirror view of a unilateral abductor paralysis. In the left side picture we see the two folds in approximation; the vocal fold on the right is atrophied, smaller than the normal fold on the left. In the righthand picture, the paralyzed fold on the right stays in the midline position while the normal fold on the left has been abducted.

Phonation Breaks

A frustrating approximation disorder for some patients is phonation breaks. A *phonation break* is a temporary cessation of phonation, which may occur suddenly as the patient is phonating. It is usually situational bound, occurring after prolonged vocal hyperfunction, and in this way differs from the phonatory interruptions described by Aronson (1980) as abductor spastic dysphonia. The typical patient with phonation breaks works to talk. He may be someone who uses his voice a lot, perhaps a teacher. After prolonged speaking, he begins to experience vocal fatigue, and starts to do something to improve the sound of his voice, such as raising or lowering voice pitch or speaking through clenched teeth. The result is increased vocal tension. Finally, while he is phonating, his vocal folds spontaneously abduct and he temporarily loses his voice. By throat clearing, coughing, swallowing water, or whatever, phonation is restored until the next phonation break. Most voice patients, even if they have occasional phonation breaks, will not exhibit this temporary voice loss during the evaluation session. Therefore, at that time the patient should be asked if he ever experiences a temporary loss of voice when he is speaking. Phonation breaks in themselves are not serious problems but may be considered as symptomatic of an unnecessary amount of effort directed toward phonation.

Ventricular Dysphonia

A very rare approximation disorder is *ventricular dysphonia:* Phonation is produced by the approximating false folds or ventricular folds. Sometimes the ventricular voice becomes the substitute voice of the patient who has a severe disease of the true folds (such as severe papilloma or large polyps). The ventricular voice is usually low pitched because of the large mass of vibrating tissue of the ventricular bands (as compared to the smaller mass of vibrating tissue of the true folds). In addition, the voice has little pitch variability and is therefore monotonous. Finally, since the ventricular bands have difficulty in making a good, firm approximation for their entire length, the voice is usually somewhat hoarse. This combination of low pitch, monotony, and hoarseness makes most ventricular voices sound unpleasant. If there is no persistent true cord pathology that continues to force the patient to use his or her ventricular voice, this disorder will usually respond well to voice therapy. Sometimes, however, there is *hypertrophy* (enlargement) of the ventricular bands, which makes their normal full retraction somewhat difficult.

Ventricular phonation is difficult to diagnose by the sound of the voice alone. On laryngoscopic examination during phonation, the ventricular folds are seen to come together, covering from view the true cords that lie below. Some ventricular dysphonias display a special form of *diplophonia* (double voice), where the true folds and ventricular bands phonate simultaneously. Identification and confirmation of what vibrating structures the patient is using for phonation can best by made by frontal tomographic X-ray (coronal) of the sites of vibration. In true ventricular phonation, the true vocal folds will be slightly abducted, with the ventricular bands above in relative approximation. In normal phonation, the opposite relationship between the true folds and the ventricular bands occurs; that is, the true folds are adducted and the ventricular bands are positioned laterally from the midline position. Once ventricular phonation is confirmed by laryngoscopy or X-ray, any physical problem of the true cords that might make normal phonation impossible should be eliminated. An occasional patient with much true fold pathology or absent true folds will need to be taught ventricular phonation (usually an impossible task). We will consider both the elimination of ventricular phonation and its occasional need to be taught as we review voice therapy for special problems in Chapter 6.

Laryngofissure, Cordectomy, and Laryngectomy

There have been dramatic advances in the surgical management and vocal rehabilitation of the patient with laryngeal cancer in recent years. Malignancy (*carcinoma*) of the larynx and upper airway can often be treated successfully by radiation therapy or limited surgery (Gates, 1980). The type of medical-surgical therapy is dictated by the size and location of the cancer. Batsakis (1979) described stages relative to the extent and site of the lesion; in cases of laryngeal cancer, stages I and II can often be successfully treated by radiation therapy alone; stage III lesions might require radiation and limited surgery; stages IV and V require total removal of the larynx or *laryngectomy* as well as radiation therapy (Gates, 1980).

In *laryngofissure* the patient loses much of the larynx on one side only; with surgical reconstruction, some of the removed structure can be replaced, a sufficient amount to enable airway valving (Batsakis, 1979). If the patient is able to use the reconstructed larynx for airway valving and not require a tracheostomy (external opening into the trachea), the laryngeal valve must be capable of tight valving during swallow so the patient does not experience aspiration of food and liquids. These kinds of partial laryngectomies require the close cooperation of the surgeon and the speech-language pathologist if the patient is to develop usable phonation. In *cordectomy*, one vocal fold is removed (sometimes only partially) and many of the postsurgical problems are related to the patient's aspiration potential and faulty voice experience. Surgical reconstruction of the removed fold is usually successful (Tucker and others, 1979).

A total laryngectomy involves the complete removal of the larynx and the creation of a permanent tracheostomy. Total laryngectomy procedures are reserved today for the patient with advanced laryngeal and airway cancer (stages IV and V). Recent modifications of the laryngectomy procedure have enabled some patients to quickly develop a substitute voice (Singer and Bloom, 1980).

The laryngectomy patient has lost his or her larynx and must learn to develop a substitute voice. The most common approach used is teaching the patient esophageal speech, where one learns to trap air in the esophagus, and uses esophageal-pharyngeal vibration as the new substitute voice. The learning procedure is much like learning to burp and using the belch as a phonation source. We shall consider the problem of laryngeal cancer, the laryngectomy patient (the *laryngectomee*) with his or her many problems, and the teaching of a substitute voice in Chapter 8, which is devoted to this problem.

SUMMARY

We have grouped organic and functional disorders of voice together, separating them into two categories: size-mass disorders and approximation disorders. When we consider therapy and management in Chapters 5, 6, and 7, we will find the designations specific to size-mass and/or approximation useful in planning therapy. Some of what we can do in therapy will alter mass-size; some approaches we use have marked effects on fold approximation. We must not forget, however, specific disorders and their etiologies. For example, for papilloma, which is both a mass-size and approximation problem, voice therapy is usually not indicated. The majority of vocal disorders are functional in origin and appear related to vocal hyperfunction, which respond well to voice therapy. Some forms of disorders, such as laryngeal web, require specific management steps by both the physician and speech-language pathologist. All successful management must depend on adequate diagnostic evaluation, which is considered in the next chapter.

4
The
Voice
Evaluation

The successful management of the child or adult with a voice disorder first requires a voice evaluation. Sometimes the child with a voice problem is discovered by the speech-language pathologist in a school screening program. These children are subsequently seen for diagnosis and possible treatment by the laryngologist before voice therapy is started. Or the speech-language pathologist may see the voice patient by direct referral from the laryngologist. An occasional patient with dysphonia may come directly to the speech-language pathologist, who then evaluates the patient and, if indicated, refers to the laryngologist for medical evaluation. The best voice evaluations are probably those in which the laryngologist and the speech-language pathologist work together as a team, each providing the assessment and data required to make the best decisions relative to overall management of the problem.

Successful voice therapy is highly dependent on how well the voice clinician can identify what the patient is doing vocally. The typical voice evaluation is completed after someone else, such as the laryngologist, has already diagnosed the problem and what may be causing it. The speech-language pathologist must make a detailed analysis of what the patient is doing with regard to respiration, phonation, and resonance. To do this, he or she makes good use of whatever medical descriptions of the problem may be available, takes a detailed history, observes the patient closely, uses those testing tools and instrumentations necessary to make an accurate assessment, and introduces to the patient various therapeutic probes to obtain clues as to what direction the voice therapy should take.

While we are presenting the voice evaluation in a separate chapter, it is important for the reader to appreciate that voice evaluation and voice therapy cannot be separated. Effective voice therapy requires continuous ongoing assessment. Evaluation and therapy are highly overlapping. What is found at the evaluation and given back to the patient as a form of feedback may also have great therapeutic value. Using various therapy approaches as diagnostic probes in an attempt to identify the patient's "best" voice can be an important part of every therapy session. Many of the evaluation procedures and tools described in this evaluation chapter are also used by the clinician in voice therapy.

VOICE SCREENING

The speech-language pathologist in the public schools is in an excellent position to develop voice screening procedures for the early identification of children with voice problems. Most school programs have speech screening programs for new children and for all children in certain grades at specified times of the year. For example, the clinician may screen in the fall all children in kindergarten and third grades. By using some kind of voice screening form, the clinician is able to make better judgments specific to parameters of voice. With but very little additional testing time per child, a voice screening program can be added to the present speech and language screening measures. Different clinicians in various settings have developed various screening forms. The items on the form usually represent the aspects of voice that the clinician feels important for helping to identify children who may be having problems of voice. The screening form aids the clinician in focusing his or her listening observations. Wilson (1979) recommends that the clinician use these tasks in voice screening; counting from one to ten; connected speech sample (one minute); reading sample (one minute); and prolongation for five seconds each of five selected vowels (high to low). Previous screening forms published by Boone (1973; 1977) have included observations specific to rating the parameters of pitch, loudness, quality, and resonance. These previous screening forms have generally been modified as they are field tested and utilized in various settings. We have found over time that the rating task must be as focal as possible to be useful. The more parameters to be rated and the more gradations of the rating, the poorer the reliability in using the form. The form shown in Figure 4-1 seems to offer the clinician the information that is needed in a screening test (Boone, 1980). The single criterion for each of the scale judgments (pitch, loudness, quality, nasal resonance, oral resonance) is whether or not the child's voice on that particular parameter sounds like the voices of peers of the same age and sex.
     If the child's voice appears lower in pitch than that of his or her peers the (−) is circled on the form; if pitch appears normal, the (N) is circled; if the pitch level is heard to be higher than the child's peers, we circle the (+). Inadequate loudness is specified as (−); normal loudness is (N); excessive loudness is characterized by (+). Any deviation of quality is

VOICE SCREENING FORM
The Boone Voice Program for Children

Name ______________________ Sex M F Grade ________

School ______________________ Teacher ________

Examiner ______________________ Date ________

VOICE RATING SCALE

Circle the appropriate symbol (s)

Pitch	– N +	Describe:
Loudness	– N +	Describe:
Quality	– N +	Describe:
Nasal Resonance	– N +	Describe:
Oral Resonance	– N +	Describe:

S/Z RATIO

Record 2 trials of [s] and 2 trials of [z] expirations

s = ____ seconds

s = ____ seconds

Longest s ÷ by Longest z = S/Z Ratio: ____

z = ____ seconds

z = ____ seconds

DISPOSITION:

☐ Complete voice evaluation required (one or more ratings of + or – or an S/Z ratio of greater than 1.2)

☐ No further evaluation required

☐ Second screening required ________ (Date)

Comments:

FIGURE 4-1
A Voice Screening Form taken from *The Boone Voice Program for Children.* Tigard, Oregon: C. C. Publications (1980).

represented by (–) or (+), with the breathy, hoarse voice marked as (–) and the tight, harsh voice as (+).

If denasality (insufficient nasal resonance) is noted, the form is checked (–); normal nasal resonance is marked (✓); and hypernasality is characterized by (+). Oral resonance deviations do not occur as often as in the other four judgment areas; however, excessive posterior tongue carriage that produces inadequate oral resonance is marked as (–); no problem in oral resonance is (N); excessive front-of-the-mouth resonance characterized by the baby voice is marked as (+). If the child on screening receives either (–) or (+) on any of the five clinical parameters, he or she should be rechecked. If problem areas are again identified, a complete voice evaluation would be recommended (Boone, 1980).

We have recently added the s/z ratio as a screening measure (Tait, Michel, and Carpenter, 1980; Eckel and Boone, 1981). The s/z ratio is a measure of how well the child can sustain a prolonged /s/ phoneme as compared with the maximum duration of the /z/ phoneme. The /s/ is a measure of expiratory control, while prolongation of the /z/ sound adds the laryngeal component to the task. Normal speakers yield maximum duration values of both /s/ and /z/ of about the same duration; however, there is a slight skewing of longer durations for the /z/ rather than for the /s/. It appears that when the laryngeal valving contributes to the task as in voicing, the glottal structure inhibits the airflow, contributing to a longer duration.

Individuals with larynges with glottal lesions (such as nodules or polyps) exhibit significantly shorter /z/ durations than normal subjects, although their maximum /s/ durations appear of normal length (Eckel and Boone, 1981). The s/z ratio is computed by dividing the maximum /z/ time into the maximum /s/ time. Eckel and Boone found that more than 95 percent of their patients with laryngeal pathologies demonstrated s/z ratios in excess of 1.4. It would appear that the s/z ratio provides a quick "software" measure which might identify those people with dysphonia who have possible laryngeal lesions.

Most screening forms allow a brief space for comments that the examiner feels necessary to add to the screening data. For example, the notation "she had a bad cold" would be helpful information to remember on the followup visit with someone previously noted as having "hypernasality" on a screening form. At the second visit, comparisons of screening data are made with present observations. For those individuals who on followup continue to show some departures in voice from their age-sex peers, arrangements should be made for a full voice evaluation.

THE VOICE EVALUATION
AND MEDICAL INFORMATION

Voice patients evaluated by the speech-language pathologist have either been "discovered" in his or her voice screening program, or are referred by teachers and other professionals in the schools, or are referred by physicians (usually laryngologists), or are self-referred. Regardless of the referral source, the speech-language pathologist in early contacts with the patient will arrange for a full voice evaluation. For those patients other than those referred by laryngologists, part of the evaluation process may include a medical evaluation. Occasional voice problems, such as the patient who does not talk loud enough or someone who is using an aberrant pitch level for what appears to be functional reasons, may not require a medical evaluation. Voice quality and resonance problems generally require some medical evaluation of the ear, nose, and throat as part of the total voice evaluation.

The most effective voice rehabilitation programs seem to have close team cooperation between the speech-language pathologist and the laryngologist. Unfortunately, in some areas of the country there are no laryngologists, and it is not uncommon for speech-language pathologists in these areas to report that there are no medical doctors available who can perform *indirect laryngoscopy* (mirror view of the vocal folds). The speech pathologist in such a situation should confer with the patient's local physician, saying, for example, "Tom seems to be hoarse every day. Could you please see that his vocal folds are examined?" It is the rare physician who will not appreciate such a request. The physician who feels that he does not possess the skills required for indirect laryngoscopy will see that the patient is referred to a laryngologist. It is not unusual for patients living in remote areas of the United States to travel several hundred miles for an examination by a laryngologist. A laryngeal examination must be made before the patient can begin voice therapy for problems related to quality or resonance. As part of the diagnostic process the speech-language pathologist may wish to use therapy approaches as diagnostic probes; for example, asking a patient to imitate the pushing approach may provide important diagnostic information as to how tighter vocal fold approximation affects voice quality. Voice therapy efforts should be deferred until after the medical examination (which would include laryngoscopy) is concluded, for there are occasional laryngeal pathologies, such as papilloma or carcinoma, for which voice therapy would be strongly contraindicated.

The laryngologist's examination includes an assessment of the larynx and related structures. The vocal folds are assessed by indirect mirror laryngoscopy, and their color, configuration, and position are noted. During the patient's quiet respiration, the laryngologist looks for the normal inverted-V position of the cords. For phonation, the patient is often asked to phonate a relatively high pitch, perhaps by extending an e-e-e for several seconds. The higher the pitch, the further the epiglottis and tongue are extended upward, permitting a relatively unobstructed view of the vocal folds. A judgment is made on the adequacy of fold approximation during phonation. Other structures examined may include the ventricular folds, laryngeal ventricle, pharynx, tonsils-adenoids, nasal cavities, velopharyngeal mechanism, glands and muscles of the neck, and so on. The laryngologist's examination is directed at finding the cause of the patient's presenting problem and evaluating the overall status of the larynx and related mechanisms. If the laryngologist wants additional information about how the patient uses his or her voice, or if the laryngologist feels voice therapy may be needed, the patient will be referred directly to the speech-language pathologist. Such referral usually requires a written statement by the laryngologist describing the patient's problem, and, in actual practice, the written referral may be supplemented by a conversation further describing the problem. The laryngologist's referral usually includes an abbreviated statement of the patient's history, a descriptive statement of the presenting problem, what was told to the patient, and a statement indicating treatment direction and probable prognosis. Taken from a clinic file is the following letter of referral from a local laryngologist who placed strong and continued emphasis on voice therapy for most of his patients with hyperfunctional voice problems:

I have asked Mrs. Pearl ———— to see you for a voice evaluation at the earliest opportunity. This forty-four-year-old woman works as a secretary to an insurance executive, a position which requires much talking on the telephone. In the past six months she reports continued hoarseness, usually worse at the end of the day, and she complains of occasional pain in the general hyoid region after prolonged speaking. She is married, the mother of three young adult sons. Until six months ago, there was no history of vocal distress.

On mirror laryngoscopy, I found the patient to have small bilateral nodes at the anterior one-third junction. Areas immediately adjacent to the nodes were characterized by increased vascularization, suggesting much irritation at this site. On cord adduction, there is noticeable open chinking on each side of the approximated nodes. Her voice, as you might suspect, is quite breathy with an audible escape of air, probably escaping through the open chinking. Inadequate voice loudness, also, appears to be a problem for her.

I am referring her to you for your ideas on what she may be doing wrong with her voice. If you feel she would benefit from voice therapy, please schedule her. I told Mrs. ———— that if you felt voice therapy were indicated, we would begin there. If not, we might attempt surgical removal of the nodules and then instruct her on proper voice usage to prevent their recurrence. She appears strongly motivated to improve her voice and will, I'm sure, gladly accept whatever you recommend.

Physicians develop different methods of describing their findings for the speech-language pathologists. Their descriptions may range from a brief "normal vocal folds" to a multi-page written evaluation. Typically, the speech-language pathologist may receive a statement from the laryngologist which appears similar to these:

Large tonsils and adenoids; no need to remove at this time. Larynx normal.

Bilateral thickening runs from the total AP distance on both folds. Could well be related to voice abuse. Could you take her on for voice therapy?

No physical basis for the tight voice. Cords show good mobility and normal function. No cord lesions. Do you think she'd be a good candidate for nerve resection?

A short, relatively immobile velum. Good symmetry. VP distance looks too excessive for normal closure. Recommend a pharyngeal flap. Could you do pressure-flow study and endoscopic photography? We'll staff her next month.

The laryngologist and the speech-language pathologist work together in planning both the evaluative procedures and remediation steps to be followed. Other professional specialties sometimes included in the evaluation, such as outlined in Chapter 7 in discussing problems of nasal resonance, may include a pediatrician, a neurologist, an orthodontist, a prosthodontist, a psychologist. Specialization today requires a team of professionals for the effective management of some patients with voice disorders. D. K. Wilson (1979) has written:

The management of voice problems requires the coordinated efforts of many specialists. A voice team approach is an efficient and effective method for examination, consultation, treatment, and follow-up. (pp. 61–62)

Some laryngologists prefer an evaluation form with a glottal figure. This allows them to quickly make their statements accompanied by a line sketch of the pathology (if present) specific to its site and size. In Figure 4–2, we see part of such a form (Boone, 1980a) that would be completed by the examining physician and returned to the speech-language pathologist.

Community health centers and university clinics routinely obtain medical information and some case history data from patients when the initial appointment is made, and, if a voice problem is indicated, schedule the patient first for a medical diagnostic evaluation. It sometimes happens, however, that a voice patient will make the initial appointment without identifying the problem as one of voice. If, for whatever reason, a patient arrives to be treated for some form of dysphonia, but has not had a previous medical examination, the speech-language pathologist must defer final disposition of the patient until the medical information is obtained. The voice evaluation by the speech clinician may begin, however, even in the absence of the medical information. The case history can be taken, respiration-phonatory-resonance observations and test data can be obtained, and only the decision about voice therapy need be deferred.

The ethics and efficacy of speech-language pathologists themselves doing indirect laryngoscopy might be discussed at this point. Some speech-language pathologists are trained to perform mirror laryngoscopy, a pro-

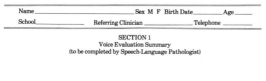

VOICE REFERRAL TO PHYSICIAN

To the physician: This child was recently seen for a voice evaluation. Voice therapy has been deferred until a medical diagnosis has been made. Please complete Section 2 of this form and return it with your recommendations.

Name_____ Sex M F Birth Date_____ Age_____

School_____ Referring Clinician _____ Telephone _____

SECTION 1
Voice Evaluation Summary
(to be completed by Speech-Language Pathologist)

SECTION 2
Summary of Medical Findings
(to be completed by examining Physician)

Indicate site and
extent of lesion

Recommendations:
____ Voice therapy recommended

____ Voice therapy not recommended

Comments:

Return this form to:

_____
_____   Physician's Signature
_____
                           Date

FIGURE 4-2
Voice Referral to Physician. Such a form as this provides a systematic way for making referrals to the physician. Used with permission from *The Boone Voice Program for Children*. Tigard, Oregon: C. C. Publications (1980).

cedure that is not difficult to master; these persons use indirect laryngoscopy primarily as a method of teaching students laryngeal function and to observe the folds directly to determine any changes during therapy. No speech-language pathologist, however, should use laryngoscopy as a diagnostic device. Primary identification of laryngeal pathology is the clear responsibility of the laryngologist, who is equipped also with the medical techniques required for the treatment of the pathology, once it is identified. It would appear, therefore, for the ethical and legal protection of the speech-language pathologist, that the voice patient who comes in for evaluation without prior medical examination should not at this first visit be given indirect laryngoscopy by the speech-language pathologist. To repeat, the diagnostic examination of the vocal cords belongs to the laryngologist. After the laryngologist has made a diagnosis, the speech-language pathologist trained in laryngoscopy may occasionally use mirror laryngoscopy to view the cords indirectly; this will facilitate the treatment of the patient by allowing him or her to make judgments about vocal cord adequacy.

THE VOICE EVALUATION
AND THE CASE HISTORY

To understand the patient with a voice disorder and to understand his or her problem, it is necessary for the clinician to assemble a case history. Most texts and manuals dealing with diagnosis and appraisal of communicative disorders present general strategies for history taking (Darley, 1965; Dickson and Jann, 1974; Nation and Aram, 1977; and Perkins, 1977).

Recent texts on management of voice disorders that offer suggestions for history taking include Aronson, 1980; Boone, 1980a; Greene, 1980; Moncur and Brackett, 1974; Polow and Kaplan, 1979; and Wilson, 1979. There are many individualized voice evaluation forms available for the clinician. Most history forms include major headings specific to description of the problem, cause of problem, consistency or variability of problem, and voice usage as seen in the headings used on the form shown in Figure 4-3.

Description of the Problem and Cause

It is valuable in understanding the patient to ask directly what he or she feels is the problem and what might have caused it. It is often effective to ask the same questions of family members or a child's teacher. The different views as to what the problem may be and the various guesses specific to probable causation may offer tips for management. The patient's description often reveals much about his or her own conceptualization of the problem. What the patient feels the problem is may not be consistent with the opinions of the referring physician or the speech-language pathologist—a discrepancy that may be due to what we call the patient's

VOICE EVALUATION FORM
The Boone Voice Program for Children
by Daniel R. Boone, Ph.D.

NAME _____ SEX M F   DATE OF BIRTH_____ AGE _____

SCHOOL _____ TEACHER _____ GRADE_____

REFERRAL SOURCE: SCREENING____TEACHER____ PHYSICIAN____SELF____OTHER____

EXAMINER _____ DATE OF EVALUATION _____

SECTION 1
History of the Voice Problem

	Child's Report	Parent's Report Informant_____	Teacher's Report
Description of Problem			
Cause of Problem			
Onset of Problem			
Variability Through Day			
Voice Usage			

Abuses:

Misuses:

Comments:

FIGURE 4-3
History taking is facilitated by obtaining reports from the child, the teacher, and the parents. This particular history format is from *The Boone Voice Program for Children.* Tigard, Oregon: C. C. Publications (1980).

"reality distance." This distance may be the result of the patient's lay background and his inability to understand adequately what had been explained. Often we hear highly discrepant reports of "what the doctor said" as the patient recounts the diagnoses of previous clinicians. More often this distance is the result primarily of the inability to accept and cope with the real problem. His defenses may force him to describe the problem in a way that is not consistent with the perceptions of others. What the patient says about his or her problem may provide the clinician with insights that no amount of observation or testing can match. This sort of reality distance is well illustrated by the following excerpts from the clinic records of this twenty-eight-year-old computer programmer:

Physician's Examination Statement: George was an extremely hard man to examine with indirect laryngoscopy. He was very fearful during our exam and gagged with the slightest touch to the posterior tongue. His vocal folds show broad-based bilateral polyps, about 4 mm wide along the anterior-middle third junction. Trial voice therapy is indicated.

Speech-Language Pathologist's Statement: Patient voices with much audible strain, characterized by diplophonia, hoarseness, and severe glottal attack. Patient participated in all phases of our evaluation with a fixed smile on his face, contrasted with tight, clenched fists. We may well need here a combined voice therapy-counseling approach.

Patient's Statement of the Problem: Now that I have recently found the Lord, I want to serve him. Whenever I go to teach at the church, I seem to lose my voice. My computer work presents no problem, because I don't need the voice much there. It's a problem of going hoarse and even losing the voice when I work with the groups at the church.

Consistently from these descriptions do we view a patient who is showing some tension signs relating to other people. He was hypersensitive during laryngoscopy attempts, his vocal patterns and facial-hand mannerisms suggested tension, and his description of his problem voicing with other people all suggest psychological tension as a possible contributing factor to his dysphonia. Aronson (1980) has written, "If the dysphonia is of greater severity or different in character than warranted by the lesion, a psychogenic component is strongly suspected" (p. 185). The bilateral polyps alone should not cause the complete voice breakdown the patient experiences while teaching groups at the church. Successful management of this man's problem necessitated a combined voice therapy and psychological counseling approach, similar to what was suggested initially by the speech-language pathologist.

Onset and Duration of the Problem

How long the patient believes he or she has had the voice problem is important. A problem of acute and sudden onset usually poses a severe threat to the patient; that is, it keeps the patient from carrying out his or her customary activities (playing, singing, acting, selling, preaching, or whatever). The aphonia or dysphonia of sudden onset deserves thorough exploration by both the laryngologist and the speech-language pathologist. Some dysphonias develop very gradually. These gradual fluctuating dysphonias are often related to varying situations in which the patient may find himself or herself, sometimes only occurring during moments of stress or after fatigue. A history of slow onset sometimes suggests a gradually developing pathology, such as the patient who develops bilateral polypoid degeneration of the vocal folds, or the occasional patient whose dysphonia is but an early developing symptom of some kind of progressive neurological disease. Long-term chronic dysphonia usually has existed for so long because the patient has never been particularly disturbed by his or her voice problem. Voice therapy, like other forms of remedial therapy, is usually more successful with those patients who are motivated to overcome their problem. The patients with a long history of indifference toward their dysphonia usually present a more unfavorable prognosis than the ones who have recently acquired the disorder, depending, of course, on the kind and relative extent of the pathology involved.

Variability of the Problem

Most voice patients can provide rather accurate timetables with regard to the consistency of their problem. If the severity of the voice problem is variable, the clinician may be able to identify those vocal situations in which the patient experiences the best voice and the worst voice. The typical patient with vocal hyperfunction reports a better voice earlier in the day, with increasing dysphonia as the voice is used more. For example, a high school social studies teacher reported a normal-sounding voice at the beginning of the day; toward the end of a day, after six hours of lecturing, he reported increasing hoarseness and a feeling of "fullness and dryness in the throat." Voice rest and then dinner at the end of the day would usually restore his voice to its normal level. Obviously, such fluctuations in the daily quality of the voice enabled the clinician easily to identify the situations contributing to the patient's vocal abuse. Another patient, whose dysphonia was closely related to an allergy and postnasal drip experienced during sleep, presented this kind of variation in hoarseness: severity in the morning upon awakening, decrease in severity with usage of the voice, complete disappearance by late afternoon, and severity again the next morning.

The variation of the voice problem can provide even more specific clues as to what situations most aggravate the disorder. A night-club singer reported that she had no voice problem during the day in conversational situations or while practicing her repertoire. She would develop hoarseness only at night and only on those nights she sang. Further investigation of her singing act revealed that the adverse factors were the cigarette smoke around her, to which she was unusually sensitive, and the noise of the crowd, above which she had to increase her volume to be heard. Her singing methods were found to be satisfactory. A change of jobs to a summer-tent theater provided her with immediate relief.

Description of Vocal Use
(Daily Use, Misuse)

Abuse, misuse, and overuse of the voice are the causes of most functional voice problems. It is important for the clinician to determine how the voice patient is using the larynx in most life situations. The voice the child or adult exhibits in the speech-language pathologist's office may in no way represent the voice used on the playground, in the classroom, or in other settings. Sometimes the patient can recreate some of his or her aversive laryngeal behaviors as a demonstration for the clinician, but more often a valid search for aversive vocal behaviors requires the clinician to visit the environment where the abuse-misuse occurs. The successful voice clinician must build into his or her schedule actual visits to the playground, or the theater, or the church, or the office. It becomes apparent that only a little voice abuse-misuse in whatever setting is all that may be needed to keep a glottal membrane inflamed or a pair of vocal nodules irritated and fibrotic. Case (1981) has demonstrated the effects of cheerleading on the larynges of teen-agers, comparing them with laryngoscopy before and after two weeks of attendance at a cheerleading camp. His data strongly suggest that continued cheerleading has a direct aversive effect on the larynges of the majority of the adolescents studied. It is obviously important for the clinician to identify the vocal use pattern of the patient.

Special attention must be given to the identification of playground screaming and yelling in children. One only has to listen to the noise level of the typical primary school playground to realize that yelling at play appears to be a normal childhood behavior. The child with a voice problem, however, often presents the history of yelling a little louder and a bit more often than his or her normal-voiced peer. Sometimes the public school clinician must enlist the help of the teacher, the child's friends, and the family to determine the everyday vocalization history of the child. Perhaps the most important part of voice therapy for children is in identifying vocal abuse and developing strategies to reduce its occurrence.

Additional Case History Information

It is important to determine at the time of the voice evaluation if the patient has ever had previous voice therapy. If so, what type of past therapy would have obvious relevance to present management? Determination of whether other members of the family have similar voice problems is helpful. We have had particular patients present a certain voice problem, only to interview members of the family and find that all or many of them have the same voicing patterns. Deviations in resonance are often the most commonly observed family patterns. The voice evaluation should include some kind of health history; an example of a health history taken from a child evaluation form (Boone, 1980) is shown is Figure 4–4. Cer-

SECTION 2
Health History

Informant _____

Birth History

Feeding Problems

Illnesses and Allergies

Accidents

Surgery

Medications

Voice Change

Family Voice Problems

Previous Voice Therapy

FIGURE 4-4. Health History. The health history may be organized under topic headings as shown in this form.

tainly for adult patients it is important to determine such conditions as allergies, medication or hormone therapy, excessive smoking, use of alcohol, and use of drugs. Once the patient is comfortable with the examiner, or perhaps after voice therapy has begun, a social history will tell the clinician useful information about the patient as a person.

THE VOICE EVALUATION
AND OBSERVATION OF THE PATIENT

Observations of our patients often tell us more about them than our histories and our test data. It is important for the speech-language pathologist to become a critical observer, attempting to describe behavior that is seen rather than merely labeling the behavior. Writing one's observations about a patient is one of the few places in the voice evaluation where the clinician can write what he or she observes. Even here, however, it is important for the clinician to minimize any subjectivity by describing only what is seen and heard, and not adding interpretation to the observation. An example of such a description of what was observed and heard is taken from this case record, which describes a sixteen-year-old boy, effeminate in appearance, who was being evaluated for a problem of an excessively high-pitched voice:

> David came into the clinic room with his arms hanging stiffly at his sides, his mouth in a tight contortion producing slight facial tics on the right side, avoiding all eye contact with the examiner. While he would freely volunteer history about himself, he seemed as if he were speaking in a high pitched (probably around E_3) monotone. About five minutes into the interview, he began to tell a long story about himself and his friend, Jamie, and their trip with Jamie's mother to Mexico. Apparently, Jamie's mother had scolded him for having such a high voice, fearing that he might make Jamie talk "that sissy way." David was quick to add, "Jamie was already into gay fun more than I ever was."

The brief preceding paragraph contains much observation with two patient quotes, communicating description of the patient better than if the clinician had attempted to label the boy's behavior.

Since voice difficulties are often symptomatic of the inability to have satisfactory interpersonal relationships, it is imperative that the clinician consider the patient's degree of adequacy as a social being. The patient who exhibits extremely sweaty palms, who avoids eye contact with the person to whom he or she is speaking, who uses excessive postural changes or sits with a masked, nonaffective facial expression, or who exhibits obvious shortness of breath, may be displaying some of the behaviors frequently considered as symptomatic of anxiety. His struggle to maintain a conversational relationship may be accompanied by much struggle to phonate. Such observed behavior in the voice patient may be highly significant to the voice clinician as he or she plans a course of voice remediation. The decision about whether to treat the problem symptomatically (that is, by voice therapy) or by improving the patient's potential for interpersonal adjustment (perhaps by psychotherapy) is often aided by a review of the observations of the patient. The patient who demonstrates friendly, normal affect is telling the clinician, at least superficially, that he or she functions well in a two-person relationship; such information may well have clinical relevance.

THE VOICE EVALUATION
AND TESTING OF THE PATIENT

A voice rating scale of some kind aids the clinician in separating the various processes contributing to voice into separate components. A children's voice-rating scale may be seen in Figure 4–5. This particular scale permits

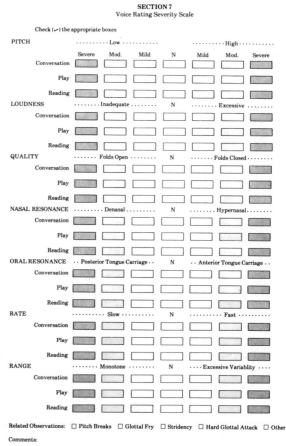

FIGURE 4-5
Voice Rating Severity Scale. This seven-point rating scale enables the clinician to rate seven parameters of voice from observations during conversation, play, and oral reading. Used by permission from *The Boone Voice Program for Children.* Tigard, Oregon: C. C. Publications (1980).

the clinician to observe each of seven parameters: pitch, loudness, quality, nasal resonance, oral resonance, speaking rate, and variability of inflection. Each of the parameters is judged for voice production in three settings: in conversation, in play, and in reading. This particular scale is basically a seven-point rating scale with normal production checked in the middle. To the left of normal are the rating slots for insufficient performance of the parameter to be rated; for example, a voice pitch that appears too low would be rated on the pitch scale to the left of normal. The individual's pitch level is compared with the pitch levels of his or her age peers. The mild, moderate, and severe boxes are checked according to the clinician's judgment. The rating scale is not a test per se but provides the clinician with a structure for systematizing his or her observations. Actual measurements of frequency, intensity, quality, and resonance are made separately, and these data can often aid the clinician in making the summary judgments placed on the voice rating scale. Because rating scales force clinicians to focus their measurements and observations into some kind of summary, many voice clinicians have developed scales and found them useful (Wilson and Rice, 1977; Perkins, 1971). Wilson (1979) describes several equal-interval appearing scales, having ratings from 1 to 7, with interjudge reliability in excess of .90. Let us consider some of the measurement instruments used by the speech-language pathologist in the voice evaluation.

The Peripheral Oral Evaluation

Some assessment of the peripheral oral mechanisms is part of the voice evaluation. While we place our focus on evaluation of the larynx and respiratory systems, some examination of facial stuctures, mouth, dentition, tongue, teeth, hard and soft palate, pharynx, and nasal cavities is required. Incorporated into the voice evaluation may be the peripheral mechanism forms offered in such evaluation-diagnosis books as written by Darley (1965), Dickson and Jann (1974), and Nation and Aram (1977). In our evaluation of the peripheral mechanisms of the voice patient, we must pay particular attention to possible signs of neural innervation problems. Every now and then we evaluate a patient who has come to us with a problem of "functional dysphonia" only to find some subtle neurological signs of fasciculation and atrophy of the tongue, or asymmetries of the velum related to neural innervation changes, and so on. Subsequent medical-neurological evaluations may find that the early dysphonia is but the beginning symptomatology of a serious neurological disease. It is important to evaluate the voice patient specific to structural and functional adequacy for all parts of the oral mechanisms.

In Chapter 2 we presented sites of possible hyperfunction where voice patients may experience some difficulty. Let us review some of these sites of hyperfunction and be sure that we look at them closely as part of our total peripheral mechanism evaluation. Beyond observing obvious problems in breathing, some attention should be given to the amount of *neck tension*. The accessory neck muscles and the supralaryngeal strap muscles in some patients literally stick out as the patient speaks. Often closely associated with neck tension is *mandibular restriction,* where the patient speaks with clenched teeth, with little or no mandibular movement. Such restricted jaw movement places most of the burden of speech articulation on the tongue, which, to produce the various vowels and diphthongs in connected speech, must make fantastic adjustments if no cavity-shaping assistance from the mandible is forthcoming. Another externally observable hyperfunction of the vocal tract is unusual *downward* or *upward* excursion of the larynx during the production of various pitches. Any unusual movement upward while phonating higher pitches, or unusual movement downward while phonating lower ones, should be noted. The *angle of the thyroid cartilage* may be digitally felt as the patient sings a number of varying pitches; typically the fingertips will feel little discernible change in thyroid angle as the patient sings up and down the scale. Sometimes, however, the thyroid cartilage can be felt to rock forward slightly in the production of high pitches, as it sweeps upward to a higher position toward the hyoid bone. Any really noticeable amount of lifting or lowering of the larynx, as well as the tipping forward of the thyroid cartilage in the production of high pitches, should be noted as possible hyperfunctional behavior.

Probably the majority of hyperfunctional behaviors associated with voice problems are not directly observable in the examination of the peripheral mechanism. For example, to determine tongue position in relation to other oral structures such as dentition or the velum, we probably have to rely on lateral view cineradiography. By using a combination of X-ray and film, a visual record can be made of the patient's intraoral movements. The oral endoscope is having increased use in our evaluation of voice patients. The scope may be introduced intraorally or intranasally; the light on the tip of the scope (which comes fiber-optically from an external light source) illuminates the nasal and oral pharynx that is viewed through a window lense on the tip of the endoscope. A drawing of a typical oral endoscope is found in Figure 7–1 in Chapter 7, where we will discuss utilization of endoscopic viewing in evaluating velopharyngeal competence. Of relevance to our voice evaluation, the window lens of the oral endoscope can be directed up at the velopharyngeal closure mechanism or down at the larynx below. For most of our observations and measures of intraoral phenomena contributing to normal and faulty voice, we are forced to use various measuring instruments that help us quantify aspects of respiratory, phonatory, and resonance function.

Respiration Testing

Since the vocal folds are activated for phonation by the outflowing air stream passing through the closed glottis, some observation and measurement of respiratory adequacy is a necessary part of the voice evaluation. The early phoniatrist placed much emphasis on breathing adequacy, particularly with regard to adequacy of singing; such a view was prominently advocated by Tarneud (1958) and frequently cited by Luchsinger and Arnold (1965). Most speech-language pathologists, but certainly not all, continue to show interest in how well the voice patient breathes, and particularly in how well the patient is able to extend and use his or her exhalation for phonation. It is commonly recognized, for example, that shortness of breath or speaking after much breath is already expired will have noticeable effects on phonation. We shall consider separately those instruments that can be used for measuring various aspects of respiratory movement and, finally, those observations and tests that we can use to assess the patient's use of respiration as it applies to phonation. Specifically, we shall consider separately four types of information: lung volume, driving air pressure, air flow, and motions of the torso.

Lung volume. It is important to determine how much of the total lung volume the patient uses in phonation. We can easily observe the patient speak or sing, and make a judgment specific to the overall adequacy of respiration while performing the task. Does she run out of her air supply before finishing the planned utterance? Is she forced to renew air intake more often than is desirable? Part of the evaluation of respiratory adequacy is determined by measuring the patient's lung volume. Specific dimensions of volume that can be measured include *vital capacity* (maximum amount of air that can be expelled from the lungs following a maximum inspiration), *tidal volume* (amount of air inspired and expired in a normal breathing cycle), *inspiratory reserve* (maximum amount of additional air inspired after a tidal inhalation is completed), and *expiratory reserve* (maximum volume of air expired after a tidal expiration). The normal speaker uses only a small amount of his total vital capacity when speaking. Hixon, Goldman, and Mead (1973) have written that the normal speaker uses only about twice the air volume for speech that he uses for a quiet, easy normal (or tidal) breath. Does the typical patient use greater or lesser volumes than this? The capacities and volumes we need to measure are best determined by using wet or dry spirometers. In the wet spirometer, a container floats in water placed in a larger container. As air is introduced to the smaller floating container, it floats higher in proportion to the volume of air introduced. The distance or rise of displacement is measured in terms of cubic centimeters or liters. A fourteen-year-old boy was recently tested on a wet spirometer and found to have these lung volumes:

Vital capacity	= 3.8 liters
Tidal volume	= .4 liters (400 cc)
Inspiratory reserve	= 3.4 liters
Expiratory reserve	= 3.3 liters

We see in this example that the normal tidal volume and the maximum amount of air the boy can expire after the tidal breath in several trials (summarized in the preceding data) approximate his vital capacity or total maximum expiration. Some spirometers are of the dry type, where a flexible container enlarges on inspiratory tasks and decreases in volume on expiratory tasks, in both instances measuring the volume of displacement.

The wet spirometer appears to have greater clinical usage and, also, appears to provide greater volume accuracy. It should be pointed out, however, that volume data does not have the clinical relevance provided by measures of expiration (pressure and flow) and data specific to neck, thoracic, and abdominal movements.

Air flow pressures.   One can hear the effects of air pressure on the perceived loudness of the voice. Greater vocal intensities require higher air flow pressures for a shorter time passing through the glottis, producing greater excursions of the vibrating vocal folds. We will further describe in the ensuing section on loudness the measurement of voice intensities by several methods, such as using a sound-level meter. In our clinical voice patients, we often hear symptoms of inadequate air flow pressure as observed in the patient who experiences varying and inadequate loudness; we also may hear quality disturbances related to inadequate pressure for normal fold vibration. There are relatively inexpensive pressure measuring gauges and manometers for the measurement of air flow pressures. In our measurement of air pressure adequacy for voice we are interested in finding the individual's oral pressures. One way of doing this is to ask the patient to produce a series of "pa" sounds; in the production of "pa" the glottis is open, with the pressure peaking during the production of the /p/ phase of the "pa." Netsell and Hixon (1978) have found that the oral pressures obtained in the "pa" production or in a blowing task (when the mouthpiece has a small air leak) correspond to the pressures found in the lungs and the glottis. They have concluded that if a patient can produce 5–10 cm of pressure over a period of five seconds in a sustained blowing task, he or she probably has sufficient expiratory pressures to produce normal voice.

Pressure measurements are used diagnostically more often when attempts are made to measure velopharyngeal adequacy, described in some detail in Chapter 7. Using some kind of manometric device, the patient is asked to produce a consonant such as /p/ or /k/; oral pressures are taken and nasal pressures (a nasal olive is inserted in the nares attached to the flow tube) are also determined. Sometimes the oral and nasal measurements are taken sequentially back to back, but such measures are perhaps more meaningful when taken simultaneously. For simultaneous oral-nasal pressures, the patient wears a face mask that is divided into oral and nasal sections, which provides separate oral-nasal pressure ratings (Hixon, Saxman, and McQueen, 1967). Oral speech should have little or no nasal pressure flow; as puffs of air escape through an inadequately closed velopharyngeal port, the sensitivity of the pressure gauge would detect such escape.

Air flow measures.   An important diagnostic measure in the voice evaluation is a measurement of air flow, which provides an indication of the volume of air passed through the glottis in a fixed period of time. For example, the normal production of a vowel requires about 100 cc of air passage through the glottis in one second. A patient with large bilateral nodules who cannot effect adequate glottal closure will exhibit much higher air flow rates and perhaps will use 100 cc in far less than a second. His or her voice would be characterized by much breathiness as we actually hear the leakage of air caused by the lack of normal glottal resistance. Poor glottal resistance to the air flow, as would be caused by the formation of nodules on the glottal margin, results in elevated air flow measures. An opposite kind of problem, where the glottis is highly constricted, such as is observed in spastic dysphonia, results in markedly reduced flow rates. Therefore, the rate of flow, particularly when combined with pressure ratings, gives us much diagnostic information about what is happening to the outgoing air at the level of the glottis. Our measurements are usually substantiated by our critical listening to the voice. If the voice appears to be produced by a relatively lax glottal closure as observed in breathiness, the flow rates are high; if the voice appears harsh and sounds constricted, there are often markedly diminished flow rates. Not only is flow rate information of diagnostic importance, it also helps us measure the effects of therapy. For example, as we attempt to move patients into more optimal phonatory behaviors, we see flow rates shift toward normal values (such as 100 cc per second). A useful device for measuring air flow is the pneumotachometer, seen in Figure 4-6. The patient produces vowel prolongations and his air flow is captured in the oral mask, with the flow rate measured by the pneumotachometer. There is much normal data available to normal flow

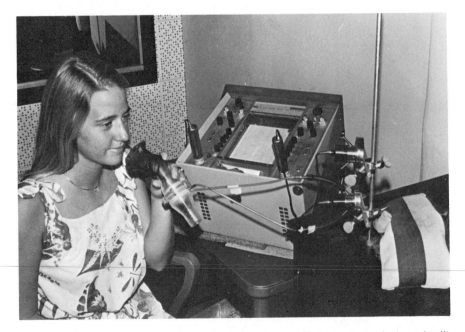

FIGURE 4-6. The pneumotachometer provides air flow data specific to pressure and volume. A split mask can be used for picking up flow separately from both the mouth and the nose.

rates both in children (Leeper, 1976) and adults (Yanagihara and von Leden, 1967) and many references looking at changes in flow for various voice disorder groups (Isshiki and von Leden, 1964; Hirano, Koike, and von Leden, 1968; Gordon, Morton, and Simpson, 1978).

Somewhat related to a measure of flow are the various duration studies that determine how long the individual can sustain a voiced or voiceless expiration (Ptacek and Sander, 1963; Bless and Saxman, 1970; Tait, Michel, and Carpenter, 1980; Eckel and Boone, 1981). One measure of differential duration measures that is used diagnostically in the voice evaluation is the s/z ratio. Here the patient is asked to sustain the /s/ as long as possible; he or she is then asked to sustain the /z/. The typical s/z ratios of normal subjects approximate 1.0, indicating that the voiceless expiration time (the /s/) closely matches maximum phonation time (the /z/) (Tait and others, 1980). In 95 percent of their patients with glottal margin pathologies (nodules, polyps, thickening), Eckel and Boone (1981) found elevated s/z ratios in excess of 1.4, indicating marked reduction in voiced duration values. The clinical value of the s/z ratio to pressure and flow measures may be seen in the application of all three measures in this clinical case:

A nineteen-year-old university singer was self-referred to the University Speech and Hearing Clinic for her continuing problem of "breathiness and hoarseness." Initial voice evaluation techniques included a pneumotachic evaluation which found air flow measurements of 240 cc/sec with oral pressure readings of 5.5 cm H_2O; her initial /s/ duration was 18, her /z/ duration was 11, and her s/z ratio was computed at 1.64. Initially, she resisted having a medical evaluation that included indirect laryngoscopy. The clinician, however, armed with the knowledge that her high s/z value may well be predictive of laryngeal disease, insisted that she have laryngoscopy. A subsequent examination found her to have bilateral vocal nodules which occupied almost a third of her total anterior-posterior glottal length. Following laryngoscopy, she was enrolled in individual voice therapy. Repeated testing after nine weeks of voice therapy revealed a lower air flow measure of 219 cc/sec and higher oral pressure readings of 7.3 cm H_2O; her s/z ratios had decreased to 1.28. These improved scores all suggested better laryngeal function. Subsequent laryngeal examination confirmed some decrease in the size of the nodules, although small bilateral nodes were still present. Her voice quality had improved. The s/z ratio as used here provided one additional measure and observation for the clinician in conducting the overall voice management of the patient.

Motions of the torso.   For many years, students of voice have been able to use the *pneumograph* for the measurement of thoracic and abdominal movements during inhalation and exhalation. The pneumograph is usually connected to a recording device, of which there are two main types, the *kymograph* and the *polygraph*, both of which provide graphic measurement writeouts. The pneumograph provided straps, which are placed around the thorax or abdomen; at the ends of the straps are rubber tubes. As the tubes are stretched, a partial vacuum is created within them, and the amount of vacuum is communicated to the recording instrument. The pneumographic recordings help the speech-language pathologist study the frequency of the respiration cycle, focusing on the regularity of the inhalation-exhalation ratio. How well the patient can sustain the exhalation can be determined very well by using the pneumograph with a kymographic or polygraphic writeout. For the study of differential movements of the thorax in inspiration-expiration, the pneumograph is used less today in favor of newer methodologies.

To study the relative coordination between abdominal movements and thoracic movements, Hixon, Mead, and Goldman (1976) have used *magnetometers* in their study of the relative "anteroposterior diameters" of both the abdomen and thorax, particularly as the two areas relate to one another. When using the magnetometers, the clinician can determine the synchrony of movements of the rib cage and the abdomen during speech breathing. Some clinical voice disorders related to problems such as cerebral palsy or other motor-speech disorders produce severe problems in this synchrony between the different parts involved in breathing. Small magnets are placed on the back and on the front chest wall and on the lower back and abdominal wall; the anterior-posterior distance varies between the magnets in each area (chest or abdomen), and this information can be traced either on an oscilloscope or on some kind of graphic printout.

The experimental use of the *electromyograph* (EMG) in investigating the use of particular muscles in breathing during speech has been explored in several studies reported by Hoshiko (1962), but there has been little regular use of the electromyograph as a clinical tool for respiration assessment. Which muscle is doing what may be determined by the clinical EMG, where recordings are made of the variations in electrical potential as detected by needle or surface electrodes inserted into or placed on a muscle. Whenever that muscle becomes active (contracts), its electrical activity is displayed on a graphic writeout.

Movement of the thorax and the downward excursion of the diaphragm can be identified very well by various X-ray techniques. The degree of inflatability, as seen by thoracic expansion and downward movement of the diaphragm, has been evaluated with convenience by *still X-ray*. We have found still X-rays taken at moments of maximum inhalation and exhalation to be helpful in identifying those sites of respiration (apical versus base of lungs) that show the most deflation or inflation, providing us with knowledge about the type of breathing the patient employs: abdominal-diaphragmatic, midthoracic, or clavicular. Similar information can be obtained by viewing the respiratory mechanism in action, assessing actual movement by the use of other X-ray techniques, namely, *fluoroscopy* and *cinefluorography*.

Other aspects of respiration testing.   The type of breathing the patient uses can sometimes be accurately determined by visual observation. The most inefficient type of breathing, *clavicular,* seems to be the easiest to identify. The patient elevates the shoulders on inhalation, using the neck accessory muscles as his or her primary muscles of inhalation. This upper chest breathing, characterized by noticeable elevation of the clavicles, is unsatisfactory for good voice for two reasons: first, the upper, apical ends of the lungs, when expanded, do not alone provide an adequate respiration; and second, the strain in using the neck accessory muscles for respiration is often visually apparent, with individual muscles "standing out" (particularly the sternocleidomastoids, as they contract to elevate the upper thorax). While there is little research evidence that clearly identifies the negative effects on speech of clavicular breathing, no serious singer would waste his or her time developing such a shallow, upper-lung reservoir of air. Clavicular-type breathing requires too much effort for too little breath. *Diaphragmatic-abdominal* breathing may well be the preferred method of respiration, especially if the patient has heavy vocal demands placed upon him or her, as in singing or acting-speaking without electronic amplification. If the patient is employing diaphragmatic-abdominal breathing, this should be noted on the voice evaluation form. This use of lower thoracic breathing is usually identifiable by the presence of abdominal and lower thoracic expansion on inspiration, with a gradual decrease in abdominal-lower thoracic prominence on expiration. When asked to "take in" a deep breath, the patient will demonstrate, upon inhaling, a relatively active expansion of the lower thorax and little noticeable upper-chest movement.

We can perhaps obtain a more accurate assessment of how the patient breathes for speech when we ask him to demonstrate various voices, such as his pulpit voice, calling the kids voice, talking-to-superiors voice, and so on. Most voice patients exhibit breathing patterns that are somewhere in between clavicular and diaphragmatic-abdominal breathing, and for these persons we use the somewhat nondescript term, *thoracic,* on our voice evaluation form. The thoracic breather is the patient who exhibits no noticeable upper thoracic or abdominal expansion on inhalation. The general mode of breathing can often be assessed if the clinician observes the patient closely as he or she speaks.

Measurement of Pitch

While our observations of voice pitch tell us whether a voice is low or high for the patient's age and sex, only when we measure pitch can we determine the exact fundamental frequency of the voice. Of the various aspects of voice, frequency as measured in cycles per second (Hz) is perhaps the most measurable. As part of the voice evaluation, the patient's total *frequency range* (lowest to highest note) should be determined as a prelude to finding the patient's *optimal pitch* (the patient's easiest and most compatible voice pitch). Measurements should be made of the patient's *habitual pitch* (the most frequently occurring or modal pitch level used by the patient). We will first discuss the instruments we have available for measuring these aspects of frequency and pitch.

The Visi-Pitch, as shown in Figure 4–7, is an excellent clinical instru-

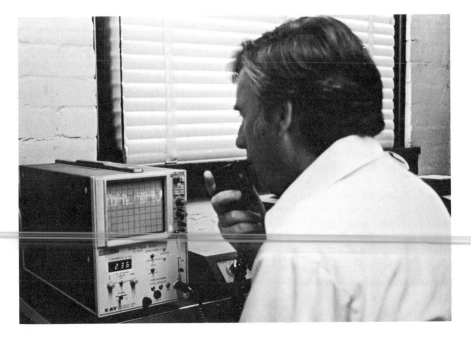

FIGURE 4-7. The Visi-Pitch provides ongoing data and feedback specific to both frequency and intensity.

ment for measuring different aspects of frequency: frequency range, optimal pitch, and habitual pitch. The Visi-Pitch offers both a digital writeout of frequency and an oscilloscopic display. For determination of range, the patient is asked to say "ah" at a comfortable pitch and loudness level and then repeat the "ah" at decreasing musical steps, down to the lowest "note" the patient can produce. He or she is then asked to produce successively higher notes until reaching the top of his or her range. While the clinician will have a digital writeout of fundamental frequency for each separate vocalization, the productions can be stored on the scope and frequency values can be determined after the patient has completed the sequence. There is a cursor feature on the Visi-Pitch that allows the clinician to search the stored tracings on the scope for determination of the exact frequency of any particular phonation. The lowest and the highest frequencies the patient is able to produce represent the patient's range. Optimal pitch can be determined using the Visi-Pitch by using both the frequency and intensity writeouts at the same time. Optimal pitch is usually the frequency that is slightly louder and clearer in quality; both relative changes in intensity and in quality can be determined by the scope tracings (greater vertical excursion indicates greater intensity, and improved sharpness of tracing line indicates better periodicity or improved quality). One way the determination of habitual pitch can be made is by playing a conversational tape jacked into the Visi-Pitch; for every eight seconds of conversation, the most frequently occurring frequency level can be spotted in the scope tracings (which can be stored until they are reviewed) and then measured. Or the patient can produce live conversation or oral reading directly into the Visi-Pitch microphone for a time period of eight seconds; the tracings of frequency can be stored on the scope and then measured. The most frequently occurring frequency can be easily identified. The Visi-Pitch has been designed as a clinical instrument that will easily provide frequency data both at the time of the evaluation and as ongoing feedback information during voice therapy.

Another useful instrument for extracting fundamental frequency from running speech and for determining pitch range is the Tonar II (Fletcher, 1972). As the patient speaks into the microphone, Tonar II automatically displays at fixed intervals the fundamental frequency of the voice. While the Tonar II is designed primarily as an instrument for training in resonance therapy, its digital writeout of frequency is helpful in the determination of modal pitch or habitual pitch. The Tonar II can also be used as an instrument for measuring fundamental frequency range.

Another instrument for measuring both pitch range and habitual pitch is the Tunemaster III (1974), as seen in Figure 4-8. When the tone switch is on, the instrument is capable of generating pitch levels over a one-octave range; for example, the instrument can generate the twelve semitones from C_3 to B_3, and by switching on the octave switch, one can extend the range up another octave to B_4. When the musical frequency is generated in step-by-step semitones, the patient is asked to match the tone with his or her own voice. For adult male subjects whose fundamental frequencies may be well below C_3 (128 cps), the clinician will have to convert the matched pitch of the patient to the instrument pitch level by dropping the machine value by one octave; for example, if the instrument is generating an F_3 and the male patient is "matching" the tone with his

FIGURE 4-8. The Tunemaster has the capability of producing a two-octave range of semitones, such as C_3 to C_5, for pitch range testing. When set at a desired frequency, the instrument can monitor the patient's production of that frequency as he or she speaks in a monotone.

lowest pitch production, the patient would be producing an F_2 pitch level. The Tunemaster III is a useful instrument for establishing a new pitch level, as described in Chapter 5. With the meter switch on, an internal microphone picks up external sounds. If the sound is within a two-semitone range of a target note that has been predetermined and set in the instrument, a "valid reading" light will light and a meter pointer will show how sharp or flat the speaker's pitch is specific to the target pitch.

It is possible to measure frequency range and make other measures specific to frequency without instrumentation other than a piano or pitch pipe. An initial voice recording is made at the time of the patient's first clinic visit and will provide a useful tool for analyzing the patient's habitual pitch level. This analysis can be made after the patient has left the clinic. One method we have used is to stop the recorder at random points and attempt to match the voice pitch level with a *pitch pipe* or a piano. After some experience with a pitch pipe, such as the type shown in Figure 4-9, it is possible to match pitch levels between the pitch pipe frequency and the patient's voice. This is facilitated by remembering key pitch values for average voices; that is, in cycles per second, the typical adult male voice will be somewhere near C_3 (128 cps), and therefore not very different from the C_3 note on a pitch pipe. Using the pitch pipe, we would start at C_3 and then go by gradations (sharps and flats) until we reached "near" the recorded level of the patient's voice. With an adult female we might select as our beginning pitch A_3 (213 cps) and go up or down to match the patient's voice. A typical starting place for a prepubertal child would be middle C (256 cps). In a two- or three-minute sample from the voice recording, we might select seven or eight voice samples for analysis of pitch level. After we have determined the approximate pitch of the patient's voice samples, we then count the various pitch levels and look for the *modal pitch value* (the pitch level that occurs most often), recording this as the patient's habitual pitch level. Using the modal pitch probably gives us a more valid habitual pitch than averaging the obtained sample values and using the mean.

The patient's pitch range can also be determined by using voice

FIGURE 4-9
A typical one-octave pitch pipe is frequently of value to the clinician and the patient in determining pitch level as part of voice therapy.

models. This may be done by asking the patient first to match a pitch level provided by the clinician. It is usually easier for the patient to match his or her own voice with another person's voice than to a generated pitch level from some instrument such as a piano, a pitch pipe, and so on. For this reason, it is most useful to have on hand some recordings of normal voices (adult male, adult female, several children's voices) producing vowels, prolonging each vowel for about three seconds. These samples can be recorded on small cassette tapes, discs, or on blank Language Master cards (1979). On playing the sample voice, which should be "close" to the patient's observed pitch level, we ask the patient to say "ah" with the sample voice, matching it as closely as he can. This allows us to provide the patient with a model, showing how we want him to sing down to the lowest note he can make, descending by one full note on the musical scale for each production. In our model sample, we prolong each note for about three seconds. The patient's performance should be recorded on tape, whenever possible, with the actual frequency analysis done later in the laboratory. He then attempts to sing down to the lowest note he can produce. The patient is then instructed to sing up, one full note at a time, until reaching the highest note he can produce, including the falsetto, and then to sing down, one note at a time, until reaching his lowest note again. Finally, when the lowest note is reached, he is asked once again to sing up to the highest note of his range. This pitch-range task is usually easiest for the patient if he is instructed to sing one note at a time, taking a breath between each three-second production. Many voice patients, and perhaps the population in general, have real difficulty in matching their own voices to a pitch model and in producing a range of their lowest to their highest pitch productions. It may be impossible for some patients with vocal fold pathology, such as nodules or polyps, to vary much the pitch of their voice. By providing various models and encouragement at the right times, the experienced voice clinician can usually obtain some pitch-range information.

For each individual, there appears to be a voice pitch level that can be produced with an economy of physical effort and energy. This relatively effortless voice production is known as *optimum pitch* and is apparently the pitch level at which the thyroarytenoids and other intrinsic muscles of the larynx can produce vocal fold adduction with only minimal muscular effort. The vibrating frequency emitted from the approximated vocal folds is directly related to the natural length and mass of the thyroarytenoids, without much lengthening or shortening. It is doubtful, however, that optimum pitch represents any exact cycles-per-second value. Optimum pitch is more often found in two or three notes somewhere at the bottom of the individual's pitch range, several notes higher than the lowest possible pitch production. The classic notion of optimum pitch is validated somewhat in using the Visi-Pitch, where we confirm a note or two toward the bottom of the patient's total range, where the periodicity of fold vibration is improved (a sharper line appears on the scope) accompanied by relative increases in intensity.

A traditional way of determining optimum pitch was described by Fairbanks (1960), which requires individual patients to phonate their entire vocal ranges, including the falsetto, from their lowest productions to their highest. The total range of full-step musical notes is then counted. For adult males, the optimum pitch level is considered to be the one located one-fourth of the way from the bottom of the total pitch range; for female adults, it might be one or two notes lower than the one-fourth level.

Although the concept of optimum pitch has been questioned (Thurman, 1958), the concept of an ''easy, natural'' pitch level is useful in voice therapy. Since so many voice patients seem to have problems of vocal hyperfunction, an attempt to have the patient produce easy, relatively effortless phonations has obvious diagnostic and therapeutic implications. If the patient can produce a good voice easily, such a voice can become an immediate therapy goal. When an optimum pitch has been determined, the patient should be asked to produce various other vowels and words at that general pitch level. A qualitative judgment should then be made as to how the voice sounds at that level. Other validating methods of optimum pitch determination may be used, including these methods described by Murphy (1964):

> (a) the loud-sigh technique: take a deep breath and intone as on expiration; (b) the grunt method: grunt ah or o, gradually prolonging the utterances until a passage is chanted at the original grunt pitch level; (c) the swollen tone technique: stop up the ears, sing ah or hum m up and down the scale until the pitch level at which the tone swells or is loudest is identified; (d) cough sonorously on an ee sound. (p. 95)

We might add to Murphy's list two other brief methods that aid in determining optimal pitch: Ask the patient to yawn and sigh (the relaxed phonation of the sigh is often the optimum speaking pitch) and also to say ''uh-huh'' (this somewhat automatically produced, affirmative utterance often approximates the optimum pitch level). The six methods—these two and Murphy's four—will usually yield pitch levels that are close to one another, even if not the same. We now also add the indications from the Visi-Pitch as part of our determination of optimum pitch. It should be remembered, however, that for clinical purposes we are interested in a particular area of the frequency range (usually a note or two, several notes above the bottom of the total range) that seems to produce the ''best'' voice with the least amount of effort.

Variations in pitch as a diagnostic aid.   An inappropriate pitch level may at times contribute to the development of a voice disorder. Some vocal fold pathologies, on the other hand, produce changes in voice pitch, often because of the weighting or increased mass-size of the involved fold(s). Some functionally produced low-pitched voices may be called ''the voices of profundity.'' The young professional person may employ an artificially low voice to assert authority and knowledge; a preacher may try to ''hit the low ones'' in his sermon; a young woman may think a low-pitched voice is more professional sounding. Conversely, the high-pitched voice is often symptomatic of general tension and difficulties in relaxation. Or, the postmutational falsetto of the postpubertal male may be the result of serious psychological problems of identity, or may serve the patient little or not at all, persisting out of habit or set. If the patient's pitch appears incongruous with his or her chronological age and sex, the clinician should first determine if the patient has the functional ability to speak at a pitch level more compatible with his or her overall organism. If pitch variation is impossible, it might be the result of cord paralysis, or of certain virilizing drugs that have permanently changed the vocal folds, or of glandular-metabolic changes.

Variations in loudness.   Some patients are observed to speak too loudly or too softly for particular vocal situations. There is no optimal loudness level for any one individual, as voice loudness will vary according to the situation. In the evaluation session, the clinician can make a judgment about the loudness of the patient's voice. If it appears to be impossible for the patient to speak in a loud enough voice, the dysphonia may be related to vocal fold paralysis, or to increases in the mass of the folds (such as with problems of vocal nodules), or to bowed vocal folds worn out from continuous use. Soft voices may be heard also in patients who feel relatively inadequate and inferior, their softness of phonation being consistent with their overall self-image. There are some neurological disorders, such as Parkinson's disease and bulbar palsy, where the patient characteristically speaks in a voice that may be barely audible. At the other end of the spectrum, there are patients who speak with voices that may be perceived as uncomfortably loud. Some dysphonic patients, particularly those who speak with hyperfunction, may have inappropriately loud voices as part of their total problem. Another intensity variation that may be observed at the time of the voice evaluation is the patient who speaks with little or no fluctuation in loudness, also, perhaps, with no variation in pitch.

Since the loudness of the voice frequently varies according to the setting, the interactions of the speaker-listener, background noise levels, and so forth, it is difficult to measure a representative intensity of the speaking voice. One of the best ways we have of measuring loudness is to use a sound pressure level meter that will give us the sound pressure level of the voice for a particular distance (from speaker's mouth to sound level microphone). To measure voice intensity, the patient is seated so that his or her mouth is about one meter from the microphone. The intensity level of the voice can be read from the sound-level-meter dial in terms of decibels. It might be remembered, however, that this laboratory measure of intensity does not have practical application to the loudness levels the patients may be using in more natural settings.

The Visi-Pitch can provide relative measures of intensities. The Visi-Pitch (1980) "screen is divided into a grid, and each vertical division represents 10 Db of sound pressure level" (p. 2–13). The Visi-Pitch can also provide data for the interaction of frequency and intensity, since the instrument allows the simultaneous plotting of both values. Typically, the speaker, or singer for that matter, uses higher intensity levels for higher frequency levels. With practice it is possible for the speaker to hold his or her pitch level constant and vary the intensity curve without altering frequency. The Visi-Pitch intensity values are relative values that one can infer from the oscilloscope display rather than from direct measurements of sound-pressure level.

Most measures of voice level intensity should be related to other information specific to air flow and air pressure, frequency, relative opening of the mouth, body position, and so on. If intensity measurements are possible, they will usually be supplemented by rating scale judgments of loudness, as discussed earlier in this chapter.

Measurement of Vocal Quality

One of the early diagnostic signs of a voice problem is the emergence of some kind of vocal quality disorder, such as hoarseness or breathiness. It is usually some form of *dysphonia* (the term used through this text for all disorders of voice quality) that signals to the patient that he or she has a voice problem. At the time of evaluation, the clinician should listen closely to how the patient speaks and make an attempt to describe what is heard. The verbal description of dysphonia is extremely difficult. Until the state of the art improves, the voice clinician will simply have to grope for terms to use to describe the voice he or she hears. Fairbanks (1960) lists three quality conditions, *breathiness, harshness,* and *hoarseness,* that may well be related to difficulties in optimal approximation of the vocal folds on phonation.

In breathiness, we can usually observe an audible escape of air as the approximating edges along the glottis fail to make optimum contact. Breathiness may be related to the patient's functional inability to bring his or her folds firmly together—he or she has the functional capability of firmer vocal fold approximation, but, for whatever reason, prefers speaking with the breathy voice. Sometimes the breathiness is related to growths on the folds, such as nodules or polyps, which prevent optimum adduction; or it may be the result of cord paralysis, which prevents optimum fold adduction. In the voice signal that is characterized as breathy, there is a reduction in the periodicity of vocal tone and an increase in aperiodicity or noise. We frequently observe at the beginning of the utterance, marked aperiodicity that decreases as the vocal folds begin to vibrate. It appears, therefore, that the breathy voice is often produced by the vocal folds approximating slowly together after the initiation of the outgoing air stream has already begun. The spectrograph shown in Figure 4–10 can provide a visual display of what we hear. In Figure 2–14, we saw that the breathy voice produces noise across the sound spectrum with less definition of a periodic soundwave, as seen in the distinct print of the first three formants in the normal voice spectrogram. Other laboratory measures for quantification of breathiness can be made, such as measuring air flow–air pressure, spectral noise levels (Sansone and Emanuel, 1970), and determining jitter (variations or perturbations in frequency) and shimmer (variations in amplitude) as described by Michel and Wendahl (1971). The perceptual judgments of the clinician and other listeners continue, however, to play an important role in the observation and diagnosis of breathiness.

FIGURE 4-10
A spectrograph used for voice analysis.

A harsh voice is usually heard by listeners as an unpleasant voice. Ainsworth (1980) described the difficulty of defining harshness when he wrote,

> Verbal descriptions of *harshness* are difficult to make without using "impressionistic" terms, i.e., grating, rasping, rough, guttural, raucous. There often are frequent and "hard" glottal catches, i.e., the initiation of tones with an explosive release of air by the vocal folds, and excessive glottal (vocal) fry which is a low-pitched "popping" sound. (Disorders of Voice, Chapter 13 in *Otolaryngology,* p. 7)

Aperiodicity of laryngeal vibration can be seen in the spectrogram for the harsh voice. There is often abrupt initiation of voice characterized by hard glottal attack. The patient sounds as if he or she is working hard to speak. A harsh voice may be described as strident, metallic, or grating, and whatever the descriptor used, it carries an unpleasant connotation. The Visi-Pitch or any kind of spectrum analyzer like the spectrograph will visualize harshness with increased aperiodicity across the spectrum, a reduction of fundamental frequency, a scatter of resonance across the spectrum, and abrupt glottal attack as observed in sudden initiation of phonation. In our judgments of harshness we often focus on the metallic aspects of resonance, where the voice seems to come out of a pharynx and oral cavity that appear to be in a state of hypercontraction; instead of hearing softness and some absorption of soundwave, we hear a hardness described by Coffin (1981) as a "voice produced by hard, reflective surfaces rather than by soft, absorbing surfaces." It is difficult to verbalize a description of the harsh voice we sometimes hear.

Hoarseness is the most common laryngeal quality disturbance, although the term is used often in a meaningless manner for labeling any kind of laryngeal problem in phonation. Anything that interferes with optimum vocal fold adduction can produce the symptom of hoarseness. Many patients exhibit it on a purely functional basis; that is, because they approximate the vocal folds too tightly or too loosely together, they produce hoarseness. Darley (1965) wrote that "hoarse voice quality combines the acoustic characteristics of harshness and breathiness and usually results from laryngeal pathology" (p. 57). The typical dysphonic patient displays the kind of hoarseness we hear in the patient who has some form of laryngitis. The hoarse voice heard in the patient with bilateral vocal nodules includes a breathy escape of air, and is often accompanied by hard glottal attack as the patient attempts to compensate for his or her phonation difficulties. Moore, in his chapter on organic voice disorders in the *Handbook of Speech Pathology* (1971), wrote that hoarseness may be related to mucus on the vocal folds, or relative flaccidity of one or both folds, or additions of mass to the folds, or sometimes to destruction of all or a part of the fold. The spectral printout of the hoarse voice in Figure 2–14 confirms the combination of breathiness and harshness, as we see increased noise across the spectrum with a heavier concentration of acoustic energy in the first formant at the bottom of the spectrogram. Many patients with hoarseness begin to compensate for their poor voices by driving the mechanism even harder; they may feel, for example, that they must have abrupt initiation of glottal attack to "get their voices started." The Visi-Pitch is an easy instrument for determining the abruptness of glottal attack combined with hoarseness. Any kind of air pressure instrument can likewise provide verification of sudden onset of expiration. The visual imprints on the oscilloscope attached to such a monitoring instrument will show sudden and abrupt phonation onsets, characterized by vertical excursions at onset, as opposed to a more gradual sloping rise of the onset curve. Clinician judgment of hoarseness must supplement any measurements we are able to make. The advantage of some kind of instrument quantification of hoarseness at the time of the initial evaluation is that the measurement data can be compared with data taken subsequently during and at the end of therapy. It has also been our experience that the instruments that provide the evaluation data can be used to provide feedback to the patient in therapy specific to a particular component of voice. For example, for the patient with hoarseness, there may be advantages for providing visual feedback on the oscilloscope relative to improvement of periodicity as the voice is heard to be "less hoarse." Like most evaluation data, it should be used not only in the diagnostic-decision process in planning therapy but actually given to the patient as a continuing feedback and confirmation of his or her therapy progress.

Other variations in vocal fold approximation may produce symptoms of *glottal fry, register variations, pitch breaks,* and *phonation breaks.* Most voice evaluation forms have checkoff lists that would include these terms. *Glottal fry* can be detected using the Visi-Pitch. Instead of getting a single tracing line representing a single fundamental frequency, the voice is represented by two or more broken lines, indicating that the patient is producing two or three simultaneous fundamental frequencies. The multiple phonation pulses are usually of low frequency and usually are observed at the bottom of one's frequency range (Hollien, and others, 1966). The phenomenon of fry is usually observed as a slight hoarseness that comes into the individual's voice toward the bottom of his or her pitch range. It has been described as sounding like an outboard motor boat, a creaking door, pop-corn popping, and so on. Moore and von Leden (1958) termed glottal fry "dicrotic dysphonia." Others have described the vocal folds during the production of fry as thick, with the ventricular bands in close contact with the superior surface of the true vocal folds. It is undoubtedly this thickness of folds that produces the lower fundamental pitch that usually accom-panies glottal fry. With some elevation of voice pitch, the fry will often decrease.

Register variations, rarely mentioned in American speech pathology texts, do appear to exist as clinical problems in some voice patients. The concept of vocal register comes from the organ stop, which in German is called "register." Luchsinger and Arnold (1965) wrote this on the subject of register:

> In chest voice, the cords vibrate over their entire breadth, whereas the falsetto voice reveals vibration limited to the inner cord margins. When phonating low tones, the cords appear rounded, full, and relaxed, while they are sharp-edged, thin, and taut for falsetto tones. These differences may readily be seen on frontal laryngeal tomo-grams. (p. 97)

Register variation is related to the relative changes in the cross-section of the vocal folds, produced by differential contraction of the vocalis section of the thyroarytenoid muscle. Negus (1957) in his classic article, "The Mechanism of the Larynx," used the terms *thick* and *thin* to correspond to the cross-sectional differences seen in the production of the chest register and the head register. Sometimes we observe voices that seem incompat-ible with the resonating bodies of the patient. Certain patients may pro-duce variations by attempting to speak at their lower pitches with vocal folds approximated in the manner typical of high-pitched head register. Conversely, sometimes higher pitches are produced with the folds approx-imated in their fullest broad dimension, the typical pattern of the low-pitched chest register. Register variation (fold approximation incompati-ble with the desired pitch level) can best be confirmed by frontal X-ray of the approximating glottal surfaces, as seen in frontal tomograms. Typical tomographic configurations for varying registers were seen in Figure 2–13.

When *pitch break* is observed, it is usually in a voice that is pitched too low. As the patient is phonating, the pitch level will suddenly break up-ward to a falsetto level, often one octave above the pitch level he or she was using. Pitch breaks may be observed in a voice pitched too high, also, and the break then is downward, usually a full octave below the previous pitch level. In an adult patient, voice breaks can be extremely embarrassing. Sometimes the pitch break is the patient's primary, and perhaps sole, reason for seeking voice therapy. Pitch breaks in children are much more common, but are rarely considered to be clinical problems. Curry (1949) found in his voice studies of adolescents that while voice breaks in males can occur in prepuberty, they are much more common at around the age of fourteen, when rapid pubertal changes take place. In eighteen-year-olds, Curry found virtually no pitch breaks. It would appear that pitch breaks in children, particularly in males at around the time of puberty, are fairly common and usually disappear with continuing physical maturation. In adults, pitch breaks are relatively rare and appear most often to be a symptom of inappropriate habitual pitch level—too low a pitch with an involuntary pitch break upward, or too high a pitch with the break occurring downward.

The *phonation break* is a temporary loss of voice that may occur for only part of a word, a whole word, a phrase, or a sentence. The individual is phonating with no observable difficulty when suddenly he experiences a loss of voice or phonation break. Patients who experience voice breaks usually exhibit some degree of voice hyperfunction as they speak. They work to talk. The typical patients with voice breaks may be people who use their voices a lot, perhaps teachers. After prolonged speaking, they begin to experience vocal fatigue. The individuals begin to do something to improve the sound of their voices, such as raising or lowering the voice pitch or speaking through clenched teeth. The result is increased vocal tension. Finally, while they are phonating, the vocal folds spontaneously abduct and the voice is temporarily lost. By throat clearing, coughing, swallowing water, or whatever, phonation is restored until the next phonation break. Most voice patients, even if they have occasional phonation breaks, will not exhibit this temporary voice loss during the evaluation session.

Resonance Testing

Our focus in this evaluation chapter has been on the evaluation of patients with phonation disorders. That is not to say that the patient may not have an accompanying resonance disorder; phonation and resonance disorders may go hand in hand. Many patients, however, have voice problems that are primarily of voice resonance. We will discuss the problems of voice resonance, their evaluation, management, and therapy in Chapter 7.

SUMMARY

The voice evaluation is the time when the clinician first meets the voice patient, providing opportunity for observation and testing. The evaluation continues as part of every therapy session, particularly as the clinician continually searches with the patient for new vocal behaviors. The speech-language pathologist must continue to evaluate and observe the patient's respiratory, phonatory, and resonance functions. Whenever possible, these functions should be quantified with instrumentation. The patient's voice data are used for comparison purposes, to quantify vocal changes between the first visit, subsequent therapy sessions, and the final outcome session. Patient's performance, both as observed and as measured, is offered back to the patient as a continuing feedback, helping the patient become aware of his or her voice performance. The evaluation enables the voice clinician to decide on what management steps to take for the patient. If voice therapy is indicated, the evaluation will help the clinician in developing a therapy plan and in predicting the patient's outcome prognosis.

5

Voice Therapy
for Problems
of Vocal Hyperfunction

Most voice disorders are related to vocal hyperfunction. The patient uses too much effort while speaking or singing. Effective voice therapy for patients with vocal hyperfunction must begin with identification of vocal abuse and misuse, followed by systematic attempts to decrease the occurrence of such abuse-misuse. The voice clinician then searches with the patient for the best voice the patient is able to produce by using therapy techniques we call facilitating approaches. Those approaches that facilitate better voice are then used in voice therapy. Twenty-five techniques that the clinician uses in the search for good "can do" voice behaviors are described here.

The first part of any voice therapy program requires that the patient become aware of any vocal abuses and misuses. As described in earlier chapters, an example of an abuse to the laryngeal mechanism would be continuous throat clearing. If throat clearing is extensive enough, it alone can produce edematous (swelling) changes of the glottal margin, causing symptoms of hoarseness and breathiness. Or the throat clearing may be the result of an additive lesion that serves as a glottal margin irritant, with the patient clearing the throat to change the feeling that "something is there." He or she may soon begin to clear the throat out of habit set. Or the continuous throat clearing can add irritation to an already irritated site, and the throat clearing itself becomes part of the production of the irritation. Efforts must be made, if voice therapy is to be successful, to reduce the occurrence of the throat clearing or any other form of vocal abuse. Similarly, voice misuse can add irritation to the glottal margin, which can contribute to the beginning and the continuation of a voice problem. An example of vocal misuse could be speaking with excessive hard glottal attack. The patient speaks with sudden initiation of voice onset, with the voice sounding forceful and strained. If one were interested in improving the quality of one's voice, speaking in such an abrupt manner would best be changed to an easier phonatory style.

There is little difference in the kind of voice therapy given for the different kinds of dysphonia related to vocal hyperfunction. A ten-year-old boy with a husky voice and a normal larynx would require about the same therapy program as his ten-year-old friend with a husky voice and a larynx with bilateral vocal nodules. The type of facilitating approaches might be different, for what helps one person may not help another. Both children would profit, however, from a voice program designed to reduce vocal abuse and misuse, and a voice production program where the clinician searches with the child, using various facilitating approaches, to find the best voice the child is able to produce with the least amount of effort. Many adult problems of dysphonia and vocal fatigue demonstrate no structural change of the laryngeal mechanism, either as a cause of the problem or as a result. Functional voice problems without pathology usually respond to the same techniques of voice therapy as dysphonias related to cord thickening, vocal nodules, polyps, contact ulcers, and so on. A differential therapy approach—that is, a certain method for nodules, a different one for polyps—is not needed for each voice disorder. Rather, our therapy might be more effective and relevant if, after analyzing the voice disorder along the dimensions of pitch, loudness, and quality, we then applied a therapy appropriate to those dimensions.

It would be easy, and very wrong, to identify for the patient the various things he or she is doing wrong vocally and then provide him or her with a series of specific remedial therapy techniques. Rather, the voice therapist must continually search for the patient's best and most appropriate voice production. This searching is necessary because so much of our vocal behavior is highly automatic, particularly the dimensions of pitch and quality. The patient cannot volitionally break vocalization down into various components and then hope to combine them into some ideal phonation. Our therapy techniques are primarily vehicles of facilitation; that is, we try a particular therapy approach and see if it facilitates the production of a better voice. If it does, then we utilize it as therapy practice material. If it does not, we quickly abandon it. As part of every clinical session, we must probe and search for the patient's best voice. When an acceptable production is achieved, we use it as the patient's target model in therapy. The patient's own best voice becomes his or her goal. This requires, of course, the continuous use of feedback to the patient of some aspect of his or her best voice production. Various kinds of feedback could include the auditory playback of one's productions using a cassette or reel-to-reel audiotape recorder, using a looptape recorder, or using a videotape recorder and presenting the patient's production back to him or her on a TV monitor, or using various kinds of biofeedback equipment so that the patient might monitor a physiologic aspect of his or her production. Biofeedback might include the monitoring of some aspect of respiration using a manometer or a pair of magnetometers, or letting the patient watch his or her velopharyngeal closure by using an endoscope attached to a video unit. Often the patient can progress in voice therapy with only the feedback of his or her own best voice as the target model; sometimes the voice feedback needs the additional feedback provided by other devices.

An example of how voice therapy works using a four-point program (identify abuse-misuse; reduce occurrence of identified abuses-misuses; search for the best voice using facilitating approaches; use the approaches that work as therapy practice techniques) may be seen in this case report of a nine-year-old boy with vocal nodules:

Eric, age 9, had a four-year history of hoarseness and occasional loss of voice. In a third-grade school screening program he was found to have a severe dysphonia by the speech-language pathologist who referred him to an ENT physician for indirect laryngoscopy. The ENT doctor found that he had "large bilateral nodules which occupied about one-third of his total glottal length." A voice therapy program was initiated which put beginning focus on identifying his vocal abuses and misuses. Eric was observed to yell continually at play, clear his throat excessively (sometimes twice a minute), and make funny animal sounds as a way of entertaining his family and friends (and himself). The reduction of abuse-misuse section of the *Boone Voice Program for Children* (1980a) was very successful in providing Eric with the insights he needed to curb his yelling and throat clearing. Various voice therapy approaches were used including chewing, open mouth, and the yawn-sigh. These approaches gave him an immediate better-sounding voice, and he subsequently enjoyed using them as therapy techniques. His better-sounding voice was his positive reinforcement. The clinician also found that Eric's intelligence and sensitivity allowed him to profit much from her explanations of his problem. Audio feedback, which confirmed for him the improvement in the way he sounded, was also critical to his progress in voice therapy. The boy saw his public school clinician for individual voice therapy twice weekly for a total of twenty-six weeks. At the end of that time, repeat laryngoscopy found "only a slight thickening on the right fold with the left fold completely normal." His voice quality began to sound like the voices of other boys his same age. When he entered fourth grade, no further voice therapy was indicated.

The successful therapy described for this boy with vocal nodules would have to be followed with a vocal hygiene approach. While there have been many vocal hygiene approaches described in the literature (Anderson and Newby, 1973; Boone, 1980c; Cooper, 1980; Fox and Blechman, 1975; and D. K. Wilson, 1979), we will present a vocal hygiene approach later in this chapter, which is particularly useful for children and adults to follow after they have completed formal voice therapy. A vocal hygiene program is basically a common sense approach in avoiding future and unnecessary vocal abuse or misuse. Voice therapy and the vocal hygiene program that follows are highly individualized endeavors.

ESTABLISHING WHERE TO START
IN VOICE THERAPY

Voice therapy must begin where the patient is able to perform. We cannot ask patients to do more than they are capable of doing. The beginning of voice therapy must relate to the final outcome of the therapy. In applying dismissal criteria to seventy-three voice patients (Boone, 1974), we found at our first therapy session that we had to determine the size of laryngeal lesion (if there is one), make a voice recording of the patient, and determine how the patient felt about his voice. These initial data are then compared to data after therapy and are used as part of the decision process in terminating therapy. The effects of subsequent voice therapy could never be fully determined without some preliminary specificity relative to the presence or absence of a laryngeal lesion. The site and size of the lesion, if one is present, will greatly determine the beginning steps of voice therapy. For example, large fibrotic vocal nodules might well require a surgical approach followed by voice rest and then voice therapy. Small, beginning thickenings at the anterior-middle third junction of the folds would offer a prompt and convincing signal for the speech pathologist to initiate a voice program to reduce vocal hyperfunction. Some beginning documentation of the lesion is necessary if we are to compare pretreatment and posttreatment effects.

Voice therapy progress can only be clearly documented if it is built upon thorough beginning diagnostic information. There are two important early steps we must make in voice therapy: make an initial voice recording, for both immediate analysis and later comparison; and determine the patient's somatic feelings of the disorder (dryness, pain). The initial voice recording should include the patient's name, the date, spontaneous conversation, oral reading, and specific vowel and phrase repetitions that best illustrate the disorder. Subsequent and final recordings should always contain basically the same spoken material. Since many voice problems related to vocal hyerfunction create physical discomfort to the patient, sometimes, in the absence of dysphonia, it is important to determine the patient's self-reports of dryness, pain, fullness, and so forth. Elimination of these symptoms often represents a real improvement to the patient. Initial time in therapy should be spent exploring the speaking conditions and situations that precipitate these self-reports of discomfort.

Most of what we do in early voice therapy is searching or probing with the patient for the best voice he can produce. Many of the facilitating approaches listed in Table 5–1 are designed to reduce vocal hyperfunction; we probe for their effects on the voice as part of the therapy. For example, we might employ the Open-Mouth Approach (facilitating approach 19) to see if opening the mouth wider has a positive effect on the production of voice. If it does, we would use opening the mouth wider as an initial therapy technique. The clinician employs various facilitating approaches to determine whether by their application, the patient's voice sounds better. If a facilitating approach is successful, it is continued; if the voice sounds the same or actually sounds poorer, the clinician goes to another approach. Sometimes, some of the steps of an approach are facilitative for good voice while others may not be. We determine both the effects of the overall approach and the steps in that approach by marking a form similar to that shown in a sample form (Boone, 1980a) in Figure 5–1.

Voice Therapy for Young Children

The speech-language pathologist in the public schools probably encounters more children with voice disorders than any other specialist. A national speech and hearing survey (Hull and others, 1976) found that

FIGURE 5–1. The voice probe. The clinician measures the effectiveness of various facilitating approaches with the patient. Each step in administering the approach is measured for its effect. Used in *The Boone Voice Program for Children*. Tigard, Oregon: C. C. Publications.

VOICE IMPROVEMENT RECORDING FORM
The Boone Voice Program for Children

Name_____ Date Therapy Initiated_____ Date Therapy Terminated_____
Check (✓) if Vocal Abuse Program is in effect_____ .

DATE	FACILITATING APPROACH #	STEP NUMBER	NEGATIVE CHANGE	NO CHANGE	SLIGHT IMPROVEMENT	GREAT IMPROVEMENT

(CHECK (✓) APPROPRIATE BOX)

about 10 percent of all school-age children (grades 1 through 12) did not have acceptable voices, with the prevalence of 25 percent at first grade and as low as 3 percent in grades 11 and 12. Most of those children who have dysphonia have their voice problem because of vocal hyperfunction, using too much effort and force as they speak. Most voice programs (Wilson and Rice, 1977; Drudge and Philips, 1976; Boone, 1980a) place early emphasis on identification of abuse-misuse, with specfic steps for reducing the occurrence of such behaviors.

Probably there is no more effective thing the clinician can do than isolate for the child those situations in which the child is vocally abusive, such as yelling at a ball game, screaming in the playground, crying, imitating noises below or above his or her speaking pitch range, and so on. Many children maintain their vocal pathologies simply by engaging in abusive vocal behavior for just brief periods each day. It is usually not possible to identify these vocal abuses through interview methods or by observing the child in the therapy room; rather, the child must be observed in various play settings, in the classroom, and at home. This need for extensive observation requires that the clinician solicit the help of the child himself to determine where he might be yelling or screaming. The teacher will provide some helpful clues about the child's vocal behavior both on the playground and in the classroom. A meeting with parents will often reveal further situations of vocal abuse, and the parents may be asked to listen over a period of time for abusive vocal behavior in the child's play or in his interaction with various family members. At times, we have had good luck in using the child's siblings or peers to help us determine what the child may be doing vocally in certain situations.

Once the abusive situations are isolated, the clinician should obtain baseline measurements of the number of times the vocal abuse is observed in a particular time unit (an hour, a recess period, a day, and so on). Figure 5-2 shows a vocal-abuse graph, plotting the number of abuses the child has recorded over a period of two weeks.

You will notice that the first plot on the abscissa is the first day's baseline measurement, which tells on the ordinate how many times the child caught herself yelling on that particular day—for this child, eighteen separate yells. The overall contour shows a linear decrement in voice yelling, which is a somewhat typical curve for young children. Having to monitor her offensive behavior seems to motivate the child to reduce it. In her pocket the child may keep a tally card on which to mark down each occurrence; at the end of the day, she tallies that day's occurrences and plots the total figure on the graph. The review of the plotting graph is a vital part of the therapy, and the child's pride in her graph (which will usually show a decrement in the behavior) helps her continue to curb the vocal abuse. Some children require assistance in making this kind of plot, and sometimes we ask the teacher, the parents, or a friend to also keep a tally card, recording the number of events they observed in a particular time period. It appears that if the child is given a proper orientation to the task and clearly knows why she must reduce the number of vocal abuses, her tally counts are higher, and perhaps more valid, than the counts of the external observers.

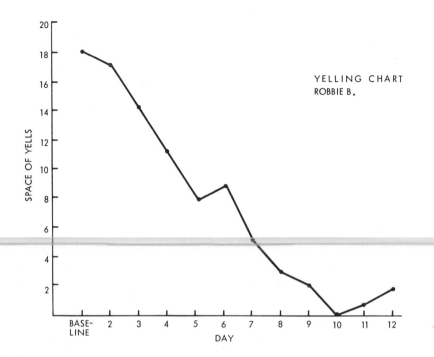

FIGURE 5-2. An eleven-year-old boy was found at the time of his voice evaluation to do a lot of screaming and yelling. He was asked to count each day the number of times he found himself yelling. Figure 5-2 charts the boy's daily tally of his yelling over a twelve-day period. On the first day a baseline count of eighteen yells was tallied. The general overall contour of the curve shows a marked decrement in the amount of yelling he recorded.

    Another method for keeping track of a child's vocal abuses (we have used the method also with a few adults) is to provide the patient with a voice tally card (Boone, 1980a). The card has a series of numbers, each perforated. For example, if a boy catches himself producing the vocal abuse, he tears off the next tally number. At the end of the day, he can quickly see how many abuses (such as throat clearings) he caught himself doing that day. Actually, the exact number of abuses is not as important as the general task of counting in helping the patient become aware of abusive vocal behavior. The tally method of counting abuses is a prominent part of therapy for children and cannot be overestimated for its importance in eliminating vocal abuse. If it is successful, often no other form of voice therapy is needed. An important prelude to the tally method—indeed to any form of speech therapy, particularly voice therapy—is for the clinician to explain to the child what the problem is, what he seems to be doing wrong vocally, and what can be done about it. Obviously, the child must first know that there is a voice problem (rarely does a child recognize such a problem independently) before he can develop any awareness of it or do anything about it. This explanation to the child is especially important when we remember that most children with voice problems are not self-referred. Their dysphonia has been discovered by someone else. To the child, there may be no problem.

Voice Therapy for Adolescents and Adults

The abusive vocal behaviors of adults are likely to be far more difficult to isolate than those of children. It is the relatively rare adult voice patient whose vocal abuses are bound only to particular situations, even though the preacher or the auctioneer whose voice problems appear only on the job may indeed be excellent examples of vocal misuse. Generally, the dysphonic adolescent or adult has a hyperfunctional set toward phonation. He or she works to talk in most situations. Sometimes the exaggerated efforts are related to a generalized feeling of tension that becomes more acute in particular settings, such as when he or she speaks to authority figures or when trying to make a favorable impression on listeners. It is this common observation—that many people with hyperfunctional voice problems exist in a milieu of tension—that has fostered the belief among laryngologists and voice clinicians that the symptomatic treatment of the voice disorder should be avoided in favor of a more comprehensive psychological approach. Gray, England, and Mahoney (1965) have described an approach that combines some elements of traditional voice therapy with an emphasis on deconditioning the patient's anxiety and tensions by using the behavioral approach of reciprocal inhibition. It is this text's point of view that while unresolved tension and anxiety contribute to the voice problems of some voice patients, most of our patients are fully capable of producing a good, optimum voice, providing someone (the clinician) will only help them "find" it.

Therefore, the primary task of the voice clinician is to explore with the patient the various therapy techniques that might produce that "good" voice. Similar to our using facilitating techniques as therapy probes with children, we use the same approach with adults. The approach that works is then used as a therapy practice approach. Once the patients are able to produce a model of their own best voice, this model and the techniques used to achieve it become the primary focus of the voice therapy. To be sure, the voice clinician also provides the patients with needed psychological support, and together they explore various facilitating techniques to be used in particular situations. Borrowing from the work of Wolpe (1973) and of Gray and his associates (1965), efforts are made to have the patients isolate those hierarchies of stress in which their phonation varies.

The voice clinician has an advantage in working with adolescents and adults in that most of them are self-referred and, at least to that extent, motivated to succeed. The average patient experiences some form of dysphonia for several months before seeking professional help from his physician or from the laryngologist to whom he has been referred. The physician, in turn, refers the patient to a speech pathologist. The patient who is disturbed enough by voice problems will seek help. In voice therapy, as in psychotherapy, if the problem makes the patient miserable enough, motivation usually will be sufficient to enable him or her to participate in the therapy very well.

The average patient with a hyperfunctional voice problem will respond well to symptomatic voice therapy. The clinician should analyze what the patient is doing with regard to vocal fold mass-size and vocal fold approximation, relating these observations to the acoustic dimensions of loudness, pitch, and quality. Loudness disorders are usually characterized by voices that are too weak to be heard or inappropriately loud. Many problems of inadequate loudness are directly related to the patient's self-image, mirroring rather closely his or her inner psychic state. However, such patients sometimes respond well to respiration exercises designed to increase subglottal air pressure for relatively short verbal units; by expending greater breath for short verbal segments, they can add considerably to their loudness. Some loudness problems may be related to inadequate vocal fold adduction and approximation, where much subglottal air pressure is wasted. We shall discuss several techniques that facilitate more optimum vocal fold approximation, which in turn helps produce more adequate loudness. Pitch problems are usually directly related to faulty mass-size adjustments of the vocal folds, although some pitch problems are the result of additive tissue to the vocal folds, a consequence of such problems as vocal nodules, polyps, cord thickening, and so on. We shall also consider techniques that help the patient establish appropriate vocal pitch levels. Quality problems, always difficult to define, appear to be those departures in total voice sound that distinguish the patient from the normal speaker. Such voices may be described variously as hoarse, husky, breathy, harsh, and so on. These quality problems are generally related to problems in fold approximation. Of the twenty-five facilitating techniques discussed in this chapter, many will be applicable to quality problems; that is, the technique will produce for the patient a good target voice. Once that voice is produced, it is the clinician's task to see that the patient practices the facilitating technique with some frequency, so that the target voice will be produced repeatedly. The best voice therapy appears to be to practice, under various conditions, the best voice one is able to produce.

VOICE THERAPY FACILITATING TECHNIQUES

A *voice therapy facilitating technique* is that technique which, when used by a particular patient, enables him or her easily to produce a good voice. Once discovered, the facilitating technique and the resulting phonation become the symptomatic focus of therapy. After the patient has achieved a voice production that approximates the target model (the therapy goal), he or she requires systematic practice in using that phonation. This use of a facilitating technique to produce a good phonation is the core of what we do in symptomatic voice therapy for the reduction of hyperfunctional voice disorders. Such an approach involves the continuous search for "can do" vocal behaviors in each particular patient. What may work (or facilitate) for one person may well not work for another. While the clinician should be familiar with a number of voice facilitating techniques and know how to use them, one's search for what works and what does not should not be based on arbitrary trial and error. Rather, each technique should be evaluated in terms of its possible effect on vocal fold mass-size and approximation, as observed in changes of voice loudness, pitch, and quality.

It should be noted that some techniques are applicable for facilitating both mass-size changes and approximation of the vocal folds. Others appear to be used primarily for promoting mass-size changes, and still others primarily for better vocal fold approximation. Similarly, certain approaches have greater facilitating effects on loudness, others on pitch, and others on quality. Some techniques, such as number 25 (the yawn-sigh ap-

TABLE 5-1. Twenty-five Facilitating Approaches in Voice Therapy

FACILITATING APPROACH	PHONATORY PROCESS AFFECTED		PARAMETER OF VOICE AFFECTED		
	MASS/SIZE	APPROXI-MATION	LOUDNESS	PITCH	QUALITY
1. Altering Tongue Position		X*		X	X
2. Biofeedback	X	X	X	X	X
3. Change of Loudness	X	X	X	X	X
4. Chant Talk		X	X		X
5. Chewing Approach	X	X	X	X	X
6. Digital Manipulation	X			X	
7. Ear Training	X	X	X	X	X
8. Elimination of Abuses	X	X	X	X	X
9. Elimination of Hard Glottal Attack		X	X		X
10. Establishing New Pitch	X			X	X
11. Explanation of Problem	X	X	X	X	X
12. Feedback	X	X	X	X	X
13. Gargle Approach		X			X
14. Hierarchy Analysis	X	X	X	X	X
15. Inhalation Phonation		X		X	
16. Masking	X	X	X	X	X
17. Negative Practice	X	X	X	X	X
18. Open Mouth Approach	X		X	X	X
19. Pitch Inflections	X	X	X	X	
20. Place the Voice	X	X		X	X
21. Pushing Approach		X	X		X
22. Relaxation	X	X	X	X	X
23. Respiration Training		X	X		X
24. Voice Rest	X	X			
25. Yawn-Sigh Approach	X	X	X	X	X

* X indicates the particular facilitating approach effective for that particular Phonatory Process or Parameter of Voice.

proach), appear applicable to most problems. Many techniques may be used in combination with one another, and the basic rule of application (when to apply) is to use the approach that works best with the individual patient.

For each of the twenty-five techniques that follow, the reader will find these areas developed:

A.   Kinds of problems for which the approach is useful;
B.   Procedural aspects of the approach;
C.   Typical case history showing utilization of the approach;
D.   Evaluation of the approach.

I.   ALTERING TONGUE POSITION
   A.   *Kinds of problems for which approach is useful.* The position of the tongue within the mouth and pharynx is a primary shaping factor of resonance. The distinguishing characteristics of vowels and consonants are produced by tongue positioning, and any group of people speaking the same language will make basically the same tongue movements; that is, if one's vowels or consonants are to be intelligible to one's listeners, he or she must make them in the same way the listeners do. In the faulty positioning of tongue that contributes to voice disorders, it is not the individual phoneme placement that is in error, but the overall carriage of the tongue. Some patients carry the tongue backward, almost occluding the pharynx, which contributes to a hollow-sounding cul-de-sac resonance; the focus of the voice appears to be pharyngeal. This author has pointed out elsewhere (1966, p. 691) that "deaf boys and girls, regardless of age, have a tendency for a pharyngeal focus in their vocal resonance." Some voice patients retract their tongues into the pharynx during moments of tension, reporting problem voices only at these times. Other patients have the opposite problem, carrying their tongues too far forward, creating what Fisher (1975) describes as a "thin quality." This is the baby-talk voice; lacking the full resonance of back vowels, it sounds immature or pathologically meek and submissive. Both the muffled voice with posterior resonance focus and the weak, thin voice with anterior carriage can sometimes be favorably improved by direct work in modifying tongue position.
   B.   *Procedural aspects of approach.*
      1.   For the patient with posterior tongue carriage, these activities will help promote a more forward tongue positioning:
         a)   Preface any exercises with a discussion and demonstration of pharyngeal tongue positioning and its effect on voice. Check the posture of the patient and be sure that the chin is neither tucked in toward the chest nor excessively extended.
         b)   Begin practice with the whispered production of tongue tip—alveolar consonants, such as /t/, /d/, /s/, and /z/.

Require that the patient whisper a rapid series of "ta" sounds, perhaps ten per breath. After several minutes of using "ta," go on to the next front-of-the-mouth phoneme. Each practice series of several minutes should be followed by some analysis with the patient of what has just been done, for example, "What does the front-of-the-mouth production feel like?" Keep the early practice confined to whispered productions. Other front consonants that lend themselves well to practice are /w/, /wh/, /p/, /b/, /f/, /v/, /θ/, /ɝ/, and /l/. The following vowels have a relatively high oral focus and lend themselves well to joint practice with the above consonants /i/, /ɪ/, /e/, /ɛ/, and /æ/.

c) After some success with whispered productions, add voice lightly. Select for oral reading those exercises that are heavily loaded with tongue-tip consonants and front vowels. Practice contrasting this new front resonance with the old posterior resonance. On recorded playback, listen to the difference critically; evaluate the difference in the "feeling" of the two productions.

2. For excessive anterior carriage of the tongue, these activities will help develop a more normal tongue position:

a) After explaining the problem, determine whether the patient is using an appropriate pitch level (often he or she is not).

b) Instruct the patient that he or she does not have to shape the tongue in any particular way. By saying the back vowels aloud in as full a voice as he or she can, the patient has usually already brought the tongue back to where it should be. These vowels should be practiced first in isolation, with some effort given to sustain each one for a period of about five seconds: /a/, /ɑ/, /o/, /ʋ/, and /u/.

c) Practice the reading of materials heavy with the back consonants /k/ and /g/, and heavy also with the back vowels. When the patient has achieved some success in posterior productions, ask him or her to contrast the old method of speaking with the new, perhaps using both methods for each work or phrase read aloud. Spend some time listening to the two and discussing the difference in sound and feeling between them.

C. *Typical case history showing utilization of approach.* F. D., a twenty-seven-year-old male teacher, found himself in situations where his voice would become muffled and almost inaudible. The voice evaluation found him to have a normal larynx and a "tendency to withdraw his tongue posteriorly into the pharynx during moments of stress." By using hierarchy analysis, facilitating technique 14, he was able to identify those situations which produced the most stress—situations in which he would almost reflexively draw his tongue back in his pharynx. The patient was taught to alter his tongue carriage to a more anterior position by practicing, in whispers, front-of-the-mouth consonants and vowels. He then practiced using this anterior tongue carriage in various situations in the hierarchy of stress, maintaining optimum tongue position with good voice production in increasingly tense situations. The patient maintained this success in most situations; he reported that only occasional situations, such as speaking up at a teacher's union meeting, were characterized by the old voice.

D.   *Evaluation of approach.* Many voice patients appear to develop faulty tongue positioning as part of their overall problem of dysphonia. Altering the main carriage of the tongue, whether it be excessively posterior or anterior, can be achieved to some degree by most patients. A slight alteration of position toward a more normal carriage usually has a profound influence in improving the quality and resonance of the voice. It would appear that proper positioning of the tongue enables the oral resonance cavities to function more naturally in their filtering of the laryngeally produced fundamental frequency. the relatively normal positioning of the tongue appears to be an important component of a normal voice.

II.   BIOFEEDBACK

A.   *Kinds of problems for which approach is useful.* As individuals speak, they become grossly aware of their voices and the things they do muscularly to speak. There are many components of talking, however, for which we do not have acute awareness. Biofeedback provides the patient with ongoing feedback specific to certain biologic systems. The Biofeedback Approach, which uses various forms of equipment, provides the patient an awareness of what he or she may be doing with a particular biologic system related to voice. For the patient working on some aspect of respiration, a manometer or spirometer may provide the patient with ongoing data, specific to the expiration task he or she may be practicing. Or television monitors may display for the patient what he or she is doing specific to mouth opening, velopharyngeal closure, tongue movements, or whatever system is being photographed. Tracings from the oscilloscope can often be stored and used by the patient for comparison of his ongoing efforts in contrast to the stored model. Sometimes the voice patient who is working on relaxation requires ongoing biofeedback specific to his or her state of relaxation, as seen in EMG pickup of muscle tension or EEG pickup of brain waves. Often, after the patient knows what "it feels like" to be relaxed, corresponding to certain levels of biofeedback information, continued use of biofeedback instrumentation is not needed. For example, in working on relaxation, once the patient observes that the heavy feeling of true relaxation is always coupled with low digital writeouts depicting low muscle potentials, the EMG biofeedback unit may no longer be needed to confirm the relaxation state.

B. *Procedural aspects of approach.*

1. We will first develop application procedures for using biofeedback to monitor an ongoing physiological event, such as monitoring one's velopharyngeal closure:

   a) We review with the patient some of the findings of Shelton and others (1975) specific to using the panendoscope coupled with a videotape recorder and television monitor. It is sometimes best to show the patient a brief videotape that shows how the patient uses the panendoscope, how the velopharyngeal closure mechanism works, and how one can distinguish the velum from the posterior and lateral pharyngeal walls.

   b) The patient is asked to place the panendoscope into the open mouth and let the instrument slide back on the superior surface of the tongue, clearing under the uvular area.

   c) Once the instrument is in place, the patient is asked to visualize the closure on the TV monitor. Various vowel and consonant combinations are used to produce closure.

   d) The patient is to focus on "what it feels like" when he or she produces the closure pattern that represents the target pattern for the session.

   e) Once effective velopharyngeal closure can be produced (there is no need to use the procedure if the patient can never produce closure), the patient practices this production, monitoring his or her velopharyngeal closure on the monitor.

2. The procedures developed here are for using instrumentation for providing biofeedback specific to relaxation:

   a) The clinician explains to the patient that the biofeedback apparatus will help him or her experience a relatively deep level of muscle relaxation that will be used in behavioral therapy such as systematic desensitization or hierarchy analysis (facilitating technique 14). The patient is introduced to the feedback components of the apparatus. When he or she is in a relaxed state, the feedback will report reduced digital counts, a reduced auditory beep signal (if auditory signals are part of the feedback unit), and a green light will light (if the feedback unit is equipped with colored visual indicators). Relative tension will produce increased digital counts, an increased rate of auditory beeps, and the visual indicators will change from green to yellow to red.

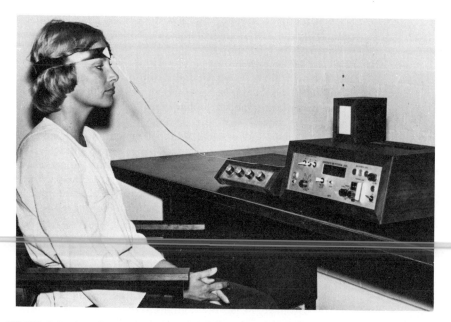

FIGURE 5-3. A biofeedback unit, featuring EMG (electromyographic) feedback, is illustrated. The patient is provided digital, auditory, and visual (changing colored lights) feedback on the amount of EMG activity coming from the electrodes placed on her left frontalis muscle.

b) Specific operation procedures are followed according to the specifications listed by the manufacturer of the feedback unit. We use a Model B-1, Bio-Electric Information Feedback System, manufactured by the Bio-Feedback Systems, Inc. This particular B-1 model is equipped for electromyographic (EMG) feedback. Our subsequent procedural steps will be listed for use with this B-1 EMG unit. Other commercially available biofeedback units will be essentially similar in operation.

c) The clinician makes the equipment operative by turning on both the preamplifier and the biofeedback apparatus. A neutral baseline is taken by placing the EMG electrodes on a "dummy fixture" to see that dummy readings are practically at a zero level. Adjustments are made, if necessary, by turning various panel controls so that there is basically no feedback activity with the electrodes attached only to the "dummy fixture." When zero levels are established, the three surface electrodes are then placed, usually on the patient's frontalis muscle on the forehead. The frontalis site, about one-quarter inch above the eyebrow, has been found to be an ideal area for patients working on speech. Speech movements of the facial and mandibular muscles appear to have very little effect on frontalis EMG output.

d)   Instructions are given to the patient to imagine various scenes representing tension and then relaxation. Tension imagery may be characterized by having the patient imagine speaking before an audience or driving on a freeway. Relaxation states are often induced by imagery of sitting on a lounge chair in front of a fire or by lying in the sun at the beach. As the patient thinks of the various scenes, she should experience some fluctuations in the feedback (digital, sound, and visual). If marked feedback changes do not take place, ask the patient to raise her eyebrows, which will, of course, actively contract the frontalis and produce considerable EMG feedback. The purpose for producing the movements at this stage is for the patient to experience the feedback effect.

e)   A baseline is then taken of the digital count after the patient is instructed to "just sit there for awhile now with your eyes closed." After there is some stabilization of the base rate count for trial periods of time (the B–2 machine has thirty-two-second trial periods, sixty-four-second trials, and so on), the training conditions may be introduced.

f)   Following the establishment of the baseline, the patient may then receive various kinds of training instructions, such as, "Now think of something very relaxing. Just relax. Feel the heaviness of relaxation." Then instruct the patient to imagine doing something that may produce tension. One patient with a stuttering problem was asked after relaxation to think he was in front of a group about to tell the assembled people his name.

g)   Once variations in feedback levels are demonstrated under the various conditions, the clinician may wish to give quantification feedback to the patient. Each patient has his or her own individual baseline, so the actual number values only have importance in their relative change or lack of change for the various conditions. For example, a woman with spastic dysphonia exhibited the following digital printouts for successive thirty-two-second trial periods:

Base rate: 3.70, 4.51, 3.90; Relax: 3.92, 2.79, 2.67;

Read spondees: 9.35, 10.01, 11.36; Relax: 7.14, 3.12, 2.89;

Read sentences: 7.97, 7.77, 9.67; Relax: 3.40, 2.95, 3.18;

Think of talking, but do not talk: 6.18, 5.73, 4.78

Activities associated with talking, actual speaking, or even thinking about talking produced increased frontalis activity over both the base rate and relax conditions during the same training session.

h) Discussion of the feedback data should be part of every training session. The clinician will couple the feedback experience with various voice facilitating approaches.

i) As soon as the patient knows what it feels like to be relaxed, as previously validated by ongoing feedback information, he or she can usually imagine and produce the relaxed state without continued need for the feedback apparatus.

C. *Typical case history showing utilization of approach.* C. S., a sixty-three-year-old librarian, was forced to retire early because of a rapidly "deteriorating voice." The patient was found to have spastic dysphonia and at the time she began voice remediation, six years after onset, her voice was found to be "so tight, she had to push to get her air out." A few situations were found in which she was able to demonstrate a relatively normal voice, all of which seemed to be when she was relatively relaxed and not "thinking" about her disorder. She began a seven-week course of voice therapy, receiving some seven sessions per week. Five of the sessions each week were focused on biofeedback practice. She was instructed to think of relaxed situations, which quickly became characterized on the biofeedback equipment by low digital counts, low frequency of auditory beep, and the green light visual indicator. Initially, when she attempted to say words or even thought of saying words, she would experience accelerated and intense biofeedback from her frontalis muscle. The illustrative values shown in step g were taken from her training chart. The patient was able to produce at the end of the training period of seven weeks, normal voice under laboratory conditions coupled with low tension levels. Attempts to generalize her phonatory gains outside of the clinic were not as successful as was hoped, despite her practicing at home three hours daily, producing normal sounding words. The patient was successfully operated on by the Dedo (1976) procedure, described in Chapter 6, and now has a much more functional voice.

D. *Evaluation of approach.* Biofeedback can provide information back to the patient specific to the biologic performance of particular systems for which the patient does not possess the receptors to self-monitor without the use of such equipment. For example, if the patient wanted to observe the differential muscle system activity between chest and abdominal breathing, he or she could be assisted in these observational attempts by being hooked up to some kind of monitoring device, such as the kymograph or thoracic and abdominal magnetometers. The tracings of his relative chest and abdominal movements would provide him with ongoing feedback specific to what he was doing physiologically. Various other biofeedback systems can provide the patient information about what he is doing as he speaks and sings in a way that he could never do without the use of such monitoring equipment. We have also shown how biofeedback can be used in developing increased relaxation. We have found that only four or five training sessions using relaxation monitoring (such as EEG or EMG) are all that are required to teach the patient relatively deep relaxation.

III. CHANGE OF LOUDNESS
   A. *Kinds of problems for which approach is useful.* Some patients have voices that are either too soft or too loud. The prolonged use of inappropriate loudness levels can result in organic pathologies of the vocal folds, such as nodules or polyps. Many of the vocal pathologies of children are related to such excesses of loudness as screaming and yelling. Weak, soft voices may develop as a consequence of the prolonged hyperfunctional use of the vocal mechanism that results in the eventual breakdown of glottal approximation surfaces, for example, the patient with vocal nodules who loses much air flow around the nodules and is unable to produce an intense enough vocal fold vibration to achieve a sufficiently loud voice. Some speaking environments require a loud voice, and the untrained speaker or singer may push for loudness at the level of the larynx rather than adjust his or her respiration. Inappropriate loudness of voice is most often not the primary causative factor of a voice problem, but rather a secondary, if annoying, symptom. Reducing or increasing the loudness of the voice lends itself well to direct symptom modification through exercise and practice, and often, if other facilitating techniques are being used, does not even require the use of loudness techniques per se.
   B. *Procedural aspects of approach*
      1. For a decrease in loudness:
         a) See that the patient has a thorough audiometric examination to determine adequacy of hearing before any attempt is made to reduce voice loudness. Once it has been established that the patient has normal hearing, the following steps may be taken.
         b) For young children, ages three through ten, the change of loudness steps in the *Boone Voice Program for Children*

(1980a) are useful. We ask the child to develop awareness of five different voices:

(1)   Voice number one is presented as a whisper.

(2)   Voice number two is presented as the voice we would use when not wanting to awaken a sleeping person, a quiet voice.

(3)   Voice number three is the normal voice we use to talk to family and friends.

(4)   Voice number four is the voice we use to get someone's attention across the room.

(5)   Voice number five is the yelling voice when we call someone outside.

c)   With patients over ten years old, we might discuss with the patient the observation that he or she has an inappropriately loud voice. The patient may be unaware of the loud voice, and, if this is the case, he or she should be asked to listen to tape-recorded samples of his or her speech. The best demonstration tape for loudness variations would include both the patient's voice and the clinician's, to provide contrasting levels of loudness. Then ask the patient, "Do you think your voice is louder than mine?"

d)   Focus on making the patient aware of his problem. Once the patient becomes aware that his voice is too loud, the clinician might ask, "What does a loud voice in another person tell you about that person?" Loud voices are typically interpreted to mean that the speaker feels "overly confident," or "sure of himself," or that the speaker is putting on a confident front when he or she is really scared, or that he or she is mad at the world, impressed with his or her own voice, trying to intimidate listeners, and so on. For the average patient, some discussion of these negative interpretations is usually sufficient to motivate him to learn to speak at normal loudness levels.

e)   We often practice using a quiet voice, the voice designated as a "2" in the preceding section b. The practice for the quiet voice can be facilitated by using instruments that give feedback specific to intensity, such as the *Vocal Loudness Indicator* (LinguiSystems, 1980) and the Visi-Pitch (Kay Elemetrics, 1980). The Vocal Loudness Indicator, for example, has a series of lights that are illuminated by increases in voice intensity. Keeping the instrument at a fixed distance, the patient can quickly learn to keep his or her voice at a lower intensity level to prevent the light (all or a few) from coming on.

f)   For practice materials there are excellent voice drill books available for controlling loudness of voice, such as

Fairbanks's *Voice and Articulation Drillbook* (1960) and Fisher's *Improving Voice and Articulation* (1975).

2. For an increase in loudness:
   a) Determine first that the inappropriate softness of the voice is not related to hearing loss, general physical weakness, or a severe personality problem; for these cases, a symptomatic approach is not indicated. The steps that follow are for voice patients who are physically and emotionally capable of speaking in a louder voice.
   b) Discuss with the patient his soft voice. A tape-recorded playback of the patient's and clinician's voices in conversation will usually illustrate for the patient the inadequacy of his loudness. After the patient indicates some awareness of his soft voice, the clinician might ask, "What does a soft, weak voice tell us about a person?" Inadequately loud voices are typically interpreted to mean that the speaker is afraid to speak louder, is timid and shy, is unduly considerate of others, is scared of people, has no self-confidence, and so on. Some discussion of these negative interpretations is usually helpful.
   c) By exploring pitch level and fundamental frequency, try to achieve a pitch level at which the patient is able with some ease to produce a louder voice. If the patient habitually speaks near the bottom of his pitch range, a slight elevation of pitch level will usually be accompanied by a slight increase in loudness. The Visi-Pitch has been found useful in helping the patient associate changes in pitch with relative changes in intensity. Certain frequencies produce greater intensities. When the patient finds the "best" pitch level, he should practice sustaining an /a/ at that level for five seconds, concentrating on good voice quality. He should then take a deep breath and repeat the same pitch at a maximum loudness level. After some practice at this "home base" pitch level, ask the patient to sing /a/, up the scale for one octave, at one vocal production per breath; then have him go back down the scale, one note per breath, until he reaches his starting pitch.
   d) Explore with the patient his best pitch, that is, the one that produces the best loudness and quality. Auditory feedback devices (such as loop-tape recorders) should be employed, so that the patient can hear what he is doing. Some counseling may be needed with regard to the practice pitch used, since the patient may be resistant to using a new voice pitch level. It should be pointed out that the practice pitch level may well be only a temporary one, and not necessarily the pitch level the patient will use permanently. It is important that the work be pur-

sued both in and out of therapy. A change in loudness cannot be achieved simply by talking about it. It requires practice.

e) Sometimes respiration training (facilitating technique 23) is necessary for the patient with a loudness problem. It should be remembered, however, that while loudness is directly related to the rate of air flow through the approximated vocal folds, there is little evidence to indicate that any particular way of breathing is the best for optimum phonation. Any respiration exercise that produces increased subglottal air pressure may be helpful in increasing voice loudness.

f) Particularly effective in functional voice loudness problems is the pushing approach (facilitating technique 21). When pushing is coordinated with phonation, there is little air wastage and firm vocal fold approximation, both of which result in louder phonation. However, if the patient can achieve adequate loudness through initial counseling, "best" pitch practice, and some help in respiration, the pushing approach and other techniques requiring physical effort should be avoided.

g) For the patient who appears to resist increasing the loudness of his or her voice, it might be necessary to introduce loud noise as a competing sound to the feedback of the patient's own voice. The Lombard effect (speaking at louder voice levels during conditions of competing noise) lends itself well therapeutically to the demonstration of greater voice loudness. The clinician may use white noise, a pure tone (such as 125 or 250 Hz), or the patient's own voice amplified on a simultaneous or delayed auditory feedback device. The procedures of the approach are as follows: (1) ask the patient to read aloud a passage of about 100 words; (2) tape-record the patient's oral reading; (3) at about word 30, introduce the loud competing auditory stimulus; the patient's voice will be heard to increase in loudness; (4) at about word 50, shut off the sound stimulus; the patient will immediately be heard to use a softer voice; (5) for the balance of the reading, alternately introduce and stop the sound source at about fifteen-word intervals; (6) complete the procedure by having the patient listen to the recorded playback, noticing the Lombard effect on the loudness of his or her voice. An extension of the approach might be to ask the patient to attempt to match his or her own loudness models.

3. A few patients demonstrate little or no loudness variation. To achieve such variation:

a) Have the patient listen to a tape recording of his or her voice. Then, after making appropriate comments, ask the patient how he or she likes his or her voice, and whether he or she thinks it should be changed. People who become aware of the monotony of their voices, and who are concerned about it, can usually develop loudness inflections with practice.

b) The maintenance of an unvarying level of loudness seems to require a great deal of energy. There appears to be less work in speaking naturally, which means speaking with a mouth well open and with pitch-loudness variations. The rare patient with hyperfunctional voice problems who speaks in a loudness monotone should be encouraged to increase loudness variation. Any good voice and diction book will include useful practice materials for developing such variation.

C. *Typical case history showing utilization of approach.* A thirty-one-year-old teacher, C. T., complained for more than a year of symptoms of vocal fatigue, that is, pain in the throat, loss of voice after teaching, and so on. Laryngoscopy revealed a normal larynx, and the voice evaluation found the man to speak at "a monotonous pitch and low loudness level, with pronounced mandibular restriction, at times barely opening his mouth." Early efforts at therapy included the chewing approach, with special emphasis given to varying pitch level and increasing voice loudness. The patient was highly motivated to improve the efficiency of his phonation; he requested voice therapy three times a week and supplemented the therapy with long practice periods at home. After nine weeks of therapy, pretherapy and posttherapy recordings were compared, and the patient agreed with the therapist that he sounded "like a new man." Speaking in a louder voice for this patient seemed to have an immediate effect on his overall self-image, resulting in an almost immediate increase in his total communicative effectiveness. Not only did the patient achieve a better-sounding speaking voice, but he reported no further symptoms of vocal fatigue.

D. *Evaluation of approach.* Inappropriate loudness of voice penalizes the patient. Happily, however, many of the facilitating techniques described in this chapter have some influence on voice loudness, and when inadequate loudness constitutes part of the patient's vocal symptomatology, it is often a variable that is highly modifiable. In fact, more often than not the use of various other facilitating techniques will have an indirect effect on voice loudness, obviating the need for loudness techniques per se.

IV. CHANT TALK

A. *Kinds of problems for which approach is useful.* Patients with functional dysphonias, particularly those who employ hard glottal attack, often profit from chant talk. Another group of voice patients who benefit from chant talk are those patients who speak in an abusive fashion, who cannot modify their present method of voicing; imitating the chant-like kind of voicing pattern is so different from their usually phonatory style that they can often produce the contrasting voice of the chant. About the only setting today where one hears the chant legitimately used is in various churches and synagogues. Characteristic of the chant is usually elevation of voice pitch, prolongation of phonation with noticeable softening of glottal attack. Dysphonic patients who may use the chant as a temporary voice practice technique will usually experience a voice free of hard glottal attack and relatively free of dysphonia. Once the patient can imitate the chant in its extreme form, he or she usually can modify it to more closely resemble everyday phonation. The chant is often used well in combination with other facilitating approaches, such as the chewing approach (5), open-mouth approach (18), and the yawn-sigh approach (25).

B.   *Procedural aspects of approach.*

1.   The chant talk approach is explained to the patient as a method of talking that reduces the effort in talking. It is important to point out to the patient that the method will only be used temporarily as a practice method and will not become a permanent and different way of talking. The clinician can best demonstrate chant talk by playing a recording of a religious chant. The clinician should then imitate the recording by producing the same voicing style while reading any reading material aloud.

2.   The patient is then urged to imitate the same chant voicing pattern. Most patients are able to do this with some degree of initial success. For those who cannot chant in initial trials, the clinician should again present a chant recording and then follow it with his or her own chant production. Some light-hearted kidding by the clinician telling the patient that the chant is indeed a different and funny way of talking is appropriate, but it will only be used temporarily as a therapy method. If the patient still cannot chant, another facilitating approach should be used. For those patients who can chant, go on to step 3.

3.   Reading materials should be read aloud by the patient, alternating with the regular voice and with the chant voice. Twenty seconds has been found to be a good time for each reading condition. Ask the patient to read aloud first in the normal voice, then in a chant, then back to normal voice, then in a chant, and so on.

4.   Record the patient's oral reading. On playback, contrast the different sound of the normal voice with the chanted voice.

Discuss the pitch differences, the phonatory prolongations, and the soft glottal attack.

5. Once the patient is able to produce chant talk with relative ease, efforts should be made to reduce the chant quality, approximating normal voice production. Slight prolongation and soft glottal attack should be retained as the patient reads aloud in a voice with only slight chant quality remaining.

C. *Typical case history showing utilization of approach.* D. S., a thirty-five-year-old football coach, developed bilateral vocal nodules with a moderately severe dysphonia. At the time of his voice evaluation, he spoke at a slightly low pitch level for his total pitch range, he had pronounced mandibular restriction, and demonstrated hard glottal attack. Therapy began with the chewing method. It was then followed with chant talk where the patient was asked to speak in a higher pitch and prolong his words as in a chant. He would record oral reading using first his usual voice, followed then by the chant. On listening to the playback, he commented on how much "easier" he sounded when he chanted. By using the chant, he was able to experience voicing without hard glottal attack. The patient attacked his problem of low pitch, mandibular restriction, and hard glottal attack simultaneously by using both the chewing and chant talk approaches. Laryngoscopic examination of his vocal folds four weeks after voice therapy began revealed "complete elimination of both nodules."

D. *Evaluation of approach.* Most patients are able to use the chant talk technique. Initially, it is important for the clinician to let the patient know that the chant is "only a means to an end," a temporary way of talking in practice sessions that helps to take the "work" out of talking. We have found the method particularly useful with children, who enjoy the different way of talking. The method lends itself well for analysis relative to pitch, phonation attack, rhythm of talking, and loudness.

V. CHEWING APPROACH

A. *Kinds of problems for which approach is useful.* The chewing method, as developed by Froeschels in 1924, has been applied as the "natural method" for developing good speech and voice for patients with many kinds of communication disorders (Weiss and Beebe, 1951). Chewing has been found as a useful therapy tool in reducing vocal hyperfunction, in that it appears to promote more optimum vocal fold size-mass adjustments and better fold approximation. Rather than working on the segments of voice, such as pitch, loudness, quality, or resonance, one is able to work holistically, which could "at the very beginning remove all the debris that habit and training had put upon the natural function" (Froeschels, 1952, p. 428). When chewing is presented properly to the patient, it can be a "fun" activity that produces immediate changes in production of voice. Both children and adults alike with voice problems related to vocal hyperfunction often profit from chewing.

B.   *Procedural aspects of approach.*

1.   First, explain to the patient that he or she is speaking with unnecessary tension. If appropriate, point out that he or she is speaking with an approximated mandible, through clenched teeth, with so little mouth opening that he or she "speaks like a ventriloquist." Use a mirror to show the patient what he or she looks like while talking. Let the patient see his or her relatively restricted mandibular movement. An explanation should follow of how relatively relaxed the jaw, throat, tongue, and lips are when one chews, and how chewing and talking simultaneously often result in a more relaxed voice. Instruct the patient that he or she will be using the chewing method in order to promote the greater oral movement, which produces a more relaxed voice. Emphasize that the chewing method will only be a means to an end. That is, make sure the patient understands that chewing in an exaggerated manner will only be temporary, to get the feeling of vigorous action, and that he or she need not worry that you want him or her to speak permanently with such exaggerated, open-mouthed postures. If patients are sufficiently warned that the method is but a temporary way of introducing a more relaxed phonation, and that it will eventually be brought down to a more normal way of talking, few will be resistant to learning it.

2.   With both the clinician and the patient facing a mirror, ask the patient to pretend that he or she is opening the mouth wide, about to bite into a handful of four or five stacked crackers, and then to pretend that he or she is chewing them. (Usually this imagery is sufficient.) Occasionally, however, the crackers are actually introduced and the patient is asked to chew them in an open-mouthed, exaggerated fashion, observing himself or herself closely. This is followed immediately by having the patient imitate the chewing that was just done. Point out to the patient the degree of mouth opening, and the movement of the jaw. Several minutes should be spent in establishing a natural and exaggerated motion of chewing.

3.   Demonstrate the chewing for the patient and add a very soft phonation. Have the patient imitate you. Brodnitz (1971b) warns that "at this stage, many patients will go through the motions of opening and closing the jaws but the tongue is left flat and motionless on the floor of the mouth. A monotonous 'yam-yam' will result" (p. 80). It is therefore important for the clinician to point out early that the tongue

must be kept moving so that a variety of sounds will emerge. The patient should stay with this exercise until he or she is able to produce chewing and voicing simultaneously, with an ever-changing number of different sounds. For the method to be effective, the natural movements of the tongue, as experienced when actually chewing food, should be retained.

4. After the patient has performed the chewing-voicing exercise satisfactorily, we introduce some special words for the patient to practice a combination chanting-chewing. In the children's voice program (Boone, 1980a) we play with the chewing approach and use funny names coupled with funny pictures that the names are supposed to represent, such as "goolagonga, ahlameterah, wandapanda, monamoona, tokalama, cucalamonga." With older patients we may use words and phrases like "lampshade, peaches and cherries, and candy chunks." Either stay with such words until the patient demonstrates that he or she can say them well, or explore with other words, starting with those that the patient is able to produce while still maintaining good chewing.

5. When a few nucleus words are established with the chewing method, ask the patient to count from one to ten, using the same technique. Some practice at this is usually necessary. If the numbers appear to reduce the patient's ability to use the method correctly, go back to an earlier level and reestablish more appropriate chewing. If the patient is able to voice well while chewing and saying numbers, have him listen to himself doing it (using some kind of auditory feedback device, such as a loop auditory tape). It is critical that the patient not only experience the relaxed "feel" of the method, but that he also receive some immediate auditory feedback showing the effect of the method on the sound of his voice.

6. After the patient has demonstrated an ability to chew and say numbers satisfactorily, he can usually tackle more extensive, connected speech. Provide the patient with verbal material to say or passages to read aloud. This chewing-connected speech should usually not begin with true conversation, but rather with neutral verbal material, such as a passage from a book.

7. The last practice step is to use the approach during conversational speech. If the patient experiences difficulty at this level, and in the beginning he or she usually will, have him or her go back to the highest successful level and guide him or her forward from there. When the patient has some success in using the method conversationally in therapy, have

him or her also use it outside of therapy in comfortable verbal settings. Good listeners in the beginning might be parents, a friend, or a spouse.

8. The great advantage of the chewing method, once it is learned, is that the patient can practice it many times, for a minute or so each time, throughout the day. The average patient's phonation will be noticeably more relaxed when using the chewing method, and because it usually facilitates a better voice, the patient will use it extensively outside of therapy. A great deal of daily practice, maybe as often as five times an hour, should be established.

9. Finally, after several weeks of practicing the method, the patient should be taught how to diminish the exaggerated chewing to a more normal jaw movement. It is important, however, as chewing is deemphasized, that the patient retain the same feeling and the same sound in his or her voice. If, when the chewing is minimized, the patient reverts to earlier faulty phonation patterns, have him or her return to the earlier chewing level where optimum performance was achieved, and proceed forward again from there.

10. Ultimately, the patient just "thinks" the method. By this time the patient has developed an awareness of what oral openness and jaw movement feel like and has experienced the vocal relaxation that accompanies the feeling.

C. *Typical case history showing utilization of approach.* David J. was a nine-year-old boy with a three-year history of dysphonia, who was found to have "bilateral fibrotic vocal nodules." He was subsequently scheduled for twice-weekly voice therapy at school. It soon became apparent to his clinician that he was working excessively hard to produce any kind of voice. Probably as a compensation for the large nodes that prevented good vocal fold approximation, when he wanted to produce a voice that could be heard, he used excessive amounts of air flow and pressure in an attempt to speak louder. His phonations were also characterized by hard glottal attack. The chewing approach was introduced as a means of using voice more optimally and with less effort. The immediate effect of chewing combined with phonation was increased hoarseness and breathiness. The clinician counseled David specific to his temporary increase in hoarseness "as a means to an end" for developing a better voice. The clinician so successfully created a fun atmosphere for the practice of chewing that the boy used the exaggerated mouth openings and easy onsets of voice in many situations outside of therapy including home self-practice. While the chewing approach was the primary therapy approach used, emphasis was also given to reducing abuse-misuse, explaining to him the probable genesis of his nodules, and reducing his overall voice loudness. After approximately six months of voice therapy, his nodules were reduced to "slight thickenings"; his air flow rates went down, which indicated firmer glottal approximation; and his voice sounded very much like the voices of his classmates. In a one-year followup with this consultant, all findings were within normal limits. Chewing was again demonstrated to be an effective method with children.

D.   *Evaluation of approach.* With a proper orientation to the chewing approach by the clinician, with emphasis given to chewing being a different and *temporary* way of talking, most patients find the method helpful in their struggle to find an efficiently produced voice. It is not a panacea for all voice problems. When involved in the somewhat automatic function of chewing, the oral structures seem to become capable of more synergic, relaxed movement. Relaxing the components of the vocal tract in this way appears also to relax the phonatory functioning of the larynx. By employing a commonly used action, chewing, the patient is able to achieve some relaxation of the vocal tract from a holistic, or gestalt, point of view, without having to fulfill such impossible directions as "relax your throat" or "relax your voice"; since no individual has volitional control over the vegetative functions of the throat and larynx, compliance with such instructions is quite impossible. More often than not, however, the patient can achieve such relaxation by combining chewing with phonation.

VI.   DIGITAL MANIPULATION

A.   *Kinds of problems for which approach is useful.* External pressure on the patient's thyroid cartilage by the clinician is sometimes effective in helping the patient establish a lower voice pitch. The external pressure tilts the thyroid cartilage slightly backward toward the vocal processes, shortening the vocal folds; this increases the mass of the folds, producing a lower fundamental frequency. Another facet of digital manipulation is for the patient to feel the movement of the larynx with the fingers; as the patient moves up and down the pitch range with the fingers placed externally on the thyroid cartilage, she will feel the larynx rise with high pitches and descend with low ones. This method of feeling the upward and downward excursion of the larynx is used for persons who may have excessive pitch variation as they speak.

B.   *Procedural aspects of approach.*

1.   With the exception of some men with falsetto voices, patients will respond to digital pressure by producing a lower voice. Ask the patient to phonate and to extend a phonation by "hanging on to an ah." As the phonation is prolonged, apply slight finger pressure to the thyroid cartilage. The patient's voice pitch will lower instantly.

2.   Then ask the patient to maintain the lower pitch, even when your fingers are removed. If the patient can do this, he or she should continue practicing the lower pitch. If he or she quickly reverts to the higher pitch, the digital-pressure

method of producing the lower pitch should be repeated. If this method is used for giving the patient some experience with the feeling and sound of a lower pitch, some time should be spent in practicing the production of the lower pitch and in providing the patient with auditory feedback of what his or her voice sounds like.

3.   A variation of the digital-pressure technique is to begin by pressing the fingers on the thyroid cartilage and then asking the patient to phonate. Once the lower pitch is produced, release the finger pressure suddenly. There may be an immediate rise in voice pitch. This rise should be monitored by the patient with his own fingers, and he should be instructed to bring his voice back to (that is, acoustically match) the lower pitch. Most patients can do this almost instantly. Only at the second of release will a break in pitch be heard. Practice with the technique is most helpful for the patient desiring to lower pitch.

4.   For a completely different kind of digital manipulation for the patient with excessive pitch variability, show the patient how to place the fingers on the external larynx and feel the upward and downward movement of the larynx. Then ask the patient to phonate a pitch level that you feel is close to his or her optimum one, and to place the fingers on the thyroid cartilage to feel the vibration. Keeping the fingers in place, the patient should then phonate one musical note at a time until reaching his or her lowest comfortably produced pitch. The lowest pitches are usually accompanied by downward laryngeal movement. If this occurs, the movement should be demonstrated again and pointed out to the patient. The patient should then be asked to phonate successive one-note steps until reaching his or her highest note, exclusive of falsetto; the patient will usually experience a continuous elevation of the larynx as when moving successively higher up the scale. This movement should be clearly described to and experienced by the patient; if pronounced movement does not occur, the method cannot be used.

5.   Around the level of his optimum pitch, the patient should feel that there is little or no upward-downward laryngeal movement. If the clinician is attempting to establish a new pitch level, whether it be lower or higher, the finger monitoring of laryngeal movement for the faulty pitch, and the absence of movement for the desired pitch, will help the patient discriminate between the two.

C.   *Typical case history showing utilization of approach.* J. F. was a seventeen-year-old male who had been raised exclusively by his mother until her sudden death about a year before. Since that time he had lived with a maternal uncle who was concerned about the boy's effeminate mannerisms and high-pitched voice. Laryngeal examination revealed a normal adult male larynx. The boy was found to have a habitual pitch level of around 200 cps, well within the adult female range, but below the level of falsetto. The most effective facilitating technique for producing a normal voice pitch was to apply digital pressure on the external thyroid cartilage. The young man was able to prolong the lower pitch levels with good success, but any attempt at conversation would be characterized by an immediate return to the higher pitch. After three therapy sessions, he was able to read aloud using the lower pitch, but was unable to use the lower voice in conversation except with his male clinician. Subsequent psychiatric evaluation and therapy were initiated for "identity confusion and schizoidal tendencies." Voice therapy was discontinued after two weeks, when it was clearly demonstrated that the patient could produce a good baritone voice (125 cps) whenever he wanted. Unfortunately, follow-up telephone conversations several months after therapy revealed that he was using his high-pitched, pretherapy voice exclusively.

D.   *Evaluation of approach.* With some problems of vocal hyperfunction, particularly cord thickening and vocal nodules, it is sometimes necessary to work toward lowering the child's or adult's (but not the adolescent's) pitch level as suggested in the writings of Aronson (1980) and Wilson (1979). Elevation of pitch may be needed for such problems as contact ulcers and voice therapy for patients with papilloma (Cooper, 1977). Digital pressure on the thyroid cartilage is an excellent facilitator for many patients in developing a lower voice pitch. If the method does not produce a lower pitch level, as it may not do for certain cases of falsetto, the method cannot be used. Even though the method may produce an immediate change of voice to a more desired, lower pitch level, as illustrated in our case history example, it may not be able to effect a permanent voice change without some counseling or psychotherapy. Digital pressure, while effective in lowering pitch level, will rarely bring about permanent success unless other therapeutic approaches are used as well.

A well-trained singing or speaking voice is produced with a minimum of physical effort, with relatively little upward-downward movement of the larynx. Some patients demonstrate excessive pitch variability demonstrating unnecessary laryngeal excursion as they speak. An excellent method of pointing this out to the patient, and of helping him or her establish a more optimum phonation with only minimal vertical laryngeal movement, is to have the patient place his or her fingers lightly on the laryngeal thyroid cartilage, feeling the downward movement as the pitch lowers and the upward movement as it rises.

VII.   EAR TRAINING

A.   *Kinds of problems for which approach is useful.* Most voice therapy involves the identification and elimination of faulty vocal habits and their replacement by more optimum ones. The basic input modality in developing appropriate phonation is the auditory system, particularly the patient's self-hearing. No individuals have much awareness of what they are doing laryngeally, whether they are approximating their folds or shortening or lengthening them, except as they hear their own voices. The surprise nearly always evoked in people at hearing their own voices on recordings is one indication of how gross our self-hearing is. This lack of voice feedback has always presented problems to the clinician, as patients literally do not know what they are doing when they phonate. Music teachers have historically attempted to circumvent the problem by using imagery in their training attempts, since the voice will often respond appropriately to psychological-anatomical instructions—for example, "put your voice forcefully down in your chest"—even though the physiology of the described event is in error. In voice therapy, we are concerned with making the patient a critical listener. The patient may need practice in learning to listen to his or her own voice. Davis and Boone (1967) report that some voice patients, like some people in the normal population, demonstrate difficulty in pitch discrimination and tonal memory as measured by subtests of the Seashore Tests of Musical Aptitude (1960). Such patients may have serious problems in voice therapy in making pitch discriminations and in remembering the sound of their own model voices. Up to a certain point, gross pitch discrimination and tonal memory can be taught by ear-training practice, wherein the patient learns how to listen critically to his or her own "good" and "bad" voices and to the voices of others. Through the use of auditory feedback devices, such as loop tape recorders, the patient learns to hear and monitor auditorily his or her own phonation. For patients who have defective listening skills, voice training must include instruction in making pitch discriminations, improving tonal memory, and learning to hear one's "good" and "bad" voices. But the clinician should first assess the patient's listening skills, for many voice patients have no problem in this area; for others, just as for some people in the normal population, listening abilities may be surprisingly deficient. It is the latter group that may profit from ear training.

B.   *Procedural aspects of approach.*

1.   Take a baseline measurement of how well the patient can make pitch discriminations. The ear-training cassette from the *Boone Voice Program for Children* (1980a) contains twenty pitch discrimination pairs that were produced with a music synthesizer and twenty singing voice pitch discriminations. Such a tape provides for easy contrast discrimination. Or the clinician may make his or her own taped or "live" discrimination presentations. Or the clinician may use the Seashore pitch discrimination subtest, or a piano or pitch pipe. Pre-

sent to the patient a pair of tonal stimuli, asking if the stimuli are the same as one another or different. This should be followed by voiced pitch discriminations, either produced by the clinician or prerecorded. If the patient is unable to discriminate between one whole note and its flat or sharp, the indication is that the patient's pitch discrimination is not normal, but not necessarily that pitch discrimination therapy is needed. In gross departures, however, such as the patient's being unable to discriminate between notes that are more than a third apart (say, between a C_4 and an F_4), some discrimination training may be needed if the patient is ever going to match successfully a target model voice.

2. Pitch discrimination training should begin at the patient's baseline "can do" performance. When the patient makes correct discriminations at this level, his or her performance should be positively reinforced. Pitch stimuli can come from a piano, a pitch pipe, or the voice itself; it is often better therapy to mix all three types of pitch stimuli into the practice sequence, rather than to use one type only. The clinician should continue this activity for as long as necessary, until the patient is able to discriminate between pitches that are one full musical note apart (for example, C_4 and D_4). This pitch discrimination approach can be effectively practiced alone, without the clinician, with the patient listening to prerecorded practice materials and making "same-different" choices as she listens. To learn the correctness of response, the patient can mark her choices down on paper and then check them against a master sheet. Simple programming equipment has also been successfully used; here, the patient indicates her "same-different" choice, and a light goes on when the choice is correct.

3. Tonal memory therapy also begins where the patient is. That is, if the patient can remember a two-note sequence (via piano, pitch pipe, or voice), the therapy should begin by presenting him or her with two two-note sequences and asking the patient to identify which note varies between the two presentations. The ear-training cassette (Boone, 1980a) also contains twenty pairs of contrasting melodies for use in tonal memory practice. It does not appear to be necessary for the patient to work beyond remembering a four-note series. When the patient can hear a four-note melody, remember it, and successfully compare it with a second four-note melody (with only one note varying between the first and second presentation), his or her tonal memory is probably good enough to recall various voice-model presentations. Tonal memory therapy is also well suited to self-practice, with the patient listening and responding to prerecorded sequences.

4. If a target model voice has been produced by the patient, can

he or she discriminate between this good production and his or her faulty one? It is essential in voice therapy that the patient use his or her own "best" voice as a therapy model whenever possible. The patient may need some practice in learning to listen for his or her own "best" and "bad" voices. The clinician should capture the patient's voice productions on recordings, editing and splicing them into contrasting pairs, and the patient should listen discriminatively to these pairings so as to learn to identify quickly and correctly his or her better phonation. Recordings of other people's voices with similar problems, also paired for discrimination listening, make excellent practice materials. When the patient is able to demonstrate a consistent ability to hear his or her "good" voice, whether or not the patient is able to produce that voice, there is little need to emphasize ear training. For some patients, just a little listening to their own voices helps; for others, even a great deal of practice is useless. For the rare patient who shows no improvement after trial ear training, further training might as well be abandoned.

C.   *Typical case history showing utilization of approach.* C. M., a nine-year-old girl with functional hypernasality, was evaluated by a local cleft-palate team and found to have adequate velopharyngeal closure (as demonstrated by cinefluorography), normal manometric pressure ratios, and normal stimulability for producing good oral resonance in isolated words repeated after the examiner. Voice therapy on a twice-weekly basis was recommended. The focus of therapy was on ear training, helping the patient to discriminate between her nasal resonance and oral resonance. The first seven weeks of therapy were spent both in this discrimination listening, which in the beginning was very defective, and in producing contrasting oral and nasal resonations. In the early phases of therapy, orality was stressed only in the therapy and practice sessions, with no attempt at any outside carry-over. Eventually, carry-over phrases and sentences were practiced in situations outside the clinic setting. As therapy progressed, the girl showed excellent auditory self-monitoring and was able to develop normal oral voice quality in all situations. Voice therapy was judged a success and terminated after eleven weeks.

D.   *Evaluation of approach.* In voice therapy, the patient must become a critical listener to his or her own voice. Some voice patients, like some people in the normal population, have real difficulty in making pitch discriminations and judgments of tonal memory. Of these patients, some will profit from ear training. The patient must learn to hear, if possible, how he or she is phonating. As Sommers and Brady (1964) have written, "improvements in phonation and resonance are heavily dependent upon the subject's ability to detect desirable changes as a function of specific voice therapy activities'' (p. 7). If the patient's listening abilities are poor, ear training should be initiated. If there is no problem in listening, ear training should be avoided.

VIII.   ELIMINATION OF ABUSES

A.   *Kinds of problems for which approach is useful.* Some vocal abuses are relatively focal and easily identifiable. They include crying, screaming, yelling, throat clearing, grunting, coughing, and focalized cases of inappropriate pitch, loudness, or quality. It appears to require only a minimal amount of vocal abuse each day to maintain a dysphonia or to develop and maintain a laryngeal pathology. By the same token, and this is especially true for children, the elimination or reduction of the vocal abuse will often be remarkably effective in eliminating the dysphonia and its accompanying laryngeal pathology. For any voice patient with approximation or mass-size problems of the vocal folds, vocal abuse, if present, should be eliminated or at least reduced.

B.   *Procedural aspects of approach.*

1.   By evaluating and observing the patient, identify the offensive vocal act. Then determine its baseline rate of occurrence. For instance, if the vocal abuse is throat clearing, try to observe the patient in various settings, such as the classroom, the playground, the therapy room, and so on, and count the number of times he or she clears the throat.

2.   Children with vocal abuse must become aware of the impact of such abuses on their voices. With children we use the ''Vocal Abuse Reduction Program'' (Boone, 1980a, p. 5), which recommends:

> an explanation of how additive lesions occur, using the story, *A Voice Lost and Found;* a review of the child's abuses; and a systematic reduction of the child's abuses, using the Voice Tally Card and the Voice Counting Chart.

The focus of the reducing abuse program is to make the child aware cognitively of the relationship of vocal abuse-misuse to increasing symptoms of voice. The story in the program is pictorially illustrated with various vocal behaviors related to changes of ''the little bumps on the vocal cords.''

3.   Discuss identified vocal abuses with the patient, emphasizing the need to reduce their daily frequency. Assign to patients the task of counting the number of times each day they find themselves engaged in a particular abuse. Perhaps a peer or sibling could be brought in, told about the situation, and asked to join in on the daily count, or, depending upon the age of the patient, a parent or teacher, or spouse or business associate, might be asked to keep track of the

number of abuses occurring in their presence. At the end of the day, the abuses should be tallied for that day.

4. Ask the patient to plot his or her daily vocal abuses on a graph, similar to the one shown in Figure 5-2. Along the vertical axis, the ordinate, the patient should plot the number of times the particular abuse occurred; and along the base of the graph, the abscissa, the individual days, beginning with the baseline count of the first day. Instruct the patient to bring these graphs to voice therapy sessions. Keeping a graph usually increases the patient's awareness of what he or she has been doing and results in a gradual decrement of the abusive behavior. The typical vocal abuse has a sloping decremental curve, indicating its gradual disappearance. Any decrement in the plots of the people observing the patient, but particularly in those compiled by patients themselves, should be greeted with obvious approval by the clinician.

C. *Typical case history showing utilization of approach.* Joyce was a twenty-seven-year-old secretary who complained of a voice that was often hoarse and a voice that tired easily every day. Subsequent indirect laryngoscopy confirmed a slight bilateral thickening at the anterior–middle third junction. A detailed history and observation of the patient found that she constantly cleared her throat. The throat clearing had become a habit. She rarely felt that she was able "to bring up any mucus" but just cleared her throat in attempt to make her voice clearer. A high-speed motion picture was shown to the patient depicting throat clearing and she was counseled to make efforts to reduce its occurrence. The patient subsequently began to tally her throat clearing and coughing as they occurred, plotting them on a graph at the end of the day. Within two weeks, she was able to change her throat clearing habit. Her vocal quality improved immediately and there was never a need for formal, long-term voice therapy.

D. *Evaluation of approach.* Identifying vocal abuses and attempting to eliminate them by plotting their daily frequency on a graph appears to be a most effective method of helping young children with voice problems. Adolescents are equally guilty of vocal abuses and profit greatly from keeping track of what they are doing. Typical adult abuses, such as throat clearing, are often eliminated in a week or two by graph plotting by motivated patients. The effectiveness of this approach, in fact, appears to be highly related to the skill of the clinician in motivating the patient to eliminate his or her abusive behavior. The value of the plotting appears to be more in the developing awareness of the problem, rather than the actual count per se. The value comes from the awareness of the need to curb the frequency of the identified aversive activity, rather than the actual counts. The success of chanting in reducing vocal abuse has made charting an important part of most reductions of vocal abuse programs such as Drudge and Philips (1976), Johnson (1976), Wilson and Rice (1977), and Boone (1980a).

IX. ELIMINATION OF HARD GLOTTAL ATTACK

A. *Kinds of problems for which approach is useful.* Hard glottal attack (the glottal stroke) is frequently among the abusive vocal behaviors of patients with hyperfunctional voice disorders. In hard glottal attack, the patient adducts the vocal folds, but does not initiate phonation until the outgoing air flow is strong enough literally to blow the glottis open. The acoustic result is an abrupt staccato initiation of phonation. This crisp style of phonation will usually take a toll on the glottal structures, and particularly on the arytenoid cartilages, whose only covering on the glottal margins is a relatively thin mucosal membrane. Hard glottal stroke is, therefore, particularly common among patients with posterior glottal pathologies, such as contact ulcers. When employed in a prolonged performance by a singer or lecturer, the hard glottal stroke will often result in generalized glottal edema (swelling), which will have noticeable effects on the quality of the voice.

B. *Procedural aspects of approach.*

1. Hard glottal attack is a fairly common phenomenon among actors, politicians, and untrained singers. Recordings of the voices of such people, and of the patient, should be played for the patient, and a contrasting demonstration should be made of the soft, easy glottal attack. The length of the demonstration will depend on the patient's insight.

2. With children we demonstrate the child's vocal attack by letting individuals hear a recording of their own voices contrasted with the normal voice of one of their peers. We then practice using words beginning with /h/, taking them from various lists, such as those in Fisher (1975), Moncur and Brackett (1975), or Boone (1980a). We select monosyllabic words, beginning with the aspirate /h/ for soft-attack practice. When the /h/ words are produced correctly, introduce other words beginning with unvoiced consonants for similar practice. We then use words beginning with vowels.

3. Use the whisper-phonation technique. Here, a few monosyllabic words are chosen, each beginning with a vowel. The patient's task is to whisper very lightly the initial vowel, prolonging it by gradually increasing the loudness of the whisper until phonation is introduced and, finally, the whole word is said. The whisper blends into a soft phonation.

4. The yawn-sigh approach (facilitating technique 25) is particularly effective in eliminating hard glottal attack.

5. The chewing approach (facilitating technique 5) almost always reduces the glottal stroke. It is nearly impossible to produce abrupt phonations while chewing.

6.   There are various instruments that are useful in providing the patient feedback specific to the severity of his or her glottal attack or suddenness of initiation of phonation. The display from a spectrograph or the Visi-Pitch will show the relative onset time of phonations; a vertical tracing at the beginning of the word indicates hard, abrupt vocal attack as opposed to a sloping onset tracing that displays a more gradual onset. Using various facilitating approaches, the clinician and the patient can confirm visually the relative suddenness of onset by the slope of the onset curve. The Voice Monitor (1977) has been found useful. The Voice Monitor can be set at various sensitivity levels to alert the patient to sudden initiation of phonation. When the patient initiates a word with abrupt initiation, a light goes on. The patient's task is to continue speaking connected speech without abruptness of attack to avoid the warning light. The Voice Monitor offers the advantage of a critical monitor to the patient's voice practice, without the necessity of the clinician being in the room.

7.   Once the patient is able to produce easier glottal attack, make an audio recording of the production. Ask the patient to listen to his or her hard-attack and soft-attack contrasts. The patient should think of the difference both in the sound of the production and the contrasting feeling between the two modes. Most patients will agree that using the hard glottal attack is a much more difficult way to speak. Whenever we have used negative practice (facilitating approach 17) with deliberate efforts made to speak with hard attack, patients will often quickly abandon permanently the old way of talking as requiring "too much effort."

C.   *Typical case history showing utilization of approach.* Marcia C., a thirty-four-year-old single woman, had a two-year history of vocal fatigue after every day of teaching high school social studies. The discomfort gradually increased, until she suffered severe pain in the hyoid area. Laryngoscopy found her to have bilateral contact ulcers, and the voice evaluation found that she had "had an inappropriately low voice pitch for her total pitch range, and pronounced hard glottal attack." From the beginning of voice therapy, she was able to use a slightly higher pitch level and reduce her hard glottal attack, producing good phonation of generally pleasant quality. She succeeded in permanently reducing the hard glottal attack by listening and learning to discriminate between hard and soft attack, by chewing, by using the yawn-sigh and whisper-phonation techniques, and by practicing word lists beginning with various unvoiced consonants. After twenty weeks of twice-weekly individual voice therapy, the patient reported no further symptoms of dysphonia and vocal fatigue, and a posttherapy laryngeal examination revealed "no further posterior pathology."

D. *Evaluation of approach.* There is probably no way of singing or speaking that is more vocally fatiguing than using hard glottal attack. Singing teachers, who have long been concerned with eliminating hard glottal stroke, have generally relied on teaching general body relaxation as a means of inducing greater vocal tract relaxation. Although the effort and force required to speak with glottal attack makes it a common symptom of patients with hyperfunctional voice disorders, many voice clinicians do not focus directly on modifying the hard glottal stroke. The reason for this is that once patients become aware of their hard glottal attack and its contrast with normal ways of beginning phonation, the old abrupt manner of phonating is usually spontaneously reduced. It is a common clinical observation that the reduction of hard glottal attack results in a corresponding improvement in voice quality.

X.   ESTABLISHING NEW PITCH

A. *Kinds of problems for which approach is useful.* Problems of mass and size of the vocal folds resulting in inappropriate voice pitch levels are sometimes helped by direct attempts to change the pitch level. A change of pitch level will often have audible effects, also, on the loudness and quality of the voice. A common characteristic of hyperfunctional voice disorders is inappropriate pitch level, the maintenance of which often requires much effort. Sometimes patients with vocal fold problems of additive mass (cord thickening, nodules, polyps) will speak at a lower pitch because of the increased amount of vibrating tissue. Other patients will use low-pitched voices purely on a functional basis, while still others will use inappropriately high-pitched voices merely as a faulty habit. Elevating or lowering the voice pitch, if this is needed in therapy, can usually be accomplished by direct symptom modification through exercises and practice.

B. *Procedural aspects of approach.*

1. If, as a result of the diagnostic evaluation, it is apparent that there is a discrepancy between the patient's habitual pitch level and his tested optimum pitch, this discrepancy should be explained and demonstrated to the patient. The methods of determining habitual and optimum pitches described in Chapter 4 can be applied here. A tape recording should be made while the patient is searching for his pitches, and when the habitual and optimum pitches have been recorded, they should be played back. The playback should always be followed immediately by a discussion comparing the sound and feel of the two pitches.

2. Most voice patients will be able to imitate their own pitch model, once it has been produced by the appropriate facili-

tating technique. There are occasional patients who cannot initiate a pitch to match a model, as Filter and Urioste (1981) discovered in testing college women with normal voices. An excellent model can be produced by having the patient extend an /a/ at the desired pitch level for about five seconds, recording the phonation on a loop tape recorder. If the loop is set for a three- or four-second playback, the patient's phonation will come back on playback while he is still producing it. This will provide the patient with a continuous model of his own preferred pitch level. There appear to be distinct advantages in using patients' own voices as the model, in that they will already have had the experience of producing the sound they are trying to duplicate. The clinician should stay on the loop model of /a/ for considerable practice before introducing a new stimulus.

3. The Visi-Pitch provides both a digital writeout of fundamental frequency and an oscilloscopic display of frequency. The clinician can display for the patient values specific to frequency and intensity. The pitch level that is computed to be the patient's optimum pitch level will usually on the Visi-Pitch yield a sharper, more periodic tracing (not like the diffuse scatter of aperiodicity) accompanied by relative increases in intensity. Both the fundamental frequency writeout and the tracing display provide the patient ongoing feedback in her attempts to establish a new pitch.

4. The Tunemaster III (see Bibliography) and the Tonar II (1972) are useful instruments for monitoring practice in establishing a new pitch level. Both instruments feature feedback information of ongoing frequency. For both instruments a predetermined pitch level should be agreed upon by both the clinician and the patient. With the Tunemaster III, the desired pitch level is set on the instrument panel; the display dial can then feed back to the patient as he or she speaks, whenever his or her fundamental frequency is within 30 cycles, sharp or flat, off the target pitch. The Tonar II can give feedback of the pitch level used during running speech, providing a digital writeout of the cycles-per-second value.

5. Work first on single words, preferably those beginning with a vowel, repeating each word in a pitch monotone. An /a/ may be used to initiate the word, blending the word into the end of the /a/. It will occasionally be observed that the patient has more difficulty in using the new pitch with certain words. Any of these "trouble" words should be avoided as practice material, for what is needed at this stage of therapy is practice in rapidly phonating a series of individual words at the new pitch level.

6. Once the patient does well at the single-word level, introduce phrases and short sentences. It is usually more productive at

this stage to avoid practice in actual conversation, since the patient is better able to use the new phonation in such neutral situations as reading single words, phrases, and sentences. When success is achieved at the sentence level, assign the patient reading passages from various voice and diction books. Success in using the new pitch level can be verified by using the Visi-Pitch, recording the actual fundamental frequency as it displays for each utterance.

7.   After reading well in a monotone, the patient may try using the new pitch in some real-life conversational situations. In the beginning he or she may have more success in talking to strangers, such as store clerks; patients often find it difficult to use the new pitch level with friends and family, since their previous ''set'' may prevent them from utilizing their new vocal behavior. Whatever conversational situation works best for the individual should be the one initially used.

8.   In establishing a new pitch, it is helpful in therapy to tape record the patient's voice as he or she searches to establish a different level. When the patient is able to produce a good voice at the proper pitch level, his or her own ''best'' voice can then become the therapy model.

C.   *Typical case history showing utilization of approach.* John K., a ten-year-old boy, was referred by his public-school speech clinician for a laryngeal examination because of a six-month history of hoarseness. The findings included a normal larynx and a ''low-pitched dysphonic voice.'' The youngster could readily demonstrate a higher phonation, which was characterized by an immediate clearing of quality. In the discussion that followed the tape-recorded playback of his ''good'' and ''bad'' voice, the boy stated that he thought he had been trying to speak like his older brother. The clinician pointed out to him that his better voice was more like that of other boys his age, and that the low-pitched voice he had been using was difficult for others to listen to. In subsequent voice therapy with his public-school clinician, the boy focused on elevating his voice pitch to a more natural level. His success was rapid, and therapy was terminated after six weeks.

D.   *Evaluation of approach.* The pitch of the voice changes constantly, according to the situation in which the speaker finds himself. In some voice patients, however, the pitch level appears to be too high or too low for the overall capability of the laryngeal mechanism. In other persons, an aberrant pitch level is but one manifestation of the total personality. Patients with additive masses to the folds (nodules, papilloma, polyps, and so on) may have lower pitch levels than normal because the thicker vocal folds vibrate slower, emitting a lower fundamental frequency. As the lesion is reduced or eliminated, the frequency of the voice will become higher, perhaps approaching normal limits. For patients with additive laryngeal lesions due to vocal hyperfunction, it is often best to work slowly toward increasing pitch level to approximate levels of the patient's peers, specific to age and sex. There are occasional voice patients who use an aberrant pitch level because of personality factors. Counseling of the patient and the patient's decision to want to change pitch level might well have to precede actual symptomatic therapy to alter pitch. The typical voice patient, however, who may need to change pitch level can usually do so rather quickly, after experiencing a marked improvement in overall voice quality because of pitch change.

XI. EXPLANATION OF PROBLEM

A. *Kinds of problems for which approach is useful.* The explanation of a problem to the patient is an important part of voice therapy. Olsen (1972) found that the experienced clinician in voice therapy spends some 20 percent of his or her therapy time explaining some aspect of the voice or voice problem to the patient. Clinical experience has taught this author that if he can help individuals know why they have the voice problem, sometimes this is all that is needed for changing a phonation style or for curbing vocal abuse-misuse. In the case of those dysphonias that are wholly related to functional causes (such as hyperfunction), it is important that the clinician not confront the patient with the implication that one "could talk all right if one wanted to." Instead of saying, "You are not using your voice as well as you could," we might say, "Your vocal folds are coming together too tightly." The latter statement absolves the patient of the guilt he or she might experience if we indicated that the patient was doing things "wrong." The patient will be much more receptive to a statement that puts the blame on his or her vocal folds. For patients with structural changes of the vocal folds, such as nodules or polyps, it may be necessary to explain that the organic pathology may well be secondary to prolonged misuse, and that by eliminating the misuse, the patient will eventually experience a reduction of vocal fold pathology.

B. *Procedural aspects of approach.* In problems of the voice related to vocal hyperfunction, it is important to identify for the patient those behaviors that help maintain his or her dysphonia. No exact procedure for this can be laid down; each case will have its own rules. For problems related to abuse and misuse of the voice, it is important that the clinician identify the inappropriate behavior and demonstrate to the patient some ways in which it can be eliminated. In the vocal abuse reduction section of our voice program for children (Boone, 1980a), we put much focus on having the child cognitively approach the problem of vocal abuse. By using comic pictures with an accompanying story text, we help the child understand the consequences of continued abuse with emphasis also given to what can be expected (a better voice) if he or she reduces or eliminates such abuses.

For truly organic problems, such as unilateral adductor

paralysis, the same explanations must be made, but in terms of inadequate and adequate glottal closure. Most voice patients want to understand what their problem is and what they can do about it. The clinician must make use of his or her medical and diagnostic information, but formulate explanations to the patient in language the patient can understand. Such imagery as "your vocal cords are coming together too tightly," or "you seem to place your voice back too far in your throat," may lack scientific validity, but may very well help the patient understand the problem. While explanations should be brief and to the point, the clinician must take care that the patient is not put psychologically on the defensive during the first visit. If, after the evaluation, it appears that some psychological or psychiatric consultation is necessary, further diagnostic-therapy sessions may have to be held before the patient is able to agree with the clinician's statements that "we need to find out more about our feelings" or "find out more about ourselves." The explanation of the problem does not have to be completed before voice therapy begins; in fact, Olsen's data (1972) suggest that an explanation of the problem is an important part of every session of voice therapy as practiced by experienced speech clinicians.

C.   *Typical case history showing utilization of approach.* Doris L., a nine-year-old girl with a one-year history of dysphonia, was found on mirror laryngoscopy to have "a nodule on the left cord at the anterior–middle third, with a corresponding thickening on the right cord." Prolonged discussion with her teacher and parents revealed that Doris was an extremely verbal, active child who made many loud and noxious noises while at play. The voice clinician was able to observe the girl on a school playground and confirm her screaming, screeching play noises. The explanation that the voice clinician gave the child described the vocal fold thickenings that were taking place, probably as a direct result of all that screaming on the playground. Doris was told,

> We are concerned about your voice getting increasingly hoarse. Often people can't understand what you are saying because they cannot hear your speaking voice. Your bad voice is the result of your screaming. The more you scream and screech, the bigger the bumps on your vocal cords will get. If they get much bigger, you won't have any voice at all. If you cut down on your screaming, those bumps will start to get smaller. If you can stop screaming altogether, the bumps will go away, and I think that your voice will become just as good as anyone else's.

> Pictures of nodules, some description of the effects of vocal abuse, and recordings of the "before-after" voices of other children who had been successfully treated for vocal nodules con-

vinced Doris of the need to reduce her screaming. In this case, the explanation of the problem proved to be a most effective motivator. The girl plotted the number of screams she made each day on a weekly graph, and succeeded in almost completely extinguishing her screaming behavior. There was a concomitant reduction in the thickening of her glottal margins, and an obvious improvement in the quality of her voice. No formal voice therapy was required.

D. *Evaluation of approach.* An explanation of the problem is an important part of voice therapy. Wilson (1979) wrote, ''During the initial part of the voice therapy program the child should be taught how voice is produced and given the basic facts about his voice problem'' (p. 96). Boone (1980a) and Thurman (1977) have written about ways of letting children know about why they are doing what they are asked to do in therapy. Adults need explanations specific to their vocal pathologies and steps to remediate the problem. All patients need these explanations from the clinician, perhaps supplemented by charts and pictures, as a continuing part of voice therapy. Voice patients who understand how the voice functions and something about their own pathologies are much more apt to show motivation toward applying the various therapy strategies offered to them by their clinicians.

XII. FEEDBACK

A. *Kinds of problems for which approach is useful.* Once the patient is able to produce a model voice—his or her own or one that matches some external model—it is important that he or she make an attempt to study what the voice feels like and how it sounds. Tactual and proprioceptive feedback are common modalities through which we get some information about our voices as we speak, but it is primarily the auditory feedback system that we use in monitoring our own phonation. We have little awareness of what our muscles are doing in the larynx, throat, palate, or tongue, which is why voice therapy relies heavily on the auditory feedback mechanism.

It is often helpful to couple auditory feedback with other kinds of feedback. There are many instruments available, such as the instruments we use in voice evaluation, which can provide the patient feedback relative to some aspect of voice production. For example, the patient who is working on respiration may profit from watching her relative chest-abdominal movements by using magnetometers and watching the movement curves on some kind of scope. Or parameters of frequency and intensity may be monitored by the patient as she practices watching the tracings of her productions on a scope. Patients working on improving oral resonance may well profit from using the Tonar II, which provides ongoing feedback about relative oral and nasal resonances of any one production. The patients can become aware that their best-sounding productions are usually coupled with a certain physiologic behavior that they have been monitoring on some kind of feedback device. Feedback is useful for any voice patient who needs to become aware of what he or she may be doing in the areas of respiration, phonation, or resonance.

B. *Procedural aspects of approach.*

1. Discuss with the patient the general concept of feedback. Tactual feedback might be illustrated by moving the fingertips lightly over the surface of a coin. Proprioception can be demonstrated by having the patient close the eyes, extend an arm, and slowly raise the arm, bending it at the elbow joint. Muscle and joint proprioceptors tell us where our arm is in space and that it is moving. But in the larynx, such proprioceptive feedback is essentially lacking; we must rely on hearing our voices as we phonate to monitor what we are doing laryngeally.

2. The conventional tape recorder has never been particularly useful as a training device for auditory feedback. All it can do, essentially, is serve as an amplifying system. By the time the clinician rewinds the tape and finds the precise recording segment, the patient has already lost his or her focus on that particular stimulus. There are many auditory tape devices available—Language Master, Phonic Mirror, Echorder, Artik (see Bibliography)—that provide an immediate auditory stimulus of an event just recorded. A loop recording device, for example, set on a three-second delay, will give the patient an immediate playback of what he or she has just said. By using such a device, patients can immediately match what they thought they sounded like with the actual playback of what they sounded like externally. Vowel prolongations, single words, and phrases are used as the stimuli in this delayed feedback practice. The clinician should remember that this practice in self-listening will be much more effective if coupled with commentary and questions about what was heard, and what was different between the old voice and the new.

3. Introduce the patient to other forms of feedback specific to voice production. The biofeedback approach described earlier in this chapter becomes very useful when coupled with auditory feedback. Feedback provides a continuous monitoring of what one is doing, requiring the use of some external devices ranging in sophistication from a mirror on the wall to a frequency-monitoring device such as the Visi-Pitch. Whichever the monitoring feedback device used, the clinician must explain to the patient how the feedback is obtained and what it means as it relates to voice production. After some beginning help by the clinician, the patient can usually learn to use feedback devices alone as part of self-practice or self-monitoring.

4. Once the patient develops an awareness of what he or she is doing with the help of feedback devices, we remove the feedback and see if the patient can then maintain the target production. For example, when the patient no longer can see on a scope the normal coordination of abdomen and thorax in breathing for speech, can the optimum pattern be maintained? Both biofeedback of some physiological system and ongoing auditory feedback eventually need to be phased out of the therapy session if we are to facilitate generalization of improved production outside of therapy.

C. *Typical case history showing utilization of approach.* Cheryl T. was a twenty-two-year-old university student with vocal nodules and a severe dysphonia. It was found at the time of her voice evaluation that she spoke at the very bottom of her limited pitch range. When she spoke one or two full musical notes higher than the bottom, her voice sounded near normal. We spent much time in therapy giving her auditory feedback of her new voice at a higher pitch level, utilizing in therapy a four-second tape loop cartridge of a Phonic Mirror (see Bibliography). This provided her immediate feedback specific to how she sounded. We then coupled the auditory feedback with the visual feedback of a Visi-Pitch scope, where she could witness the increased periodicity of her voice as seen by a sharper tracing line on the scope. Not only did she sound better to herself, she could also see that one or two notes higher than where she had been voicing produced a smoother, better sounding voice. The focus of the voice therapy used the auditory and visual feedback coupled with some practice in reducing excessive glottal attack, opening her mouth more, and so forth. At the end of fifteen weeks of twice-weekly voice therapy, her nodules were gone and we all (including the patient) judged her voice as normal.

D. *Evaluation of approach.* As Van Riper and Irwin have written, "Unlike articulation training, in which visual, tactual, and kinesthetic cues can be used to guide the revision of phonemes, vocal training relies primarily on the ear" (1958, p. 283). If the voice patient is to be successful in identifying and producing his or her target phonation, it is important that he or she develop the capacity for self-hearing. In the beginning, to make the task easier, the clinician should introduce the patient to the delayed auditory feedback of his or her own phonations. After the patient has had some success in monitoring these delayed reproductions, we may introduce other feedback systems, such as an oscilloscope or TV monitor, coupled to some kind of measuring device. The goal in feedback is to provide the patient with some ongoing monitoring about some aspect of voice production. With the aid of such feedback, the patient is often able to produce the target model voice. Once the optimal voice is produced, we begin to withdraw the feedback. It is hoped that the patient will have learned to maintain the better voice without the extra information the feedback systems had been providing.

XIII. GARGLE APPROACH

A. *Kinds of problems for which the approach is useful.* For the past several years we have been using the gargle approach as a method for finding voice for the aphonic patient or finding a normal voice for someone with functional dysphonia. The approach helps facilitate normal vocal fold approximation and phonation on expiration. Gargling produces a peculiar phonation that most people were taught to do as children, providing a rinsing of the oral cavity, the oropharynx, and the hypopharynx. The individual takes a small amount of liquid, such as water, extends the chin, tilting the head back; as the head is tilted backward, the individual begins a voiced expiration that apparently keeps the liquid in the hypopharynx from being aspirated. The phonation of the gargle sound appears to be a way of ensuring that the gargle is on expiration, bubbling the liquid in the throat. For occasional patients with functional aphonia, the phonation they produce while gargling may be the first real phonation they have had since the onset of their aphonia. The gargle method was once used successfully with a child who, after prolonged voice rest, had "forgotten" how to phonate on expiration; by using the gargle, he was able to develop prolonged expiration with phonation. For patients with functional dysphonia, we have also found the method useful for developing a greater mouth opening and promoting ease in phonation.

B. *Procedural aspects of approach.*

1. The clinician demonstrates the procedure of gargling with water, stressing the prolonged phonation and the outgoing voice. The use of voice is explained to the patient as a method for ensuring that the gargle is on expiration, not inspiration. Care should be taken to keep the water on the tongue until the head is tilted back, and as the water is introduced to the pharynx, phonation is begun.

2. Following the clinician's demonstration, the patient produces the gargle. Emphasis must be given to the timing of the parts so that phonation does not begin until the tilting of the head. The patient who is able to gargle is asked to sustain the gargle for approximately five seconds. If the patient cannot gargle with phonation, the clinician should repeat the demonstration followed by another request for the patient to gargle.

3. If the patient can gargle, the clinician demonstrates how the mouth is open, the head is back, and the voiced expiration keeps producing the bubbling and water gurgling in the pharynx. After several attempts, if the patient cannot gargle, the method should be abandoned by the clinician.

4. Posterior consonants and low back vowels are introduced to

use at the "top" of the gargle. The patient might produce a prolonged "gʌ" combination. First we couple the gargle with liquid as the patient prolongs the "gʌ." Then, if successful, we prolong the voiced consonant-vowel combination without any water bubbling in the hypopharynx. In general, as soon as the patient can maintain the voice without water, we no longer use the true "liquid gargle."

5. Once voice can be established without the gargle, the gargle phase of the practice is eliminated. We work on back consonants and low back vowels, first with single words and then short phrases, maintaining the easy voice first produced by the gargle.

C. *Typical case history showing utilization of approach.* Sister Catherine was a forty-two-year-old nun who lost her voice while on a month-long renewal tour, where she had to give daily lectures at a number of parochial schools. Subsequent laryngoscopy found her to have a normal larynx and the speech-language pathologist found her to have "functional aphonia." Attempts at coughing and inhalation phonation were unsuccessful in early therapy attempts to help her "find" her voice. The gargle approach was introduced with immediate results. She was able to produce an expiratory phonation while gargling, with her head tilted back and her mouth wide open. The clinician rewarded her early gargle phonations with statements like "now your cords are coming together." The Sister was reassured that her vocal folds could come together well and produce voice on expiration. After several repetitions with the gargle, voice was sustained without the need of gargling water. At the first therapy session when gargle was successfully introduced, counseling and explanations about voice were all provided; toward the end of the session, the Sister was able to produce good voice consistently, coupling her phonation attempts with chanting and the open-mouth approach. Within four therapy sessions, she reported having her normal voice back again.

D. *Evaluation of the approach.* It appears that the extended position of the head, the open mouth, and the easy voice experienced by most patients while gargling provides the patient with a relatively relaxed way of phonating. The Gargle Approach is used only temporarily to help the patient find a voice that is "lost" in functional aphonia or to help a patient experience easy voice on expiration for occasional problems of functional dysphonia. Once the method facilitates the production of voice, it is no longer used and is replaced by other therapy approaches. It has been our experience measuring the fundamental frequency of patients while gargling that the voice frequency produced closely approximates the patient's tested optimal pitch level. The voice produced while gargling does not appear to be too far away from the voice the patient is able to produce eventually with the least amount of effort.

XIV.   HIERARCHY ANALYSIS
   A.   *Kinds of problems for which approach is useful.* In hierarchy analysis,
        the patient constructs lists of various situations in his or her life
        that ordinarily produce some anxiety, arranging the situations in
        a sequential order from the least to the most anxiety provoking.
        Or the individual patients may prepare a hierarchy of situations,
        ranging from those in which they find their voices best to where
        they find their voices worst. This technique is borrowed from
        Wolpe's method of reciprocal inhibition (1973), wherein the pa-
        tient is taught relaxed responses to anxiety-evoking situations;
        after identifying a hierarchy of anxiety-evoking situations, the
        patient begins by employing the relaxed responses in the least
        anxious of them, and, in therapy, works his or her way up the
        hierarchy, eventually deconditioning his or her previously estab-
        lished anxious responses. The identification of hierarchical situa-
        tions (less anxiety–more anxiety; worst voice–best voice) appears
        to be a useful therapeutic device for most patients with hyper-
        functional voice problems, which by definition imply excessive
        overreacting. Patients with functional dysphonia, or with
        dysphonias accompanied by nodules, polyps, and vocal fold
        thickening, frequently report that their degrees of dysphonia
        vary with the situation. Such patients may profit from hierarchy
        analysis.
   B.   *Procedural aspects of approach.*
        1.   Begin by developing in the patient a general awareness of the
             hierarchical behavior to be studied. If, for example, the pa-
             tient is to be asked to identify those situations in which he
             feels most uncomfortable, discuss with the patient the symp-
             toms of being uncomfortable. Or if the patient is going to
             develop a hierarchy of situations in which he experiences
             variation of voice, discuss and give examples of what is a
             good voice or a bad voice. Explain to the patient that he must
             develop a relative ordering of situations, sequencing them
             from "good" to "bad." Some patients are initially resistant
             to this sort of ordering, perhaps never before having realized
             that there are relative gradations to their feelings of anxiety
             or relative changes in their quality of voice. They may not be
             aware that the degree of their anxiety or hoarseness is not
             constant.
        2.   While the majority of voice patients are soon able to arrange
             situations into a hierarchy, a few require some practice with
             the clinician in sequencing some neutral stimuli. On one oc-
             casion, a woman was taught the idea of sequential order by
             arranging five shades of red tiles from left to right, in the
             order of the lightest pink to the darkest red. Having done
             this, she was then able to sequence her voice situations, pro-
             ceeding gradually from those in which her voice was normal
             to those in which it was extremely dysphonic.

3. As a home assignment, have the patient develop several hierarchies with regard to his or her voice. One hierarchy might center on how the patient's voice holds up with the family, another on how it is related to the work situation, and a third on what happens to it in varying situations with friends. An excellent example of hierarchical situations developed by a woman with vocal nodules is given in an article by Gray, England, and Mahoney (1965). After these hierarchies have been developed by the patient at home, review them in therapy.

4. In therapy, use the "good" end of the hierarchical sequence first. That is, begin by asking the patient to recapture, if he or she can, the good situation. It is the goal of therapy to duplicate the feeling of well-being or the good voice that the patient experienced in the situation he or she rated as best. Efforts should be made in therapy to recall the good factors surrounding the more optimum phonation. If the patient is successful in recreating the optimum situation, his or her phonation will sound relaxed and appropriate. The recreated optimum situation thus serves as an excellent facilitator for producing good voice. After demonstrating some success in recreating the first situation on the hierarchy, capturing completely his or her optimum response (whether this be relaxation or phonation or both), the patient will then be able to move on to the second situation. There again the goal will be to maintain optimum response. The rate of movement up the hierarchy will depend entirely on how successfully the patient can recreate the situations and maintain optimum response. By using the relaxed response in increasingly more tense situations, the patient is conditioning himself or herself to a more favorable, optimum behavior.

5. While some patients can recreate situations outside the clinic with relative ease, some cannot. As soon as possible, have the patient practice his or her optimum reponse outside the clinic under good conditions, so that the patient will eventually be able to use it in the real world in more adverse situations. The patient must not lose sight of the goal of maintaining the good response in varying situations outside the clinic.

6. Some patients succeed in going just so far up the hierarchy, only to reach a situation in which they continuously have a maladaptive response. When this occurs, the patient should drop back to a lower hierarchical level and attempt once more to capture the optimum response under more favorable conditions. When a good response is again maintained, efforts at the next level should be resumed.

C. *Typical case history showing utilization of approach.* Laurie L. was a twenty-four-year-old forest conservationist who worked in an office with ten male conservationists. For six months she had experienced recurring dysphonia, particularly when on the telephone at work. Laryngoscopic examination found her to have an "early nodule formation on her left vocal cord"; during the voice evaluation she demonstrated a relatively normal voice. The patient's dysphonia appeared to fluctuate, becoming particularly severe, she reported, in certain anxiety-provoking situations. As part of her three months of voice therapy, she was asked to develop several hierarchical scales, listing the situations in order, from those in which she experienced a normal voice to those in which she became all but aphonic. Here is the hierarchy she developed for her vocal responses at the office:

Best Voice
1. Calling mother on the phone every day from the office.
2. The female secretary at the office is easy to talk with, particularly when the older men in the office are not around.
3. Dictating on the dictaphone and talking to the secretary are about the same.
4. Bill W. talks to me a lot at the office and on dates.
5. The younger men kid me about going out with them on field trips.
6. The older conservationists at the office keep reminding me that I have only school and no field experience, which always makes me clear my throat.
7. Talking about forestry projects on the phone is hard.
8. I lose my voice entirely when talking to our regional manager, and if I can't get over this, I will lose my job.

Worst Voice

As voice therapy developed, hierarchy analysis and counseling with the speech pathologist gave this patient greater insight into her difficulties in various interpersonal relationships. Her varying dysphonia was but a symptom of the discomfort she felt with certain people. Voice therapy was terminated after three months in favor of psychotherapy.

D.   *Evaluation of approach.* Voice patients typically report marked inconsistencies in the severity of their dysphonias. In one situation they will phonate with relative ease, and in other situations, usually those in which they feel some stress, their voices may break down completely. These vocal inconsistencies can be studied effectively through hierarchy analysis. This use of hierarchy analysis differs considerably from Wolpe's (1973), although the principle of maintaining an optimum response under varying conditions of stress is the same. Wolpe teaches his patients relaxation techniques to apply during various hierarchical situations, beginning with low-on-the-hierarchy situations where the patient is relatively free of stress. The relaxation response is established at the lower levels and gradually conditioned to occur at higher ones. With voice patients, we establish optimum phonation at lower levels and gradually condition it to occur at higher levels. In one sense, we are teaching the patient to react optimally to various situational cues, a method often used for establishing and maintaining effectiveness of communication under varying situations. By analyzing the hierarchical situations in which the patient becomes more anxious and more dysphonic, the voice patient learns what situational cues trigger an ineffective response, a poorer voice. By using various facilitating techniques and recapturing the relaxed phonation the patient may use in low-on-the-hierarchy situations, he or she learns to produce more relaxed phonation at all levels of the hierarchy.

XV. INHALATION PHONATION

A. *Kinds of problems for which approach is useful.* When voice is produced on inhalation, this is always produced by true fold vibration. Lehmann (1965) demonstrated radiographically that high-pitched vocalization produced on inhalation is always the result of true fold vibration. Inhalation phonation should only be used diagnostically or as a probe in searching for true fold vibration. Williams and others (1975) have written that reverse phonation provides an excellent view of the vibrating folds as viewed by fiberoptic endoscopy. It has been found to be an excellent method for eliciting true phonation in patients who are experiencing functional aphonia. Greene (1980) writes that inhalation phonation can be effectively used as a therapy approach with the occasional patient who exclusively uses "the ventricular band voice." The method is also used with the occasional patient who is experiencing a functional puberphonia, maintaining an inappropriately high-pitched voice despite a vocal mechanism that has matured beyond puberty. The ease with which most patients are able to produce the high-pitched inhalation voice makes the method useful in establishing or reestablishing true vocal fold vibration.

B. *Procedural aspects of approach.*

1. For this particular approach, similar to masking (facilitating approach 16), it is perhaps better for the clinician to demonstrate the approach rather than explain it. The clinician demonstrates inhalation phonation by phonating a high-pitched hum while elevating the shoulders. It is important to time the initiation of the inhalation with shoulder elevation. The shoulder elevation is done so the clinician can mark and stress for the patient the contrast between inhalation (shoulders raised) and exhalation (shoulders lowered).

2. After demonstrating several separate inhalations with simultaneous shoulder elevation and phonation, the clinician then says, "Now, we'll match the high-pitched inhalation voice with an expiration voice." The clinician then inhales, raising the shoulders and simultaneously humming in a high pitch, then dropping the shoulders on exhalation and producing the same sound of voice. He or she repeats the inhalation-exhalation matched phonations several times.

3. The patient is then asked to make an inhalation phonation. He or she should repeat the inhalation phonation several times. Now the clinician again repeats the inhalation-exhalation matched phonation, taking care to make the associated shoulder movements. Then the patient may be told, "Now drop your shoulders on expiration, making the same high-pitched voice as you do it." With a little trial practice, the typical patient is able to do it.

4. The clinician then says, after the patient has produced the matching hum, "Now, let us extend the expiration like this." The clinician demonstrates a continuation of the high pitch, sweeping down from what is the falsetto register to his or her regular chest register on one long, continuous expiration. The clinician should repeat this several times. He or she then might say to the patient, "Once I've brought my vocal cords together at the high pitch, I then sweep down, keeping them together, down to the pitch level of my regular speaking voice."

5. If the patient is unable to produce this shift from high to low, then the first four steps should be repeated. For those patients who can make the shift down to their regular speaking register, the clinician could say, "Now you're getting your vocal cords together for what sounds like a good-sounding voice." Care must be given at this point not to rush the patient into attempting to use the "new" voice functionally. Rather, some similar hum phonations can be practiced. After some practice just phonating the hum, the clinician might give the patient a word list containing simple monosyllabic words for "true" voice practice.

6. Stay at the single-word practice level until normal voicing is well established. We will often spend several therapy periods practicing the new phonation as a motor practice drill with no attempt at making the voice conversationally functional. The clinician might say, "Now we're getting the vocal folds together the way we want them." This places the previous aphonia or ventricular phonation "blame" on the mechanism, rather than on the patient per se. Counseling with the patient at this time is important. The motor practice gives the patient time to adjust to the more optimum way of phonating.

C. *Typical case history showing utilization of approach.* D. S., a five-year-old boy, was found to have small bilateral vocal nodules. His speech clinician placed him on complete voice rest, which unfortunately was enforced for five continuous months. At the end of five months, the nodules had disappeared, and the child was instructed by both the physician and the speech pathologist to resume normal phonation. Despite all efforts by the child, he could only whisper. He became completely aphonic, but conversed easily with all people with much animation and relative comfort. This functional aphonia remained for two months after he was instructed, "Go back and talk the normal way, Davey." The child gestured that he wanted to use his voice but he could not "find it." Therapy efforts for restoring phonation were begun some seven months after the child's phonations had ceased. Inhalation phonation was initiated, and at the first therapy session the boy was able to produce a high-pitched inhalation sound and followed his clinician well by matching the inhalation with an expiration sound. He was able to use an expiration phonation, appropriate in both quality and pitch, by the end of the first therapy session. He was scheduled for two other appointments within a twenty-four-hour period, during which he practiced producing his regained normal voice. He was counseled that his "voice is working now and you'll never have to lose it again." The boy has had normal phonation since his voice was restored using the inhalation phonation technique. Incidentally, counseling to curb yelling and other vocal abuses appeared to be successful, as he has experienced no return of the bilateral vocal nodules.

D. *Evaluation of approach.* It would appear that some patients who experience either aphonia or ventricular phonation for any length of time lose their ability to initiate normal true fold phonation. The longer the aphonia or dysphonia persists, the harder it might be to use normal voice. Inhalation phonation is a simple way for producing true cord approximation and voicing. The high-pitched voice on inhalation probably is the result of the vocal folds being longer in their inhalation posture, and even though they may adduct on command, they remain in their longer configuration. This elongated posture thins them, resulting in the higher-pitched phonation. The patient is able to match the inspiration sound with an expiration sound.

XVI. MASKING

A. *Kinds of problems for which approach is useful.* There are occasional voice patients who experience real difficulty monitoring their own voices. They may demonstrate particular difficulty monitoring the loudness of their voices or exhibit problems maintaining normal vocal quality in certain situations. Most of these patients have functional dysphonia without organic pathology. A useful voice technique in helping these patients utilize a louder, clearer voice is employing the voice-reflex test, known by audiologists as the Lombard test (Newby, 1972). In fact, the Lombard test was first introduced as a method of finding voice in patients with functional aphonia. When asked to phonate in a loud noise background, patients with functional aphonia were sometimes heard to use light voice. In the voice-reflex situation, the patient wears earphones and is asked to read a passage aloud. As the patient is reading, a masking noise is fed into the earphones. The louder the masking, the louder the patient's voice. At loud masking levels the patient cannot monitor well either the loudness or the clearness of his or her voice. Some patients with functional dysphonias actually experience clearer voices when they cannot monitor their productions because of loud masking. The clinician may make a tape recording of all of the patient's oral reading, with and without masking, and then play back the results to the patient. The patient may well experience the "proper" set for more optimal phonation during the masking conditions and be able to maintain this improved production without the need for continued masking.

B. *Procedural aspects of approach.*
1. The masking approach is best used without any prior explanation. Since an increase of voice loudness comes about with increased intensities of masking on a reflexive, nonvolitional basis, there is no need to discuss the method in advance. In fact, there is some evidence that some patients can override the voice-reflex and maintain constancy of voice loudness despite fluctuations in masking intensity.
2. The patient is seated next to an audiometer. He or she then puts on headphones and is asked to listen to a bilateral presentation of masking at a low level, roughly 40 dB SPL. Once the patient acknowledges hearing the masking, the masking stimulus is discontinued. The patient is then instructed to read aloud and to keep reading, no matter what kind of interruption he or she may hear in the headphones.
3. All of the patient's oral reading is recorded on an audiotape recorder.
4. Five- or ten-second exposures to masking are introduced to the patient bilaterally. The intensity levels should be in excess of 90 dB SPL, which is sufficiently loud to mask out the patient's own voice. Whenever the patient hears the loud masking, his or her voice will become louder. Some patients will also experience some clearing of their dysphonia under the masking conditions. Typically, the patient is asked to read aloud for a total period of about two minutes, with the masking fluctuating off and on throughout the reading. Variations in loudness of the patient's voice on playback will usually signal when the masking noise is introduced and when it ceases. If the patient demonstrates a marked im-

provement in loudness and quality, it is sometimes useful to let the masking continue uninterrupted for thirty seconds or more.

5. For those few voice patients who do not demonstrate the voice-reflex effect, the method should not be tried beyond the trial stage. If it works well, producing voice improvement, the method may be used as part of every therapy period. The clinician might then experiment by having the patient listen to tapes of himself or herself, seeing whether the patient can match volitionally his or her voice under masking conditions. Recordings can then be made of the voice without masking (attempting to recreate the same voice as heard under masking) contrasted with the voice with masking. Attempts should be made to have them sound alike.

6. A patient may profit from reading aloud under masking conditions, and then having the clinician abruptly end the masking to see if the patient can maintain his or her better voice. Many variations using the masking noise can be initiated by the inventive clinician.

C. *Typical case history showing utilization of approach.* Sarah R., an eight-year-old, experienced multiple airway papilloma, requiring a series of four operations. After several papilloma were removed from her vocal folds, she experienced postoperatively a continuing and severe dysphonia. About six months after the last surgical procedure, her vocal folds were examined and found to "have normal motility with the membranes well healed and free of any recurring papilloma." A severe, persisting dysphonia did not seem compatible with the relatively normal larynx. Under conditions of masking in voice therapy, she was able to produce a relatively normal voice, a voice with sufficient loudness and relatively free of dysphonia. She was able to match the tape-recorded samples of her voice under masking, and this approach became the primary method of therapy. A subsequent removal of a tracheal papilloma had no adverse effect on her phonation, which has remained at relatively normal loudness and quality levels.

D. *Evaluation of approach.* It would appear that occasional voice patients overmonitor their voices. They become so aware of some aspect of phonation that they seem to lose naturalness of production. For these patients, the masking approach is useful. If the masking noise is loud enough, in excess of 90 dB SPL, the patient cannot hear his voice to monitor his phonation. If required to continue speaking by reading aloud under conditions of masking, the patient will often produce a relatively normal voice under the masking condition. The clinician should use some care in confronting the patient on audiotape playback with his "good" voice. The improved voice under conditions of masking should be used as the patient's own model for his own imitation phonation. The clinician should use the masking approach with some degree of eclecticism, that is, if the approach works, we use it, and if it does not, we should quickly abandon it.

XVII. NEGATIVE PRACTICE

A. *Kinds of problems for which approach is useful.* In voice therapy we use various facilitating techniques to develop new, desirable, target voices. While it is comparatively easy to produce optimum phonation in therapy, the patient is often resistant to using the new phonation outside in the everyday world. Negative practice, the intentional use of a previously incorrect response, is a helpful method for facilitating the carry-over of new voice patterns to out-of-clinic situations. Negative practice of an old voice is relatively easy for most voice patients and appears to be particularly useful for patients attempting to change voice pitch and loudness. In using negative practice with children, Wilson (1979) writes, "negative practice is used conservatively and in limited amounts to bring undesirable vocal practices to a conscious level" (p. 101). We have found negative practice to be useful for voice patients of any age who have developed a new and better method of phonation; to go back intentionally to the old method of production seems to show the patient the unneeded and unwanted effort involved in that old method.

B. *Procedural aspects of approach.*

1. Once the patient is able to produce target phonations freely in the clinical situation, ask him or her to voice deliberately an old phonation pattern. Make a tape recording contrasting the new phonation with the old, perhaps no more than twenty seconds in total length. Then evaluate the playback with the patient, having the patient analyze what the two phonations "feel" like in contrast to one another and how they differ in sound.

2. Ask the patient about those situations in which she is best able to produce the new voice, and, after the patient has identified them, have her make specific plans to use deliberately the old voice pattern at certain times within those situations. It appears to be most useful to confine negative practice to those situations in which the patient is comfortable and in which she can use the new phonation pattern any time she wishes.

C. *Typical case history showing utilization of approach.* A thirty-five-year-old teaching colleague of this writer had a long history of vocal fatigue (pain and dysphonia) after prolonged lecturing. His laryngoscopic examination was normal. His only observed faulty speaking habit was pronounced mandibular restriction—most of the time he literally talked through clenched teeth and with a closed mouth. The chewing approach was used successfully with this man, and shortly after establishing good chewing behavior, he began to use negative practice. In situations where he found chewing an easy and relaxing aid to maintaining good phonation, he would deliberately revert to his previous style of speaking with little or no jaw movement. The effort required to speak in this old way became immediately apparent to him, and in only a few weeks he developed a lasting enthusiasm for the open-mouthed, relaxed, chewing method. His problem of vocal fatigue after lecturing was greatly reduced.

D. *Evaluation of approach.* Negative practice is a useful approach for anyone attempting to establish a new behavioral response in place of an old one. In the case of the voice patient, the old response is faulty and generally requires a great deal of hyper-functional effort; the patient works to talk. After a more optimum method of phonation has been established, negative practice reinforces for the patient how much easier it is to talk in the new way. Negative practice, a useful approach also with such problems as articulation defects and stuttering, is equally beneficial with various voice problems.

XVIII. OPEN–MOUTH APPROACH

A. *Kinds of problems for which approach is useful.* Encouraging the patient to develop more oral openness will often reduce generalized vocal hyperfunction. Opening the mouth more while speaking and learning to listen with a slightly open mouth allow the patient to use his or her vocal mechanisms more optimally. The open-mouth approach promotes more natural size-mass adjustments and more optimum approximation of the vocal folds, aiding in problems of loudness, pitch, and quality. For the patient wanting to increase oral resonance as part of improvement in overall voice quality, opening the mouth more appears to increase oral resonance. The voice also sounds louder. Development of greater openness should be part of any voice therapy program where the patient is attempting to use the vocal mechanisms with less effort and strain.

B. *Procedural aspects of approach.*

1. Have the patient view himself or herself in a mirror (or on a videotape playback, if possible) to observe the presence and absence of open-mouth behavior. Any lip tightness, mandibular restriction, or excessive neck muscle movement should be identified for the patient by the clinician.

2. Children seem to understand quickly the benefits of opening the mouth more for the production of a better-sounding voice. In our voice program for children (Boone, 1980a), we use a brief story that illustrates two boys, one who talks with his mouth closed and one who speaks with his mouth open. We then introduce a hand puppet and ask the child if he's ever been a ventriloquist. The clinician portrays the ventriloquist as one who does not open his mouth, as contrasted with the puppet who makes exaggerated, wide-mouth openings.

3. The ventriloquist-puppet analogy also works well with

adults. Let the patient observe the marked contrast between talking with a closed mouth and an open one. Ask the patient to watch himself speak the two different ways in a mirror. The patient should be instructed that what is attempted will at first feel foreign and inappropriate. The initial stages of letting the jaw relax are frequently anything but relaxed.

4.   To establish further this oral openness, ask the patient to drop his head toward the chest and let the lips part and the jaw drop open. Once this can be done, have the patient practice some relaxed /a/s. When the head is tilted down and the jaw is slightly open, a more relaxed phonation will often be achieved.

5.   In order for patients to develop a feeling of openness when listening, and as a pre-set to speaking, they must in the beginning develop a conscious awareness of how often they find themselves with a tight, closed mouth. One way to develop this awareness is to have patients mark down, on cards carried with them, each time they become aware that their mouths are closed unnecessarily. The marking task itself is often enough to increase the patient's awareness, and his number of mouth closings over a period of a week will decrease notably. Another way of developing an awareness of greater orality is to have patients place in their living environment (on a dressing table, desk, or car dashboard) a little sign that says "OPEN," or perhaps has a double arrow (↕), or any other code that might serve as a reminder.

6.   Once the patient has achieved oral openness, such oral resonance practice materials as those set down by Fisher (1975), Moncur and Brackett (1974), and Fairbanks (1960) will be helpful in establishing a carry-over between greater orality and the speech-voicing task itself. Practice in steps 3 and 4 under this open-mouth approach will usually help produce a more optimum voice and should precede the reading of actual speech materials.

C.   *Typical case history showing utilization of approach.* J. J., a seventeen-year-old high school girl, was examined by a laryngologist about one year after an automobile accident in which she had suffered some injuries to the head and neck. Laryngoscopic examination found all visible laryngeal structures normal in appearance and function, despite the fact that since the accident the girl's voice had been only barely audible. The speech pathologist was impressed "with her relatively closed mouth while speaking, which seemed to result in extremely poor voice resonance." Voice therapy combined both the chewing and the open-mouth facilitating approaches. It was discovered in therapy that for three months after the automobile accident the girl had worn an orthopedic collar that seemed to inhibit her head and jaw movements. It appeared that much of her closed-mouthmandibularly restricted speech was related to the constraints imposed upon her by the orthopedic collar. When using the open-mouth approach with her head tilted down toward her chest, she was immediately able to produce a louder, more resonant voice. The open-mouth approach was initiated before beginning chewing exercises, and both achieved excellent results. Therapy was terminated after six weeks, with much voice improvement in both loudness and quality.

D. *Evaluation of approach.* As the normal speaking and singing voice improves in resonance and loudness when the mouth is open, so does the dysphonic voice. The effects on voice from opening the mouth a bit more are immediate. Not only does the typical voice patient sound better with a more active opening of the mouth; he or she will also usually report that his or her voice feels more relaxed. Besides opening the mouth more while speaking, the approach also encourages slight mouth opening while listening. In describing a vocal hygiene approach Boone (1980b) has written about mouth opening, "A gentle opening of less than one finger wide between the central incisors keeps the teeth apart and generally fosters a relaxed oral posture" (p. 40). This approach has been found particularly effective with performers who often open their mouths well during performance (singing, acting) but forget the importance of opening their mouths during conversation.

XIX. PITCH INFLECTIONS

A. *Kinds of problems for which approach is useful.* The normal voice will vary below and above its habitual pitch, which is the pitch level used most often. But in some voices this pitch variation is lacking. Such a monotonous pitch, which for the average speaker would be impossible to maintain, requires the inhibition of natural inflection and is observed usually in overcontrolled persons who display very little overt affect. Fairbanks (1960), who describes pitch variation as a vital part of normal phonation, defines inflection and shift, "An *inflection* is a modulation of pitch during phonation. A *shift* is a change of pitch from the end of one phonation to the beginning of the next" (p. 132). Voice therapy for patients with monotonic pitch seeks not only to establish more optimum pitch levels, but also to increase the amount of pitch variability. Any voice patient with a dull, monotonous pitch level will profit from attempting to increase his or her pitch inflections. Cooper (1977) has written that optimum usage of the voice is facilitated by the patient using the correct pitch level with pitch inflections below and above the optimum pitch.

B. *Procedural aspects of approach.*

1. Listen, with the patient, to recorded samples of the patient's voice, contrasting these perhaps with samples of a few voices with excellent pitch variation, and follow this listening with

direct comment on the problem. The patient must be made aware of his or her lack of pitch variation.

2. Begin working on downward and upward inflectional shifts of the same word, exaggerating in the beginning the extent of pitch change. Most voice diction books provide excellent practice materials for enhancing inflection.

3. Using the same source material, have the patient practice introducing pitch shifts within specific words.

4. For patients desiring to work on pitch inflection, both the Tonar II (1972) and the Visi-Pitch (1980) provide feedback information to the patient so that he or she might work on inflection in self-practice sessions.

5. Record the patient's oral reading and conversation from time to time, critically analyzing these productions with regard to pitch variability.

C. *Typical case history showing utilization of approach.* Ralph M., a fifty-two-year-old farm implement salesman, had a two-year history of recurring dysphonia with occasional aphonia. Laryngeal examination found him to have "an edematous larynx with early polypoid formation on the right vocal fold at the junction of the anterior third–middle third." His voice evaluation revealed an inappropriately low-pitched voice with almost no pitch variation. Trial voice therapy suggested that the patient experienced more relaxed phonation when he used pitch inflections and spoke at a higher pitch level (D_3 instead of B_2). The patient terminated voice therapy after four sessions, leaving behind recordings that clearly demonstrated that the use of pitch inflection helped him maintain a slightly higher voice pitch and noticeably improved his overall voice quality. It was the clinician's opinion that had the patient continued in voice therapy, practicing a slightly higher voice pitch and the use of pitch inflection, he would have experienced a marked reduction of his dysphonia and a gradual clearing of his polypoid formation.

D. *Evaluation of approach.* In voice therapy, anything that can be done to reduce the amount of effort used by the patient to speak usually has a positive effect on the laryngeal mechanism and its vocal product. Increasing pitch variability in a monotonic voice usually contributes to increased vocal relaxation. Patients are easily taught to increase their pitch inflections, and such an approach should be used in any case where pitch variability is lacking.

XX. PLACE THE VOICE

A. *Kinds of problems for which approach is useful.* Many patients with voice problems have long histories of concern about their voice problem. Many of them focus on their throats as the anatomical site of their problems. Such patients may profit from this approach, place the voice, by shifting the focus from the throat to the upper vocal tract. Perkins (1981) has written that "voice that feels focused high in the head'' is a more efficient voice and one that can survive extensive vocalization. The clinician helps the patient focus on the area of his or her face under the cheeks and across the bridge of the nose. Most patients with chronic dysphonia experience difficulty finding their voices; they experience much continued expectancy of vocal failure. They clear their throats continually, they make phonation rehearsals, and they worry about the poor vocal quality they are likely to have the next time they attempt to speak. For these patients the successful voice clinician often employs two techniques, respiration training and placing the voice in the facial mask, for two reasons: (1) improving respiratory control and resonance; (2) transferring the patient's mental focus away from the larynx and placing it with the activator (respiration) and the resonator (supraglottal vocal tract).

B.   Procedural aspects of approach.

   1.   In working with children, we use the pictures shown in the drawing of the facial mask shown in Figure 5-4. As described in the Boone Voice Program for Children (1980a), we follow these steps: "Give the following explanation to the child, pointing to the appropriate places on the picture. (Point to the shaded area on the boy in the picture.) 'A good sounding voice is made right here. We'll do some things today that will put your voice right here.' (Point to the bridge of the nose in the picture, then touch the child in the same place.) 'Then we'll put some voice right here.' (Point to the cheeks in the picture, then touch the child in the same place)." (p. 111)

   2.   With adults we use a similar procedure, perhaps not requiring the pictures (although this writer uses this same picture with voice patients of any age).

FIGURE 5-4.   Place the Voice. The imagery of "placing" the voice in the middle of the face is helped by using the two pictures above. Used with permission from C. C. Publications, Inc. Tigard, Oregon, taken from *The Boone Voice Program for Children.*

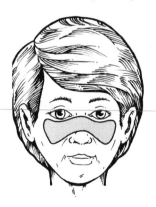
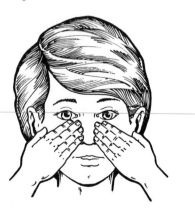

3. The clinician demonstrates the method by saying "me" and "one" in an exaggerated manner, which will create sufficient nasal resonance to produce some vibration on the bridge of the nose and above the maxillary sinuses.

4. The patient is requested to produce the "me" and the "one" in the same manner. Ask the patient if he or she can feel the vibration on his or her nose and high cheeks.

5. If the patient confirms feeling the vibration produced by the nasal consonant, we then add a few more words that permit the exaggeration of the nasal consonant. Words like *man, mean, many, went* lend themselves well for this beginning work. If this is done correctly, one should hear an improvement in vocal quality. The nasal consonants are used not to increase nasal resonance, but to place a higher vocal tract focus for the voice than where the patient had been previously experiencing.

6. If there is an audible improvement in the sound of the voice using the words with nasal consonants, we then introduce other words, such as *baby, beach, take,* and so on, emphasizing the resonance in the facial mask area. Any words may be used at this point.

7. After the patient has had some success in placing the voice "higher," we discuss with the patient the imagery of what we are doing. We discuss how this is similar to the singing teacher who uses such imagery (we cannot really "place" the voice anywhere), knowing that when the singer has the imagery of "putting his or her voice somewhere," there are often audible measurable effects. This is a good place to use some kind of feedback device, such as a spectrograph or the Visi-Pitch to confirm any changes in voice quality using the approach.

8. Oral reading and conversation in the voice clinic setting, focusing on the feeling and the "set" for using place the voice is an important requisite for generalization of the approach outside the clinic.

C. *Typical case history showing utilization of approach.* Richard H. was a forty-four-year-old lawyer who developed a functional dysphonia while still maintaining "a normal larynx." At times, he experienced a normal voice and often at meetings or talking on the telephone, he would experience severe hoarseness, pain in the laryngeal area, and the feeling that to talk at all required much effort. The place-the-voice technique worked better for him than all the other facilitating approaches we used. He found that the imagery of placing his voice "in his face" seemed to free the tightness he experienced in his throat. Increased periodicity of laryngeal vibration and improvement in overall laryngeal function appeared directly related to shifting his voice focus concern away from his larynx. From our explanation of phonation, he began to understand that the vocal folds come together "slightly," with the real activator of voice being the outgoing air flow and the real sound and quality of the voice being formed in the vocal tract above the larynx. The explanations and the practice in placing the voice in the facial mask had lasting effects. Place the voice, used with respiration training and explanations of the vocal physiology, appeared to restore normal voice in this professional man. A one-year followup quickly confirmed that he had maintained his normal voice.

D.   *Evaluation of approach.* The goal in using this approach is to transfer the patient's focus from the larynx to the upper vocal tract. The approach is not used to increase nasal resonance; the heavy utilization of nasal resonance in the beginning steps of the approach are used only to develop focus on the area of the nose and face. Teachers of singing have long successfully used such imagery approaches (Coffin, 1981). The method is similar to Cooper's (1977) *um-hum* technique, in which the patient experiences a "tingle or buzz" near the lips or the bridge of the nose. Improvement in vocal quality, using nasal consonants as a method of focusing the voice out of the throat, is part of therapy procedures developed by Wilson (1979, p. 150) and McClosky (1977, p. 143). Once the patient experiences the nasal vibration of production, the clinician shifts to oral productions, keeping, however, focus on the same somatic site. It has been our experience that the approach is helpful to most voice patients except those whose problems have a hypernasality component.

XXI.   PUSHING APPROACH

A.   *Kinds of problems for which approach is useful.* Pushing exercises are useful for the patient with problems of vocal fold approximation, and may be helpful in increasing loudness and improving the quality of voice. Froeschels (1955), who introduced the pushing approach, first used the method for increasing the strength of the soft palate, later adapting it to problems of cord paralysis and to voices worn out from continued hyperfunction (hypofunctional voices). We have found the pushing approach useful with patients with weak voices related to such varied causes as generalized systemic fatigue, myasthenia, unilateral cord paralysis, and traumatic injury to the larynx, and especially effective with patients who have bowing of the vocal folds as a result, usually, of prolonged hyperfunctional use of the voice. The pushing method is useful for any patient who needs improved activation and firmer closure of the vocal folds.

B.   *Procedural aspects of approach.*

1.   First demonstrate the pushing method by raising the patient's fists to about shoulder height, and then pushing the arms down suddenly in a rapid, uninterrupted motion until the hands, fully extended, reach to just below the hips. Then instruct the patient to do the same thing by himself. Occa-

sionally a patient may require some active assistance from the clinician so as to ensure that the patient achieves the rapid, downward movement required.

2. After the patient can perform the pushing well, ask him to push and phonate simultaneously. It usually requires only short practice for the patient to synchronize the two actions. Phonations produced while pushing are usually louder and have better resonance.

3. Another variation of the pushing approach is to ask the patient to grasp the seat of a chair, and, while gripping the chair, to push down firmly with his arms. Next, ask the patient to add phonation while pushing in this way. Short successive bursts of pushing-phonation should then be practiced.

4. Another variation of the pushing approach using a chair is to ask the patient to sit down, grip underneath the chair, and attempt to lift himself or herself as he or she is seated up from the floor. While lifting up, the patient should simultaneously phonate. Phonation under this condition is usually characterized by firmer approximation (less dysphonia) and increased loudness.

5. Once better phonation has been produced through pushing, have the patient listen to it on some kind of auditory feedback loop system. While the pushing may be the primary facilitator in producing the better voice, the patient should soon attempt to match the same loudness and quality of phonation without pushing. A useful approach would be to have the patient listen discriminatively to his or her two phonations, one with pushing and one without, and see how closely he or she can match them in subsequent imitative attempts.

6. Once the patient is able to extend the good voice into a series of practice phrases, the pushing should be stopped. It is generally advisable to terminate pushing as soon as the same voice loudness and quality can be achieved without using it. The primary benefit of pushing is its initial facilitating role.

C. *Typical case history showing utilization of approach.* Marvin M., a fifty-two-year-old attorney, had a two-year history of a "tired" voice that could not be heard during his courtroom appearances. On laryngoscopic examination, he appeared to have "severe posterior bowing of the cords, with the vocal processes in a fixed state of slight abduction." Voice therapy focused on a slight lowering of pitch level and on the pushing approach. On the first day of evaluation-therapy, the patient was able to produce a louder, more resonant voice by combining arm-extension pushing with the lowered phonation. In four therapy sessions, he was able to combine pushing with the more vigorous phonation of practice phrases. The patient continued in voice therapy for a total of eight weeks, seeing the clinician for thirty-minute practice sessions twice a week. He was soon able to produce good matching phonations without pushing. As for carry-over to the courtroom, the setting where his difficulty had been most penalizing to him, he was able to achieve this by occasionally pushing down hard on his chair while speaking. Laryngeal examination at the end of therapy found "normal vocal fold approximation, with no evidence of vocal process abduction." Voice loudness and quality appeared to be highly adequate at the time that therapy was discontinued, but no follow up evaluation could be made to determine the permanence of these gains.

D.   *Evaluation of approach.* For pushing to be effective, the push must be perfectly synchronized with the onset of voice. One of the primitive functions of the larynx is its valve closing during particular physiologic states of the organism, such as during heavy physical effort. The pushing approach, which requires the person to use the upper extremities in a forceful pushing manner, is usually accompanied by glottal closing. This glottal closure is observed in heavy lifting efforts, which are frequently accompanied by primitive vocalizations, indicating relatively firm approximation of the vocal folds. When the patient employs intentional vocalization timed with primitive sphincteric closure, the result is often a phonation of good loudness and quality. Pushing exercises have been found useful for hyperfunctional voice conditions and paralytic conditions by Froeschels, Kastein, and Weiss (1955) and Brodnitz (1971).

Pushing exercises should be thought of as only a facilitating approach for producing firmer vocal fold approximation, which will result in a louder, more resonant voice. Once the patient is able to match his or her "pushing" voice without pushing, the exercises should be progressively minimized. The pushing method is useful for the occasional patient with a hypofunctional, "wornout" voice. The method provides such a patient with an immediate increase in both loudness and quality. It should be remembered, however, that most hypofunctional voices have developed that way after prolonged periods of vocal hyperfunction. Therefore, once the stronger voice has been elicited with pushing, the clinician should seek to maintain the same vocal quality and loudness without the pushing, employing other therapy approaches.

XXII.   RELAXATION

A.   *Kinds of problems for which approach is useful.* Most dysphonias and laryngeal pathologies are related to prolonged and continued vocal hyperfunction, the reduction of which is a frequent goal in voice therapy. It does not necessarily follow, however, that with all these hyperfunctional problems we teach general body relaxation. Using such methods as the chewing approach or the yawnsigh approach achieves vocal tract relaxation without working on it systemically. It is usually futile in therapy to imply to tense patients that if they would "just relax," all would be well. If patients could relax, they would; if their tension did not in fact serve them in some way, they would get rid of it. A certain amount of psychic tension and muscle tonus is normal and healthy, of course, but there are individuals who overreact to their environmental stresses; instead of "running at a slow idle," they are like "fast idle engines," expending far more energy and effort than the situation requires. By relaxation, therefore, we mean a realistic responsiveness to the environment with a minimum of needless energy expended. Some, but certainly not all, voice patients profit from a therapy program designed to reduce unnecessary tension by using relaxation techniques. Relaxation procedures focused on breathing and speaking have been found effective as developed by Jacobson (1957), Filter (1974), Mc-Closkey (1977), and Wilson (1979). Whenever excessive tension appears to contribute to a voice problem, direct work on relaxing tension in the patient's arms, chest, neck, and oral and pharyngeal cavities may be helpful.

B.   *Procedural aspects of approach.*

1.   The classical method of differential relaxation might be explained to the patient and applied. Under differential relaxation, the patient concentrates on a particular site of the body, deliberately relaxing and tensing certain muscles, discriminating between muscle contraction and relaxation. The typical procedure here is to have the patient begin distally, away from the body, with the fingers or the toes. Once the patient feels the tightness of contraction and the heaviness of relaxation at the beginning site, he or she moves "up" the limb (on to the feet or hands, and thence to the legs or arms), repeating at each site the tightness-heaviness discrimination. Once the torso is reached, the voice patient should include the chest, neck, "voice box," throat, and on through the mouth and parts of the face. With some patients, we start the distal analysis with the head, beginning with the scalp and then going to the forehead, eyes, facial muscles, lips, jaw, tongue, palate, throat, larynx, neck, and so on. Some practice in this progressive relaxation technique can produce remarkably relaxed states in very tense patients.

2.   The clinician may wish to use biofeedback in teaching relaxation. If so, he or she should use facilitating approach 2, biofeedback (see p. 119), in conjunction with other relaxation procedures.

3.   Wolpe (1973) combines relaxation, once it is taught, with hierarchy analysis (facilitating technique 14). The patient responds to certain tension-producing cues by deliberately employing a relaxed response, such as a feeling of heaviness in certain parts of the body, and this in turn enables him or

her to maintain a degree of relaxation despite the presence of anxiety-provoking stimuli.

4. Head rotation might be introduced as a technique for relaxing components of the vocal tract. The approach is used in this way: The patient sits in a backless chair, dropping the head forward to the chest; the patient then ''flops'' his or her head across to the right shoulder, and then lifts it, again flopping it (the neck is here extended), along the back and across to the left shoulder; he or she then returns to the anterior head-down-on-chest position and repeats the cycle, rolling the head in a circular fashion. A few patients will not find head rotation relaxing, but most will feel the heaviness of the movement and experience definite relaxation in the neck. For this latter group, once the patient reports neck relaxation, he or she should be asked to phonate an ''ah'' as the head is rolled. The relaxed phonation might be recorded and then analyzed in terms of how it sounds in comparison to the patient's other phonations.

5. Open-throat relaxation can also be used. Have the patient lower his head slightly toward the chest and make an easy, open, prolonged yawn, concentrating on what the yawn feels like in the throat. The yawn should yield conscious sensations of an open throat during the prolonged inhalation. If the patient reports that he can feel this open-throat sensation, ask him to prolong an ''ah,'' capturing and maintaining the same feeling experienced during the yawn. Any relaxed phonations produced under these conditions should be recorded and used as target voice models for the patient. Encourage the patient to comment and think about the relaxed throat sensations experienced during the yawn.

6. In D. K. Wilson's *Voice Problems of Children* (1979, pp. 127–130) is an excellent presentation on various relaxation procedures for use with children, developed by Wilson and other authors, which seem to have equal applicability to adults. Most of the procedures described can provide the patient with immediate experience of increased relaxation and reduced tension associated with speaking.

7. Ask the patient to think of a setting he or she has experienced, or perhaps imagined as the ultimate in relaxation. Different patients will use different kinds of imagery here. For example, one patient thought of lying in a hammock, but for another person the suggestion of lying in a hammock produced a set of anxious responses. Settings typically thought of as relaxed are lying on a rug at night in front of a blazing fire, floating on a lake, fishing while lying in a rowboat, lying down in bed, and so on. The setting the patient thinks of should be studied and analyzed; eventually, the patient should try to capture the relaxed feelings he im-

agines he might have, or may actually have experienced, in such a setting. With some practice—and some tolerance for initial failure in recapturing the relaxed mood—the average patient will be able to find a setting or two that he or she can recreate in his or her imagination and use in future tense situations.

C.   *Typical case history showing utilization of approach.* M. Y., a thirty-four-year-old missile engineer, developed transient periods of severe dysphonia when talking to certain people. At other times, particularly in his professional work, he experienced normal voice. Mirror laryngoscopy revealed a normal larynx. During the voice interview, the speech pathologist was impressed by the man's general nervousness and apparently poor self-concept. In exploring the area of interpersonal relationships, the patient confided that in the last year he had seen two psychiatrists periodically, but had experienced no relief from his tension. Further exploration of the settings in which his voice was most dysphonic revealed that his biggest problem was in talking to store clerks, garage men, and persons who did physical labor; some of his more relaxed experiences included giving speeches and giving work instructions to his colleagues. Subsequent voice therapy included progressive relaxation. Once relaxed behavior was achieved, the patient developed a hierarchy of situations, beginning with those in which he felt most relaxed (giving instructions to colleagues) and proceeding to those in which he experienced the most tension (talking with car mechanics). After some practice, the patient was able to recognize various cues that signaled increasing tension. Once such a cue occurred, he would employ a relaxation response, which more often than not enabled him to maintain normal phonation in situations that had previously induced dysphonia. As this consciously induced response continued to be successful, the patient reported greater confidence in approaching the previously tense situations, knowing he would experience little or no voice difficulty. Voice therapy was terminated after eleven weeks, with the patient reporting only occasional difficulty in phonating in isolated situations, and developing increased self-confidence in all situations.

D.   *Evaluation of approach.* While many psychological and psychiatric therapists today advocate symptomatic therapy for the relief of psychological tension, there is the other view that symptomatic therapy treats only the symptom and not the true cause of the disorder. Representing the latter view, Murphy (1964) writes

> To focus therapeutic energy on the tensions as such does not bring us closer to the factors producing the tensions. Therefore, any effort to erase tension and to induce relaxation directly is likely to be only temporarily effective or to fail altogether. (p. 118)

Some of the thinking supporting the other view, direct symptom modification, is presented in Chapter 1 of this text and need not be repeated here. It should be added, however, that there appears to be a growing body of clinicians who feel that direct symptom modification, such as teaching relaxed responses to replace previous tense responses, breaks up the circular kind of behavior that characterizes so much of what we do as human beings; that is, we respond in a certain way now because we responded in the same way before. Aronson (1980) feels that relaxation is a required part of voice therapy for both organic and nonorganic voice disorders:

> *All patients with voice disorders, regardless of etiology, should be tested for excess musculoskeletal tension, either as a primary or as a secondary cause of dysphonia.* The degree of voice improvement following therapy for musculoskeletal tension is directly proportional to the contribution of the musculoskeletal tension to the dysphonia or aphonia. (p. 198)

It appears that even a slight decrease of unnecessary vocal tract tension replaced by an increase in relaxation has a positive influence in producing a more relaxed, optimum phonation.

XXIII. RESPIRATION TRAINING

A. *Kinds of problems for which approach is useful.* Back in the first part of the twentieth century, some of the earliest articles about voice therapy supported the view that most voice disorders were related to poor breathing patterns—and, indeed, the singing teacher and the dramatic coach to this day include breathing exercises and breathing technique as part of their instruction. The modern-day voice clinician, whether a laryngologist or a speech pathologist, places far less emphasis on faulty respiration than his or her predecessors did. However, there are some voice patients, described in earlier chapters, who profit from some attention given to improving their control of respiration, especially their control of the expiratory phase of the breathing cycle. While general improvement in total respiration, such as an improvement in vital capacity, appears to have little effect on the voice, any marked departure in the inspiratory-expiratory cycle may produce noticeable voice alterations. As Greene (1980) writes:

> I am quite unable to envisage how to teach control of expiration and adjustment of glottal resistance without recourse to, first, obtaining an adequate intake of air and, secondly, by training of expiration in production of short and long vowels of varying pitch, volume and resonance, thus reinforcing the patient's awareness of how he is producing voice. (pp. 182–183)

B. *Procedural aspects of approach.*

1. Give the patient a simple explanation of phonatory physiology, emphasizing that it is the flow of the outgoing air stream that sets the approximated vocal folds into vibration. If the patient demonstrates a problem in this area (and work on respiration should be avoided if no problem exists), the problem and what can be done about it should be described by the clinician.

2. Demonstrate a slightly exaggerated breath, as used in sighing. The sigh is characterized by a slightly larger-than-usual inhalation followed by a prolonged open-mouth exhalation. The type of breath used to produce the sigh can be described to the patient as the ''breath of well-being,'' the kind of easy breath one might take when comfortable or happy—the sigh of contentment.

3. Demonstrate the quick inhalation and prolonged exhalation needed for a normal speaking task. Take a normal breath and count slowly from one to five on one exhalation. See if the patient can do this; if he or she can, extend the count by one number each time, at the rate of approximately one number per half second. This activity can be continued until the patient is able to use his or her ''best'' phonation during the number counts. Any sacrifice of vocal quality should be avoided, and the number count should never be extended beyond the point where good quality can be maintained.

4. Practice extending an even phonation such as an /a/ or similar open vowel, for as long as possible without any noticeable phonation break or change of quality. Take a baseline measurement in the beginning, such as number of seconds the phonation can be maintained, and see whether this can be extended with practice. Avoid asking the patient to ''take in a big breath''; rather, ask him or her to take in a normal breath of well-being, initiating a lightly phonated sigh on exhalation. See if the patient can extend this for five seconds. If so, progressively increase the extension, to eight, twelve, fifteen, and finally twenty seconds. The voice patient who can hold on to an extended phonation of a vowel for twenty seconds has certainly exhibited good breath control for purposes of voice. Such a patient would not have to work on breath control per se, but he or she might want to combine work on exhalation control with such approaches as hierarchy analysis (to see if he or she can maintain such good breath control under varying moments of stress).

5. Select from various voice and articulation books reading materials designed to help develop breath control. Give special attention to beginning phonation as soon after inhalation as possible, not wasting a lot of the outgoing air stream before phonating. Practice quick inhalations between

phrases and sentences, taking care not to take "a big breath."

6. With young children who need breathing work, the clinician might begin with nonverbal exhalations. One way to work on breathing exhalation with little children is to use a pinwheel, which lends itself naturally to the game, "How long can you keep the pinwheel spinning?" With practice, the child will be able to extend the length of his or her exhalations (the length of time the pinwheel spins). Another method of enhancing exhalation control is to place a piece of tissue paper against a wall, begin blowing on it to keep it in place when the fingers are removed, and keep blowing on it to see how long it can be kept in place. Both the pinwheel and tissue-paper exercises lend themselves to timing measurements; these measurements should be made and plotted graphically for the child; when a certain target length of time is reached, the activity can be stopped.

7. When the clinician working with a singer, actor, or lecturer decides that some formal respiration training should be given, the following steps might be taken:

    a) Discuss the importance of good posture, for normal posture is one of the best facilitators of normal breathing. Any real departure from good posture, such as leaning forward with the head (kyphosis), may contribute to faulty breathing.

    b) Demonstrate abdominal-diaphragmatic breathing. First, have the subject lie supine, with his or her hands on the abdomen, directly under the rib cage. In this position, there will be observable distention of the abdomen upon inspiration. The downward excursion of the diaphragm, which increases the vertical dimension of the chest, cannot be viewed directly (since the diaphragm attachments are behind and inside the ribs); its effect can only be viewed by the outward displacement of the abdomen. On expiration, as the diaphragm ascends, the abdominal distention lessens. In this form of breathing, then, the patient should try deliberately to relax the abdominal muscles during inspiration and contract them during exhalation. If this can be done successfully in the supine position, the patient should try to duplicate the procedure while standing with the back flat against a wall. Continuing to clasp his or her hands on the abdomen in the beginning will help the patient develop some awareness of the difference between abdominal relaxation-distention and abdominal contraction-flattening. As soon as the subject learns to breathe by this relaxation—contraction of the abdominal muscles—introduce some phonation activities to be done on expiration. The voice patient who has been speaking "from the level of his or her throat," without adequate breath support, will often "feel" the difference that a bigger breath makes only when phonation is added. The voice patient who needed respiration training in the first place needs to have respiration and phonation combined into practice activities as soon as possible.

8. For serious problems in respiration, often related to illnesses like emphysema or bronchial asthma, the voice clinician should enlist the help of other specialties for aiding the patient in improving respiratory efficiency. Physical therapists, inhalation therapists, and pulmonary medical specialists may have the expertise required for assisting the patient. The voice clinician can often offer the patient ways of phrasing and using expiratory control to better match what the patient is trying to say, supplementing the respiration therapy of these other specialists. For example, we have coordinated a breathing-for-speech program for quadriplegic patients, in which the speech pathologist and the physical therapist work closely with the patient, improving both general respiration and expiratory control for speech phrasing and better voice.

C. *Typical case history showing utilization of approach.* M. M., a twenty-two-year-old first-grade teacher, complained of losing her voice at the end of each teaching day. While mirror laryngoscopy found her to have a normal larynx, voice testing revealed that most of the time she spoke on supplemental air. She seemed to take in an adequate inhalation, only to exhale a major part of it before beginning to phonate. Much of her phonation appeared to be forced, with inadequate air flow behind it. Voice therapy focused on introducing her to the necessity of "getting some air behind her voice." First the myoelastic theory of phonation was demonstrated. Then the method of abdominal-diaphragmatic breathing was demonstrated, and the patient was instructed in its use. Her roommate was also instructed in the method, so that she could help the patient during home-practice periods. Exhalation-phonation exercises were initiated, wherein the patient would practice extending both phonations and number counts on one breath. After six weeks of twice-weekly voice therapy and home practice, the patient was able to employ adequate breathing methods, and her improved breathing produced a louder voice of better quality, which did not tire with daily teaching use. Before therapy was concluded, however, the patient was in a severe automobile accident, requiring many months of hospitalization. Thus, no long-term followup was possible to see if her improved voice had been maintained.

D. *Evaluation of approach.* One has only to scan early books about speech remediation toward the beginning of this century to quickly see the great focus that was given to respiration training for many speech and voice disorders. The European-trained phoniatrist and clinician, according to Greene (1980), continues to give more emphasis to respiration training than most American voice clinicians. Greene writes that "the swing away from breathing techniques arises, it seems, out of the experimental research regarding air flow through the glottis and study of the aerodynamics of phonation" (p. 181). There are a number of voice patients who profit from some training in respiration, particularly with focus on getting air into the lungs quickly and efficiently while learning to parcel out an extended expiratory flow. Gordon, Morton, and Simpson (1978) found in their treatment of functional dysphonia that almost 80 percent of their patients had demonstrated serious problems in maintaining expiratory air flow. Determination of adequacy of respiration and expiratory control should be an important part of the voice evaluation, and those patients demonstrating some respiration problem may require breathing work as part of their overall voice therapy.

XXIV.   VOICE REST

    A.   *Kinds of problems for which approach is useful.* Voice rest is indicated in cases of acute laryngitis or after surgery involving the larynx. Voice rest is of little benefit to the various hyperfunctional pathologies of voice, because once the patient resumes his or her faulty phonation patterns, the dysphonia and related pathologies may return. For the patient with acute laryngitis, infectious or traumatic in etiology, voice rest does prevent further irritation of already irritated folds, and the cessation of irritation does promote healing. After a surgical procedure, such as the removal of polyps or nodules, it is essential that the irritated glottal surfaces be free of vibration, and this can only be accomplished by total cessation of voicing. The voice rest prescribed after surgery should always be as brief as possible, perhaps three to seven days in the case of the average surgery, and two weeks of maximum for something like the removal of rather large polyps. The length of voice rest after surgery is the decision of the surgeon. There are occasional patients with vocal hyperfunction who, as part of their total treatment, benefit from a few hours of self-imposed voice rest each day. If the clinician and the patient have identified periods of vocal excess, often where the patient speaks unnecessarily and without stopping, ceasing such periods of phonation during a part of the day may help the patient give the vocal mechanism a little rest from overuse.

    B.   *Procedural aspects of approach.*

        1.   If voice rest is to be initiated, it must be complete. Explain the need for voice rest to the patient, insisting that he or she *not even whisper.* It is almost impossible for anyone to whisper

without some glottal closure, despite evidence that the patient is producing his or her whisper orally or buccally. For this reason, total abstention from speech should be enforced. Communication will have to rely on gesture or writing.

2. The patient should also be counseled about no coughing, throat clearing, or laughing. Any of these phonations will have the same deleterious effect as speech.

3. Some patients with vocal hyperfunction, particularly adult patients, may profit from situational voice rest. For example, perhaps the patient is asked not to use voice each morning but is able to resume speaking the rest of the day. The clinician should identify with the patient those situations where voice rest might be initiated. For example, a professional singer found if she avoided talking several hours before her evening performance, she had a better-sounding voice.

C. *Typical case history showing utilization of approach.* Claude B., a six-year-old boy, was found by his laryngologist to have bilateral vocal nodules. He was subsequently placed on voice rest in an attempt to make the nodules disappear. The boy followed the physician's instructions completely, making no attempt to whisper or use voice. He communicated well, completely by gesture. The family elected not to return to the doctor, and the boy unfortunately continued his voice rest for almost five months. He was subsequently treated by a school speech-language pathologist for his problem of "functional aphonia." After two therapy sessions, the boy "found" his voice again and was able to speak with normal voice. Incidentally, on follow-up consultation at a university hospital clinic, his bilateral nodules had disappeared. This case illustrates well how even a young child can learn to follow complete voice rest, but it also illustrates one danger of prolonged voice rest, that is, the loss of set for phonation with a resulting aphonia even after "wanting" to resume voice.

D. *Evaluation of approach.* The primary value of voice rest is in its use for individuals who have acute laryngitis or for patients following laryngeal trauma or surgery. It is occasionally used as a temporary measure to reduce the amount of phonation one is doing; voice rest each day for a period of several hours may sometimes be of value for an occasional patient. Voice rest should not be used as a treatment for most problems of vocal hyperfunction; after resuming phonation, the individual will usually revert back to his or her hyperfunctional way of talking. However voice rest is used, it only appears effective when the individual makes no attempt to speak, avoiding whispering and using only gestures and writing for communication. Voice rest is a difficult task to impose on anyone and should only be used when it appears absolutely necessary.

XXV.   YAWN–SIGH APPROACH

    A.   *Kinds of problems for which approach is useful.* Over the years that this writer has applied various facilitating approaches for problems of vocal hyperfunction, the yawn-sigh approach has been found to be consistently useful. It helps the patient produce an easy voice with very little effort. For problems of functional dysphonia with no laryngeal pathology or with problems of nodules, polyps, or fold thickening, the approach is most helpful. For the patient who needs to develop an easier glottal attack, the approach usually works. Yawn-sigh has been found useful in a vocal hygiene program developed for the patient who desires to develop optimal phonation with far less effort (Boone, 1980b). Yawn-sigh is easily combined with many of the other facilitating approaches and is, therefore, rarely used alone.

    B.   *Procedural aspects of approach.*

        1.   With children we give an explanation to the child using the pictures and narrative from our voice program (Boone, 1980a). Showing the child the appropriate pictures, we read

> This girl usually has a tight mouth. She uses too much effort when she speaks. Her voice does not sound good. (Demonstrate) This girl is opening her mouth wide and yawning. She is very relaxed. When she sighs at the end of the yawn, it will be her best voice. (p. 127)

        2.   With teen-agers and adults we explain generally the physiology of a yawn, that is, that a yawn represents a prolonged inspiration with maximum widening of the supraglottal airways (characterized by a wide, stretching, opening of the mouth). Then we demonstrate a yawn and talk about what the yawn feels like.

        3.   After the patient has yawned, following the clinician's example, ask the patient to yawn again and then to exhale gently with a light phonation. In doing this, many patients are able to feel an easy phonation, often for the first time.

        4.   Once the yawn-phonation is easily achieved, instruct the patient to say words beginning with /h/ or with open-mouthed vowels, one word per yawn in the beginning, followed eventually by four or five words on one exhalation.

        5.   Demonstrate for the patient the sigh phase of the exercise, that is, the prolonged, easy, open-mouthed exhalation after the yawn. Then, omitting the yawn entirely, demonstrate a quick, normal, open-mouthed inhalation followed by the prolonged open-mouthed sigh.

        6.   As soon as the patient can produce a relaxed sigh, have him or her say the word *hah* after beginning the sigh. Follow this with a series of words beginning with the glottal /h/. Addi-

tional words for practice after the sigh should begin with middle and low vowels. Care should be given to blending in, toward the middle of the sigh, an easy, relaxed, relatively soft phonation. This blending of the phonation into the sigh is often difficult for the patient initially, but is the most vital part of the approach for the elimination of hard glottal contacts.

7.   Finally, once the yawn-sigh approach is well developed, have the patient think of the relaxed oral feeling it provides. Eventually, he or she will be able to maintain a relaxed phonation simply by imagining the approach.

C.   *Typical case history showing utilization of approach.* Jerry A., a forty-seven-year-old manufacturer's representative, had a two-year history of vocal fatigue, often losing his voice toward the end of the work day. After a two-week period of increasing dysphonia and slight pain on the left side of the neck, the man was found by a consulting laryngologist to have "slight redness and edema on both vocal processes." The subsequent voice evaluation found him to speak with pronounced hard glottal attack in an attempt to "force out his voice over his dysphonia." By using the yawn-sigh approach, the patient was able to demonstrate a clear phonation with relatively good resonance. His yawn-sigh phonations were recorded on loop tape and fed back to him as the voice model he should imitate. Because the patient reported some stress in certain work situations, the hierarchy analysis approach (facilitating technique 14) was used, isolating those situations in which he felt relaxed and those in which he experienced tension. Thereafter, whenever he was aware of tense situational cues, he employed the yawn-sigh method to maintain relaxed phonation. Combining yawn-sigh with hierarchy analysis proved to be an excellent symptomatic approach for this patient, as his voice cleared markedly with no recurrence of the periodic aphonia. Twice-weekly therapy was terminated after twenty-two weeks, with the patient demonstrating a normal voice and a normal laryngeal mechanism.

D.   *Evaluation of approach.* The yawn-sigh is another approach that makes use of a normal, vegetative function, at which time the patient can phonate in a more natural, relaxed manner. Luchsinger and Arnold (1965) describe yawning as a "prolonged and deepened inspiration with maximal widening of the upper airways. The act of yawning is an *inborn reflex pattern.* . . ." (p. 152). The advantage of the yawn as a prelude to phonation is that during the initial stages of the yawn, the oral-pharynx is open and relaxed. With but little practice, the average patient can produce a relaxed, easy phonation if he or she couples the phonation with a yawn. The sigh, a relaxed and extended exhalation, provides an excellent environment for the initiation of an easy phonation. As the patient extends his or her sigh, he or she begins a soft phonation with very gentle approximation of the vocal folds. This easy phonation is often in sharp contrast to the hard, abrupt type he or she may regularly use.

SUMMARY

Successful voice therapy requires that the clinician identify the patient's aversive vocal behaviors and subsequently reduce the occurrence of such abuses-misuses. Voice therapy for most voice problems requires continuous assessment of what the patient is able to do vocally. By using various therapy approaches as diagnostic probes, the clinician searches for the best voice the patient is able to produce. Twenty-five facilitating approaches have been presented, with specific procedures of application followed by an illustrative case history showing the particular effects of each approach.

6
Voice Therapy for Special Problems

Not all problems of voice are related to vocal hyperfunction. Some particular problems, such as spastic dysphonia, require distinctive management and individualized voice therapy. In this chapter we shall consider voice therapy for the hard-of-hearing and deaf; for problems of dysarthria, aphonia, ventricular phonation, spastic dysphonia, vocal fold paralysis; for problems related to aging, falsetto and puberphonia, diplophonia, pitch breaks, and phonation breaks. The chapter concludes with a vocal hygiene program applicable for any serious user of voice and for most of our patients with voice problems.

VOICE THERAPY FOR THE HARD-OF-HEARING AND DEAF

Voice problems are commonly observed in children and adults with severe hearing loss or deafness. The greater the hearing loss, the greater the likelihood of voice problems related to elevated pitch, to faulty resonance, and to variations in loudness. Ling (1976) stresses that most voice problems can be minimized in the hearing-impaired child in ''all except totally deaf children if hearing aids are worn'' (p. 217). Early amplification and proper teaching methods can do much to help the young hard-of-hearing or deaf child develop relatively normal voicing patterns. The majority of oral deaf children and adults continue, unfortunately, to show symptoms of faulty voice resonance (Boone, 1966; Monsen, Engebretson, and Vernula, 1979), elevations of pitch (Nickerson, 1975; Wilson, 1979), and variations in loudness (Ling, 1976; Monsen, 1978). The poor voices frequently heard among the deaf, sometimes unwisely called ''deaf speech,'' can frequently be improved by direct work on some of the symptoms. Because of the primary role of voice in the production of the suprasegmentals of language and in particular in the prosodic aspect of language (Ross and Mesulam, 1979), the earlier the clinical intervention to correct voice differences, the greater the impact on communication effectiveness.

Pitch Changes.   While there is some controversy over whether or not very young deaf children exhibit elevated fundamental frequencies, there appears to be common agreement (Boone, 1966; Ling, 1976; Wilson, 1979) that as deaf children get older, their voices appear inappropriately high in pitch when compared with normal hearing children. Wilson, in his excellent chapter on "Voice Problems of Children with Hearing Losses" (*Voice Problems in Children,* Second Edition, Baltimore: The Williams and Wilkins Co., 1979), develops useful procedures for both changing pitch levels and for working on the changing pitch levels of intonation. Apparently, the lowering of voice pitch as one moves from childhood through adolescence and then to adulthood requires some acoustic monitoring to match one's normal peer group. The deaf child, or adult, who lacks this auditory feedback appears to need some external guidance in using the acceptable pitch levels of his or her age peers. What are some of the things that the teacher of the deaf or the voice clinician can do to help the deaf child develop a normally pitched voice as he or she grows older?

Any attempt to change the pitch level of a deaf child must begin with a discussion about the need for such a change. This discussion should focus on the tested fundamental frequency of the child as compared to normative values for the child's age and sex. The inventive clinician might prepare a chart or graph demonstrating for the child where his pitch is and where it ought to be. Lacking an adequate auditory model for his or her pitch target, the deaf child must rely on various visual devices as signals for whether his or her voice pitch is too high or too low. Instruments such as the Tonar II, Tunemaster III, and Visi-Pitch can be used by the clinician with the deaf child who needs feedback about his or her ongoing pitch level. Oscillograph display panels can isolate the child's fundamental frequency and provide a locked-in display pattern of the frequency he or she has just spoken. Most clinical programs working with deaf children and adults seem to lack the hardware needed for providing individuals with continuous feedback about their pitch levels.

Innovative clinicians, however, have found several effective ways of making the deaf child or adult aware of pitch level and possible pitch variability. One useful device for altering the pitch level of the deaf is to provide "cue arrows" pointing in the desired direction of pitch change. For example, for the typical deaf child attempting to lower the voice pitch, cards should be printed with an arrow pointing down. These cards should be placed wherever possible in the child's environment—in the wallet, on the bureau or desk, and so on. Also, the classroom teacher and voice clinician can give the child finger cues by pointing toward the floor. Another method for developing an altered pitch level is to have the child place his or her fingers lightly on the larynx and feel the downward excursion of the larynx during lower pitch productions and the upward excursion during higher ones. The ideal or optimum pitch produces very little vertical movement. Any noticeable upward excursion of the larynx, except during swallowing, will immediately signal to the child that he or she may be speaking at an inappropriately high pitch level. In therapy, once an appropriate pitch level has been established, the child may be asked to read aloud for a specified time period, placing his or her fingers lightly on the larynx and trying to read so as not to feel any downward or upward movements.

Following any practice period using a desirable pitch level, there should be some consideration of what that new pitch level feels like. The deaf voice patient should try to analyze what he or she is doing while producing a good pitch level, particularly what is happening to his or her breathing, what the throat feels like, what the tongue is doing, how open the mouth is, and so on. The clinician should not ask such vague questions as, "What does it feel like?" for this can only be followed by a vague, useless response. Of more use would be, "Did you feel any difference in your throat? If so, can you describe it?" While the tactual, kinesthetic, and proprioceptive feedback systems give us only vague information about what we are doing when we speak, for the deaf person, who lacks adequate auditory feedback, they are vital and must be used. Any successful alteration of pitch production, therefore, must be followed by some attempt by the patient to analyze what he or she has produced. In the beginning, the deaf child attempting to modify his or her voice will need some guidance in developing these analytic abilities.

It appears that improving an inappropriate pitch level is one task that can be achieved by the average deaf child or adult. When the need for changing (usually lowering) the voice pitch is pointed out to the patients, they are able to do a great deal by themselves by using a pitch meter or some form of visual feedback system that can signal the inappropriateness of a pitch production. It might be added that since the average pitch level of most voices is under 250 cps, as much low-frequency amplification should be provided as possible. If deaf children or adults have any residual hearing available to them, it is usually the lower frequency range, below 250 cps, and amplification here might well permit them to achieve some auditory monitoring of their own fundamental frequencies. The clinician should make use of any self-hearing available, since this will prove most helpful in the deaf individual's struggle to alter his pitch level.

Of the facilitating techniques described in Chapter 5, the following may be useful in altering pitch levels of deaf children and adults: altering tongue position (1), chewing (5), digital manipulation (6), establishing new pitch (10), open mouth (18), relaxation (22), respiration (23), and yawn-sigh (25).

Resonance. The typical voice of the deaf child who has had no training in developing a good voice seems to be characterized by alterations in nasal resonance, often accompanied by excessive pharyngeal resonance, producing the cul-de-sac voice. It would appear that the major contributing factor for these resonance alterations is the excessive posterior posturing of the tongue in the hypopharynx, producing a marked lowering of the second formant (Boone, 1966; Monsen, 1976). The tongue is drawn back into the hypopharynx, which produces the cul-de-sac resonance focus in the hypopharynx, creating the peculiar resonance heard in deaf speakers; this back resonance sounds similar to what is sometimes heard in the resonance of speakers with athetoid cerebral palsy, or oral verbal apraxia. The cul-de-sac voice has a back focus to it. In addition, the hard-of-hearing or deaf child or adult may demonstrate marked variations in nasal resonance, with too much nasal focus (hypernasality) or insufficient nasal resonance (denasality); such nasal resonance variations may be due in part to the posterior carriage of the tongue, as well as to the inability to monitor acoustically the nasalization characteristic of the normal speaker. In the few cinefluorographic studies focused on velopharyngeal closure in deaf speakers, both Crouter (1962) and McClumpha (1966) found that posterior tongue carriage and insufficient velopharyngeal closure were typical findings among deaf speakers. Ling feels that with early amplification and using the teaching model proposed in his 1976 text that excessive nasalization can be avoided. It does appear possible to minimize variations in resonance by direct symptom modification with young children before faulty resonance patterns become well established.

Some of the methods described in Chapter 5 under facilitating technique 1, altering tongue position, are applicable in promoting a more forward carriage of the tongue in deaf children. The following quotation from an earlier work (Boone, 1966) may provide the clinician with helpful methodology for improving the resonance characteristics of a deaf speaker's voice:

Emphasis given to articulation training, particularly for tongue-alveolar sounds such as /t/, /d/, /s/, and /z/ will often promote a higher, forward carriage of the tongue. It would be particularly beneficial to require the child to whisper a rapid series of phonemes such as "ta, ta, ta, ta, ta," etc. The whispered alveolar tongue-tip sounds appear to give the deaf child a tactual feeling of "front-of-the-mouth" speech. A drill of about five minutes duration using alveolar tongue-tip sounds in a rapid series four or five times daily appears to be an effective method of developing a higher, more forward carriage of the tongue. The child follows the whispered production of these phonemes by adding voice. Usually the teacher can hear the difference in the resonance quality of the child's "ta, ta" productions as contrasted to his general conversational voice quality. Sometimes the child himself "feels" a difference when he achieves good oral resonance which then seems to give him the muscle "set" required for increased oral resonance.

It would appear that the teacher can best help the child develop oral resonance by using speech drills rather than exercises per se. It would appear that little can be achieved by giving the child such things as isolated respiration training, exercises for parts of the oral mechanism, etc. Rather, the use of speech materials appears to be most beneficial in increasing oral resonance. The following consonants would lend themselves well for front-of-mouth-resonance: /w/, /wh/, /p/, /b/, /f/, /v/, /θ/, /ɝ/, /t/, /d/, /s/, /z/, and /l/. The following vowels have a high oral focus and might lend themselves well for practice sessions coupled with the above consonants: /i/ as in deed, /ɪ/ as in bit, /e/ as in bait, /ɛ/ as in set, /æ/ as in bat. (p. 689)

Any instrument that can provide the deaf speaker visual feedback specific to his or her relative oral-nasal resonance can be most useful. One such useful instrument is the Tonar II (Fletcher and Daly, 1976), which when used with the deaf provides feedback specific to relative oral and nasal resonance. The normal range of nasality as measured on the Tonar is between 5 and 20 percent if the consonants /m/, /n/, and /ŋ/ are eliminated from the test passage. Denasality would register less than 5 percent; efforts to make the reading above 5 percent would lessen the denasality sound. While the majority of deaf patients are denasal, some individuals demonstrate true hypernasality. Hypernasality on the Tonar is said to exist if levels excluding the three nasal consonants exceed 20 percent. The Tonar is particularly effective as a therapy instrument for these patients, providing direct feedback specific to hypernasality. Once the deaf child is able to produce an oral-sounding voice, the clinician should help him or her become aware of the contrast between his or her oral and pharyngeal resonance. The contrasting resonances should be produced repeatedly by patients until they develop the ability to self-monitor what they are doing when they produce good oral resonance. Through practice in producing front-of-the-mouth phonemes, the patient must develop an awareness of what it feels like to use the lips, the tongue against the alveolar process, and so forth. It would appear that front tongue positioning is best encouraged by intensive *speech* drills, requiring the subject to produce a rapid series of high front consonants and vowels (tongue exercises exclusive of speech practice seem to be ineffective here). The following facilitating techniques, described in Chapter 5, are also helpful in establishing better vocal resonance in the deaf: altering tongue position (1); chewing (5), negative practice (19), once good resonance has been established; open-mouth (18); relaxation (22); respiration (23); and yawn-sigh (25).

Excessive Loudness.   Because of the inability to monitor loudness of the voice, the typical deaf individual speaks too loud. In investigation of forty-four deaf children, compared with forty-four normal hearing children, Boone, (1966) found excessive loudness prominent among the deaf speakers as well as elevations in pitch, cul-de-sac resonance, and a speaking rate that was excessively slow. Excessive expiratory air flow, producing symptoms of excessive loudness, was further altered by the deaf children's tendency to speak with prolonged duration and marked diphthongizations. Forner and Hixon (1977), in their study of respiratory kinematics in ten deaf young adults, males ranging from nineteen to twenty-four years, found that although the deaf men demonstrated normal tidal volumes, they exhibited marked variation in expiratory control. They would often begin speaking late in the tidal expiration and would seldom match their linguistic message with a sustained and controlled expiration. The deaf males would often take breath refills or exhibit breath holding while attempting to produce connected speech on one expiratory utterance.

Most deaf speakers can profit from voice therapy that develops easy onset of phonation matched with the beginning of the expiratory cycle. Instruments, like the Visi-Pitch, which can provide the deaf speaker with an oscillographic display specific to voice intensity, can often provide the necessary feedback the speaker needs to develop a match between easy onset of voice with the beginning of tidal expiration at loudness levels that are appropriate. Ling (1976) states that normal hearing people, such as teachers, need to provide the deaf child with monitoring specific to appropriateness of loudness. The steps outlined in Chapter 5 specific to change of loudness (3) work well with hard-of-hearing youngsters and adults, particularly when supplemented by voice intensity feedback devices such as the Voice Loudness Indicator (1980), the Visi-Pitch (1980), or the typical VU-meter from a speech audiometer or audio tape recorder.

Voice Therapy for Patients with Dysarthria

Most patients with dysarthria show some variations in voice. *Dysarthria* is observed in changes in speech and voice secondary to central nervous system (CNS) or peripheral nervous system (PNS) involvement of muscles of respiration, phonation, and speech. The degree and type of dysarthric symptom is dependent on where the particular nervous system disease or disorder is located. The most common cause of dysarthria comes from cerebral vascular accidents (CVAs) where the patient experiences a stroke (thrombosis, embolus, or hemorrhage) resulting in weakness or paralysis of muscles essential for normal speech. Other causes of dysarthria may include trauma to the nervous system, tumors, and degenerative diseases (like muscular dystrophy or Parkinson's disease). Aronson (1980) described six types of dysarthria which may be interpreted as:

Flaccid. "Flaccid (meaning flabby) label implies weakness, lack of normal muscle tone, and reduced or absent type reflexes" (p. 415). We usually see this kind of lesion when the injury is to the brain stem and the cranial nuclei or in the peripheral nerve itself, causing a lower motor neuron type lesion.

Spastic. The lesion is in the pyramidal or extrapyramidal systems (cortical or subcortical) causing "muscular weakness, greater than normal muscular tone, slow movements, limited range of motion, and hyperactive reflexes" (p. 421). This is the most common type of dysarthria we see in the patient who has had a CVA.

Ataxic. This is a relatively rare dysarthria where the damage is confined to the cerebellum, causing "difficulties in regulating force, speed, range, timing, and direction of volitional movements" (p. 422).

Hypokinetic. Parkinson's disease is the most prevalent kind of disease that produces this kind of dysarthria, the result of insufficient dopamine in the basal ganglia. The symptoms include loss of automatic movements, at rest (non-intention) tremor, alterations in movement of muscles of respiration and speech, and increased muscle tone. Patients in time may demonstrate problems in initiating movements (such as oral imitations, walking through doorways, etc.).

Hyperkinetic. Lesions at various sites of the extrapyramidal system from the cortex, down through the tracts, and in the basal ganglia may produce symptoms of acceleration and myoclonus of movements. The patient's speech is jerky, accompanied by severe alterations of voice and resonance. Huntington's chorea is among the more common of the hyperkinetic diseases, although some of these patients show a slowing or hypokinetic muscle patterning (McDowell and Lee, 1973).

Mixed. A mixture of flaccid or spastic dysarthria may be seen in the same patient, particularly one with diffuse CNS disease. Such diseases as amyotrophic lateral sclerosis and multiple sclerosis often produce speech and voice symptoms that are the result of both flaccidity and spasticity of various muscles.

If one were to group all of the speech and voice symptoms under general headings, as Darley, Aronson, and Brown (1969) did, we see that dysarthria can manifest itself in symptoms of pitch, loudness, vocal quality, respiration, prosody, articulation, and a general impression of intelligibility and bizarreness. We sometimes see patients for a voice evaluation whose problem at the time of the evaluation is but the beginning of a serious neurological disease. For example, several times a year in our large hospital with many out-patients, we see a patient who comes in with a "functional voice problem" who is actually showing the early symptoms of a degenerative disease, such as muscular dystrophy or amyotrophic lateral sclerosis. The man described in the following case represents the typical patient with the beginning of a serious CNS disease, which was first masked as a functional voice disorder:

John V., a forty-six-year-old college professor of hydrology, began to experience increased hoarseness after lecturing. At times, he would lose his voice completely after a busy, vocally demanding day. Indirect laryngoscopy found him to have "normal vocal folds with good motility, free of lesions." During the peripheral oral evaluation it was noted that he "seemed to have some tongue atrophy with surface fasciculations whenever the tongue was extended." He was subsequently referred for a neurological evaluation where testing, including muscle biopsy of thigh muscles, confirmed that the patient had "lower motor neuron disease or amyotrophic lateral sclerosis." Over a twenty-four-month period, the patient was found to experience an increasingly severe dysarthria accompanied by marked involvement of all four extremities. Although the patient is still alive, his progressive disease continues.

The preceding case illustrates how some alteration of voice, either in phonation, or resonance, or both, may be the early symptom of a neurological disease or disorder. Patients with neurological disorders frequently voice alterations of pitch, quality, loudness, or resonance as part of their symptoms of dysfunction.

Many patients with dysarthria require primary medical-surgical management, particularly since the speech-voice symptoms are but part of a much larger symptom complex. Usually, the muscle impairment that produces the dysarthria also produces problems of muscle movement in the extremities. Some dysarthrias related to disease can be treated with medication. For example, in Parkinson's disease many patients experience a remarkable lessening of symptoms with the administration of L-Dopa; this provides the patient with the needed dopamine he or she is lacking, reducing the hypokinetic symptoms and improving the clarity of speech. Patients whose dysarthrias are related to tumors are sometimes helped by neurosurgical intervention with the removal of the tumor. Many dysarthric patients experience severe hypernasality, requiring the combined therapies of the prosthodontist and the speech pathologist who focus on improving velopharyngeal closure (see Chapter 7). The typical dysarthric with hypernasality has a weak or paralyzed soft palate, which may require a palatal-lift prosthesis to make contact with the pharyngeal wall. Those patients with degenerative diseases, even severe ones like amyotrophic lateral sclerosis (ALS), can maintain function and life itself with help from habilitative therapies like physical therapy and inhalation therapy (McGuirt and Blalock, 1980). Speech pathology services with heavy emphasis on voice therapy can often improve the intelligibility of dysarthric patients, both those with static and fixed conditions (like CVA) and those with degenerative diseases (like ALS).

For some dysarthric patients, speech and voice can be markedly helped by determining whether either volitional or involitional behaviors are facilitative. Some of the dysarthrias are related to diseases that produce greater symptoms during nonintention or automatic function (like Parkinson's), while others are exacerbated by intention (like multiple sclerosis). We see the effects of nonintention and intention clearly when we ask the patient to count one to fifteen forward and then backward. The Parkinson patient with nonintention symptoms counts forward with a light voice, rapidly, with poor articulation; however, when the patient counts backward (which requires more intention), the dysarthric symptoms may be markedly less. The opposite situation is seen in the multiple sclerosis patient with his or her intention pathologies; the patient's count forward sounds clearer than his or her attempts to count backward. The voice clinician should probe with the patient to see if the type of verbal stimulus, nonintention (counting, days of week, and so on) or intention (speaking with an accent, or speaking inappropriately loud) will facilitate improvement in voice. If there is a difference between nonintention and intention, the voice clinician should use this information in helping the patient minimize his or her dysarthria. The patient needs much practice using the best intention mode. If there appears to be no improvement of speech function with one intention mode or the other, the clinician must work on the various parameters of voice, using in many cases the same kind of voice-facilitating approaches used with the various voice disorders described in this text.

Altering tongue position (facilitating approach 1), particularly bringing the tongue forward, is often useful. We have found that rapid production and forward carriage of the tongue is often facilitated when the patient replaces voice with whisper. Some patients with whisper or light voice have better intelligibility than when they use voice. Many biofeedback devices, such as the panendoscope showing velopharyngeal closure on a TV monitor or the Visi-Pitch showing fluctuations in vocal frequency, are useful with dysarthric patients. Sometimes, Gestalt modeling, providing the patient with the prosody or pitch inflection needed to sound "more normal," can produce change; the procedures outlined under ear training (7) are useful to follow. Sometimes hieararchy analysis (14), coupled with relaxation (22) and easy phonation, enables the dysarthric patient to minimize his or her voice symptoms. Much of what we do in voice therapy with dysarthric patients is to teach them speaking tricks, ways of using the speech and vocal mechanism in an easy, efficient way. Examples of "tricks" to facilitate better speech include speaking with less intensity, making deliberate efforts to employ more nonintention or intention vocal responses, speaking with greater (or less) oral opening, and so forth. Besides focusing on voice and resonance, the speech pathologist gives obvious attention to improving the patient's articulation and developing a more normal rate of speech, improving overall speech-voice prosodic patterns.

Voice Therapy for Functional Aphonia

In aphonia, the patient has *lost* his or her voice completely. The terms *conversion aphonia, hysterical aphonia,* and *functional aphonia* are used interchangeably to signify the loss of phonation independent of any true laryngeal disease. Thus, the patient with bilateral vocal fold paralysis who cannot phonate does *not* have functional aphonia, although he or she is aphonic. In the following discussion, we will be talking about the patient without voice, but with a normal larynx. We prefer the term *functional aphonia* to *conversion* or *hysterical aphonia*, because the latter suggest a psychiatric dimension that may not exist for the particular patient under consideration. Aronson (1980) writes that "eighty percent of patients with conversion aphonia are female," while Greene (1980) labels the condition as hysterical aphonia "more common in women than men, occurring in the ratio of 7 to 1." The functional aphonic patient demonstrates a normal larynx, perhaps riding a bit higher than normal toward the hyoid bone; when the patient is asked to phonate "eeh" during indirect laryngoscopy, the vocal folds are observed to abduct further apart rather than come together for midline approximation. Most clinical reports of functional aphonia report a sudden onset of the disorder, sometimes precipitated by an extreme fright, or a major disappointment, or a temporary illness characterized by a loss of voice. The patient will usually retain such nonverbal phonations as coughing or crying, but all speech attempts will be characterized by whispering with normal speaker affect (good eye contact, facial expression, and so on). The striking observation about patients with functional aphonia is how well, despite their voicelessness, they maintain their communicative contact with the people around them. It is the rare patient who allows his aphonia to isolate him from everyday speaking contacts.

As stated in Chapter 3, it appears that in functional aphonia the patient is easily conditioned to continue to speak without voice. Whatever the original cause, the behavior is maintained by the reactions of the people around him or her. The patient soon develops a *no voice* set toward speaking, and a habitual response is established; he speaks this way today because he spoke this way yesterday. Most patients with functional aphonia express a strong desire to regain their normal voice. (There are a few patients whose aphonia serves them well, and they will resist all therapeutic attempts at voice restoration.) The bias of this writer, developed from following aphonic patients over time, is that symptomatic voice therapy is usually effective in restoring normal voices in these patients. Once phonation is reestablished, it remains, and the patient does not develop substitute symptoms to take the place of the previous aphonia. A similar lack of symptom migration is reported by Stevens (1968), who, in his study of 300 patients with conversion hysteria, found that not one developed a new substitute symptom. It would appear that a trial period of voice therapy might well restore the aphonic patient's normal voice.

Successful voice therapy for functional aphonia must begin with the clinician explaining and discussing the problem with the patient. In the physiologic description of the aphonia, the clinician must avoid implying to the patient that one could phonate normally if one wanted. Rather, a description of what the patient is doing ("keeping the vocal cords apart") will make it clear that the clinician knows what the problem is. Following the physiological description, the clinician should say something like, "We will do things in therapy that will bring the cords together again to produce normal voice." The clinician should not (at the first session, at least) ask or show interest in *why* the patient is not phonating. After the explanation and discussion of the problem, the clinician should evaluate whatever nonverbal phonations the patient may have in his coughing, grunting, laughing, and crying repertoire, and then describe them to the patient as normal phonatory activities "where the vocal cords are getting together well to produce these sounds." These nonverbal phonations should then gradually be shaped into use for speech, at first confining any speech attempts to nonsense syllables, and then moving on to single words, but with no early attempts at phonating during real communication. Attempts at phonating in conversational situations (that is, in the real world of talking) should be deferred until good, consistent phonation has been reestablished under laboratory, practice conditions. This approach is illustrated in the following report of the case of a seven-year-old child with functional aphonia, reprinted from a report by Boone (1966):

M. P., age seven
Problem: Functional aphonia
History: The girl had a history of hoarseness since infancy with no medical investigation of the problem until the age of seven. All other areas of growth and development were considered normal.

Medical findings: At age 7, the child on indirect laryngoscopic examination was found to have "bilateral vocal nodules and cord thickening at the anterior 1/3 junction." The nodules were removed with a bilateral "cord stripping" followed by a 10-day period of enforced voice rest. Following the 10-day period of voice rest, despite the laryngologist's urging, the child was unable to resume phonation. After seven additional days of complete aphonia, she was referred to the speech pathologist with this note from the laryngologist. "This child has functional aphonia with normal appearance and good motility of both vocal cords."

Speech evaluation: This cooperative girl answered all questions by using whispered speech, more oral in type than glottal. Articulation and language functions were found to be normal. When asked to cough, she produced a firm true-cord cough. She could cough repeatedly on instruction. Other attempts at achieving nonverbal phonations, such as yawning, gargling, and inhalation-phonation were not successful. Hearing was normal. Both the mother and the child's teacher reported that the girl faithfully followed the laryngologist's recommendation of "no talking": no one had heard her phonate during the 10-day voice rest or in the seven days of continued aphonia.

Voice therapy: The first therapy session was scheduled for the afternoon following the initial evaluation; second and third therapy periods were scheduled for the following day. The child whispered to the speech pathologist during the first therapy period that she "wanted to talk." The speech pathologist described briefly to the girl how her vocal cords had been repaired, explaining why the physician wanted her to keep the cords apart (and not talk) until the cords had healed. It was further explained that if we keep the cords apart too long, we sometimes experience trouble getting them together to make a voice, although we can still make other sounds. This type of imagery explanation appeared comforting to the child, perhaps demonstrating to her that the "speech doctor" knew why she could not talk.

On command and in rapid response to a red signal light, the girl was asked to produce a cough. She was able to produce well a series of light coughs (phonations) and could make a soft squealing sound on inhalation. We then found she could contrast and make a similar sound on exhalation. She then practiced a rapid series of sounds on inhalation and matched these with similar-sounding noises on exhalation. Attempts at this time to extend these exhalation phonations into monosyllabic words were not successful. We then returned to the nonverbal phonations and after listening to animal noises on a phonograph recording, she voiced the "meow" of a cat.

Following the first afternoon voice-therapy session, the girl practiced at home the coughing sound, the inhalation-exhalation noises, and the "meow" sound. The mother was instructed not to ask the child to attempt to voice anything beyond these. The following morning she demonstrated to the clinician that she could produce easily the exhalation phonations, no longer requiring the inhalation-phonation as a model. After five minutes, she was able to produce good sustained phonation shaping it easily into prolonged /a/ and /o/. At this point, the clinician commented, "Your vocal cords are beginning to move well." After she produced good strong phonation on open-mouth vowels, we introduced our first actual words, requesting the child to repeat separately, "all, are, oh, oak, open, arm." On the first request to say the words, she whispered that she did not think she would be able to say them. After a few awkward attempts, she did produce the words. Her success in producing these first words again received relatively passive reinforcement by the clinician who stated, "The cords are definitely stronger now." The clinician in no way placed any of the responsibility of the aphonia on the child and frequently used the impersonal "they" or "the cords." The girl, a first-grader, was asked to repeat after the examiner a series of single words, each beginning with a peculiar phoneme, from the *Voice and Articulation Drillbook* (Fairbanks, 1960). These she repeated with surprisingly clear, strong phonation. Her pitch level, according to the mother, was slightly elevated compared with her pre-surgery voice. However, with the removal of bilateral nodules and cord-stripping, some elevation in pitch level was expected because of the reduction of cord mass.

Since the child came for her afternoon appointment with normal phonation, no formal clinic session was needed. Counseling was given to both child and parents about the need for the girl to minimize screaming and yelling to prevent recurrence of the nodules. There has been no recurrence of hoarseness or aphonia in this child during the past two years of follow-up consultation. (pp. 70–71)

Of the facilitating techniques described in Chapter 5, the following are useful for functional aphonia: chewing (5), gargle (13), hierarchy analysis (14), inhalation phonation (15), masking (16), pushing (21), relaxation (22), and respiration (23). If the voice clinician has any doubt about the patient's general emotional stability, as indicated perhaps by the patient's continued inability to produce some phonation, he or she should refer the patient for psychological or psychiatric consultation. Sometimes the aphonic patient profits most from symptomatic voice therapy concurrent with psychotherapy. If psychotherapy is needed, however, the typical case involves a fairly rapid recovery of voice with relatively brief voice therapy and a much longer period of psychotherapy.

Voice Therapy for Ventricular Phonation

Ventricular phonation is a rare vocal event. In its pure form, called *dysphonia plicae ventricularis,* the patient uses his or her false folds instead of the true vocal folds for phonation. A frontal X-ray tomogram is the best way to confirm the adduction of the false folds, as is well demonstrated in a series of illustrative tomograms in Arnold and Pinto's classic report on ventricular phonation (1960). Using the fiberoptic panendoscope, Brewer and McCall (1974) described a woman who had tight ventricular approximation with a severe and persistent dysphonia. It is difficult for the typical patient to produce true ventricular voice, and most cases of *dysphonia plicae ventricularis* referred to this clinician have proved to be patients who were using their true folds inappropriately, producing a functional dysphonia. Because the ventricular bands are mounted superiorly and quite laterally on the arytenoids, it is difficult for them to approximate in the midline for phonation unless they have become hypertrophied. It would appear that patients who have enlarged ventricular folds sufficient to produce phonation usually end up producing a double voice (diplophonia), with both the false and true folds vibrating simultaneously (Ward and others, 1969). From clinical observation, it would appear that the rare patient who demonstrates ventricular voice or diplophonia is a patient who has had extensive scarring from previous lesions and surgery. Diplophonia, however, is more likely found in the patient with unilateral true fold paralysis, where the involved fold is atrophied and vibrating at a different rate of vibration than the normal fold, producing the double-sounding voice.

Since the ventricular voice is usually low pitched, monotonous, and hoarse, this kind of phonation is frequently described as *ventricular dysphonia*. In the absence of true cord pathology, voice therapy is often effective in "finding" true cord phonation, which usually provides the patient with a much more satisfactory voice than the false folds can. Successful therapy for ventricular phonation, as for most other voice disorders, should begin with a frank explanation to the patient of what the problem is. Frontal tomogram X-rays are helpful in demonstrating normal abduction-adduction of both true and false vocal folds. Even with this explanation, however, the patient may not be able to produce true cord phonation volitionally. If that is the case, the best therapy approach is to have the patient practice making prolonged inhalations with an open mouth, followed by sustained exhalations, with no attempt at phonation. (See inhalation phonation, facilitating approach (15).) This is followed by having the patient make an effort to phonate on inhalation. With some practice, most patients can produce some inhalation phonation. Inhalation phonation is usually true cord phonation, according to the radiographic observations of Lehmann (1965), who found true fold adduction and marked retraction of the ventricular bands on inhalation phonation. Once inhalation phonation is achieved by the patient, efforts can be made to produce a matching exhalation phonation, usually a high-pitched squeaky sound. This is the difficult part of the therapy. Patients will be able to make the inhalation voice with relative ease, but will have a great deal of difficulty in producing the matched exhalation. It seems to be easier, however, if the patient attempts inhalation-phonation-exhalation-phonation on the same breath cycle. Perseverance in this task will usually be the key to eliminating the ventricular dysphonia; several of our therapy failures with ventricular dysphonia seem to have been related to our not sticking with the matched inhalation-exhalation phonations long enough.

While the frontal X-ray tomogram is the only sure way of confirming true cord phonation (or ventricular voice, for that matter), once the patient is able to produce an exhaled phonation, he or she should be asked to produce varying pitches. True cord phonation has the capability of pitch variation; false cord phonation usually does not. Once true cord phonation is established, the patient must abandon the inhalation-exhalation squeak and blend it down to a more acceptable pitch level.

Occasionally, a patient with laryngeal disease—for example, extensive true cord involvement with papilloma, or unilateral adductor paralysis—will need to develop a vicarious phonatory mechanism. One such mechanism would be the ventricular folds adducting for ventricular production. It is difficult to *teach* someone to use ventricular voice. Rather, for patients who want to develop ventricular phonation, all we can usually do is encourage them to produce various voices, if they can. If true cord adduction is not possible, the phonations produced after such urging will usually be ventricular in origin. If a better ventricular voice can be produced, it will usually be possible to improve it by working on optimal control of exhalation, keeping the mandible open and relaxed, and so on. Increasing both loudness and pitch variability are the usual therapy goals in improving the sound of ventricular voice, but the clinician must realize that both these goals with ventricular voice can be only minimally achieved.

Voice Therapy for Spastic Dysphonia

The patient with spastic dysphonia speaks with a strained, hoarse voice accompanied by much physical effort, trying to force out air flow for phonation. The voice of the spastic dysphonic patient sounds similar to that of the normal speaker attempting to phonate while lifting a very heavy object. The primitive valving action of the larynx cuts in on the normal speaker when doing heavy lifting, and his or her vocal cords adduct so tightly that he or she can hardly speak. The same mechanism seems to operate for the patient with spastic dysphonia, except that the vocal fold overadduction occurs in the absence of any physical lifting. The tense, tight voice appears to be produced by the patient's attempting to phonate while the vocal folds are adducted too tightly. As such, spastic dysphonia is an excellent example of a severe vocal fold approximation disorder. Why the patient speaks this way is not clearly known.

There may be more than one cause of spastic dysphonia. Bloch (1960) wrote that spastic dysphonia was a conversion reaction symptom; that is, because of severe psychological problems patients choke off their attempts to communicate, and despite their good intentions for voice, their vocal folds overadduct, preventing normal communication or voicing. Aronson and Hartman (1981) feel that some forms of spastic dysphonia may actually be symptoms of essential tremor of laryngeal muscles accompanied by voice arrest. Others feel that the disorder may be the result of other central nervous system or peripheral nervous system pathologies, perhaps in the brain stem or involving fiber differences or demyelinization of the recurrent laryngeal nerve (Dedo and others, 1978; Bocchino and Tucker, 1978; Izdebski and others, 1977). Regardless of the cause of spastic dysphonia, neither speech pathology, laryngology, nor psychiatry-psychology were traditionally able to help most patients with this disorder. Not until Dedo (1976) first reported his surgical cutting of the recurrent laryngeal nerve in thirty-four patients with spastic dysphonia had there been any convincing reports for improving the voices of such patients.

Before the procedure reported by Dedo (which we will soon describe), our voice therapy attempts searched with the patient situationally for those situations where he or she might enjoy normal voice. Like the stutterer and his reports of fluency, the patient with spastic dysphonia may demonstrate a normal voice when talking to a pet animal, or to a baby, or aloud to himself. When listeners are introduced, particularly those the patient thinks are evaluative, his voice will tighten and phonation will be difficult. With some self-study and inquiry from the clinician, the patient can develop for himself a hierarchy of situations, ranging from those in which his voice is normal to those few in which he can barely phonate. The patient must analyze his normal vocal behavior and the situations that surround it. The clinician can use the therapy periods to help the patient recreate those environments where relaxed phonation is best achieved. For example, if the patient has a normal voice when talking to his dog, efforts must be made in therapy to create a situation in which the dog seems actually to be there. This recreating of optimum situations requires much practice if the patient is going to be able to employ normal phonation (as if he or she were actually talking to the dog). If the hierarchy analysis, as developed in Chapter 5 under facilitating technique 14, is going to be effective, it is essential that a great deal of time be spent in attempting to capture the environmental factors that permit the patient to phonate normally. Without a normal, relaxed phonation to produce at will, the patient will not have an optimum response to use at various levels of the hierarchy.

While most speech pathologists report generally poor results with therapy for spastic dysphonia, Cooper (1977) reports "direct vocal rehabilitation" as being helpful. His rehabilitation includes working on pitch, quality, breath support, volume rate, and "vocal psychotherapy." Our symptomatic therapy working to help the patient produce easy phonations has been less successful, employing such facilitating approaches as chanting (4), chewing (5), place the voice (20), and yawn-sigh (25), coupled with hierarchy analysis (14) and biofeedback (2). Our attempts for generalization using desensitization approaches have only had sporadic results. One patient was observed to say, "I just cannot understand why I can talk to you and my husband with normal voice, but I cannot talk to the next-door neighbor." The inconsistencies of these patients' voices are influenced by the setting, the listener, the focus of the response, similar in many ways to what the speech pathologist experiences in working with stutterers. Normal phonation, like normal fluency, may be easier to demonstrate in the clinical laboratory than it is in the outside, *real* world of talking.

If trial symptomatic voice therapy is unsuccessful for the patient with spastic dysphonia, referral may be made to the laryngologist for consideration of unilateral recurrent laryngeal nerve (RLN) resection. A thorough diagnostic evaluation by both the surgeon and the speech pathologist is followed by injection of Xylocaine into the RLN, which produces a temporary unilateral adductor paralysis. The patient's air flow, relative ease of phonation, and change of voice quality are assessed. If there is marked improvement in air flow (greater flow rates with less glottal resistance) and improvement in both ease and quality of phonation, the decision may be made to cut the RLN permanently. Postoperatively then, the patient usually has an easily produced but breathy voice, similar in sound to the patient with unilateral adductor paralysis. Voice therapy focusing on a slight elevation of pitch (10), some ear training (7), increasing glottal attack, and pushing (21) have all been found effective for developing a better-sounding voice.

Followup of patients with RLN resection emphasizes the importance of selecting patients carefully for this procedure. Aronson and De Santo (1981) in following thirty-three patients a year and a half after resection, found that "61 percent were still improved while 39 percent had failed." The patients who fail to improve often experience a return of the spastic dysphonia for different reasons. For some, the normal vocal fold overcompensates and produces excessively firm approximation with the paralyzed fold. Some patients probably did not have true spastic dysphonia, but perhaps had some condition similar to tremor. Wilson, Odring, and Mueller (1980) described a woman who, thirteen months postoperatively, had the RLN grow back together again, producing the return of spastic dysphonia, requiring a second RLN cut, which produced an immediate relief from her struggle phonation. It has been our experience with eleven spastic dysphonia patients who experienced RLN resection that nine demonstrated a marked and continuing improvement in vocal quality, and that all eleven experienced great relief from the amount of effort they had previously expended to phonate. As Aronson and De Santo (1981) have written, "Relief from effortful phonation is as much a benefit from surgery as is voice improvement" (p. 6).

Voice Therapy for Vocal Fold Paralysis

Voice therapy is often the treatment of choice for aphonias and dysphonias related to vocal fold paralysis. Sometimes medical-surgical management is the primary treatment, perhaps supplemented by voice therapy. While most vocal fold paralyses, particularly unilateral paralysis, are related to trauma or cutting of the recurrent laryngeal nerve, about 10 percent of vocal fold paralyses are central in origin from a low lesion in the central nervous system. We shall consider separately the four kinds of vocal fold paralysis: *unilateral adductor paralysis* (the most common type), *bilateral adductor paralysis, unilateral abductor paralysis,* and *bilateral abductor paralysis.* These terms are less confusing to the student of voice if one remembers that the name of the paralysis describes what the vocal folds cannot do; for example, if the paralyzed fold is paralyzed in the out or paramedian position, it cannot adduct to midline (we call this a unilateral adductor paralysis).

Unilateral Adductor Paralysis.   In this condition, usually caused by unilateral involvement of the recurrent laryngeal nerve, one vocal fold works normally and reaches the midline, while the involved cord remains in a fixed, retracted position. There is usually a pronounced dysphonia or aphonia characterized by severe breathiness, the severity of which is dependent on the degree of glottal closure possible. As in all cases of paralytic dysphonia or aphonia, the decision regarding management belongs to the laryngologist, whose first concern is to preserve the patient's airway. In unilateral adductor paralysis, the air flow for breathing is threatened only minimally, but some attention must be given to ensuring the patient's adequacy of laryngeal valving (which, as the basic function of the larynx, protects the airway from foreign bodies). If airway patency becomes a primary problem, the laryngologist may well have to consider some surgical procedure, such as the injection of teflon into the abducted, paralyzed fold (Lewy, 1976). This use of teflon increases the girth of the involved cord—usually permitting actual contact with the normal cord—and affords some valve closure of the airway. Of secondary importance to the laryngologist, but of prime interest to the patient and the speech pathologist, is the patient's voice. Lewy (1976) reported that 96 percent of his patients showed voice improvement after teflon injection, with none of his patients reporting problems with aspiration. Reich and Lerman (1978) found that patients with unilateral adductor paralysis after teflon injection experienced a general reduction of perceived hoarseness with an "enhancement" of perceived pleasantness of phonation. There have been several innovative surgical approaches that have also had positive impact on voice. Isshiki, Tanade, and Sawade (1978) wrote that teflon often does not guarantee good results, particularly for patients with a wide glottal opening; they, therefore, surgically pull the muscular processes of the arytenoids with sutures, simulating the action of the lateral cricoarytenoids, rotating the arytenoids so that the paralyzed fold is closer to a midline position. Tucker (1977) reported success in six out of nine patients with unilateral adductor paralysis after taking the nerve-muscle pedicle from the omohyoid muscle on one side and inserting it into the paralyzed thyroarytenoid. It should be noted that no surgical approach should be attempted for at least nine months after onset, with hope in the interim for some nerve regeneration. Many patients experience a return of nerve function, with a restoration of function because of nerve regeneration. The nerve grows back together again. Voice therapy, however, is often effective in giving the patient a temporary voice while waiting hopefully for nerve regeneration to take place.

The preferred method of voice therapy for the problem, independent of any medical-surgical management, is the pushing approach, as described in Chapter 5 under facilitating technique 21. Under conditions of pushing, the best possible adduction of the true folds occurs; if there is any flicker of adduction capability remaining in the involved cord, it will show itself under pushing conditions. In unilateral adductor paralysis, the involved cord, despite its paralysis and lack of movement to the midline, still vibrates somewhat due to the force of the passing air stream. It would appear that under conditions of pushing, the air-flow rate is accelerated and thus produces a greater vibration of the involved cord, resulting in a slightly better-sounding voice. The best voice possible with unilateral adductor paralysis seems to be achieved in voice therapy that focuses on increasing breath control (facilitating technique 23), on deliberately increasing hard glottal attack by ear training, and on practicing pushing exercises.

Bilateral Adductor Paralysis. With both cords fixed in an open, abducted position, the patient will be aphonic. Bilateral adductor paralysis is more often than not the result of central brain stem impairment than of bilateral destruction of the recurrent laryngeal nerves. The patient's primary problem—more important than the aphonia—is the inability to close the airway. The aphonia resulting from bilateral cord paralysis is frequently accompanied by other symptoms of cerebral dysfunction, such as weakness or paralysis of the tongue, pharynx, or palate. Medical therapy might well include a tracheostomy to improve the efficiency of the airway as a temporary measure, since many cases of bilateral adductor paralysis eventually improve spontaneously. A permanent bilateral adductor paralysis is sometimes treated surgically. Such surgery can be employed only when the bilateral adductor problem is secondary to peripheral nerve damage and not the result of a central lesion. Voice therapy does very little for the patient with bilateral cord paralysis, except when the paralysis tends to diminish (if it does). Then the voice clinician can usually strengthen the whisper by employing some pushing exercises and respiration drills. Froeschels, Kastein, and Weiss (1955), working with forty patients with bilateral adductor paralysis, reported that the patients' voices were improved through pushing exercises. However, unless there is some spontaneous return of cord functioning, voice therapy may not be effective.

Unilateral Abductor Paralysis. In this condition, one of the vocal cords remains fixed in a central, adducted position, while the other cord functions normally. Phonation is rarely affected, since the two cords approximate one another quite well. Quiet, at-rest breathing is usually normal, and only when the patient becomes physically active is he or she likely to experience some shortness of breath because of the narrowing of the airway. Half of the airway is occluded by the fixed midline cord, requiring marked abduction of the normal cord to achieve an adequate glottal opening for normal breathing. The primary concern of the laryngologist is that the airway be sufficiently open to permit normal breathing; rarely in these cases of unilateral abductor paralysis is surgery necessary. An occasional patient demonstrates a fixed fold in the median position, which interferes with the airway, necessitating a surgical rotation (Bull and Cook, 1976) of the involved arytenoid to create a larger glottis. A problem in surgically lateralizing the involved vocal fold is that edema and scar tissue secondary to the operation often contribute to the overall glottal configuration (Woodman and Pollack, 1950). The wider the glottis is open after surgery, the poorer the voice. For a detailed description of vocal fold paralyses and their symptoms and occasional surgical treatment, the reader is advised to read pages 79–93 in Aronson's *Clinical Voice Disorders* (1980).

Most surgical approaches for abductor paralysis should be deferred until, at least, nine months after onset for two reasons. Many times the patient with unilateral vocal fold paralysis will initially experience a midline paralysis (abductor) that begins to lessen, with the paralyzed vocal fold migrating eventually to the paramedian position which may well cause increased hoarseness. Secondly, the injured or severed recurrent laryngeal nerve may regenerate, producing a return of function of the involved fold. Some patients experience voice symptoms with unilateral abductor paralysis, temporarily or permanently. For example, the singer or actor or professional user of voice may suffer from loss of pitch range, a double voice (diplophonia), and problems in pitch register. Effective voice therapy for these patients would be probing with various facilitating approaches to find the approach that seems to work best. We have found ear training (7), establishing new pitch (10), relaxation (22), and respiration training (23) to be often the most effective approaches for developing the best voice possible with a unilateral abductor paralysis.

   Bilateral Abductor Paralysis.   Bilateral paralysis of both vocal folds in the midline position requires immediate medical assistance to help the patient breathe. Emergency medical management of bilateral abductor paralysis includes a tracheostomy. If the symptoms of closure persist for more than a week or so, a medical decision must be made as to whether or not to construct surgically a new airway within the larynx. Bull and Cook (1976) have described some success in immediate surgery for these patients followed by some voice therapy. "Success" in the surgical treatment of bilateral abductor paralysis means that the patient is able to breathe once again through the larynx, although not necessarily that he or she regains a normal voice; the dysphonia is but a small price to pay for the ability to breathe adequately again. However, voice therapy is often found useful for those patients who, after surgery, experience varying degrees of dysphonia due to the surgically produced open glottis.

   Since airway patency is the primary need of these patients, voice therapy should never be started unless the newly constructed glottal mechanism can "take it." If the surgeon feels that voice therapy is needed and that the patient can tolerate it, the approach used is very similar to that used in adductor paralysis. The patient must learn to use his or her voice as efficiently as possible. Pushing exercises, breathing exercises, and the trial-and-error use of various facilitating techniques may help in producing a better-sounding voice.

   The reader interested especially in the aphonias and dysphonias associated with various forms of laryngeal paralyses will find Luchsinger and Arnold's comprehensive description of various aspects of paralytic dysphonia (Chapter 4, 1965) and Aronson's description of various laryngeal paralyses (Chapter 5, 1980) most useful.

Voice Therapy for Special Voice Symptoms

   Aging.   The older person does not typically have a voice problem. Although there are characteristic changes of the voice in the aged, they do not usually require voice therapy. According to an early investigation of voice changes in aging, Mysak (1959) found that fundamental frequency began to elevate slightly with increasing age from ages fifty to eighty-five. A later study by Hollien and Shipp (1972) confirmed that fundamental frequency of male speakers at different ages is characterized by a saucer-type curve, with decreasing fundamentals for each decade in life until after age fifty, when a slight increase of fundamental occurs for each decade. In several studies of aged women (McGlone and Hollien, 1963; Charlip, 1968), the opposite findings were found; that is, as women get older, they seem to demonstrate increasingly lower fundamental frequencies. Some of the confusion from the results of studying voice pitch in aging was clarified by a study by Honjo and Isshiki (1980), who studied twenty men and twenty women with a mean age of seventy-five years, finding that the men had "vocal fold atrophy and/or edema" with higher fundamental frequency than younger men while the women had "fold edema and slight hoarseness with a lower fundamental frequency" than younger women. If the patient exhibits a marked departure in pitch level from his or her age peers, symptomatic voice therapy using such facilitating approaches as biofeedback (2), change of loudness (3), establish new pitch (10), and respiration training (23) may be helpful.

As aged people pass the age of seventy, there may be an increase in hoarseness or dysphonia. The atrophy in the folds of men and the edema in the folds of women may well contribute to observed dysphonia (Honjo and Isshiki, 1980). In studying jitter (perturbations in fundamental frequency) in the voices of twenty young adults and twenty older adults, Wilcox and Horii (1980) found significantly greater jitter in the older adults. Measures of jitter provide one measurement of dysphonia. It does not appear unusual for an aged person to have some hoarseness of voice. Diagnostically, it may be important for the speech-language pathologist to rule out possible causes of the hoarseness other than normal aging, such as related to possible lesions (leukoplakia, carcinoma), or to weakness or paralysis (part of a dysarthria), or to endocrinal problems perhaps related to the side-effects from excessive hormones, vitamins, or medications. If there appears to be no cause of hoarseness other than the tissue changes of the vocal folds observed in normal aging, voice therapy might be warranted for those patients who seek such help. The quality of the voice may be improved by such methods as biofeedback (2); ear training (7); establish new pitch (10); feedback (12); and relaxation (22).

Falsetto.   A mutational falsetto, or *puberphonia,* is the persistence of a high pitched, soprano-sounding voice, observed in some young men. In cases of falsetto, the patient speaks with an inappropriately high, soprano-type voice. The falsetto is actually a false soprano voice and therefore is not found in prepubescent children or in most adult females, where such pitch levels are within the normal voice range. Falsetto voices, then, exist primarily in postpubertal adolescent and adult males, and the pitch level may well be around middle C (256 cps) or higher. The social penalties for a male using such an inappropriately high voice are obvious, with the individual often judged as effeminate and inadequate. Whatever the psychological factors are that cause the emergence and continuation of the falsetto, the large majority of these patients can be relieved from their problems permanently with but a brief exposure to voice therapy. Those few who persist in hanging on to their falsetto voices as a symptom that somehow serves them well should be referred for psychological or psychiatric therapy, particularly if they profess a desire to eliminate the falsetto voice but are unable to do so.

The laryngeal characteristics of men with falsetto voices are essentially normal, and endocrinologic factors such as the completeness of secondary sexual signs (body hair, beard, and so on) are rarely indicators of the problem. Usually there is a nonphysical reason that the young man continues to use his prepubertal voice, often at slightly higher pitch levels than he used as a child. Whatever the reason he began talking this way, we see evidence (primarily from the usual rapidity in acquiring a normal voice pitch in therapy) that he soon develops a set for phonating in the higher pitch, talking this way today because he did so yesterday. As in voice therapy for most other problems, the search for more optimum ways of phonating should be prefaced by a discussion and explanation of the problem.

Symptomatic voice therapy is highly successful with most problems of mutational falsetto. As Aronson (1980) has written, "It is one of the easiest and most rewarding disorders to treat" (pp. 147–148). In her treatment of puberphonia, Greene (1980) continues to give the disorder more of a psychological emphasis than most current writers, describing puberphonias under discussion of the Oedipus complex, narcissus complex, hero worship, homosexuality, and transsexualism. Greene then develops specific exercises for the clinician to use in helping the young man with puberphonia to develop a lower pitch. Similar approaches are outlined by Wilson (1979) and Aronson (1980).

One possible way of helping the patient produce a lower pitch level is to place your fingers externally on his thyroid cartilage and then ask him to phonate an extended *ah*. When the *ah* begins, press lightly on the thyroid cartilage (decreasing the length and increasing the mass of the vocal folds) to produce an immediate lowering of pitch; when the finger pressure is released, the pitch may revert back. Repeat the procedure and ask the patient if he can maintain the lower pitch level. This finger pressure, as mentioned under digital manipulation in Chapter 5, is not always effective with falsetto voices. But it is worth trying—and if it works, use it. Most of these patients can also demonstrate normal male pitch levels when they produce such nonverbal phonations as throat clearing, coughing, grunting, and so on. If the patient can produce a normal-pitched, nonverbal phonation, he should then be instructed to prolong the sound, extending it as an "ah" for several seconds. His early attempts to phonate should not involve actual words, but only the nonverbal sounds. Depending on the patient's success in producing nonverbal phonation and his attitude toward doing this, move gradually into having him phonate words with the lower voice. One successful way of doing this is to blend a prolonged nonverbal phonation into the production of a word that begins with a similar-sounding vowel. Most patients will make the transition from nonverbal phonation to production of a few practice words without too much resistance. In the beginning, it is wise to stay on the practice level, using only a few words, before having the patient try to use the lower voice in conversational situations. When the patient is able to produce a few practice words with normal voice, record the new voice and let him hear it. It does very little good to record both the falsetto and normal voices, using them for contrast discrimination, since hearing his falsetto as contrasted perhaps with a normal baritone often puts the patient on the defensive. Rather, listen critically with the patient to the lower voice pitch, ignoring the falsetto when analyzing the new production. When the patient listens to his new voice, we often determine what pitch level it is and then show him how this fits into the normal adult male range. If the lower pitch level is in that normal range, we make sure the patient realizes this. The typical patient with puberphonia is "hungry" to develop a more normal-sounding voice. With this excellent motivation, a direct symptom modification approach produces very rapid changes, requiring only brief voice therapy (four or five sessions).

Voice Pitch Breaks.   There is no voice symptom more annoying than to be speaking in an apparently normal voice and then suddenly experience a pitch break. The typical abnormal pitch break is a one or two octave break, one or two octaves higher or lower than the normal voice. We are not talking about the typical voice breaks experienced primarily by boys as their voices are changing; these temporary breaks usually disappear as the laryngeal mechanism matures and the youngster has had continued practice in using his new adult voice. Rather, we are considering the adult patient who complains of the voice breaking upward or downward while speaking. This individual has no warning that the pitch break will occur. When it does, he or she often is embarrassed and sometimes will avoid speaking situations rather than face the uncertainty and tension of the pitch break. Pitch breaks are almost invariably related to individuals' speaking at an inappropriate pitch level. In the male, speaking at the bottom of his pitch range, his voice will break upward, about one octave. But by elevating his habitual pitch level slightly above the very bottom of his pitch range the pitch breaks will usually "miraculously" disappear. Similarly, downward pitch breaks in the female are usually found in women who are speaking at too high a habitual pitch level, so that a slight lowering of pitch to a more optimum level will usually eliminate the problem. Pitch breaks tend to go in the direction of the optimum pitch level, and therapy directed toward bringing the voice nearer that level will usually markedly reduce them or eliminate them entirely.

Among the facilitating techniques in Chapter 5 that have been found useful in eliminating pitch breaks are: alternating tongue position (1), chant talk (4), chewing (5), ear training (7), eliminating hard glottal attacks (9), open-mouth (18), relaxation (22), respiration (23), and yawn-sigh (25).

Phonation Breaks.   In phonation breaks, the patient is speaking with a relatively normal voice when the vocal folds suddenly separate, and he or she is temporarily without voice. This sudden and fleeting loss of voice is sometimes called abductor spastic dysphonia (Aronson, 1980), characterized by a laryngospasm; instead of the folds having a midline spasm with a tight sphincteric closure, as in adductor spastic dysphonia (the typical spastic dysphonia), the folds suddenly abduct apart. These sudden abductions of vocal fold and the resulting aphonia are usually noticed after the patient has been exposed to a long period of talking, perhaps with continued strain in an atmosphere of tension. While Zwitman (1979) also labeled such behavior as "abductor type spastic dysphonia," the symptoms are the opposite of what is seen in typical spastic dysphonia and the disorder presents a far more favorable voice prognosis. It was later proposed by Shipp, Mueller, and Zwitman (1980) that the term "intermittent abductory dysphonia" be used for these spasmodic "moments of unvoicing" that appear similar to what we here consider as phonation breaks. It has been our experience that these brief phonation breaks usually begin after prolonged hyperfunction. If hyperfunctional behaviors can be identified and reduced, the phonation breaks are usually minimized. For example, a local hard-rock disc jockey suffered from phonation breaks when he was attempting to give the news "straight" for five minutes on the hour. It was soon discovered that his broadcasting style away from the news was extremely "hyper" and false, producing obvious strain on his vocal mechanisms. Voice therapy was directed toward producing a disc-jockey style that was less aversive, with the happy result that he was able to read the news copy free of phonation breaks. These intermittent losses of voice while one is voicing are usually the result of prolonged vocal hyperfunction. Once the hyperfunction can be reduced, the phonation breaks usually disappear.

A Vocal Hygiene Program for Optimum Use of the Larynx

Patients who have experienced various kinds of voice symptoms often profit from using their larynges as optimally as possible. Professional users of voice, such as the singer or teacher, must often use the laryngeal mechanism as optimally as possible if they are to get "mileage" out of their voices. Froeschels (1943) first used the phrase "hygiene of the voice" to develop a list of behaviors designed to provide for the heavy user of voice or the patient with a voice problem guidelines for achieving efficiency of laryngeal function. Cooper (1977) and Wilson (1979) both provide patients who have voice problems with good rules for using the voice with greater ease, avoiding laryngeal strain and excessive effort while vocalizing.

A vocal hygiene program developed for professional users of voice was presented by Boone (1980b) who described these twelve steps:

1. Identify vocal abuse and misuse (shouting, throat clearing, laughing, etc.).
2. Reduce or eliminate the identified abuse and misuse.
3. Develop an easy glottal attack.
4. Use a speaking level that is where you should be. Avoid singing at extreme voice levels.
5. Keep your speaking voice at the lower end of your loudness range.
6. Take an easy, relaxed breath when speaking.
7. Reduce vocal demand as much as possible. Speak or sing less.
8. While listening, keep your teeth separated with a slight lip opening.
9. Avoid talking in loud settings (disco, airplanes, cars, boats, etc.).
10. Avoid smoking and excessive use of alcohol.
11. Avoid odd sounds with your voice, such as imitating engines, funny voices, etc.
12. Keep the membranes of your mouth and throat as moist as possible. (p. 36)

The vocal hygiene program just listed is a common-sense application for preserving good vocal function. The speech pathologist must take a pragmatic approach in applying the twelve steps to the individual patient. While obviously some patients may profit from following all twelve suggestions, only a few of the guidelines may apply to the typical patient. For any user of voice, however, who experiences some voice symptoms after much voice usage, the vocal hygiene program provides a ready list of possible situations where the patient may be experiencing voice strain. Many of the program steps are natural extensions of the philosophy and therapy-facilitating approaches presented in Chapter 1 and Chapter 5. Let us further consider some of the steps of the program.

Identifying abuse-misuse and reducing its occurrence is an important requisite for successful management of any voice problem. Speaking with excessive glottal attack employs an unnecessary amount of strain on the laryngeal mechanism (good voice can be produced without such precision). Singing at the extremes of one's pitch range for extended periods of time should be avoided whenever possible; for example, sometimes tenors or sopranos may complain of throat discomfort after a three- or four-hour rehearsal where they have had to sing at the limits (usually upper) of their frequency range. "Laying off the highs" has been demonstrated as a way of preserving good voice throughout a long and difficult rehearsal. Reducing loudness of voice, as detailed in facilitating approach 3, often reduces strain associated with phonation. Efficient respiration for phonation appears to be present when the individuals can match what they want to say or sing with the perfect timing of their expiratory air flow; some help in improving respiration (approach 23) may help the patients use the larynx more efficiently for phonation. Some voices are destroyed from overwork. Sometimes the performer gets in a situation where acting or singing rehearsals become prolonged, demanding full voice in all the dimensions of frequency, intensity, and quality. Such prolonged voice usage should be minimized, if possible. Perhaps a more subtle form of voice strain comes from the speaker who continually talks. Reducing vocal output is sometimes a helpful strategy for the patient who is experiencing symptoms of voice strain. Chewing (5) and the open-mouth approach (18) have all been found useful for the occasional patient who rarely opens his or her mouth while listening and speaking. "Developing an awareness of oral opening versus oral tightening both in oneself and others is often a needed beginning for developing greater oral relaxation" (Boone, 1980b, p. 40). Avoiding extended talk in noisy situations like discos, around power motors, and in noisy, excited crowds would probably help the larynx of anyone who is experiencing voice symptoms. If one is to review the tables and descriptions of the prevalence of laryngeal and lung cancer as presented by the American Cancer Society (1980), one can quickly appreciate the overall hazard of smoking versus nonsmoking in the genesis of these airway cancers. Less known, however, is that cigarette, cigar, and pipe smoke is a drying agent for the airway and an obvious irritant to the membranes of the larynx. It would appear that a vocal hygiene approach would be lacking if it did not suggest that the serious user of voice (or a patient with a voice problem) cannot afford the "luxury" of continued smoking. Related to this observation of dryness, the membranes of the larynx must be kept moist for efficient vocalization. Performers who live or perform in low humidity climates, or in settings requiring heavy air conditioning and heating, may require additional moisture (use of a vaporizer or humidifier). Serious users of voice should check out both their homes and performing arenas (office, theater, school) to determine the relative humidity. Humidity levels below 30 percent (Boone, 1980b) may require the additional use of a vaporizer or humidifier by patients with voice problems.

Any vocal hygiene program is basically a common-sense application of ways for using the larynx and producing voice that avoid unnecessary demands on the mechanism.

SUMMARY

Because there are many voice problems not related to vocal hyperfunction, we have considered some of these separately in this chapter. We have discussed the voice problems of hard-of-hearing and deaf children and adults, with suggestions for managing these problems. We considered the pitch, quality, and resonance problems of various dysarthrias, recommending several approaches that are sometimes helpful. Therapy approaches were developed for functional aphonia and ventricular phonation with or without diplophonia. New management strategies were presented for the difficult problem of spastic dysphonia. Vocal fold paralyses were described with focus given to the medical-surgical management and voice therapy approaches that are useful for the different types of paralyses. We considered special voice problems related to aging and puberphonia, with voice therapy suggestions for pitch breaks and phonation breaks. Finally, we presented a vocal hygiene program that has been found helpful for the serious user of voice and for the patient with a voice disorder.

7

Therapy for Resonance Disorders

The most common resonance disorders are problems of nasal resonance. The majority of nasal resonance problems are related to structural abnormalities that may require, in addition to voice therapy, some kind of surgical-medical-dental management. Occasionally nasal resonance problems are functional in origin and highly responsive to voice therapy. We will present voice therapy procedures for problems of hypernasality, denasality, and assimilative nasality. We will then consider problems in oral and pharyngeal resonance, with our focus given to methods for improving the resonance of such voices.

The periodic vibrations leaving the vocal folds are filtered in the supraglottal space of the pharyngeal, oral, and nasal cavities, or the upper airway. We discussed the phenomenon of resonance in Chapter 2, finding that the F-shaped upper airway amplifies and filters the sounds coming into it from the larynx, depending on the frequency of the soundwaves and the shape of the particular cavity. The pharyngeal cavity constantly changes its horizontal and vertical dimensions by active movement of muscles, changing its overall configuration. An open coupling between the pharyngeal cavity and the oral cavity (particularly when the velopharyngeal mechanism is closed) enables the traveling soundwave to be further filtered by the continuous modifications of oral cavity size that occur during speech. What emerges as voice resonance is the fundamental frequency (laryngeal vibration) modified by the natural resonant frequencies occuring at the various supraglottal sites above the vocal folds, within the pharynx, and through the oral cavity. When the velopharyngeal port is open, the pharyngeal-oral coupling with the nasal cavity is then possible where soundwaves are further absorbed and filtered as they pass through the chambers of the nasal cavity, as for the production of /m/, /n/, and /ŋ/ in English. Problems in pharyngeal-oral coupling, structural and functional, cause the most common resonance problems, disorders in nasal resonance. We shall consider the evaluation, management, and therapy of nasal resonance problems.

NASAL RESONANCE PROBLEMS

Under the broad heading of nasal resonance fall three types of disorders, *hypernasality, denasality,* and *assimilative nasality.* While panels of individuals listening to speakers with these problems might only be able to say, "the voices all sound nasal," there are distinct differences between the three types, each requiring a differential management and voice therapy approach. As a prelude to our discussion of separate approaches, let us define the three terms:

> *Hypernasality.* Hypernasality is an excessively undesirable amount of perceived nasal cavity resonance during the phonation of vowels. Vowel production in the English language is primarily characterized by oral resonance with only slightly nasalized components. If the oral and nasal cavities are coupled to one another by lack of velopharyngeal closure (for whatever reason), the periodic soundwaves carrying laryngeal vibration will receive heavy resonance within the nasal cavity. Only three phonemes of the English language should receive the degree of nasal prominence produced by an open velopharyngeal port: /m/, /n/, and /ŋ/.
>
> *Denasality.* Denasality is the lack of nasal resonance for the three nasalized phonemes /m/, /n/, and /ŋ/. In the strictest sense, therefore, denasality could be categorized as an articulatory substitution disorder. Generally, denasality also affects vowels, in that the normal speaker gives some nasal resonance to vowels. A voice with this inadequate nasal resonance sounds like the voice of the normal speaker suffering from a severe head cold.
>
> *Assimilative Nasality.* In assimilative nasality, the speaker's vowels appear nasal when adjacent to the three nasal consonants. It would appear that the velopharyngeal port is opened too soon and remains open too long, so that vowel resonance preceding and following nasal consonant resonance is also nasalized.

Normal English consonants are produced with high intraoral pressures (3–8 cm H_2O) with essentially no nasal air flow except for the three nasal consonants that have low intraoral pressures (0.5–1.5 cm H_2O) and high rates of nasal airflow (100–300 cc sec.), as reported by Mason and Warren (1980). Aerodynamic studies looking at cleft palate and problems of nasality have provided some needed quantification to help us differentiate patients with excessive nasal resonance from patients lacking sufficient nasal resonance (Warren, 1979). By studying air pressures and airflow patterns, Warren reported estimates of the size of the velopharyngeal port. While most normal speakers demonstrate tight velopharyngeal closure with no air leakage (Thompson, 1978), Warren has written that openings as small as 5 mm or less may still permit voice quality that is perceived by listeners as normal (Mason and Warren, 1980). Patients with nasal voices who produce high nasal air-flow rates are perceived as having hypernasality with denasality, accompanied by low nasal air flows.

There is probably no area of voice therapy more neglected or more confusing than therapy for nasal resonance problems. Historically, the implication in the early literature was that most problems of nasality (usually hypernasality) could be successfully treated by voice therapy, that is, by ear training, as described by Bell in 1890, or by blowing exercises (Kantner, 1947), or by the exercises for the velum suggested by Buller (1942), or by the treatment Williamson used for seventy-two cases of hypernasality, which put some emphasis on relaxing the entire vocal tract (1945). Most of these early approaches were developed for functional hypernasality, but were later applied by various clinicians to problems of palatal insufficiency and cleft palate. For most of these structural problems, however, such approaches as blowing and relaxation were found to be ineffective. If the velopharyngeal mechanisms were structurally unable to produce velopharyngeal closure, no amount of relaxation or exercise could have much effect in reducing excessive nasal resonance. Realistic management and therapy for any problem in nasal resonance, therefore, requires that the patient have a thorough differential evaluation, including a detailed examination of the mechanism, aerodynamic studies, functional speech-voice testing, and a detailed acoustical analysis of voice.

The Evaluation of Nasal Resonance Disorders

There are more similarities than differences between patients with resonance disorders and those with phonation disorders. For this reason, the evaluational procedures outlined in Chapter 4 are equally relevant here. In addition to obtaining the necessary medical data, the clinician must pursue case history information (description of the problem and its cause, description of daily voice use, variations of the problem, onset and duration of the problem, and so on). The clinician must observe closely how well the patient seems to function as a person in the clinic and in out-of-clinic situations. Considering how subjective our judgments of resonance disorders are, it is crucial that the clinician know how the patient perceives his or her own voice. A mild resonance problem, for example, can be perceived by the patient and, or, others as a severe problem, while a severe resonance problem is occasionally ignored by the patient and, or, the people about him or her.

Analysis of Voice in Speech. An obvious way to begin the evaluation of a person with a nasal resonance disorder is to listen carefully to his or her voice during spontaneous conversation. This can provide a gross indication of what the problem may be (assimilative nasality, hypernasality, etc.). It should be recognized that it is extremely difficult to make a clinical judgment about nasality by listening to someone as he or she speaks; in fact, such a judgment is likely to be wrong. For example, Bradford,

Brooks, and Shelton (1964) found that neither a group of four experienced judges nor one of four inexperienced judges could reliably judge the recorded voice samples of children producing /a/ and /i/ with nares open and closed (by digital pressure). The judges were similarly unreliable when judging nasality from conversational speech samples. While the judgment that "there is something nasal about the speech" is usually correct, there are few examiners who can quickly and reliably differentiate the type of nasality (hypernasality, assimilative nasality, denasality) on the basis of such a conversational sample. It would appear that voice quality judgments are more accurate if made on the basis of a tape-recorded sample of the patient's conversational speech, his or her vowels in isolation, and his or her sentences (some with only oral phonemes and some loaded with nasal phonemes). The taped sample allows the clinician repeated playback, permitting him or her to focus on a specific parameter (loudness, pitch, quality) on each playback, which may increase his or her objectivity. To counter the "halo" effect, the influence of a speaker's articulation on the judgment of his or her nasality, Sherman (1954) developed a procedure of playing the connected speech sample backward on the tape recorder, thus precluding the identification of any articulation errors. Reverse playback is most helpful in differentiating between hypernasality and denasality. Spriestersbach (1955) found that the reverse playback of speech samples of cleft palate subjects reduced the correlations between articulation proficiency–pitch level and judgments of nasality. We have found that asking patients to repeat or read aloud passages that are totally free of nasal consonants, such as "Betty Takes Bob to the Show" (Boone, 1980a), or passages that are loaded with nasal consonants, such as "Many Men in the Moon" (Boone, 1980a), were helpful in differentiating hypernasality, denasality, and assimilative nasality from one another.

Patients with hypernasality often have laryngeal abnormalities as well. Therefore, the clinician must not only make judgments relative to resonance abnormality, he or she must also listen closely to voice quality. For example, children with velopharyngeal closure problems have been found to have a high incidence of vocal cord nodules and polyps (McWilliams, Lavorato, and Bluestone, 1973). The voice sample then should be analyzed for resonance, for vocal quality, and for articulation. Besides listening to the voice, the clinician must employ stimulability testing and other testing techniques.

Stimulability Testing.   Although stimulability testing was designed for use with problems of articulation, it is also effective with problems of voice. The basic purpose of stimulability testing, as described first by Milisen (1957), was to see how well the patient can produce an errored sound when he or she is repeatedly presented with the correct sound through both auditory and visual stimuli. One way of distinguishing between true problems of velopharyngeal structure (where the mechanism is wholly incapable of adequate closure) and functional velopharyngeal inadequacy (where the mechanism has the capability of closure) is to see if the patient can produce oral resonance under stimulability conditions

(Morris and Smith, 1962). Obviously, the patient's success in producing oral resonance would be a strong indication that velopharyngeal closure is possible. Shelton, Hahn, and Morris wrote,

> If repeated stimulation consistently results in consonant productions which are distorted by nasal emission and vowels which are unpleasantly nasal, the inference can be drawn, at least tentatively, that the individual is not able to change his speaking behavior because of velopharyngeal incompetence. (1968, p. 236)

Success in producing oral resonance under conditions of stimulability would be a good indicator for voice therapy and, also, a favorable prognostic sign.

Articulation Testing.   Articulatory proficiency can provide a good index of a patient's velopharyngeal closure. Nasal emission, the aperiodic escape of noise through the nose, is a most common articulation error on plosive and fricative phonemes among subjects with inadequate velopharyngeal closure. Even though the patient may have his or her articulators in the correct position, vis-à-vis their lingual-alveolar-labial contacts, the error is produced because increased oral pressure escapes nasally through the incomplete posterior palatal closure. The presence or absence of nasal emission, therefore, is a most important diagnostic sign with regard to velopharyngeal adequacy. It is important in articulation testing to distinguish between errors that are the result of faulty articulatory positioning and errors related to inadequacy of the velopharyngeal structure.

Any standardized articulation test will be found useful for determining those phonemes that are distorted because of inadequate velopharyngeal closure. The clinician must closely assess the identified errors to determine if lingual placements are accurate to make the target phoneme correctly. Many younger children with velopharyngeal problems will exhibit sound substitutions and omission errors in addition to the nasal emission and nasal snort distortion they produce because of inadequate velar closure. Older children and adults with nasal emission problems may well have correct articulatory lingual placements, with their distortions being a product of posterior nasal escape of the air stream. It may be noted that following successful pharyngeal flap surgery or after the proper fitting of an appliance, nasal emission will sometimes continue until it is modified through speech remediation. The past learning and the muscular "set" for making distorted nasal emission may continue even though the closure mechanism may now be considered normal. It is usually possible, however, to eliminate nasal emission through therapy, once structural adequacy has been achieved. An excellent articulation test for assessing competency of velopharyngeal closure is found in the forty-three special test items from the Templin-Darley Tests of Articulation (1980), known as the Iowa Pressure Articulation Test (1980), a test that is particularly sensitive for identifying the presence of nasal emission during the production of certain consonants.

Denasality in its purest and most overt form would be exhibited on an articulation test with these substitutions for the nasal phonemes: b/m; d/n; g/ŋ. Assimilative nasality would be observable only for vowels in words containing a nasal phoneme. Nasal emission would be most commonly observed in patients with palatal insufficiency in affricates (such as tʃ), fricatives (such as s), and plosives (such as p). Hypernasality per se would not be isolated on an articulation test. The clinician should be alert to the relatively high number of articulation errors often present in the speech of patients with cleft palate. In fact, from a speech therapy point of view, there is often more merit in focusing on articulation errors in cases of cleft palate than on resonance per se; as speech intelligibility improves, the hypernasality of these patients interferes less and less with effective communication. The type of articulation test or tasks used to assess articulatory proficiency is a matter of clinical choice. With the increasing availability of diagnostic aids for determining adequacy of velopharyngeal closure, the clinician must not abandon his or her articulation assessment, which may well be one of the most valid tools for diagnosing velopharyngeal inadequacy.

The Peripheral Oral Examination.   By direct visual examination, the clinician can make a gross observation of the relationship of the velum to the pharynx, note the relative size of tongue, make a judgment of maxillary-mandibular occlusion, view the height of the palatal arch, survey the general condition of dentition, and determine if there are any clefts or open fistulas in the palate. It should be remembered that direct visualization of palatal length and movement provides only a gross indication of velopharyngeal closure, since the anatomic point of closure is superior by some distance to the lower border of the velum. That is, a lack of velar contact with the pharynx at the uvular-tip end of the velum is not an indication of lack of closure further up where closure usually occurs. A markedly short palate or a palate with obvious pharyngeal contact can be noted on direct inspection of the oral cavity, and such a notation would be diagnostically important. The less obvious problems of borderline closure cannot be determined by direct inspection and probably require cinefluorographic and panendoscopic confirmation, which we will discuss in the next section.

The degree of velar movement can be determined with some validity by directly viewing the soft palate, and is extremely important to know when crucial management decisions are being made, that is, when it is being decided whether a child should have a pharyngeal flap or an appliance, or speech therapy (to be discussed in our section on the treatment of hypernasality). Velar movement is sometimes impaired in what might appear to be a normally symmetrical palate; here, the patient has a sluggish palate, sometimes as a symptom following a severe infectious disease (influenza, encephalitis, and so on). Pharyngeal movement is almost impossible to determine by direct oral examination; it is best seen by lateral-view cinefluorographic film. In some problems of nasality, particularly those not associated with palatal insufficiency, the relative size and carriage of the tongue may have some diagnostic relevance. For example, some problems of "functional" nasality may be related to inappropriate size of tongue for the size of the oral cavity, or to innervation problems of the tongue.

The clinician should make a thorough search for any openings of the hard or soft palate that might contribute to an articulation distortion or to some problem of nasal resonance. Some patients will have a small opening (fistula) or lack of fusion around the border of the premaxilla, particularly in the area of the alveolar ridge; in some individuals such a fistula may produce airstream noises, creating articulatory distortion, but almost never will such an isolated opening this far forward on the maxilla produce nasal resonance. The absence or presence of soft-palate and hard-palate clefts should be noted; if such clefts have been previously corrected surgically, the degree of closure should be noted. In the case of a bony-palate defect, for example, sometimes the bony opening has been covered by a thin layer of mucosal tissue, not thick enough to prevent oral cavity soundwaves from traveling into the nasal cavity. This same observation applies to the occasional submucosal cleft seen usually at the midline of the junction of the hard and soft palates. Any other structural deviations—of dentition, occlusion, labial competence, and so on—should be noted and considered with regard to their possible effects on speech production and nasal resonance.

Evaluation Measures.   There are many instruments available today that can assist the clinician in evaluating various aspects of nasal resonance. These instruments can aid us in the decision-making process concerning what to do for the patient with a nasalization problem. We will consider separately instruments that provide aerodynamic data, acoustic information, radiographic visualization, and visual probe information:

Aerodynamic instruments. Pressure transducers and pneumotachometers have proven to be instruments of choice for measuring the relative air pressures and air flows emitting simultaneously from the nasal and oral cavities during speech (Warren, 1979). Pressure and flow data are measured from the two channels simultaneously, permitting relative comparisons. In normal speakers, except for the production of nasal consonants, there is relatively no nasal pressure or flow. In speakers with nasality problems, there will be deviations in the relative amount of nasal and oral flows, as is well documented in the recent work of Mason and Warren (1980) and Warren (1979). The aerodynamic procedures basically provide the clinician information relative to possible leakage through the nose when the velopharyngeal mechanism should be closed. Manometers have also been found useful for measuring relative nasal-oral air flows. Manometers measure the amount of pressure of the emitted air stream and do not measure resonance per se. There are two types of manometers used clinically, the water-filled U-tube and the mechanical pressure gauge. Both of these measure airflow pressure, and not nasality; however, in comparing oral with nasal readings, some indication of velopharyngeal competence is given, which may, of course, have some relevance to the judgment of nasality. The water-filled U-tube works in this way: A glass U-tube is partially filled with a colored liquid, and one end of the tube is fitted into a rubber hose. The free end of the hose is fitted with a nasal olive. The olive is emplaced nasally, and any utterance of the patient that is characterized by nasal emission will displace the liquid, providing the patient and clinician with some visual evidence of nasal emission.

The second type of manometer, a mechanical pressure gauge, is available commercially as the Hunter Oral Manometer.[1] This small instrument has three pressure dials that can provide pressure readings for the patient under two conditions, nares open and nares pinched closed. It is used in this way: With nares open, the patient blows into the mouthpiece, which produces a pressure peak value; the patient is then asked to pinch his or her nostrils and blow again through the mouthpiece; if he or she has some velopharyngeal inadequacy, the pressure value will be higher under the condition of nostril pinching, which in effect impedes the flow of air through the nasal cavity, producing an increased oral pressure value. In a subject with a normal velopharyngeal mechanism, the nares-open/nares-closed ratio would be 1.00; if dividing the nares-closed reading into the nares-open reading produces a value of less than 1.00, the indication is that there is some nasal escape of air under the nares-open condition. Such information would be added to other clinical knowledge about the patient, since manometric pressure ratios alone, with no other clinical testing data, would not tell us very much.

Acoustic instruments. The Tonar II was designed by Fletcher (1972) to provide relative data of the acoustic signal emitting from both the oral and nasal cavities. How much of the perceived voice signal is "coming" through the nose, how much from the mouth? The Tonar II provides for a running speech sample, a continuous feedback of the oral-nasal acoustic ratio, which is displayed on the instrument display panel. Because the oral-nasal acoustic ratio fluctuates with each utterance, a one-second or ten-second averaging may be set on the instrument by the clinician. The patient is asked to read or repeat a continuous verbal passage, speaking directly into the two separate microphones, one receiving the oral signal and one the nasal signal. The oral signal value is divided into the nasal signal value to yield the actual oral-nasal acoustic ratio, a process that is done automatically at one- or ten-second intervals (depending on the interval set by the clinician) by the Tonar II (Fletcher, 1972). The typical speaker with normal nasal resonance will experience a "top" oral-nasal ratio of under 10 percent. Speakers with severe hypernasality will experience ratios in excess of 80 percent. One advantage in using the Tonar II for analyzing relative nasality is that it provides a continuous value specific to relative nasal and oral resonance in running speech.

Spectrographic and acoustic analysis have had increased use in the evaluation of patients with various voice disorders (Takahashi and Koike, 1975; Murry and Doherty, 1980) but have not been found particularly useful in differentiating the types of nasal resonance deviations, such as hypernasality from denasality. It has been demonstrated spectrographically that speakers with increased nasalization demonstrate more prominent third formants with an increase in formant bandwidth, accompanied by a rise in fundamental frequency. Dickson (1962), in his acoustic study of nasality using the spectrograph, concluded there was no way to "differentiate nasality in cleft-palate and non-cleft palate individuals either in terms of their acoustic spectra or the variability of the nasality judgments" (p. 111). It is doubtful that the visual writeout provided by the spectrograph can provide the clinician with any more information about the type of nasality he or she hears than would be obtained from listening carefully to the same samples. The spectrograph is helpful in identifying the aperiodic noise of nasal emission, but beyond this it is most difficult to differentiate between spectrograms of speakers with hypernasality and of those with denasality or assimilative nasality. As clinicians learn to use what spectral

[1] Hunter Oral Manometer, Hunter Manufacturing Company, Iowa City, Iowa.

analyses the spectrograph can provide, however, the instrument may well become a most useful tool for studying various parameters of nasality.

Radiographic instruments. Radiographic studies of the velopharyngeal mechanism during speech provide ready information about structural and physiological limitations of the mechanism in those patients who demonstrate velopharyngeal incompetence. For example, through a lateral-view film we can determine the relative amount of velopharyngeal opening during speech, the length of the velum, relative movements, and so on (Skolnick and others, 1975; Bowman and Shanks, 1978). However, there are limitations to the use of lateral views attempting to view closure, since lateral wall movement of the pharynx, which may contribute heavily to velopharyngeal closure, cannot be visualized. Sometimes the patient is asked to swallow barium and as the barium passes through the pharynx, measurements can be made of the relative pharyngeal opening as it may relate to the velopharyngeal closing mechanism (Skolnick, Glaser, and McWilliams, 1980). It appears that the most useful radiographic views of velopharyngeal closure require the patient to make some speech utterances, including phrases and sentences which include pressure consonants. The speech-language pathologist needs to work closely with the radiologist, presenting the speech tasks as the films are made and "reading" the films when they are completed. Sometimes a radiographic display can demonstrate a problem in velopharyngeal closure that cannot be detected by any other method.

Visual probe instruments. Shelton and Trier (1976) have written that direct measures of velopharyngeal competence through the use of "endoscopes, nasopharyngoscopes, and ultrasound apparatus" offer some advantages in making treatment decisions. The oral endoscope (Zwitman, Gyepes, and Ward, 1976) has been found to be a useful instrument for determining the degree and type of velopharyngeal closure. The body of the fiberoptic scope is extended above the tongue within the oral cavity so that the lighted tip and viewing window lie just below the uvula and within the oropharyngeal opening. By turning the viewing window up toward the velopharyngeal area, the velum, the lateral pharyngeal walls, and the posterior pharynx may be visualized. Incidentally, if the viewing window's tip is turned down, the clinician may visualize the vocal folds. While young children are not able to tolerate the panendoscopic exam well without severe gagging, most subjects over nine years of age seem to tolerate the procedure very well. Shelton and his colleagues (1975) have used the oral panendoscope for providing subjects visual feedback about their particular closure patterns; by viewing their panendoscopically viewed closure patterns by watching a TV monitor, subjects have been able to modify their closure pattern. Distinct variations in patterns of velopharyngeal closure have been demonstrated by Zwitman, Sonderman, and Ward (1974); some subjects have only velar movement without associated pharyngeal wall movement, some subjects primarily have lateral and posterior pharyngeal wall constriction, while some subjects appear to achieve closure by a combination of velar and pharyngeal movements. A nasal fiberoptic endoscope has been developed that places a small flexible scope through the nose and down into the pharynx, offering a view of velopharyngeal closure from above the closure site (Miyazaki, Matsuya, and Yamaoka, 1975). The primary advantage of the nasoscope is that it is not invasive to the oral cavity and consequently does not impede tongue or lip movements (a limitation of the oral endoscope); a disadvantage is that the nasal instrument may be painful and uncomfortable to some subjects, often requiring a physician to assist in its application. The oral and nasal fiberoptic probes have proven to be effective instruments for assessing velopharyngeal competence in

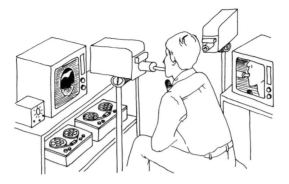

FIGURE 7-1. A display of a panendoscopic examination unit showing the subject with the panendoscope in place with two TV monitors showing the velopharyngeal closure pattern and the procedure, both being taped on separate video recorders. (*After a drawing from "Panendoscopic Feedback in the Study of Voluntary Velopharyngeal Movements," by Ralph L. Shelton, Andrew Paesani, K. D. McClelland, and Shari S. Bradfield, in* Speech Hearing Disorders 40, *232–44* [1975].)

patients with nasal resonance problems, offering direct observation of velar length and movement, degree of lateral and posterior pharyngeal wall movement, and the kind of velopharyngeal closure the patient is using.

Treatment of Hypernasality

The presence of excessive nasal resonance (hypernasality) is relatively dependent upon the judgment of the listener. That is, some languages and regional dialects require heavy nasal resonance and therefore consider pronounced nasalization of vowels to be normal. Others, however, such as general American English, tolerate little nasal resonance beyond the three nasal consonants. Thus, a native New Englander with a nasal "twang" exhibits normal voice resonance in Portland, Maine, but when he travels to New Knoxville, Ohio, the people there perceive his voice as excessively nasal. There will be variations in the degree of nasality among the voices of the people in Ohio, of course, but a certain amount of resonance variability can exist among any particular population without anyone being bothered by it. If, however, a particular voice in Ohio (or any other place) stands out as "excessively nasal," then that voice will be considered as having a resonance disorder. The judgment of hypernasality, then, is as dependent upon the speech-language milieu of the speaker and his or her listeners as it is upon the actual performance of the speaker.

The speaker who is judged to be hypernasal increases the nasalization of his or her vowels by failing to close his or her velopharyngeal port. This failure to close the velopharyngeal opening may be related to structural-organic defects, or it may have a functional etiology. Hypernasality frequently accompanies unrepaired cleft palate or a short palate. Among other organic causes of the disorder are surgical trauma, accidental injury to the soft palate, and impaired innervation of the soft palate as a result of poliomyelitis or some other form of bulbar disease. Sometimes temporary hypernasality may follow tonsillectomy as the child attempts to minimize the pain by not moving his or her velopharyngeal mechanism (Hanley and Manning, 1958). There are some people who speak with hypernasal resonance for purely functional reasons, perhaps maintaining a lingering internal model of a previously acceptable form of resonance, or perhaps imitating the voice of someone they consider particularly attractive (such as a famous political figure). While it is possible that the majority of persons with hypernasal voices have some structural basis for their lack of velopharyngeal competence, the ease of imitating a hypernasal voice tells us that it could be relatively easy to become hypernasal with perfectly adequate and normal velopharyngeal equipment. Hypernasality is one voice problem in which the distinction must be made between organic and functional causes, as the treatment recommended will be quite specific to the diagnosis.

If there are any indications of physical inadequacy of velopharyngeal closure, the primary role of the speech pathologist would be to refer the patient to a specialist who could provide the needed physical correction—a plastic surgeon, say, or a prosthodontist. There is very little evidence that voice therapy to improve resonance will have any positive effect in the presence of physical inadequacy. In fact, there is some indication that voice therapy to improve the oral resonance of patients with palatal insufficiency (those who lack the physical equipment to produce closure) will usually not only fail, but that this failure will be seen by the patient as his or her own fault—as a defeat indicating low personal worth—and thus will take an obvious toll on the patient's self-image. An example of the uselessness of speech therapy in the presence of a severe inadequacy of velopharyngeal closure is provided by this case of a teen-aged girl who had received speech therapy for both articulation and resonance for a period of seven years:

B. B., aged fourteen, had received seven years of group and individual speech therapy in the public schools and in a community speech and hearing clinic for "a severe articulation defect characterized by sibilant distortion, and for a severely nasal voice." The mother became upset because of the girl's continued lack of progress and her tendency to withdraw from social contact with her peers, which, the mother felt, was related to her embarrassment over her continued poor speech. The child was evaluated by a comprehensive cleft palate team, which, after reviewing her history, found that her nasality could be dated from a severe bout of influenza when she was six years old. The influenza had been followed immediately by a deterioration of speech. Subsequent speech therapy records were incomplete, although the mother reported that the therapy had included extensive blowing drills, tongue-palate exercises, and articulation work. Physical examination of the velar mechanism found the child to have good tongue and pharyngeal movements, but bilateral paralysis of the soft palate; even on gag reflex stimulation, there was only a "flicker" of palatal movement observed. Lateral cinefluorographic films confirmed the relatively complete absence of velar movement. The examining speech pathologist found the girl to have normal articulation placement of the tongue for all speech sounds, despite severe nasal emission of air flow for fricative and affricate phonemes. Low back vowels were relatively oral in resonance, while middle and high vowels became increasingly nasal. It was the consensus of the evaluation team that, with her structural inadequacy, this child was (and had been) a poor candidate for speech therapy. It was recommended that she receive a pharyngeal flap and be evaluated again several weeks after the operation. The surgery was successful and had an amazingly positive effect on the child's speech. While hypernasality disappeared, some slight nasal emission remained. The girl was subsequently enrolled in individual speech therapy, where she·experienced total success in developing normal fricative-affricate production.

Such a case dramatically shows the futilty of continued speech therapy when real structural inadequacy exists. Indeed, whenever this author wishes to give students a vivid illustration of the point, he plays recordings of this young lady's voice made before and after her operation. Without that operation, she could have received speech therapy for the rest of her life, with no effect whatsoever on her speech. If velopharyngeal insufficiency is found, there appear to be two primary alternatives for treatment, surgical or dental. When structural adequacy is achieved, remediation services of the speech-language pathologist can produce further changes in the patient's speech and resonance.

Surgical Treatment for Hypernasality.   The evaluation may reveal the existence of such structural inadequacies as open fistulas, open bony and soft tissue clefts, submucous clefts, and short or relatively immobile soft palates. The plastic surgeon is usually the medical specialist most experienced in making decisions about the time of surgical closure of palatal openings and about the type of surgery required. For those individuals who have been found to have cleft palate, the primary surgical procedure usually involves closing the cleft and still maintaining adequate palatal length. Most patients with cleft palate, however, require multiple secondary surgical procedures at later times, such as rebuilding structures or eliminating earlier surgical scars. Many patients with hypernasality demonstrate velums that are too short for closure or velums that do not move adequately for closure. Such patients often profit from a surgically constructed pharyngeal flap. Here, the surgeon takes a small piece of mucosal tissue from the pharynx and uses it to bridge the excessive velopharyngeal opening, attaching the tissue to the soft palate. This tissue appears to act as an excellent diverting structure, deflecting both air flow and soundwaves into the oral cavity. Bzoch (1964), discussing the physiological and speech results for forty patients who had received pharyngeal flap surgery, reported that the procedure was most effective in reducing both hypernasality and nasal emission (if present) in most of the subjects. While pharyngeal flap surgery, or any other form of palatal surgery, must not be thought of as a panacea for all resonance problems, it will often help align oral-nasal structures in such a way that, for the first time, speech and voice therapy can be effective.

Dental Treatment of Hypernasality.   Both the orthodontist and the prosthodontist may play important roles in the treatment of individuals with hypernasality, particularly those with a problem of cleft palate. The orthodontist may face the problem of expanding the dental arches so that the patient can experience more normal palatal growth. The prosthodontist, by constructing various prosthetic speech appliances and obturators, may be able to help the patient preserve his or her facial contour, filling in various maxillary defects with prostheses to cover open palatal defects such as fistulas and clefts, and may also be able to build speech training appliances to provide posterior velopharyngeal closure. In evaluating twenty-one adults with acquired or congenital palate problems, Arndt, Shelton, and Bradford (1965) found that both groups made significant "articulation and voice gains with obturation." Many cleft palate subjects are fitted by the prosthodontist with acrylic bulbs at the end of their appliance; if the bulb is well positioned against the posterior and lateral pharyngeal walls, there will often be a noticeable reduction of both nasality and air escape. Many patients with problems of dysarthria, which may include a hypernasality component, have problems with immobile velums, lacking sufficient velar movement to achieve closure. Such patients who experience weakened or paralyzed soft palates might well profit from consultation with the prosthodontist about the possibility of being fitted with a lift appliance to hold the immobile palate in a higher position so that some pharyngeal contact will be possible (Mazaheri, 1979). For nasality problems related to velopharyngeal inadequacy, the speech pathologist should freely consult both the orthodontist and prosthodontist for their ideas on how to achieve adequate functioning of the oral structures.

Voice Therapy for Hypernasality.   Any attempts at voice therapy for hypernasality should be deferred until both the evaluation of the problem and attempts at physical correction have been completed. The primary requirement for developing good oral voice quality is the structural adequacy of the velopharyngeal closing mechanism. Without adequate closure, voice therapy will be futile. However, there are individuals who, for functional reasons, speak with hypernasality, and for these people voice therapy can be helpful in developing more oral resonance. Added to this group are occasional patients who have had surgical or dental treatment that has left them with only a marginal velopharyngeal closing mechanism; in voice therapy, this mechanism may be trained to work more optimally.

Fletcher (1972) has described the Tonar II as a useful instrument for helping the patient to reduce his or her hypernasality. The instrument was designed to provide the patient with ongoing feedback information about his or her oral-nasal ratio. Fletcher recommends that the clinician set for the patient a ratio "goal." A reinforcement panel can then be connected to the Tonar panel so that the patient can be "systematically and instantaneously notified of success each time he meets the specified goal ratio and criterion of performance" (Fletcher, 1972, p. 331). If the patient has the capability of developing greater oral resonance, he or she works incrementally, using the Tonar feedback system, toward the goal of acceptable oral resonance. Until Tonar instruments or instrumentation similar to them are more readily available, however, the clinician might well use some of the following facilitating approaches for improving orality of resonance:

1. *Approach 1, Altering Tongue Position.* A high, forward carriage of the tongue sometimes contributes to nasal resonance. Efforts in developing a lower, more posterior carriage may have some effect in decreasing the perceived nasality.

2. *Approach 3, Change of Loudness.* A voice that has been perceived as hypernasal will sometimes be perceived as more normal if some other change in vocalization is made. One change that often accomplishes this is an increase in loudness; by speaking in a louder voice, the patient will frequently sound less hypernasal.

3. *Approach 7, Ear Training.* If the patient is motivated to reduce his or her hypernasality, a great deal of therapy time should be spent in learning to hear the differences between his or her nasal and oral resonances.

4. *Approach 10, Establishing New Pitch.* Some patients with hypernasality speak at inappropriately high pitch levels, which contributes to the listener's perception of nasality. Speaking at the lower end of one's pitch range seems to contribute to greater oral resonance.

5. *Approach 11, Explanation of Problem.* No voice therapy should ever be started without first explaining to the patient what the problem seems to be.

6. *Approach 12, Feedback.* Developing an aural awareness of hypernasality and some oral-pharyngeal awareness of what hypernasality "feels" like is a most helpful therapeutic device.

7. *Approach 18, Open Mouth.* Hypernasality is sometimes produced by an overall restriction of the oral opening. In such cases, efforts at developing greater oral openness may have some effect in reducing the listener's perception of excessive nasality.

8. *Approach 20, Place the Voice.* While for some patients, using the focus on the facial mask area seems to increase nasality, there are noticeable improvements in resonance for some patients, particularly those whose hypernasality is of functional origin.

9. *Approach 23, Respiration.* Increased loudness is often achieved by respiration training.

Treatment for Denasality

Beyond the nasal resonance required for /m/, /n/, and /ŋ/, vowels in American English require a slight nasal resonance. Lack of nasal resonance in severe cases produces actual articulatory substitutions for the three nasal phonemes as well as slight alterations for vowels. Denasality (hyponasality) is characterized by the diversion of soundwaves and air flow out through the oral cavity, permitting little or no nasal resonance. More often than not, this problem appears to be related to some kind of nasopharyngeal obstruction, such as excessive adenoidal growth, severe nasopharyngeal infection as in head colds, large polyps in the nasal cavity, and so on. Some patients who are hypernasal before surgical or dental treatment emerge from such treatment with complete or highly excessive velopharyngeal obstruction; perhaps the pharyngeal flap is too broad, permitting little or no ventilation of the nasopharynx, or an obturator bulb may fit too tightly, resulting in no nasal air flow or nasal resonance. Such obstruction is the usual reason for a denasality problem, and the search for it must precede any attempt at voice therapy.

Nasal air-flow competence can be tested simply as part of the overall resonance evaluation: Ask the patient to take a big breath, close his or her mouth; exhale through the nose. Then test the air flow through each nostril separately, compressing one nostril at a time by compressing the nares with a finger. If there is any observable decrement in air flow, the nasal passages should be investigated medically. Appropriate medical therapy should precede any voice therapy.

Only rarely will patients have markedly denasal voices for wholly functional reasons. While their denasal resonance in the beginning may have had a physical cause, that cause is no longer present, and the denasality may remain as a habit, a "set." Occasionally a patient has chosen a denasal voice as a model, for whatever reason, and has learned to match its denasality with some consistency. Voice therapy for increasing nasal resonance might include:

1. *Approach 7, Ear Training.* Considerable effort must be expended in contrasting for the patient the difference between the nasal and oral production of /m/, /n/, and /ŋ/. Oral and nasal resonance of vowels can also be presented for listening contrast.

2. *Approach 11, Explanation of Problem.* The resonance requirements for normal English must be explained to the patient, and his or her own lack of nasal resonance, particularly for /m/, /n/, and /ŋ/, pointed out. If the patient's problem is wholly functional, this explanation is of primary importance.

3. *Approach 12, Feedback.* Emphasis must be given to contrasting what it sounds like and "feels" like to produce oral and nasal resonance. The patient should be encouraged to make exaggerated humming sounds both orally and nasally, concentrating on the "feel" of the two types of productions.

Treatment for Assimilative Nasality

The nasalization of vowels immediately before and after nasal consonants is known as assimilative nasality. Performance on stimulability testing will provide a good clue as to whether such nasal resonance is related to poor velar functioning or is functionally induced. There are a few neurological disorders, such as bulbar palsy or multiple sclerosis, in which the patient is unable to move the velum quickly enough to facilitate the movements required for normal resonance. His or her velar openings begin too soon and are maintained too long, lagging behind the rapid requirements of normal speech and producing nasalization of vowels that occur next to nasal phonemes. Most cases of assimilative nasality, however, are of functional origin, with the patient showing good oral resonance under special conditions of stimulability.

It is important to remember here that in connected speech, all sounds are interdependent; as one sound is being produced, articulators are positioning for the next sound. This phonemic interdependence allows for a certain amount of assimilation, even in normal speech. In assimilative nasality, therefore, we are dealing once again with a perceptual problem; that is, whether the speaker's nasalization of vowels adjacent to nasal phonemes is excessive or not depends on the perception of the listener. The perception of assimilative nasality is of course related to the perception of excessive nasality; a normal, minor amount of nasality in the vowels following nasal phonemes would not be perceived, and increased amounts of nasal resonance would be judged quite differently by different listeners, according to their individual standards and experience. Therapy for assimilative nasality is likewise highly variable, being related largely to the locale (in some areas such resonance is a normal voice pattern), the standards of the speaker or his or her clinician, their motivations, and so on. It might well be that the Tonar II (1972) would be a useful therapy instrument for the patient desirous of reducing his or her assimilative nasality. The clinician and the patient can set oral-nasal ratio goals that favor orality and then work incrementally toward the goal of eliminating the assimilative nasal resonance. Voice therapy for assimilative nasality is best attempted only by those patients who have strong motivations to develop more oral resonance. These approaches might be used:

1. *Approach 7, Ear Training.* Ear training should help patients discriminate between their nasalized vowels and their oral vowels. They might profit from listening to recordings of their own oral-consonant/vowel/oral-consonant words as contrasted with their nasal-consonant/vowel/nasal-consonant words, such as these pairs: bad–man, bed–men, bead–mean, bub–mum, and so on. Voice and diction books often contain certain word pairs matching monosyllabic words using /b/, /d/, and /g/ with those using /m/, /n/, and /ŋ/. Once the patient can hear the differences between oral and nasal cognates, see if he or she can produce them.

2. *Approach 11, Explanation of Problem.* Since nasal assimilations are difficult to explain verbally, any attempt at explanation should be accompanied by demonstration. The best demonstration appears to be in presenting the contrast between oral and nasal resonance of vowels that follow or precede the three nasal phonemes.

3. *Approach 12, Feedback.* While feedback can certainly be attempted with the problem of assimilative nasality, experience has found that few patients can monitor well what they are doing during conditions of ongoing feedback. Learning to listen to oneself critically with delayed feedback provided by some kind of auditory loop tape device has been found to be helpful.

Therapy for Oral-Pharyngeal Resonance Problems

Although both the oral and pharyngeal cavities during speech are constantly changing in size and shape, the oral cavity is the most changeable of all the resonance cavities. Speech is possible only because of the capability for variation on the part of such oral structures as the lips, mandible, tongue, and velum. The most dramatic of all oral movements in speech are those of the tongue, which makes various constrictive-restrictive contacts at different sites within the oral cavity to produce consonant articulation. Vowel and diphthong production are possible only because of size-shape adjustments of the oral cavity, requiring a delicate blend of muscle adjustment of all oral muscle structures. While there are many individuals who display faulty positioning of oral structures for articulation, and thus are heard to articulate "badly," there are fewer individuals who are recognized to have problems in positioning their oral structures for resonance. Slight departures in articulatory proficiency are much more easily recognized than are minor problems in voice resonance. While an articulation error may be viewed consistently as a problem, faulty oral-pharyngeal resonance is usually accepted as "the way he or she talks." Nasality problems are more likely to be recognized by lay and professional listeners as requiring correction than are oral-pharyngeal resonance departures. Any judgment of resonance is going to be heavily influenced by the appropriateness of pitch, the degree of glottal competence as heard in the periodic quality of phonation, and the degree of accuracy of articulation. Since quality of resonance, then, appears basically to be a subjective experience, the goal in resonance therapy must be to achieve whatever voice "sounds best."

Singing teachers have long been aware of the vital role the tongue plays in influencing the quality of the voice, devoting considerable instructional and practice time to helping the singing student develop optimum carriage of the tongue (Coffin, 1981). While the postures needed to produce various phonemes will attract the tongue to different anatomic sites within the oral cavity, with noticeable changes of oral resonance, more objective evidence of the role of the tongue in oral resonance may be obtained through spectrographic and cinefluorographic analysis. In the spectral analyses afforded by the spectrograph, one can study the effects of tongue positioning and the distribution of spectral formants. The second formant seems to "travel" the most, changing position up and down the spectrum for various vowel productions. The primary oral shaper for production of vowels appears to be the tongue. It should be pointed out that decisions about quality resonance (for example, is the voice hypernasal or denasal) are almost impossible to render from the visual inspection of spectrograms. It is most difficult to quantify formant variations and relate them to variations in voice quality. In describing the difficulty of spectrographic analysis, Moll has written that "this presumably more 'objective' measure involves human judgments which probably are more difficult than those made in judging nasality from actual speech" (1968, p. 99). Visual inspection of the spectrogram is a difficult task, particularly when one attempts to relate formant positioning to judgments of voice quality. As for the cinefluorograph, its use for studying tongue, velar, mandibular, and pharyngeal movements, when such movements apply to voice quality, becomes far more effective when a voice track is added. The addition of the speaker's voice not only enables the viewer to match the sound of the voice to the filmed analysis of the speaker's movements, but, more important, provides him or her with the primary vehicle for determining whether a problem of quality exists; quality judgments cannot be made from the visual study of oral movements alone, but depend primarily on hearing the sound of the voice. By using both the pitch and intensity readings at the same time on the Visi-Pitch (1980), we have found that the stored tracings on the Visi-Pitch scope give useful information specific to better resonance. Often the resonance that sounds better to the ear is represented on the scope as being less aperiodic (the frequency writeout has less scatter) and shows greater intensity (greater amplitude of the intensity curve). The "better-sounding" voice often comes quite unexpectedly as the clinician and the patient use various facilitating approaches in their search for good oral resonance. Once the "good" voice is achieved, the Visi-Pitch offers useful feedback for the patient, often confirming by improvement in the scope tracings the subjective judgments the clinician and patient have heard.

Reducing the Strident Voice

One of the most annoying oral-pharyngeal resonance problems is the strident voice. We shall use the term *stridency,* which means the unpleasant, shrill, metallic-sounding voice that appears to be related to hypertonicity of the pharyngeal constrictors. Fisher (1975) described the strident voice as having brilliance of high overtones sounding "brassy, tinny, blatant." Physiologically, stridency may be produced by the elevation of the larynx and hypertonicity of the pharyngeal constrictors, resulting in a decrease of both the length and the width of the pharynx. The surface of the pharynx becomes taut because of the tight pharyngeal constriction. The smaller pharyngeal cavity, coupled with its tighter, reflective mucosal surface, produces the ideal resonating structure for accentuating high-frequency resonance. Such a voice may be developed deliberately by the carnival barker or the dimestore demonstrator for its obvious attention-getting effects; for another person, stridency may only emerge when he or she becomes overly tense, constricting the pharynx as part of his or her overall response. The person who has this sort of strident voice—and who wants to correct it—can, in voice therapy, often develop some relaxed oral-pharyngeal behaviors that will decrease pharyngeal constriction, lessening the amount of stridency. Anything that the individual can do to lower the larynx, decrease pharyngeal constriction, and promote general throat relaxation will usually result in a reduction of stridency. The reader is referred back to the twenty-five facilitating techniques described in Chapter 5; from that list we have selected those approaches that appear to be most helpful in reducing stridency:

1. *Approach 5, Chewing.* It is almost impossible to produce strident resonance under conditions of chewing. The various steps of chewing, detailed in Chapter 5, should be most helpful in reducing stridency.
2. *Approach 7, Ear Training.* Explore various vocal productions with the patient, with the goal of producing a nonstrident voice. When the patient is able to produce good oral resonance, contrast this production with recorded strident vocalizations by using loop tape feedback devices and following the various ear-training procedures.
3. *Approach 10, Establishing New Pitch.* The strident voice is frequently accompanied by an inappropriately high voice pitch. Efforts to lower the pitch level will often result in a voice that sounds less strident.
4. *Approach 11, Explanation of Problem.* Although it is difficult to explain problems of resonance to someone else, sometimes such an explanation is essential if the patient is ever to develop any kind of self-awareness about the problem.
5. *Approach 14, Hierarchy Analysis.* For the individual whose voice becomes strident whenever he or she is tense, it is important to try to isolate those situations in which his or her nonstridency is maintained.
6. *Approach 17, Negative Practice.* Once the patient is able to produce good oral resonance voluntarily, it is sometimes therapeutically valuable for him or her to produce the strident resonance intentionally, in order to contrast the "feeling" and sound of it with the new resonance pattern.
7. *Approach 18, Open Mouth.* Since stridency is generally the product of overconstriction, oral openness is an excellent way to counteract these tight, constrictive tendencies.
8. *Approach 22, Relaxation.* It is difficult to produce strident resonance under conditions of relaxation and freedom of tension. Either of the approaches, general relaxation or a more specific relaxation of the vocal tract, is helpful in reducing oral-pharyngeal tightness.
9. *Approach 25, Yawn-Sigh.* Since the yawn-sigh approach produces an openness and relaxation that is completely the opposite of the tightness of pharyngeal constriction, it is perhaps the most effective approach in this list for reducing stridency.

Improving Oral Resonance

There are two problems of oral resonance related to faulty tongue position, a *thin* type of resonance produced by excessively anterior tongue carriage and a *cul-de-sac* type produced by backward retraction of the tongue. The thin voice lacks adequate oral resonance, making its user sound immature and unsure of himself or herself. It is characterized by a generalized oral constriction with high, anterior carriage of the tongue and only minimal lip-mandibular opening. The user of such a voice appears to be holding back psychologically, either withdrawing from interpersonal contact by demonstrating all the symptoms of withdrawal, or retreating psychologically to a more infantile level of behavior by demonstrating a babylike quality. The first type, who withdraws from interpersonal contact, employs his or her thin resonance situationally, particularly at times when he or she feels most insecure; the second type uses the thin voice, the "baby resonance," more intentionally, in situations where he or she wants to appear cute, to "get his or her own way," and so on. The following facilitating approaches have been found useful in promoting a more natural, oral resonance:

1. *Approach 1, Altering Tongue Position.* The problem of the thin voice was first discussed in Chapter 5. Specific procedures are developed there to promote more posterior tongue carriage.

2. *Approach 2, Biofeedback.* For those patients whose anterior resonance focus appears related to situational tensions, biofeedback apparatus may help the patient to become aware of his or her varying states of tension. Biofeedback is best used with Relaxation (22) and Hierarchy Analysis (14).

3. *Approach 3, Change of Loudness.* When the resonance problem is part of a general picture of psychological withdrawal in particular situations, efforts at increasing voice loudness are appropriate for overall improvement of resonance.

4. *Approach 5, Chewing.* Chewing promotes a more natural carriage of the tongue.

5. *Approach 10, Establish New Pitch.* The thin voice is perceived by listeners to be drastically lacking in authority. Frequently, the pitch is too high. Efforts at lowering the voice pitch will often have a positive effect on resonance.

6. *Approach 14, Hierarchy Analysis.* Symptomatic voice therapy is based on the premise that it is often possible to isolate particular situations in which we function poorly with maladaptive behavior, and other situations in which we function comparatively well. By isolating the various situations and their modes of behavior, we can often introduce the more effective behavior into the "bad" situations, to take the place of the maladaptive kind. For those individuals who use a thin voice in specific situations, particularly during moments of tension, hierarchy analysis may be a necessary preliminary step in eliminating the aberrant vocal quality.

7. *Approach 18, Open Mouth.* The restrictive oral tendencies of the thin-voiced speaker may be effectively reduced by developing greater oral openness.

8. *Approach 22, Relaxation.* If the thin vocal quality is highly situational and the obvious result of tension, relaxation approaches may be helpful, particularly when used in combination with hierarchy analysis.

9. *Approach 23, Respiration Training.* Sometimes direct work on increasing voice loudness requires some work on increasing control of the air flow during expiration.

10. *Approach 25, Yawn-Sigh.* The yawn-sigh approach is an excellent way of developing a more relaxed, posterior tongue carriage.

The cul-de-sac voice may be found in individuals representing various etiologic groups: The "different" sound of the voice of the patient with oral apraxia may be of this type; the cerebral palsied child, particularly the athetoid type, has a posterior focus to his or her resonance added to his or her dysarthria; some patients with bulbar or pseudobulbar type lesions have a pharyngeal focus to their vocal resonance; and cul-de-sac resonance is a typical characteristic of the deaf child. The cul-de-sac voice, regardless of its physical cause, is produced by the deep retraction of the tongue into the oral cavity and hypopharynx, sometimes touching the pharyngeal wall and sometimes not. The body of the tongue literally obstructs the escaping air flow and the periodic soundwaves generated from the larynx below. While such a voice is often found in individuals with neural lesions who cannot control their muscles, and among deaf children and adults, it is also produced situationally by certain individuals for wholly functional reasons. Such posterior resonance is very difficult to correct in those patients who have muscle disorders related to various problems of innervation, particularly the dysarthric patient. Resonance deviations in the deaf may be changed somewhat in voice therapy as described in Chapter 6. For those individuals who produce cul-de-sac resonance for purely functional reasons (whatever they are), the following facilitating approaches will be useful:

1. *Approach 1, Altering Tongue Position.* Speech tasks designed to promote front-of-the-mouth resonance are helpful here. The reader is advised to review the section on resonance changes in the deaf in Chapter 6. The approaches described there for altering tongue position in deaf children apply for anyone working for more forward resonance.

2. *Approach 2, Biofeedback.* Posterior focus of voice resonance may for some patients be situationally related to tension. For these patients, biofeedback is often useful for helping the patient to monitor his or her varying tension states.

3. *Approach 7, Ear Training.* If, in the search for a better voice, the patient is able to produce a more forward, oral-sounding one, this should be contrasted with his or her cul-de-sac voice.

4. *Approach 14, Hierarchy Analysis.* If cul-de-sac resonance occurs only in particular situations, perhaps at those times when the individual is tense and under stress, the hierarchy approach may be useful. If the individual can produce good oral resonance in low-stress situations, he or she should practice using the same resonance at levels of increasing stress, on up the hierarchy.

5. *Approach 17, Negative Practice.* Once the patient can produce good oral resonance volitionally, he or she might undertake some negative practice, deliberately producing the cul-de-sac voice. In negative practice, efforts must be made to contrast the feeling and sound of the new voice with the old; indeed, the real value of the approach is in making this contrast.

6. *Approach 20, Place the Voice.* The forward focus in resonance required in placing the voice in the facial mask makes the approach a useful one for patients with a cul-de-sac focus. High front vowels and front-of-the-mouth consonants are particularly good practice sounds to use with the place the voice approach.

7. *Approach 22, Relaxation.* Posterior tongue retraction during moments of stress is often a learned response to tension. The patient who can learn a more relaxed positioning of the overall vocal tract may be able to reduce excessive tongue retraction.

SUMMARY

Resonance deviations of the voice are often produced by physical problems of structure or function at various sites within the upper airway. Primary efforts must be given to identifying any structural abnormalities and correcting these problems by dental, medical, or surgical intervention. The speech-language pathologist plays an important role in the early evaluation and diagnosis of the resonance problem, as well as providing needed voice therapy to correct the problem. For both organic and functional resonance problems, specific facilitating approaches were listed that can help the patient develop better oral and nasal resonance.

8

Voice Therapy for the Patient Who Has Had Cancer of the Larynx

Cancer of the larynx, a life-threatening disease, may dramatically alter or take away completely the patient's voice. Surgical treatment may include partial removal of the larynx or its total removal (laryngectomy). We shall consider in this chapter various voice remediation procedures for patients who have had partial or complete laryngeal surgery, including descriptions of using the artificial larynx and teaching esophageal speech.

The overall management of the patient with cancer of the larynx has changed markedly in recent years. Primary for successful management of laryngeal carcinoma is its early diagnosis and appropriate medical-surgical treatment. The patient first comes to the physician with such symptoms as hoarseness, difficulty in swallowing, and, or, pain. By use of mirror examination (laryngoscopy) or the fiberoptic endoscope, the physician may identify a laryngeal lesion; the tumor is subsequently studied by direct laryngoscopy and a biopsy (taking a sample of the lesion for microsopic examination). If the lesion is found to be cancerous, an overall medical-surgical management program will be initiated by the physician. The earlier or the sooner the diagnosis of laryngeal cancer can be made, the more favorable the outcome prognosis (Johnson, Newman, and Olson, 1980). The patient with laryngeal cancer will join a growing body of people who are diagnosed to have the disease; for example, in 1975, there were 9,100 new cases of laryngeal cancer annually in the United States, as compared with an estimated 10,700 new cases in 1980 (ACS, 1980). These 1980 data suggest a male-to-female ratio for laryngeal cancer of about five males for every female. The importance of early diagnosis is seen in the survival rate data (live more than five years) for laryngeal cancer and cancer in several other sites: larynx, 79 percent; breast, 85 percent; lung, 33 percent; oral, 67 percent (ACS, 1980). Patients whose lesions were detected early have less chance of the spreading (metastasis) of the disease to other sites. It might be pointed out, however, that while 79 percent of the patients with laryngeal cancer survive at least five years after the diagnosis of their disease, some 32 percent of them experience some metastasis to other body sites.

The type of medical treatment for laryngeal cancer depends on the site and extent of the tumor. A small tumor may invade only one vocal fold and can be successfully treated by radiation therapy alone, while an extensive cancer invasion of the larynx and the cervical lymph nodes may well require radiation therapy and a total laryngectomy. Because of the variety of tumor types at different sites in and adjacent to the larynx, a joint committee of otolaryngologists and other physicians (radiologists, oncologists) developed a staging category system that according to the extent and site of the tumor places it in a particular staging category (Batsakis, 1979). A lettering-numbering system is used for categorization of the tumor, enabling communication between specialists who know where the tumor is and relatively how extensive it is by its classification number; an example of a Stage I tumor is a T1 tumor where the "tumor is confined to one vocal cord with motility of cord maintained" (Batsakis, 1980, p. 137). Stage I and Stage II tumors are often successfully treated by radiation therapy alone, requiring no surgery. Such patients might experience temporary voice problems related to their tumor mass and the effects of radiation therapy; however, the management of their voice problem for the speech pathologist would be entirely different from what would be required for the patient with a total laryngectomy. In our discussion, therefore, of management by the speech pathologist of the patient who has had laryngeal cancer, we will discuss separately three types of patients: first, the patient with an altered larynx (but who still has one); secondly, we will place our focus on the management of the patient with a conventional but total laryngectomy; we will then discuss some new surgical procedures for the patient with a total laryngectomy, which permit the injection of pulmonary air into the esophagus for purposes of producing a new voice.

VOICE THERAPY FOR THE PATIENT
WITH AN ALTERED LARYNX

One of the primary functions of the larynx is to protect the airway. Therefore, any lesion or neoplasm that grows on a portion of the larynx must be evaluated in terms of its possible threat to the airway. Often, small tumors that occupy a portion of the supraglottal structure (such as the epiglottis) can be successfully treated with radiation therapy, with little or no effect on either respiratory function or on voice. A combined radiation-surgery approach is often effective in permanently eradicating a supraglottal tumor. Less extensive glottal carcinomas can often be treated similarly with radiation-surgery without the need for the total removal of the larynx (laryngectomy). Any surgical procedure, however, which compromises one of the vocal folds and its function may cause airway difficulties, with aspiration the most common complaint. That is, the partially or totally excised vocal fold cannot play its normal closure role, which may result in both aspiration and faulty voice. The surgeon evaluates how much laryngeal tissue must be cut away to remove the invading cancer, hopeful that some respiratory valving and voice can remain. Sometimes vocal fold carcinomas are successfully removed but require some surgical reconstruction of the involved fold to restore its functional capabilities (Som and Arnold, 1960). Various procedures have been used to build up the involved fold, including Teflon injection, tissue grafts, and muscle transplants (Ogura and Biller, 1969; Tucker and others, 1979). Some patients require an extended hemilaryngectomy, in which there is a vertical cutting away of one-half of most of the soft tissues of the larynx (Pearson, Woods, and Hartman, 1980), requiring major surgical reconstruction of the involved portion in order to effect sphincteric closure capability. Tucker and others (1979) report success with some patients who have had near total laryngectomy, reconstructing the larynx by utilizing the epiglottis as the primary tissue source for reconstructing a new glottis, capable of valving and for producing voice.

Patients who have had successful laryngeal surgery for carcinoma, short of having a total laryngectomy, are often referred to the speech-language pathologist for a voice evaluation and voice therapy. Each patient is unique and voice problems are primarily related to the particular glottal configuration present after surgery. The patient has survived a serious operation for laryngeal cancer and, upon the referral of his or her surgeon to the speech pathologist for voice improvement, we find the patient "high" and receptive to what we are able to do. In most cases, we begin by explaining to the patient that the primary function of the larynx, valving, now appears to be present. After conventional voice evaluation testing (case history, peripheral evaluation, respiration measurements, frequency and intensity measurements, and determinations of voice quality), the focus of the evaluation is in searching with the patient by using various therapy facilitating approaches (Chapter 5) to determine which seems to produce the better-sounding voice. The patient often needs some counseling specific to the observation that the goal is to produce "the best voice possible, and not necessarily the same kind of voice he or she had before." Such patients require the clinician to spend much time explaining what can be accomplished in voice, using the altered mechanism as optimally as possible. Beyond an explanation of the problem (11), there are other facilitating approaches that we have found useful:

2. **Biofeedback.** Using some kind of feedback device, such as viewing one's respiratory cycle on an oscilloscope or looking at voice frequency level using a Visi-Pitch, seems to help the patient establish an awareness of a new compensatory way of producing voice.

3. **Change of Loudness.** Direct work on increasing loudness will often produce a clearer, more acceptable voice. It may take greater transglottal pressures to produce optimal vibration of the altered glottis.

7. **Ear Training.** The patient will usually require an ongoing auditory feedback of his or her various voice productions. The best voice he or she is able to produce by using any new method should be captured on some kind of audiotape and fed back to the patient. The patient must learn to listen for the best voice he or she is able to produce with the least amount of effort.

16. **Masking.** Some patients volitionally cannot produce a voice loud and strong enough to be heard. The use of masking sometimes facilitates the production of the stronger voice, following the procedures developed in Chapter 5.

20. **Place the Voice.** The patient who has had laryngeal cancer naturally has much focus on the "throat." Placing the voice in the area of the facial mask, more imaginary than real, does help the patient divert his or her attention away from the laryngeal area, often permitting the larynx to function in a more natural manner.

21. **Pushing Approach.** Many patients who have had various operative procedures on the larynx lack firm vocal fold approximation for phonation. The pushing approach encourages tighter, almost sphincteric glottal closure, resulting in these patients having more normal sounding voices. The approach should be abandoned once clear (less aperiodic) phonation can be established.

23. **Respiration Training.** The patient with an altered larynx may have to increase the optimization of his or her respiratory patterns for speech. The lack of an efficient or normal mechanism may require increased air flows and transglottal pressures to produce normal-sounding phonation.

The successful voice clinician with a patient who has an altered larynx is forced to be eclectic, trying to find what works to produce the best voice and avoiding those approaches that are not facilitative. The voice therapy for such patients is highly individualized.

VOICE THERAPY FOR THE PATIENT
WITH A TOTAL LARYNGECTOMY

In this section we are considering the patient who has had a total laryngectomy, utilizing a conventional surgical procedure with no fistulas or shunts surgically constructed to introduce air into the esophagus. The patient is told that he or she will have a total laryngectomy and following the surgery will have to be taught to use voice again. We shall consider the patient with the conventional laryngectomy from the points of view of the preoperative and postoperative visit by the speech-language pathologist, the patient's postoperative medical care and problems, and types of voice therapy.

The Preoperative and Postoperative Visits

Surgeons vary in their views toward the advisability of having preoperative or postoperative visits for the patient about to have a laryngectomy. A patient, by the way, who has had a laryngectomy is known as a *laryngectomee*. The decision for a preoperative visit by a speech pathologist or by a laryngectomee who demonstrates a well-adjusted, functioning personality must belong to the surgeon. There may well be some patients who, because of too much tissue removal or because of intellectual or personality problems, will never learn to use esophageal speech. To expose such a patient before surgery to a good esophageal speaker is in fact implying to the patient that he or she, too, will be able to speak again with a little training. After the operation, the patient may interpret his or her own faulty voice, as compared with the excellent voice of the speaker who came to visit, as a sign of personal failure. As Diedrich and Youngstrom (1966) have written, "When a successfully speaking laryngectomee pre- or postoperatively visits a patient there is the implication that the patient will learn to speak as the visitor does. Obviously, this is not true" (p. 138). It might be better at the time of the preoperative visit, if such a visit is requested, to include both a speech pathologist and a laryngectomee, the latter coming along to demonstrate overall successful adjustment (he is back in the community at his former job), rather than good speech per se.

A brief preoperative visit by the speech pathologist and a laryngectomee of his or her choice is perhaps the best way to provide the most relevant information about the patient and also give the patient some psychological support. It is important for the speech pathologist to assess how the patient speaks *before* the operation. Through conversation, the speech pathologist should roughly evaluate the patient's articulatory proficiency and overall speech intelligibility, and, since the long-term goal will be to help the patient achieve intelligible speech, he or she should evaluate the patient's performance (independent of obvious voicing problems) in terms of rate of speech, dialect or accent, articulation errors, degree of mouth opening when speaking, eye contact, and so on. In the brief preoperative contact with the patient and his or her family, it is important that we convey to them confidence that the "patient *will* talk again." In assuring the patient that a method will be found that he or she will be able to use, the speech pathologist should describe several methods of therapy and give a brief demonstration of the artificial larynx. He might tell the patient that as soon as the surgeon gives the "go ahead," he or she will be provided temporarily with an artificial larynx, so that he or she will be able to talk to people instead of writing out messages (as so many laryngectomees have been instructed to do, as if using the artificial larynx would "contaminate" their chances of learning esophageal speech).

The speech pathologist should then introduce his laryngectomee companion, stressing in the introduction the laryngectomee's employment, social milieu, and so on. The laryngectomee should then discuss how life after the operation has closely paralleled life before it (hopefully, this will be the case). He or she may answer a few of the patient's questions about learning to speak again, or about the local laryngectomee club, and so on. The laryngectomee should make it clear to the patient that after the operation he or she will come back and visit a bit longer. The speech pathologist should conclude the preoperative visit by saying that speech instruction will be started as soon as the surgeon gives the word, and that un-

til that time, after the operation, it will probably do little good to carry out
any kind of speech practice.

The surgeon usually requests the postoperative visit six or seven days
after surgery. It is at this time that the speech pathologist and, or, the
laryngectomee visitant often realize that their role in the rehabilitation of
the patient is far more than teaching the patient to use a new voice. It is not
until after the operation, when the patient actually begins to experience its
many overwhelming effects, that he or she may be frightened and de-
pressed, requiring realistic and straightforward answers to the questions
posed to visitors. Diedrich and Youngstrom (1966) vividly describe the
laryngectomee's new problems:

> Laryngeal amputation is much more subtle than losing an arm or leg. In fact, just to
> say the word amputation gives one a different feeling about what is lost than to say the
> word laryngectomy. The full impact of amputation of the larynx is not ordinarily ap-
> parent. A fully clothed laryngectomee walking down the hall does not look much dif-
> ferent from anyone else. It is not until he is asked to speak, cough, breathe, eat, smell,
> bathe, lift, cry, or laugh that his differences become apparent. In other words little is
> left unaffected in the laryngectomee's physical, psychological, and social behavior.
> (p. 66)

The first postoperative visit, therefore, should have a certain amount
of flexibility, so that the visitors can respond to whatever questions the patient may have about these physical and psychological changes, and
perhaps alleviate some of the patient's concerns about talking again. There
is some advantage to bringing along some printed material, such as a few
of the pamphlets on laryngectomy problems provided by the American
Cancer Society. These materials offer the patient and family answers to
many problems they may be facing. Selected laryngectomees from local
laryngectomy clubs are often effective at the time of the postoperative visit
in relating their firsthand experiences in meeting some of the postoperative
problems the patient may have; for example, the physical problem of
mucus in the stoma is often an early complaint, and it should be pointed
out to the patient that successful control of excessive mucus at the stoma
site is usually developed early. Just as with the preoperative visit, the combination team of the speech pathologist and the laryngectomee visitant appears to be most appropriate for the first visit after surgery.

Some patients are bothered by the physical disfigurement they begin
to become aware of postoperatively. The open stoma in the neck is often
the first anatomic disfigurement of which the patient becomes aware. The
patient who has additional radical neck surgery for the removal of
cancerous lymph nodes experiences additional disfigurement with large
vertical scarring in the lateral neck area in addition to the laryngectomy. In
the immediate postoperative period, the patient's surgical sites are well
covered with bandages. As dressings are removed during the days that
follow surgery, some patients experience violent feelings toward the
dramatic alteration in appearance. Both the patient and the family may
need some guidance by the physician and nursing staff to help them accept

the physical changes in appearance as well as in function of respiration and phonation.

Before the first visit to the new laryngectomee, the speech pathologist should ask the surgeon when the patient will be able to begin speech-voice training and when he or she will be able to use the artificial larynx. The decision as to when to begin either speech training or artificial larynx usage is dependent on the overall surgical healing of the patient. Sometimes difficulty in healing or the development of fistulas will be aggravated by speech practice or by using the artificial larynx. Training should begin, whenever possible, as soon as the patient's physical condition permits. Several studies by questionnaire (Horn, 1962; Diedrich and Youngstrom, 1966) have found that the average time lapse between the operation and the beginning of speech training is from two to four months. In this interim, the average patient relies primarily on writing as the method of communication. Horn further reports that adequate speech proficiency is not acquired until seven months after surgery, while Diedrich and Youngstrom place the time at up to one year. During this protracted time of acquiring adequate speech, usually of the esophageal type, the typical patient relies on writing as an auxiliary aid to communication. Diedrich and Youngstrom make a strong argument for utilizing the artificial larynx as a regular training device before the patient learns esophageal speech. Why have the patient write his communications before or during the early learning stages of esophageal speech when the artificial larynx can provide actual speech practice and oral communication right from the beginning? It would appear that the artificial larynx helps the patient develop an early awareness of the relative independence of voice from articulation (he or she can still articulate), appreciate the need for phrasing, and develop articulatory skill postoperatively (the reduction in articulation proficiency that some patients experience after surgery responds well to practice). The clinician should demonstrate for the patient the use of an electronic larynx, such as the Western Electric artificial larynx[1] or the Cooper-Rand artificial larynx[2] (both shown in Figure 8–1), which most patients can learn to use with relative ease. However, *learning* to use an instrument is required, since few patients are able to use it well without some formal instruction. We shall discuss artificial larynx instruction under the heading of Voice Therapy in a later section of this chapter.

The postoperative visit should also, whenever possible, include the spouse of the patient. If the visit includes both the speech-language pathologist and a good laryngectomee speaker (who usually represents a local laryngectomee club sponsored by the International Association of Laryngectomees), time should be given for the patient and spouse to ask the visiting laryngectomee some questions directly. Many patients report that the postoperative visit by the laryngectomee provided them with the inspiration and motivation needed to learn esophageal speech. As more

[1] The Western Electric artificial larynx is distributed through any local Bell Telephone office.

[2] The Cooper-Rand artificial larynx is distributed through Luminaud, Box 257, 7670 Acacia Avenue, Mentor, Ohio 44060.

FIGURE 8-1. Two artificial larynges. The Western Electric artificial larynx is shown in the top photograph. It is held in the hand and the vibrating head is placed firmly against the neck, permitting its sound vibrations to be introduced through the skin into the patient's hypopharynx. The Cooper-Rand artificial larynx, shown in the bottom photograph, is carried in the pocket with a connecting wire attached to the vibrating oscillator; the oscillator is held in the hand and is attached to a small plastic tube that introduces the voice sound directly into the patient's mouth.

than one laryngectomee has said, ''When I heard that he could speak so well without a larynx, I knew that I could, too.'' The postoperative visit usually concludes with some arrangements made for future voice therapy and perhaps the laryngectomee's promise to the patient that a return visit will be made.

Postoperative Medical Care and Problems of the Laryngectomee

As important as voice restoration may be, and as important as the speech pathologist's role may become, the primary consideration during and immediately after surgery is the preservation of life. Control of bleeding, preservation of the airway, prevention of infection, and nourishment of the patient are of primary concern to the medical team caring for the patient. In the typical laryngectomy, the entire laryngeal mechanism is removed, including the hyoid bone (see Figure 8-2). The hypopharyngeal opening into the esophagus and the esophagus itself are usually well preserved, although some of their sphincteral functions may be somewhat diminished by the removal of their attachments (hyoid bone, thyroid and cricoid cartilages). The trachea, which loses its connection with the pharynx and mouth, is brought to the skin surface and attached directly

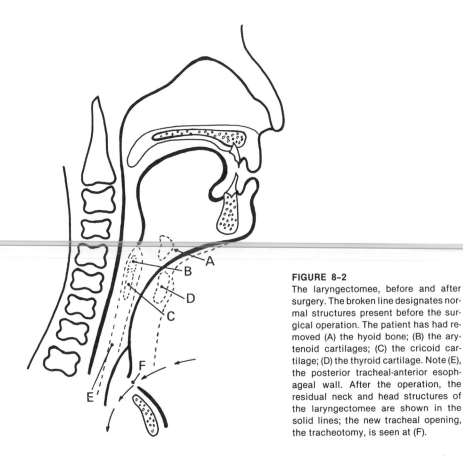

FIGURE 8-2
The laryngectomee, before and after surgery. The broken line designates normal structures present before the surgical operation. The patient has had removed (A) the hyoid bone; (B) the arytenoid cartilages; (C) the cricoid cartilage; (D) the thyroid cartilage. Note (E), the posterior tracheal-anterior esophageal wall. After the operation, the residual neck and head structures of the laryngectomee are shown in the solid lines; the new tracheal opening, the tracheotomy, is seen at (F).

superior to the suprasternal notch at this level, a permanent opening (tracheostomy) is constructed, through which the patient will forever breathe. After surgery an L-shaped plastic tube (cannula) is placed in the stoma (opening) to keep the stoma open, preventing natural healing. The stoma must be kept open to permit unobstructed breathing. The inverted L-shaped cannula is used in this way: The tube is placed through the opening with the down shaft of the cannula going below the stoma into the trachea, with the horizontal shaft remaining within the stoma opening. Some patients wear the cannula tube only for a few weeks after surgery; some laryngectomees prefer to wear the cannula all the time. If there were known or suspected cancerous nodes in the neck, the patient may have had, in addition to the laryngectomy, a radical neck dissection. This procedure involves the removal of the cervical lymph nodes as well as many of the normal-appearing nodes adjacent to the suspected cancer site. The dissection is usually done initially on one side only, sometimes followed later by the same procedure on the other side. Radical neck dissection greatly increases the site of surgical alteration, and the postsurgical medical and nursing care required is usually more intensive.

The new laryngectomee usually requires a day or two of absolute bedrest following surgery. The head of the bed should be slightly elevated so that the patient's head will be slightly flexed toward the chest, thus avoiding any tension on the sutures. Ambulation is started as soon as the patient's condition permits, frequently on the second or third day. The patient's fluid and caloric intake require constant monitoring, and attention must be given to his or her vital cardiac, pulmonary, and urinary functions. The patient will receive various antibiotics and analgesics (pain killers) as required. To prevent the patient from swallowing, and thus give the pharyngeal and esophageal structures time to heal, the patient is fitted with a feeding tube inserted through the nose and going directly through the pharynx into the esophagus and hence into the stomach. The feeding tube is usually removed on the eighth to the tenth postoperative day, if there is no unhealed fistula (small opening) between the esophagus and trachea or between the pharynx and the outer skin. It is about the time that fistulas are healed that the surgeon gives approval for starting voice-speech instruction. The referral to the speech pathologist and the beginning of voice instruction should be started, if possible, before the patient leaves the hospital. Before the patient is discharged, also, he or she usually will have received detailed nursing instructions on the care of the excision sites, maintenance of the airway, and how to keep the cannula clean.

Some laryngectomees are more concerned about some physical changes and problems after surgery than they are about their inability to have voice. The overall health of the patient eventually becomes about the same as it was before surgery. Typical problems that patients report may be related to air intake, changes in digestion, diminished taste and smell, and problems of social adjustment.

Air Intake Problems.   Many new laryngectomees are bothered a great deal by the natural increase of mucus in the trachea and at the stoma site. It is physiologically desirable for pulmonary air to be relatively warm and moist, which is the basic reason for the increase of tracheal mucus in the laryngectomee. In low humidity surroundings there needs to be increased mucus; this problem can be reduced somewhat by moistening the air in the home with a humidifier or steam inhalation device. Coughing is a frequent problem for the laryngectomee. Since the cough is more of an aspirate wheeze, a few people often react negatively to it. Most laryngectomees report that they try to avoid coughing in public, excusing themselves, if necessary, to cough and clean their stomas of excessive mucus in private. The collection of mucus in the stoma area presents a situation that requires systematic care by the laryngectomee. He or she is instructed always to wear some protective covering over the stoma, such as a crocheted bib, a gauze bib, or a foam or plastic screen guard, as shown in Figure 8–3B. This covering protects the airway from irritants and also provides a site where moisture (mucus, air stream) can collect to help moisten stoma inhalations. The patient develops a regular schedule for cleaning the stoma covering and removing excessive mucus, using a gauze pad or handkerchief (a lint-type paper tissue should be avoided). Most laryngectomees

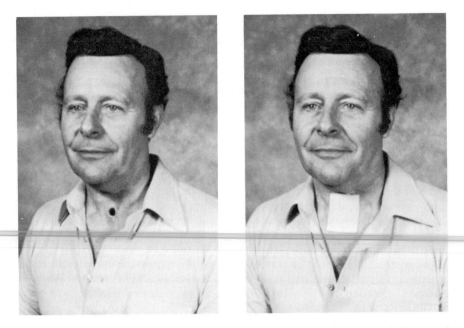

FIGURE 8-3 A & B. A laryngectomee displays his neck with an open tracheostomy; in the second picture the stoma is covered with a foam self-adhesive covering (manufactured by Radio House, Inc., Nampa, Idaho, 83651). Used by permission of Dean Rosecrans.

soon discover that while bathing and showering, they must take special care to protect the stoma from water; the relative ease with which water can enter the neck stoma makes such activities as swimming, boating, and stream fishing extremely hazardous. Care must be taken to avoid the buildup of mucus crustings at the stoma site; the use of a water-soluble salve, such as K-Y, applied to the stoma will often prevent these crusts from occurring. For more detailed descriptions of stoma care, such as cleaning the cannula, the reader should refer to materials provided by the American Cancer Society, such as articles on the subject in the IAL *News* (published by the International Association of Laryngectomees). Some of the breathing problems and special needs of the laryngectomee are outlined in *First Aid for Laryngectomees* (1978); for example, if artificial respiration is ever necessary for the laryngectomee, these warnings are given: Keep the neck opening clear, avoid twisting the head to one side, apply oxygen only to the stoma, avoid throwing water on the head, and use mouth-to-stoma resuscitation.

Digestive Difficulties. The trapping of air in the esophagus for esophageal speech carries with it the possibility that some esophageal air will move down into the stomach and into the intestinal tract. Gardner (1961) reported that among fifty-four laryngectomees with no gastrointestinal symptoms before surgery, forty-one (76 percent) acquired such symptoms chronically after surgery. Gardner believed that one of the negative features of the swallow method is its high frequency of gastric complaint. The patient swallows air into the stomach, experiencing the subsequent symptoms of bloating, pain, and flatulence. Diedrich and Youngstrom (1966) found that 71 percent of their questionnaire respondents reported an increase of gastrointestinal symptoms, often trapping "more air than they utilize in the phonation of phrases and short sentences" (p. 122). Other findings specific to digestive problems in the same questionnaire were that about one-third of the respondents had difficulty in swallowing and sucking, about half had difficulty in drinking from a fountain or in drinking soup with a spoon, more than one-third permanently took longer to eat, and the majority reported an increase of heartburn. Another feeding problem that the laryngectomee must learn to accommodate is that simultaneous eating and talking (difficult and undesirable in normal people) is almost impossible for the esophageal speaker. Some patients who have had extensive pharyngeal surgery experience problems in swallowing; for many the hypopharynx and the cricopharyngeus opening is too small. These patients often require esophageal dilation by the surgeon using esophageal dilators (bogies) placed intraesophageally to stretch the esophagus to a desired diameter. Patients experiencing esophageal dilation may well experience temporary setbacks in their mastery of esophageal voice.

Diminished Taste and Smell.   Related to the problem of feeding is the possibility that after surgery the patient will experience diminished taste. Forty-one percent of the laryngectomees in the Horn report (1962) and 31 percent of those in the Diedrich and Youngstrom sample (1966) indicated that their taste was less accurate after surgery. In elaborating on the taste problem, Diedrich and Youngstrom wrote that only 4 percent of their group had no sense of taste and that for many patients only strong sweet or acid tastes could be detected. The sense of smell, however, is usually diminished or wholly absent; the inability to smell normally was reported by 79 percent of Horn's respondents and 95 percent of Diedrich's and Youngstrom's. Over time, however, some laryngectomees do report a gradual increase in their ability to smell, although for the majority of patients the sense of smell remains permanently impaired. Such warning smells as smoke or leaking gas may not be recognized by the laryngectomee.

Problems of Social Adjustment.   The emotional trauma of losing one's voice is particularly poignant in the early postoperative period, when the patient is still in the hospital. It is at this time that the visit by a lay laryngectomee is so important. Whitler (1961) described the typical patient's reaction to this visit:

> One of the first persons to come to see me when I had regained a little strength was a man who had a similar operation some years ago. He walked into the room and with a cheery, broad grin said, "Hello, Mr. Whitler, you have now joined a rather ex-

clusive group!'' I was astounded. Here was a man who obviously lived by breathing through a tube in his neck, exactly like myself, did not have a larynx as I did not have one, and yet here he was talking to me . . . I knew then that if he could so could I. (p. 3)

The great value of the laryngectomee club, usually a chapter of the International Association of Laryngectomees, appears to be the early encouragement it gives the new laryngectomee. Eventually, if his or her total rehabilitation is successful, the laryngectomee no longer *takes* from the organization, but belongs to it for what he or she is able to contribute to new laryngectomees in their first few postoperative months.

The Horn study (1962) of 3,366 laryngectomees offers some interesting data on the psychosocial adjustment of laryngectomees: One of the primary problems the patient faces is financial loss. For example, the average laryngectomee who was employed at the time of his or her operation lost 153 work days (five months). The patient's major resources during this recovery period were found to exist in this order of frequency: personal savings, own full salary continuing, spouse's salary, company sick benefits, medical insurance. One out of five laryngectomees who answered Horn's question about borrowing stated that they had to borrow money to cover some of their medical costs. Horn reported that two out of three respondents reported a drop in income following the operation, with 60 percent of those reporting a drop attributing it to their laryngectomy and their impaired facility for communication. The percentage of those who retired doubled from 12 percent before the operation to 24 percent soon after, and the percentage of those unemployed rose from 2 percent before to 8 percent after. The greatest job and economic changes, usually to lower income levels, occurred in managerial, sales, clerical, skilled-labor and semiskilled occupants (professional and unskilled-labor occupations reported little change in status).

Many new laryngectomees are embarrassed about using various forms of alaryngeal speech, particularly with strangers. In the study by Diedrich and Youngstrom (1966), 50 percent of the seventy-two patients who responded to the question of embarrassment replied that there were continuing situations in which they experienced acute embarrassment over the way they spoke. Some situations probably become tense because of awkward, insensitive listeners whose inept responses embarrass the speaker. There is little laryngectomees can do to reconstruct their listening world, but after continued success they learn to adjust and take in stride the occasional bad situation. The speech pathologist may sometimes have to counsel the laryngectomee to focus on good speech and effective communication, rather than on the occasional breakdown that may come when speaking with inadequate loudness in a noisy situation or to a person with less than adequate hearing. The laryngectomee's sensitivity to how well he or she will be received by others is a highly individual thing, perhaps a matter of long-established personality. Diedrich and Youngstrom reported that the most frequently listed factors in overcoming self-consciousness were the patient's ''determination to talk,'' the feeling that ''there was no other choice,'' and his or her conviction that ''one had to make the best of it'' (p. 75).

Some counseling of both patient and family before the operation, as well as after, seems to promote optimum long-range rehabilitation. The patient should be clearly told by the surgeon what to expect after the operation with regard to such things as breathing through the stoma, feeding by tube, inability to voice, or postoperative communication aids (writing pad, artificial larynx, gestures). The family, also, must be given a clear picture of what the patient's postoperative problems will be. While the family should be understanding and concerned, it will be helpful for the patient if they avoid becoming overly protective (such as by cleaning the stoma for the patient); they should allow the patient to become thoroughly independent, taking care of his or her own nursing needs and making his or her own rehabilitational and vocational plans. The more that can be done to approximate the living patterns experienced by the patient before the surgery, the greater the likelihood of successful rehabilitation.

VOICE TRAINING
OF THE LARYNGECTOMEE

The primary goal of the speech pathologist working with a laryngectomee is to help the patient develop functional speech. The term *alaryngeal speech,* first introduced by Kallen (1934), refers to any kind of nonlaryngeal phonation, whether it be esophageal, buccal, via an electronic larynx, or whatever. The focus of early voice therapy is to help the patient develop a phonation source, and the most difficult task in therapy is usually to teach the patient to make the first satisfactory sound. Once the patient is able to achieve some form of phonation, using some type of alaryngeal mechanism, subsequent therapy consists of refining the method employed. In esophageal speech, for example, the most difficult task in therapy is to get the patient to take in air esophageally and then be able to release it for phonation.

Voice training of the laryngectomee will usually begin at the time of the first postoperative visit. Before the actual initiation of voice training, it may be helpful to determine the adequacy of the patient's hearing. If some hearing loss is indicated, particularly the high-frequency loss often found in older persons, some use of amplification may be helpful in therapy. We have also found that testing the hearing of the patient's spouse can provide helpful information; because the patient will be generating a less-than-optimal voice signal, his or her overall speech intelligibility is going to be impaired. The spouse may need, therefore, audiological testing and may require some kind of amplification and speech-reading training.

As part of our overall voice training for the laryngectomee, we shall first begin with some consideration of the artificial larynx. Procedures for using the artificial larynx will be presented, followed by the step-by-step procedures required for teaching esophageal speech to the patient with a conventional laryngectomy, using three methods of instruction: injection, inhalation, and swallow.

Using the Artificial Larynx

There has yet to be invented a totally satisfactory artificial larynx for the laryngectomee, although there are many good commercially available artificial instruments.

One kind of artificial larynx is the pneumatic type, which requires the passage of air from the stoma through the vibrating body of the instrument and on into the oral cavity opening. Perhaps one of the best pneumatic type artificial larynges is the Tokyo artificial larynx which was reported by Weinberg and Riekena (1973) to be easy to use with excellent intelligibility. The second form of artificial larynx is the electronic type, either the mouth-type instrument (such as the Cooper-Rand shown in Figure 8–1) or the neck-type instrument (such as the Western Electric, also shown in Figure 8–1). The electronic larynx is a battery-powered, transistorized vibrator, and is activated by a button switch. Its vibration usually makes a continuous buzzing sound, not unlike the sound of an electric razor. Some models have the capability of pitch variation, which is controlled by the amount of finger pressure applied to the activating switch. The neck-type instrument has a vibrator at one end, which must be placed snugly against the skin of the neck at a particular anatomic site; this site will vary for each individual. After some demonstration and practice, the typical laryngectomee can effectively master the artificial larynx. There continue to be developed new artificial larynges. For example, Zwitman, Knorr, and Sonderman (1978) report the development of a new intraoral electrolarynx housed in a patient's denture and activated by a hand switch. As of this writing, the instrument is still in the experimental stage and not commercially available.

The biggest problem in using the artificial larynx is the resistance that many laryngectomees, physicians, and speech pathologists offer to the patient who wants to use one. It is frequently stated that if the new laryngectomee uses an artificial larynx before learning esophageal speech, he or she will never develop good esophageal speech. Furthermore, the argument may proceed, not learning esophageal speech is tantamount to a personal defeat. Today, however, it would appear that there is far less resistance by professionals to patients using the artificial larynx. We have found that the artificial larynx is usually an aid in learning esophageal speech. Rarely has this clinician found new laryngectomees becoming dependent on the artificial larynx when it is presented to them as part of their total speech training program. Some may well continue to use the electronic larynx for part of every speaking day, particularly when they do not feel well or are fatigued. An occasional patient may even prefer to use the artificial larynx exclusively. These occasional patients may find some reassurance from the work of Bennett and Weinberg (1973), who reported that judges generally rated the speech intelligibility of speakers who used the artificial larynx to be superior to the intelligibility of esophageal speakers. Most laryngectomees prefer to use esophageal speech, particularly after they have developed some proficiency at it. The speech pathologist might introduce the artificial larynx to the new laryngectomee by following these steps:

1. In telling the patient that efforts will now begin to help him or her learn to talk again, point out that he or she faces two problems—first, learning to articulate (pronounce) words again, and second, finding a new source of voice—and that at this time it is the articulation that will be tackled. Next, demonstrate to the patient that he has basically the same capability of articulation that he had before the operation, but that he may have to make some sounds a bit differently, employing intraoral pressure for some plosive and sibilant sounds instead of the usual pulmonary air stream. If possible, demonstrate the intraoral whisper, articulating to produce a "sound" with no pulmonary air stream. Then ask the patient to imitate these intraoral productions (which are, in fact, easier for the laryngectomee to produce than for the normal person with a larynx). Warn the patient not to try to push the sounds out by using pulmonary air (the use of pulmonary air will be indicated by excessive stoma noises). The level of complexity of the discussion and the amount of positive reinforcement provided the patient for his or her correct productions are individual matters that must be decided upon by the clinician. It would appear, however, that the simpler the explanation and the more focus given to the actual demonstration, the easier the learning task will be.

2. When the patient is able to produce an intraoral whisper, introduce him or her to an orderly presentation of consonants, perhaps having him or her whisper each one five to ten times. The best presentation seems to be along the general order of acquisition of consonants (/m/, /p/, /b/, and so on), first practicing the phonemes that are easiest to produce, and then going on to more difficult ones. The patient should work for clarity of articulation. Point out to the patient his or her relative lip, tongue, and palatal competencies, as demonstrated by accurate whispering of the consonants. Then go back to the first point made in the therapy, that learning to talk again is a twofold process: articulation and voice. Tell the patient that success in practicing the whispered productions means that he or she is doing very well in the first area. The whispering practice will vary in length, depending on the intelligibility and motivation of the patient.

3. Now is the time to introduce the artificial larynx, either the pneumatic or electronic type. We will limit our suggested procedures to the electronic larynx, both the neck type and the oral type. For the neck type, the clinician should place the vibrating surface of the instrument tightly on his or her own neck at a site where he or she has previously determined the best voice to be. The clinician might well repeat some monosyllabic words that in-

clude some of the phonemes the patient has just finished using in articulation practice. To these articulations, the clinician should explain, the artificial larynx will introduce the second phase of speech, voicing. The clinician might also use the artificial larynx to demonstrate some connected speech. For the oral-type larynx, care should be made to show that the intraoral tube does not interfere with the movement of the tongue. We have found that introducing the tube toward the corner of the mouth with the tube angled high toward the palate seems to provide the best placement.

4.　Next, in offering the instrument to the patient, a great deal of care must be taken to achieve a good *seal* between the neck skin of the patient and the surface of the neck vibrator. The vibrator head must be firmly buried against the neck, or the sound source will escape freefield and not be directed into the oral cavity. This optimum site of contact, such as just above the site of the laryngeal excision in the midline, will be found best by trial and error. The patient should say the same monosyllabic word repeatedly as he searches for the site of contact where the intraoral speech or voice sounds best. Much time should be given to achieving this optimum contact of vibrator and neck, for a great deal of early disillusionment with the artificial larynx can come from improper positioning of the instrument. Patients with extensive scarring, such as those who have had radical neck dissections, may experience real difficulties at first in finding the optimum site of contact. No practice in using the instrument should begin, however, until this critical contact point has been found. Also, once a good sound has been established, the patient will require some practice in working the on-off switch to match his or her articulations. Most patients can learn to do this rather quickly. For the oral instrument, care must be exercised in having the patient place the tube optimally within the mouth and ensure that it not interfere with tongue movement. We use first the phrase "How are you?" This can be made with relatively little tongue interference. Following this phrase, we generally use number counting as the practice words for finding an optimal oral placement of the tube. Trial-and-error placement can usually find the best place to introduce the tube (again, we find that toward the side of the mouth with the tube angled high toward the palate is the best placement).

5.　The patient should then practice saying single monosyllabic words in a series, and after that go on to phrases and short sentences. At this point, the clinician should remind the patient that he or she is now practicing speech. The sharper and clearer one can articulate, the more intelligible the speech will be. The patient should be instructed to discard his or her writing pad and begin talking to everyone. The tremendous advantage afforded by the artificial larynx is that it permits the patient to talk shortly after the operation, providing valuable articulation practice. The more one talks using the artificial larynx, the better his or her speech will usually become. Point out to the patient that the artificial larynx is providing him or her with a voice source while he or she practices improving articulation. After a few days of practice using the instrument, the patient will start learning how to supply his or her own voice by using some form of esophageal voice. Make it very clear to the patient that the artificial larynx and esophageal speech are not competitive forms of voice, but that he or she will find them compatible with one another in helping to achieve good functional speech *whenever there is a need to talk.*

Teaching Esophageal Speech

Three methods of teaching esophageal speech may be employed: injection, inhalation, and swallow. We usually begin with the injection method, which is the easiest method to teach and quite compatible with the articulation practice the patient may have used with the artificial larynx.

All three methods, however, employ the same basic principle of compressing air within the oropharynx and injecting this denser air into the more rarefied space of the esophagus. Denser air within a body moves in the direction of the less dense body of air whenever the two bodies are coupled together. Some of the compressed air within the oral cavity undoubtedly escapes through the lips, some through the nasopharyngeal port, and some (particularly if the opening of the esophagus is open) into the esophagus. All three methods for esophageal voice bring compressed air into the esophagus; once the air is in the esophagus, external forces compress the air within it and expel it. It is hoped that the esophageal expulsion sets up a vibration of the pharyngeal-esophageal segment with the patient experiencing an eructation or "voice." We shall consider separately the procedures for teaching the injection method (we try this one first), the inhalation method (sometimes we combine it with injection), and the swallow method (this combines the first two plus the swallow, which may open up the esophagus).

The Injection Method. Certain consonants appear to have a facilitating effect in producing good esophageal voice. While individual patients may have their own favorite facilitating sound, it is more often than not a plosive consonant (/p/, /b/, /t/, /d/, /k/, and /g/) or an affricative containing a plosive (/tʃ/ or /dʒ/). Stetson (1937) reported many years ago that /p/, /t/, and /k/ were the easiest sounds for the new laryngectomee to use and Moolenaar-Bijl (1953) reported that the same phonemes produced esophageal speech faster in most patients than the traditional swallow method of teaching. Diedrich and Youngstrom (1966) recommended the voiceless /p/, /t/, /k/, /s/, /ʃ/, and /tʃ/ phonemes as good sounds to employ in the injection method of air intake. The injection of air is best accomplished by using speech that employs some of the consonants identified above. As the patient whispers monosyllabic words with a facilitating consonant before and after the vowel, the patient will sometimes spontaneously inject air into the esophagus and produce an "unplanned" esophageal voice. The production of the consonant facilitates the transfer of air into the esophagus. The injection method is the preferred method for teaching esophageal voice. Specific steps for teaching injection might include the following:

1. Discuss with the patient the dynamics of air flow, explaining that compressed, dense air will always flow in the direction of less dense, rarefied air. Explain also how the movements of the tongue in the injection method increase the density of the air within the mouth, enabling the air to move into the esophagus. Then demonstrate how the whispered articulation of a phoneme, such as a /t/ or a /k/, is the kind of tongue movement that produces the injection of air into the esophagus. After producing the whispered /t/, demonstrate for the patient an esophageal voice for the word "tot."

2. Now ask the patient to produce the phoneme /p/ by intraoral whisper. Care must be taken that the sound is made by good firm compression of the lips, with no need for stoma noise. Make sure that the patient avoids pushing out the pulmonary exhalation or using tongue and palatal-pharyngeal contact as the noise source. The intraoral whisper can be effectively taught by having the patient hold his breath and then attempt to "bite-off" a /p/ by compressing the air caught between his abruptly closed lips. The patient should continue practicing this until the idea of true intraoral articulation is clearly grasped. This will be demonstrated when he or she is able consistently to produce a precise-sound /p/. Once the patient can do this, he or she should move to the next voiceless plosive, /t/. Here, the tongue tip against the upper central alveolar process is the site of contact, and practice should be continued until the patient is able to produce a precise, clear /t/. The same procedure should be repeated for /k/, again first demonstrating for the patient the different site of contact.

3. When good intraoral voiceless plosives have been produced, the patient is ready to add the vowel /a/ to each plosive. With /p/, for instance, he or she makes the plosive, and then immediately attempts to produce an esophageal phonation of /a/, producing in effect the word "pa." If this is successful, the patient may combine the /p/ with a few other vowel combinations before going on to the /t/ and /k/. If the patient fails to produce the esophageal voice at this point, he or she should go back and work for even crisper articulation of the plosive sounds. If the patient is still unsuccessful after increased practice in articulation, he or she should attempt to adopt the inhalation method as the primary means of

air intake. (The swallow method is generally used only if the other two approaches have proved nonproductive.)

4. The average laryngectomee experiences some success with the injection method when using the /p/, /t/, and /k/ phonemes. Therefore, he or she might be provided with about five monosyllabic words for each of the phonemes—for example, for /p/, the words *pat, pip, pack, pot,* and *pop*. The task is now to say each word, one at a time, renewing his esophageal air supply *as he or she speaks,* which is an obvious advantage in using the injection method. It is through the mere process of articulation that the patient takes in air. After the patient has demonstrated success with these phonemes, the clinician should introduce their voiced cognates, /b/, /d/, and /g/. The same procedure should be repeated, ending with about five practice words for each new phoneme.

5. Additional phonemes, such as /s/, /z/, /ʃ/, /tʃ/, /ʒ/, and /dʒ/, may be introduced for practice. It is most important as the patient gains phonatory skill with each new consonant that he or she spends extra time learning to improve both the quickness and the quality of production. Too many patients err in trying to develop functional conversation too early. Considerable practice should be spent at the monosyllabic word level, practicing one word at a time and making constant efforts to produce sharp articulation and a good-sounding voice.

6. At this point, if the patient has been successful, the inhalation method can be introduced as a means of further improving air intake and esophageal phonation. The patient should produce a normal inhalation and, at the initial moment of exhalation, produce the consonant and say the word. Beyond the single words alone, we often couple the words together in phrases, such as "bake a cake, stop at church, park the black cart," and so on. Once plosive-laden phrases are mastered, we then use the oral reading materials from voice and diction books, including when possible the facilitative consonants we have been using.

The Inhalation Method. The flow of air in normal respiration is achieved by the transfer of air from one source to another because of the relative disparity of air pressure between the two sources. For example, when the thorax enlarges because of muscle movement, the air reservoir within the lung increases in size, rarefying (decreasing) the air pressure within the lung. Since the outside atmospheric air pressure is now greater, the air rushes in until the pressure within equals the outside pressure. The flow of air is always from the more dense to the less dense air body, and the flow continues until the two bodies are equal in pressure. It is by this same airflow mechanism that the esophagus inflates in the inhalation method of air intake. The patient experiences a thoracic enlargement during pulmonary inhalation, which reduces the compression on all thoracic structures, including the esophagus. If the cricopharyngeus opening into the esophagus is slightly open at the time of the slight increase in the size of the esophagus, air from the hypopharynx will flow into the esophagus. During the exhalation phase of pulmonary respiration, when there is a general compression of thoracic structures, the esophagus also experiences some compression, which aids in the expulsion of the entrapped air. As this air passes through the approximated structures of the lower pharynx–upper esophagus (the pharyngo-esophageal segment), a vibration is set up, producing esophageal phonation. The advantage of the inhalation method of esophageal air intake is that it follows the patient's natural inclination of pulmonary inhalation followed by exhalation-phonation. Simply to take a breath and then talk is the most natural way of speaking, and for this reason the inhalation method offers the patient learning esophageal speech some early advantages.

In proceeding to the following steps for teaching the inhalation method, the reader should remember that the approach is best used in combination with the injection method.

1. Explain and demonstrate to the patient some aspects of normal respiration. Many normal speakers, for example, have never thought much about normal respiration, and many do not know that their voicing has always been an exhalation event. Explain to the patient that when the chest is enlarged by muscle action, the air flows into the lungs, and that in the laryngectomee's case, the air comes through the stoma opening in the trachea and down into the lungs. The clinician might point out that the chest enlarges by muscle action, not by air inflation; thus, the air comes in as the chest enlarges. When the laryngectomee's chest enlarges, there is usually a concomitant enlargement of the esophagus, and when the esophagus is enlarged, there is a greater chance for air to come into it. When the chest becomes smaller, the pulmonary air is forced out, and the air within the esophagus is also more likely to be forced out. If possible, the clinician should demonstrate esophageal voice by using this method.

2. Before making any attempt to produce voice, the patient should practice conscious relaxation and correct breathing methods. He or she should become aware of thoracic expansion and abdominal distention on inhalation and of thoracic contraction on exhalation. Respiration practice should only be long enough to permit the patient to develop this kind of breathing awareness, since patients do not seem to benefit much from extended breathing exercises per se.

3. Now the patient should attempt to add air into the esophagus during his or her pulmonary inhalation. Diedrich and Youngstrom (1966) recommended that "the patient be told to close his mouth, imagine that he is sniffing through his nose, and to do so in a fairly rapid manner" (p. 112). While the sniff is basically a constricted inhalation, it is frequently accompanied by esophageal

dilation (the normal person often swallows what he or she sniffs). As an extension of the sniff, the patient should be asked to take a fairly large pulmonary breath (through the stoma, of course). When his or her lungs appear to be about half inflated, the patient should say "up" on exhalation. This procedure can be repeated until the patient experiences some phonatory success.

4. For the patient who does not experience success on step 3, the following variation of the inhalation method sometimes produces good esophageal air: Ask the patient to take a deep breath, and, as he or she begins the inhalation, to cover the stoma. While the muscular enlargement of the thorax continues (despite the patient's lack of continuing inhalation), there will be a corresponding enlargement of the esophagus, perhaps permitting air to flow into the esophagus. For the patient who can get air into the esophagus but cannot produce the air escape to produce phonation, the same mechanism applies in reverse. Here, the patient takes a deep inhalation and, as he or she begins to exhale, occludes the stoma; as the thorax begins to decrease in size, there will be increased pressure on the esophagus, which might well result in expulsion (and phonation) of esophageal air.

5. If esophageal phonation is achieved by either of the last two steps, the patient should proceed from his or her "up" response to single monosyllabic words beginning and ending with /p/, /b/, /t/, /d/, /k/, and /g/. Considerable time should be spent practicing at this single-word level, until the technique is mastered in terms of loudness, quality of sound, and articulation. The patient who masters the basic techniques of air intake and phonation at the single-word level may well become the best esophageal speaker.

6. At this level, we now use steps 4–7 from the injection method.

The Swallow Method.   If after five or six voice therapy sessions, neither the injection nor the inhalation methods have produced the slightest esophageal eructation, we introduce the swallow method. During normal swallow we elevate the tongue against the hard palate and sweep the tongue body backward toward the pharynx. In the laryngectomee this is a form of injection; that is, the tongue pressing against the hard and soft palates produces some air compression. During the swallow, the esophagus opens up, permitting the entry of denser air into the esophagus. Carbonated beverages or water may be needed to assist in forming a pocket of air in the esophagus. External forces on the esophagus, such as thoracic compression on expiration of pulmonary air, forces the air out of the esophagus similar to what occurs in the injection and inhalation methods. Actually, the swallow method combines with the injection-inhalation methods, adding the component of an open esophagus. We use the method today only when we have to, primarily because continuous volitional swallowing is tedious, it is slow, and it frequently produces pharyngeal-esophageal grunt noises (klunks). For a detailed description of the physiology of esophageal voice, including some references to the swallow method, the reader will find comprehensive data with literature citation in Diedrich's "The Mechanism of Esophageal Speech" (1968). When we add the swallow method of instruction, the following steps might be used:

1. Provide the patient with some explanation and demonstration of the swallow method. The basic purpose of swallowing is to trap air within the esophagus to make it available for the new voice. After demonstrating the swallow method of air intake, follow immediately with the production of a word. This demonstration is best performed by the teacher, either a speech pathologist or a laryngectomee.

2. Ask the patient if he or she ever belched or burped before the operation. If one can remember belching or burping, some time should be spent on trying to recreate what it felt like to do so. Can the patient remember how it felt to belch? Can he or she belch voluntarily? With the occasional patient who can belch voluntarily, one can considerably shorten the time needed to teach the first sound; it is not difficult to skip ahead and add speech articulation *on top* of the belch to produce some monosyllabic words. If, after considerable exploration, the patient relates no history of belching or is unable to produce a belch voluntarily, the clinician should go on to the next step.

3. Ask the patient to open his or her mouth, close the mouth, deliberately swallow (air) and open the mouth and say, "tot." Monosyllabic words beginning and ending with /t/, /d/, /k/, and /g/ seem particularly effective to start with, perhaps because they aid in the injection of air into the esophagus as effectively (or more so) than the swallow method. The open mouth-close mouth-swallow procedure should be repeated several times in rapid sequence; the steps are almost overlapping. If, after the swallow, the patient is unable to produce the "tot," the clinician might introduce other phonemically similar combinations. The procedure may have to be repeated several times before the patient achieves a sound. If the method is still unsuccessful, ask the patient to take a small swallow of ginger ale or water, and then, immediately after swallowing it, say the word. If, with the additional help of a swallowed beverage (which aids in opening the esophagus), the patient is still unable to produce sound, we go back to the practice of precise articulation as we did in the injection method. The articulation practice not only takes the patient's focus away from esophageal voicing (and the frustration from not achieving it), but also provides sharper articulation for purposes of injection.

4. We go back and repeat swallowing a liquid quickly followed by a production of a plosive-vowel-plosive word, such as "tot." The patient who is successful in producing "tot" should continue saying the word in a series of productions, each requiring its own swallow sequence. The "tot" sequence should be followed by

practice with other monosyllabic words beginning with /t/. Words beginning and ending with /d/, /k/, and /g/ can be used if the patient can successfully say them. At this stage of training the clinician should avoid any phoneme sequence that the patient cannot produce easily. Emphasis should be given to saying one monosyllabic word at a time, one word per swallow, until the patient achieves relative success on each attempt.

5.   Once the patient can produce a few monosyllabic words in combination with swallow and injection, we are then basically able to use the injection method. Deliberate swallow should be phased out as soon as productions can be maintained without the swallow. We go on at this point to use steps 4–7 of the injection method.

Voice Therapy for the Patient with a Total Laryngectomy with Some Surgical Modification

It has long been the hope of surgeons and speech pathologists that the patient with a total laryngectomy will one day be able to have a surgically created pseudoglottis that can provide a good and useful voice. Such a pseudoglottis would enable the patient to speak after total laryngectomy with very little speech training and with a minimum of problems (Shedd and Weinberg, 1980). While many surgical attempts have been successful in the creation of a mechanism that can produce voice, there have been many serious problems associated with such attempts, the most common of which has been aspiration. The patient can produce voice on expiration with very little difficulty, but during swallowing, liquids sometimes enter the airway. It has been observed that often the procedures that seem to have the best communication between the airway and the esophagus, producing the best voice, often prove to be the ones that have a greater propensity for aspiration (Sisson, McConnel, and Logemann, 1974). The most comprehensive reference text on historical and new surgical and prosthetic approaches for voice rehabilitation may be found in *Surgical and Prosthetic Approaches to Speech Rehabilitation* (Shedd and Weinberg (Eds.), 1980).

One of the earliest successful prosthetic devices for the production of esophageal voice after laryngectomy was developed by Taub (1975). An external, tubelike apparatus was attached to the chest for conducting pulmonary expiration directly into the esophagus (Taub and Bergner, 1973). The patient was able to have esophageal voice with no training. Another prosthetic approach by Sisson, McConnell, and Logemann (1974) enabled the patient to have voice using a flapper valve placed at the base of the hypopharynx that would vibrate on expiration, requiring no hand activation. The authors felt the prosthesis was particularly effective for those laryngectomy patients who had extensive radiation therapy; because of the edema and tenderness associated with the radiation, the patients had been unable to tolerate using either the electrolarynx or esophageal speech. A surgically innovative approach was developed by

Asai (1972), who developed a dermal tube superior to the trachea, which would conduct pulmonary expiration (when the open stoma was occluded by the patient's finger) into the hypopharynx. The end of the tube in the hypopharynx would vibrate, producing voice. While some patients experienced good success with the Asai method, many complained of severe aspiration, continued hair growth within the skin tube, and other problems related to maintenance of the open tube. Recent approaches have been developed that take pulmonary air from the trachea and introduce it by way of a shunt directly into the esophagus, such as the Staffierei approach (Griffiths and Love, 1978). Once again, some patients were able to demonstrate good esophageal voice by this method, while many seemed to experience symptoms of aspiration, scar closure of the shunt, wound complications, and infection. The tracheal-esophageal shunt approach (Saito and others, 1977) requires the patient to occlude the stoma opening with a finger so that the outgoing tracheal air can be diverted through the shunt into the esophagus; once the air is in the esophagus, it produces vibration of the pharyngeal-esophageal segment similar to the normal mechanism of esophageal voice. Recently, Singer and Blom (1980) reported a two-year experience with a valved prosthesis that is placed after total laryngectomy in a tracheal-esophageal shunt. The insertion of the small prosthesis (about 3 cm. long, called the "duckbill") into the shunt, prevents aspiration while swallowing and eliminates any stenosis of the surgically created tissue shunt. Fifty-four of sixty of their patients experienced "fluent voices" after only minimal speech therapy postoperatively. One limitation of the Singer-Blom approach is that it does require the patient to use a finger to cover his or her stoma opening, diverting the pulmonary air through the prosthesis into the esophagus. Of the many surgical and prosthetic innovations in recent years, however, we seem to have the best luck with the Singer-Blom approach (the patients demonstrate good voice without problems of aspiration).

It appears to be the individual patient who can make one procedure look good and another one look poor. The individual differences of patients appear to have much to do with success in good speaker intelligibility after laryngectomy, using either esophageal speech (conventional or by way of shunt) and artificial larynx speech (Kalb and Carpenter, 1981). For the speech-language pathologist who works with laryngectomy patients it is important to keep abreast of new surgical approaches with and without the use of prostheses. It would appear that methods developed for introducing tracheal air via a shunt into the esophagus are going to have continued use with the laryngectomee. While only minimal training should be required for these patients, let us review a few management steps:

1. The speech-language pathologist should review for himself or herself the procedures the patient has had. The Shedd-Weinberg (1980) book is helpful here in that it summarizes most of the surgical procedures available at the time the book was edited.

2. A review of how normal voice is produced is helpful for the pa-

tient who may never have realized, for example, that all speech is produced on pulmonary expiration.

3. Practice should be given for producing precise articulation. The patient should be encouraged to practice intraoral whisper so that the words are distinct and can be well understood by listeners.

4. The patient is asked to take in a normal breath, occlude his stoma with a thumb or a finger, and say a monosyllabic word on expiration. It is important that the patient be counseled to use the thumb or finger only as a diverting body to the air stream. Sending the air through the shunt (or the appliance in the shunt) does not require heavy finger pressure. Only very light touch is required to divert the air from the stoma on expiration. If voice is achieved on the single word, we go to the next step. If not, the patient should practice the timing of inspiration (open stoma) and expiration (closed stoma) in synchrony with saying one word. Trial-and-error repetitions may be needed here. Most patients can produce an effortless esophageal voice with but very little difficulty. It has been our observation that patients who cannot successfully divert tracheal air through the shunt are pushing too hard with their fingers. Only light touch on the stoma opening is needed.

5. Go from single words to phrases as soon as the patient can do so. It is important to keep the inspiratory breath a normal one. The patient needs no more breathing effort than he or she ever did. It takes some practice to time the inspiratory-expiratory phonation to match the words or phrases one is attempting to say.

6. Once the patient can say phrases, it has been our observation that by use of natural articulation he begins injecting air into the esophagus from above as well as using the pulmonary air passing out through the esophagus. Therefore, some patients can speak some words and phrases without occluding their stomas, obviously renewing their air reservoir within the esophagus by injection. It requires extended daily practice of several hours for a week or two before the patient with a tracheal-esophageal shunt is able to use his or her new esophageal voice conversationally.

7. Review with the patient that the best voice seems to be produced with the least amount of effort, that is, a normal speaking breath, light finger touch, and so on.

Avoiding Certain Problems in Teaching Esophageal Speech

Regardless of the method of getting air into the esophagus (injection, inhalation, swallow, tracheal-esophageal shunt), many esophageal speakers develop poor speaking habits that diminish their overall speech effectiveness. These faulty forms of behavior need to be identified early, before they become habituated. Some of the more common problems include:

1. *Unnecessary stoma noise.* It is not necessary for any laryngectomee to have to force out air from his or her tracheal stoma when attempting to speak. Some laryngectomees do this, particularly those who use the inhalation method of air intake. A few make the stoma noise on inhalation, but it is observed primarily on exhalation, usually as part of the normal pulmonary exhalation. The patient is often trying to speak too loudly. He uses too much force. Often, the identification of the problem is enough to make the patient eliminate stoma noise. However, an occasional patient will have to practice holding his breath while attempting to speak, or practice fixing his thorax, which slows down the rapidity of exhalation. Either breath holding or thorax fixing will eliminate the problem, particularly when it has been identified early and not yet become a habitual response.

2. *Excessive swallowing of air.* Some laryngectomees, and many who use the swallow method of air intake, swallow too much air in their attempt to inflate the esophagus. Many patients thus become bloated, experiencing a great deal of stomach and intestinal gas with the typical discomforts of abdominal-chest fullness, pain, and heartburn. One way of eliminating the problem is to change the patient's method of air intake from the swallow to either the inhalation or the injection method. Another is to work with the patient to help him or her become less tense while attempting to speak, putting less effort into voice production.

3. *Distracting noises.* Gurgling esophageal noises are occasionally related to poor sphincteric action at the distal (bottom) end of the esophagus and are difficult to control. Patients with these low gurgling noises should avoid the swallow method. A few will profit from using antacids as a method of reducing the esophageal gurgle. A more common noise is the klunking sound that characterizes too rapid an air intake. The pharyngeal noise must be extinguished immediately by the clinician, as it can quickly become habitual. The best method of eliminating it is to have the patient practice taking in air in an easier manner, producing single words free of the "klunk." Klunking is often the result of too much effort, particularly for the patient who is attempting to increase the loudness of his or her voice. The patient must be asked what it feels like to speak with the klunk as opposed to speaking without it; the typical patient can feel the difference, and from that point on can monitor himself so that the klunk will not be produced. Once the klunk has been established for several months, it is most difficult to eliminate.

4. *Facial grimacing.* Some laryngectomees early in their training pro-

gram begin to do some unnecessary things in the attempt to get air into the esophagus. For instance, they may purse their lips, make exaggerated facial movements, double pump with their lips, or clench their teeth. Such extraneous behavior must be quickly pointed out and eliminated. Many laryngectomees get started with some facial posture, thinking that this helps them speak, and from that point on they assume the posture as a habit whenever they proceed to speak. A frank, frontal assault should be made by the clinician to eliminate this undesirable facial behavior. Like any other undesirable behavior, it is much easier to eliminate during its formative stages than after it has become habitual.

SUMMARY

Most patients survive cancer of the larynx, often requiring radiation therapy and surgery, a partial or a total laryngectomy. We have reviewed the importance of the preoperative and the postoperative visit by the speech-language pathologist. Voice training after partial removal of the larynx usually requires searching with the patient for the best voice he or she can produce using various facilitating approaches. After total laryngectomy, the patient may use the artificial larynx, or use esophageal speech produced by the injection, inhalation, or swallow method or by introducing air into the esophagus through a tracheal-esophageal shunt.

References

AINSWORTH, S., Disorders of voice, English, G. M. (ed.): *Otolaryngology*. Philadelphia: Harper & Row (1980), Vol. 4, Chap. 13.

AMERICAN CANCER SOCIETY, *Cancer Facts and Figures, 1980*. New York: American Cancer Society (1980).

AMINOFF, M. J., H. H. DEDO, and L. IZDEBSKI, Clinical aspects of spasmodic dysphonia, *J. Neurology, Neurosurgery and Psychiatry, 41,* 361–365 (1978).

ANDERSON, V. A. and H. A. NEWBY, *Improving the Child's Speech*. 2nd Edition. New York: Oxford University Press (1973).

ARNDT, W. B., R. L. SHELTON, and L. J. BRADFORD, Articulation, voice, and obturation in persons with acquired and congenital palate defects, *Cleft Palate J., 2,* 377–383 (1965).

ARNOLD, G. E., Disorders of laryngeal function, *Otolaryngology,* eds., M. M. Paparella and S. A. Shumrick. Philadelphia: W. B. Saunders (1973).

ARNOLD, G. E. and S. PINTO, Ventricular dysphonia: new interpretation of an old observation, *The Laryngoscope, 70,* 1608–1627 (1960).

ARONSON, A. E., *Clinical Voice Disorders*. New York: Brian C. Decker Division, Thieme-Stratton, Inc. (1980).

ARONSON, A. E. and L. W. DE SANTO, Adductor spastic dysphonia: 1½ years after recurrent laryngeal nerve resection, *Annals Otolaryngo, 90,* 2–6 (1981).

ARONSON, A. E. and D. E. HARTMAN, Adductor spastic dysphonia as a sign of essential (voice) tremor, *J. Speech Hearing Disorders, 46,* 52–59 (1981).

ARONSON, A. E., H. W. PETERSON, and E. M. LITIN, Psychiatric symptomatology in hypernasality in cleft palate children, *Cleft Palate J., 1,* 329–335 (1964).

ARTIK (Arion Products, 1022 Nicollet Avenue, Minneapolis, Mn. 55403).

ASAI, R., Laryngoplasty after total laryngectomy, *Arch. Otolaryngol. 75,* 114–119 (1972).

BARTON, R. T., The whispering syndrome of hysterical dysphonia, *Annals Oto-Rhino-Laryngo, 64,* 156–164 (1960).

BARTON, R. T., Treatment of spastic dysphonia by recurrent laryngeal nerve section, *Laryngoscope, 89,* 871–878 (1979).

BATSAKIS, J. G., *Tumors of the Head and Neck*. Baltimore: Williams and Wilkins (1979).

BELL, A. M., The 'nasal twang,' *Modern Language, 5,* 75–76 (1890).

BENNETT, S. and B. WEINBERG, Acceptability ratings of normal, esophageal, and artificial larynx speech, *J. Speech Hearing Research, 16,* 608–615 (1973).

BILLER, H. F., M. L. SOM, and W. LAWSON, Laryngeal nerve crush for spastic dysphonia, *Annals Oto-Rhino-Laryngo, 88,* 531–532 (1979).

Bio-Feedback Systems Model B-1 (Bio-Feedback Systems, Inc., Boulder, Colorado.)

BLESS, D. and J. MILLER,   *Influence of mechanical and linguistic factors on lung volume events during speech.*
American Speech and Hearing Association Convention paper (1972).

BLESS, D. and J. H. SAXMAN,   *Maximum phonation time, flow rate, and volume change during phonation:
normative information on third-grade children.* American Speech and Hearing Convention paper (1970).

BLOCH, P.,   New limits of vocal analysis, *Folia Phoniatrica, 12,* 291–297 (1960).

BOCCHINO, J. V. and H. TUCKER,   Recurrent laryngeal nerve pathology in spastic dysphonia, *Laryngoscope, 88,* 971–978 (1978).

BOONE, D. R.,   Dismissal criteria in voice therapy, *J. Speech Hearing Disorders, 39,* 133–139 (1974).

BOONE, D. R.,   Modification of the voices of deaf children, *Volta Review, 68,* 686–692 (1966).

BOONE, D. R.,   *The Boone Voice Program for Children.* Tigard, Oregon: C. C. Publications (1980a).

BOONE, D. R.,   The optimal use of the larynx, *J. Research in Singing, 4,* 35–43 (1980b).

BOONE, D. R.,   Treatment of functional aphonia in a child and an adult, *J. Speech Hearing Disorders,
31,* 69–74 (1966).

BOONE, D. R.,   Voice disorders, *Introduction to Communication Disorders,* eds. T. Hixon, L. Shriberg,
and J. Saxman. Englewood Cliffs, N.J.: Prentice-Hall (1980c).

BOONE, D. R.,   Voice remediation: an eclectic approach, *Asha, 21,* 912–914 (1979).

BOONE, D. R.,   Voice therapy for children, *Human Communication, 1,* 30–43 (1974).

BOONE, D. R.,   Voice therapy in children, *Voice Disorders in School Children,* ed. by F. Garbee. Los
Angeles: California State Department of Education (1972).

BOUHUYS, A., D. F. PROCTOR, and T. MEAD,   Kinetic aspects of singing, *Applied Physiology, 21,*
483–496 (1966).

BOWMAN, S. A. and J. C. SHANKS,   Velopharyngeal relationships of /i/ and /s/ as seen cephalometri-
cally, *J. Speech Hearing Disorders, 43,* 185–191 (1978).

BRADFORD, L. J., A. R. BROOKS, and R. L. SHELTON,   Clinical judgment of hypernasality in cleft
palate children, *Cleft Palate J., 1,* 329–335 (1964).

BREWER, D. W. and G. McCALL,   Visible laryngeal changes during voice therapy. Fiberoptic study.
Annals Otolaryngo, 83, 423–427 (1974).

BROAD, D. J.,   Phonation, *Normal Aspects of Speech, Hearing, and Language,* eds. F. D. Minifie, T. J.
Hixon, and F. Williams, Englewood Cliffs, N.J.: Prentice-Hall (1973).

BRODNITZ, F. S.,   Hormones and the human voice, *Bulletin of the New York Academy of Medicine, 67,*
183–191 (1971a).

BRODNITZ, F. S.,   *Vocal Rehabilitation.* Rochester, Mn.: Whiting Press (1971b).

BRODNITZ, F. S.,   Voice problems of the actor and singer, *J. Speech Hearing Disorders, 19,* 322–326
(1954).

BULL, T. and J. COOK,   *Speech Therapy and ENT Surgery,* Oxford: Blackwell Scientific Publications
(1976).

BULLER, A.,   Nasality: cause and remedy of our American blight, *Quarterly J. of Speech, 28,* 83–84
(1942).

BZOCH, K. R.,   The effects of a specific pharyngeal flap operation upon the speech of forty cleft-
palate persons, *J. Speech Hearing Disorders, 29,* 111–120 (1964).

CALCATERRA, T. and D. ZWITMAN,   Vocal rehabilitation after partial or total laryngectomy, *California Medicine, 117,* 12–15 (1972).

CARPENTER, R. J., J. L. HENLEY-COHN, and G. G. SNYDER,   Spastic dysphonia: treatment by selec-
tive section of the r.l.n., *Laryngoscope, 89,* 2000–2003 (1979).

CARPENTER, R. J., T. J. McDONALD, and F. M. HOWARD,   The otolaryngologic presentation of
myasthenia gravis, *Laryngoscope, 89,* 922–928 (1979).

CASE, J.,   Vocal abuse in adults. In Mowrer, D. E. and Case, J. L., *Clinical Management of Speech Disorders,* Rockville, Md.: Aspen Systems Corp. (1982).

CHARLIP, W. S.,   *The Aging Female Voice: selected fundamental frequency characteristics and listener judgments.*
Unpublished doctoral dissertation. Purdue University, West Lafayette, Ind. (1968).

CHERRY, J. and S. MARGUILIES,   Contact ulcer of the larynx, *Laryngoscope, 78,* 1937–1940 (1968).

CLERF, L. S.,   Bilateral abductor paralysis of the larynx: results of treatment by modified King operation. *Annals Oto-Rhino-Laryngo, 59,* 38–46 (1955).

COFFIN, B.,   *Overtones of Bel Canto.* New Jersey: The Scarecrow Press (1981).

COMROE, J. H.,   *The Lung.* Chicago: The Year Book Publishers (1956).

COOPER, M.,   Direct vocal rehabilitation. *Approaches to Vocal Rehabilitation,* eds. M. Cooper and
M. H. Cooper. Springfield, Ill.: Charles C Thomas (1977).

COOPER, M.,   Papillomata of the vocal folds: a review, *J. Speech Hearing Disorders, 36,* 51–60 (1971).

Cooper-Rand Electrolarynx   (Luminaud, P.O. Box 257, 7670 Acacia Avenue, Mentor, Ohio 44060.)

CROUTER, L. A., *A cinefluorographic comparison of selected vowels spoken by deaf and hearing subjects.* Master's thesis, University of Kansas (1962).

CURRY, E. T., Hoarseness and voice change in male adolescents, *J. Speech Hearing Disorders, 16,* 23–24 (1949).

DAMSTE, P. H., Voice change in adult women caused by virilizing agents, *J. Speech Hearing Disorders, 32,* 126–132 (1967).

DANILOFF, R. G., Normal articulation processes, *Normal Aspects of Speech, Hearing, and Language,* eds., F. D.Minifie, T. J. Hixon, and F. Williams, Englewood Cliffs, N.J.: Prentice-Hall (1973).

DARLEY, F. L., *Diagnosis and Appraisal of Communication Disorders.* Englewood Cliffs, N.J.: Prentice-Hall (1965).

DARLEY, F. L., A. E. ARONSON, and J. R. BROWN, Differential diagnostic patterns of dysarthria, *J. Speech Hearing Research, 12,* 246–269 (1969).

DARLEY, F. L., A. E. ARONSON, and J. R. BROWN, *Motor Speech Disorders.* Philadelphia: W. B. Saunders (1975).

DAVIS, D. S. and D. R. BOONE, Pitch discimination and tonal memory abilities in adult voice patients, *J. Speech Hearing Research, 10,* 811–815 (1967).

DEAL, R. E., B. McCLAIN, and J. F. SUDDERTH, Identification, evaluation, therapy, and follow-up for children with vocal nodules in a public school setting, *J. Speech Hearing Disorders, 41,* 390–397 (1976).

DEDO, H. H., Recurrent laryngeal nerve section for spastic dysphonia, *Annals Oto-Rhino-Laryngo, 85,* 451–459 (1976).

DEDO, H. H., J. J. TOWNSEND, and K. IZDEBSKI, Current evidence for the organic etiology of spastic dysphonia, *J. Otolaryngol., 86,* 875–880 (1978).

DELAHUNTY, J. and J. CHERRY, Experimentally produced vocal cord granulomas, *Laryngoscope, 78,* 1941–1947 (1968).

DICKSON, D. R., Acoustic study of nasality, *J. Speech Hearing Research, 5,* 103–111 (1962).

DICKSON, S. and G. R. JANN, Diagnostic principles and procedures, *Communication Disorders, Remedial Principles, and Practices,* ed. by S. Dickson. Glenview, Ill.: Scott, Foresman & Co. (1974).

DIEDRICH, W. M., The mechanism of esophageal speech, *Sound Production in Man,* ed. by M. Krauss. New York: New York Academy of Sciences, 303–317 (1968).

DIEDRICH, W. M. and K. A. YOUNGSTROM, *Alaryngeal Speech.* Springfield, Ill.: Charles C Thomas (1966).

DRUDGE, M. K. and B. J. PHILIPS, Shaping behavior in voice therapy, *J. Speech Hearing Disorders, 41,* 398–411 (1976).

EBLEN, R. E., Limitations on use of surface electromyography in studies of speech breathing, *J. Speech Hearing Research, 6,* 3–18 (1963).

Echorder and Echordette (RIL Electronics Inc., Street Road and Second St. Pike, Southhampton, Pa. 18966.)

ECKEL, F. C. and D. R. BOONE, The s/z ratio as an indicator of laryngeal pathology, *J. Speech Hearing Disorders, 46,* 147–150 (1981).

ELLIS, P. D. M. and J. BENNETT, Laryngeal trauma after prolonged endo-tracheal intubation, *J. Laryngol., 91,* 69–76 (1977).

EYSENCK, H., Ed., *Handbook of Abnormal Psychology.* New York: Basic Books, Inc. (1961).

FAIRBANKS, G., *Voice and Articulation Drillbook.* New York: Harper and Brothers (1960).

FARMAKIDES, M. F. and D. R. BOONE, Speech problems of patients with multiple sclerosis, *J. Speech Hearing Disorders, 25,* 385–390 (1960).

FILTER, M. D., Proprioceptive-tactile-kinesthetic feedback in voice therapy, *Lang. Speech Hear. Services Schools, 5,* 149–151 (1974).

FILTER, M. D. and K. URIOSTE, Pitch imitation abilities of college women with normal voices, *J. Speech Hearing Assoc., Virginia, 22,* 20–26 (1981).

FINK, R. R. and R. J. DEMAREST, *Laryngeal Biomechanics.* Cambridge, Mass.: Harvard University Press (1978).

First Aid for Laryngectomees (New York: American Cancer Society) (1980).

FISHER, H. B., *Improving Voice and Articulation,* 2nd edition. New York: Houghton-Mifflin (1975).

FLACH, M., H. SCHWICKARDI, and R. SIMON, What influence do menstruation and pregnancy have on the trained singing voice? *Folia Phoniatrica, 21,* 199–205 (1969).

FLETCHER, S. G., Contingencies for bioelectronic modification of nasality, *J. Speech Hearing Disorders, 37,* 329–346 (1972).

FLETCHER, S. G. and D. A. DALY, Nasalance in utterances of hearing impaired speakers, *J. Communication Disorders, 9,* 63–73 (1976).

FORNER, L. and T. J. HIXON,   Respiratory kinematics in profoundly hearing-impaired speakers, *J. Speech Hearing Res., 20,* 373-408 (1977).

FOX, D. R. and M. BLECHMAN,   *Clinical Management of Voice Disorders.* Lincoln, Neb.: Cliffs Notes (1975).

FOX, D. R. and D. JOHNS,   Predicting velopharyngeal closure with a modified tongue-anchor technique, *J. Speech Hearing Disorders, 35,* 248-251 (1970).

FRABLE, M. S.,   Hoarseness, a symptom of pre-menstrual tension, *Arch. Otolaryngol., 75,* 66-67 (1972).

FROESCHELS, E.,   Chewing method as therapy, *Arch. Otolaryngol., 56,* 427-434 (1952).

FROESCHELS, E.,   Hygiene of the voice, *Arch. Otolaryngol., 37,* 122-130 (1943).

FROESCHELS, E., S. KASTEIN, and D. A. WEISS,   A method of therapy for paralytic conditions of the mechanisms of phonation, respiration, and glutination, *J. Speech Hearing Disorders, 20,* 365-370 (1955).

FRY, D. B. and L. MANÉN,   Basis for the acoustical study of singing, *J. Acoustical Society of America, 29,* p. 680 (1957).

GARDNER, W. H.,   Problems of laryngectomees, *Rehabilitation Record,* 15-18 (1961).

GATES, G. A.,   *Effects of Laryngeal Cancer and Its Treatment upon the Voice.* Short Course, American Speech-Language-Hearing Assoc. Convention, Detroit (1980).

GORDON, M. T., F. M. MORTON, and I. C. SIMPSON,   Airflow measurements in diagnosis assessment and treatment of mechanical dysphonia, *Folia Phoniatrica, 30,* 372-379 (1978).

GOULD, W. J.,   Quantitative assessment of voice function in microlaryngology, *Folia Phoniatrica, 27,* 190-200 (1975).

GRAY, B. B., G. ENGLAND, and J. L. MAHONEY,   Treatment of benign vocal nodules by reciprocal inhibition, *J. Behavioral Research Therapy, 3,* 187-193 (1965).

GREENE, M. C. L., *The Voice and its Disorders* (Fourth Edition). Philadelphia: J. B. Lippincott Company (1980).

HIRANO, M., J. OHALA, and W. VENNARD, The function of laryngeal muscles in regulatory fundamental frequency and intensity of phonation, *J. Speech Hearing Research, 12,* 616-628 (1969).

HIXON, T. J. and J. H. ABBS,   Normal speech production, *Introduction to Communication Disorders,* eds. Hixon, Shriberg, and Saxman. Englewood Cliffs, N.J.: Prentice-Hall (1980).

HIXON, T. J., M. D. GOLDMAN, and J. MEAD,   Kinematics of the chest wall during speech production: volume displacements of the rib cage, abdomen, and lung, *J. Speech Hearing Research, 16,* 78-115 (1973).

HIXON, T. J., D. KLATT, and J. MEAD,   *Influence of forced transglottal pressure changes on fundamental frequency.* Presented at Acoustical Society Meeting, Houston (1970).

HIXON, T. J., J. MEAD, and D. GOLDMAN,   Dynamics of the chest wall during speech production: function of the thorax, rib cage, diaphragm, and abdomen, *J. Speech Hearing Research, 19,* 297-336 (1976).

HIXON, T. J., J. H. SAXMAN, and H. D. McQUEEN,   The respirometric technique for evaluating velopharyngeal competence during speech, *Folia Phoniatrica, 19,* 203-219 (1967).

HOLLIEN, H.,   Vocal fold thickness and fundamental frequency of phonation, *J. Speech Hearing Research, 5,* 237-243 (1962).

HOLLIEN, H.,   Vocal pitch variation related to changes in vocal fold length, *J. Speech Hearing Research, 3,* 150-156 (1960).

HOLLIEN, H. and R. F. COLEMAN,   Laryngeal correlates of frequency change: a STROL study, *J. Speech Hearing Research, 13,* 271-278 (1970).

HOLLIEN, H. and J. F. MICHEL,   Vocal fry as a phonational register, *J. Speech Hearing Research, 11,* 600-604 (1968).

HOLLIEN, H. and G. P. MOORE,   Measurements of the vocal folds during changes in pitch, *J. Speech Hearing Research, 3,* 157-165 (1960).

HOLLIEN, H. and T. SHIPP,   Speaking fundamental frequency and chronologic age in males, *J. Speech Hearing Research, 15,* 155-159 (1972).

HONJO, I. and N. ISSHIKI,   Laryngoscopic and voice characteristics of aged persons, *Arch. Otolaryngol., 106,* 149-150 (1980).

HORII, Y. and B. WEINBERG,   Intelligibility characteristics of superior esophageal speech, *J. Speech Hearing Research, 18,* 413-419 (1975).

HORN, D.,   Laryngectomees: survey report, *International Assoc. Laryngectomees News, 7* (1962).

HOSHIKO, M. S.,   Electromyographic investigation of the intercostal muscles during speech, *Archives Physical Medicine & Rehabilitation, 43,* 115-119 (1962).

HULL, F. M., P. W. MIELKE, J. A. WILLEFORD, and R. J. TIMMONS,   *National Speech Hearing Survey.* Final report, Project 50978, Bureau of Education for the Handicapped, OE, HEW (1976).

Hunter Oral Manometer   (Hunter Manufacturing Co., Iowa City, Iowa.)

ISSHIKI, N., M. TANADE, and M. SAWADE,   Arytenoid adduction for unilateral vocal cord paralysis, *Arch. Otolaryngol., 104, 555-558* (1978).

ISSHIKI, N. and H. VON LEDEN,   Hoarseness: aerodynamic studies, *Arch. Otolaryngol., 80, 206-213* (1964).

IZDEBSKI, K., J. J. TOWNSEND, M. M. MERZENICH, and H. H. DEDO,   Laryngeal nerve in spastic dysphonia, *Proceedings of 17th International Congress of Logopedics and Phoniatrics, 1,* 117-121 (1977).

JACOBSON, E.,   *You Must Relax.* New York: McGraw-Hill Book Co. (1957).

JOHNSON, T. S.,   *Vocal Abuse Reduction Program.* Logan, Utah: Utah State University (1976).

JOHNSON, J. T., R. K. NEWMAN, and J. E. OLSON,   Persistent hoarseness: an aggressive approach for early detection of laryngeal cancer, *Postgrad Med., 67,* 122-126 (1980).

JUDSON, L. S. and A. T. WEAVER,   *Voice Science.* New York: Appleton-Century-Crofts (1965).

KALB, M. B. and M. A. CARPENTER,   Individual speaker influence on relative intelligibility of esophageal speech and artificial larynx speech, *J. Speech Hearing Disorders, 46,* 77-80 (1981).

KALLEN, L. A.,   Vicarious vocal mechanisms, *Arch. Otolaryngol., 20,* 460-503 (1934).

KANTNER, C. E.,   The rationale of blowing exercises for patients with repaired cleft palates, *J. Speech Disorders, 12,* 281-286 (1947).

KLEINSASSER, O.,   *Microlaryngoscopy and Endolaryngeal Microsurgery.* Trans. by P. W. Hoffman. London: Saunders (1968).

KLEINSASSER, O.,   *Microlaryngoscopy and Endolaryngeal Microsurgery: Technique and Typical Findings.* Baltimore: University Park Press (1979).

Language Master   (Bell and Howell Co., 7100 N. McCormick Rd., Chicago, Ill.)

LEEPER, H. A.,   Voice initiation characteristics of normal children and children with vocal nodules: a preliminary investigation, *J. Commun. Disorders, 9,* 83-94 (1976).

LEHMANN, Q. H.,   Reverse phonation: a new maneuver for examining the larynx, *Radiology, 84,* 215-222 (1965).

LEVINE, H. L., B. G. WOOD, M. RUSNOW, E. BATZA, and H. M. TUCKER,   Recurrent laryngeal nerve section for spasmodic dysphonia, *Annals Oto-Rhino-Laryngo., 88,* 527-530 (1979).

LEWY, R. B.,   Experience with vocal cord injection, *Annals Oto-Rhino-Laryngo., 80,* 440-450 (1976).

LING, D.,   *Speech and the Hearing Impaired Child: Theory and Practice.* Washington, D.C.: Alexander Graham Bell Assoc. for the Deaf (1976).

LUCHSINGER, R. and G. E. ARNOLD,   *Voice-Speech-Language Clinical Communicology: Its Physiology and Pathology.* Belmont, Ca.: Wadsworth (1965).

MACKWORTH-YOUNG, G.,   *What Happens in Singing.* London: Newman-Neame (1953).

MANUJA, S. L.,   Complications of long-term nasal & oral endotracheal intubation, *J. Laryngo. & Otology, 93,* 369-372 (1979).

MARTENSSON, A.,   The functional organization of the intrinsic laryngeal muscles, *Sound Production in Man,* ed. by M. Krauss. New York: New York Academy of Sciences, 91-97 (1968).

MASON, R. M. and D. W. WARREN,   Adenoid involution and developing hypernasality in cleft palate, *J. Speech Hearing Disorders, 45,* 469-480 (1980).

MAZAHERI, M.,   Prosthodontic care in *Cleft Palate & Cleft Lip: A Team Approach,* eds. Cooper, Harding, Krogman, Mazaheri, and Millard. Philadelphia: W. B. Saunders (1979).

McCLOSKY, D. B.,   General techniques and specific procedures for certain voice problems, *Approaches in Vocal Rehabilitation,* eds. M. Cooper and M. H. Cooper. Springfield, Ill.: Charles C Thomas, 138-152 (1977).

McCLUMPHA, S.,   *Cinefluorographic Investigation of Velopharyngeal Function in Selected Deaf Speakers.* Unpublished Master's thesis. University of Florida (1966).

McDOWELL, F. H. and J. E. LEE,   Extrapyramidal diseases, *Clinical Neurology,* 4, eds. A. B. Baker and L. H. Baker. Hagerstown, Md.: Harper and Row, Chapter 26 (1973).

McGLONE, R. E. and H. HOLLIEN,   Vocal pitch characteristics of aged women, *J. Speech Hearing Research, 6,* 164-170 (1963).

McGUIRT, W. F. and D. BLALOCK,   The otolaryngologist's role in the diagnosis and treatment of amyotrophic lateral sclerosis, *Laryngoscope, 90,* 1496-1501 (1980).

McWILLIAMS, B. J., A. S. LAVORATO, and C. D. BLUESTONE,   Vocal cord abnormalities in children with velopharyngeal valving problems, *Laryngoscope, 83,* 1745-1753 (1973).

MICHEL, J., H. HOLLIEN, and G. P. MOORE,   Speaking fundamental frequency characteristics of 15, 16, 17 year-old girls, *Language and Speech, 9,* 46-51 (1966).

MICHEL, J. F. and R. WENDAHL,   Correlatives of voice production, *Handbook of Speech Pathology and Audiology,* ed. by L. E. Travis. Englewood Cliffs, N.J.: Prentice-Hall (1971).

MILISEN, R.,   Methods of evaluation and diagnosis of speech disorders, *Handbook of Speech Pathology,* ed. by L. E. Travis. New York: Appleton-Century-Crofts (1957).

MINIFIE, F. D., T. J. HIXON, and F. WILLIAMS   (editors), *Normal Aspects of Speech, Hearing, and Language.* Englewood Cliffs, N.J.: Prentice-Hall (1973).

MIYAZAKI, T., T. MATSUYA, and M. YAMAOKA,   Fiberscopic methods for assessment of velopharyngeal closure during various activities, *Cleft Palate J., 12,* 107–114 (1975).

MOLL, K. L.,   Speech characteristics of individuals with cleft lip and palate, *Cleft Palate and Communication,* eds. D. C. Spriestersbach and D. Sherman. New York: Academic Press (1968).

MONCUR, J. P. and I. P. BRACKETT,   *Modifying Vocal Behavior.* New York: Harper and Row (1974).

MONSEN, R. B.,   Second formant transitions in the speech of deaf and normal-hearing children, *J. Speech Hearing Research, 19,* 279–289 (1976).

MONSEN, R. B.,   Toward measuring how well hearing-impaired children speak, *J. Speech Hearing Research, 21,* 197–219 (1978).

MONSEN, R. B., A. M. ENGEBRETSON and N. R. VERNULA,   Some effects of degrees on the generation of voice, *J. Acoust. Soc. Amer., 66,* 1680–1690 (1979).

MOOLENAAR-BIJL, A.,   The importance of certain consonants in esophageal voice after laryngectomy, *Annals Otol, Rhin., and Laryngo, 62,* 979–989 (1953).

MOORE, G. P.,   Have the major issues in voice disorders been answered by research in speech science? A 50-year retrospective, *J. Speech Hearing Disorders, 42,* 152–160 (1977).

MOORE, G. P.,   Voice disorders associated with organic abnormalities, *Handbook Speech Pathology,* ed. by L. E. Travis. New York: Appleton-Century-Crofts (1957).

MOORE, G. P. and H. VON LEDEN,   Dynamic variations of the vibratory pattern in the normal larynx, *Folia Phoniatrica, 10,* 205–238 (1958).

MORRIS, H. L. and J. K. SMITH,   A multiple approach for evaluating velopharyngeal competency, *J. Speech Hearing Disorders, 27,* 218–226 (1962).

MOSES, P. J.,   The psychology of the castrato voice, *Folia Phoniatrica, 12,* 204–215 (1960).

MOSES, P. J.,   *Voice of Neurosis.* New York: Grune and Stratton, Inc. (1954).

MURPHY, A. T.,   *Functional Voice Disorders.* Englewood Cliffs, N.J.: Prentice-Hall (1964).

MURRY, T. and E. T. DOHERTY,   Selected acoustic characteristics of pathologic and normal speakers, *J. Speech Hearing Research, 23,* 361–369 (1980).

MYSAK, E. D.,   Pitch and duration characteristics of older males, *J. Speech Hearing Research, 2,* 46–54 (1959).

NATION, J. E. and D. M. ABRAM,   *Diagnosis of Speech and Language Disorders.* St. Louis: C. V. Mosby (1977).

NEGUS, V. E.,   The mechanism of the larynx, *Laryngoscope, 67,* 961–986 (1957).

NETSELL, R.,   Speech physiology, *Normal Aspects of Speech, Hearing, and Language,* eds. F. D. Minifie, T. J. Hixon, and F. Williams. Englewood Cliffs, N.J.: Prentice-Hall (1973).

NETSELL, R. and T. HIXON,   A noninvasive method for clinically estimating subglottal air pressure, *J. Speech Hearing Disorders, 43,* 326–330 (1978).

NEWBY, H. A.,   *Audiology.* New York: Appleton-Century-Crofts (1972).

NICKERSON, R. S.,   Characteristics of the speech of deaf persons, *Volta Rev., 77,* 342–362 (1975).

OGURA, J. H. and H. F. BILLER,   Glottal reconstruction following extended frontolateral hemilaryngectomy, *Laryngoscope, 74,* 2181–2184 (1969).

OLSEN, B. D.,   *Comparisons of Sequential Interaction Patterns in Therapy of Experienced and Inexperienced Clinicians in the Parameters of Articulation, Delayed Language, Prosody, and Voice Disorders.* Unpublished doctoral dissertation. University of Denver (1972).

OTIS, A. B. and R. G. CLARK,   Ventilatory implications of phonation and phonatory implications of ventilation, *Sound Production in Man,* ed. by M. Krauss. New York: New York Academy of Sciences, 122–238 (1968).

PEACHER, G. M.,   Vocal therapy for contact ulcer of the larynx. A follow-up of seventy patients, *Laryngoscope, 71,* 37–47 (1961).

PEARSON, B. W., R. D. WOODS, and D. E. HARTMAN,   Extended hemilaryngectomy for T3 glottic carcinoma with preservation of speech and swallowing, *Laryngoscope, 90,* 1950–1961 (1980).

PERKINS, W. H.,   *Preventing Functional Dysphonia.* Los Angeles: Center for the Study of Communication Disorders. (ASHA Convention Scientific Exhibit.) (1981).

PERKINS, W. H.,   *Speech Pathology, an Applied Behavioral Science,* 2nd ed. St. Louis: C. V. Mosby (1977).

PERKINS, W. H.,   Vocal function: assessment and therapy, *Handbook of Speech Pathology and Audiology,* ed. by L. E. Travis. Englewood Cliffs, N.J.: Prentice-Hall, 505–534 (1971).

PETERSON, G. E. and H. L. BARNEY, Control methods used in a study of the vowels, *J. Acoustical Society, 24,* 175–184 (1952).

Phonic Mirror (H. C. Electronics, Inc., Belvedere-Tiburon, California 94920.)

POLOW, N. G. and E. D. KAPLAN, *Symptomatic Voice Therapy.* Tulsa, Okla.: Modern Education Corp. (1979).

PTACEK, P. H. and E. K. SANDER, Maximum duration of phonation, *J. Speech Hearing Disorders, 28,* 171–182 (1963).

RAVITS, J. M., A. E. ARONSON, L. W. DESANTO, and P. J. DYCK, No morphometric abnormality of recurrent laryngeal nerve in spastic dysphonia, *Neurology, 29,* 1376–1382 (1979).

REICH, A. R. and J. W. LERMAN, Teflon laryngoplasty: an acoustical and perceptual study, *J. Speech Hearing Disorders, 43,* 496–505 (1978).

ROBE, E., J. BRUMLIK, and P. MOORE, A study of spastic dysphonia, *Laryngoscope, 70,* 219–245 (1960).

ROSS, E. and M. MESULAM, Dominant language functions of the right hemisphere: prosody and emotional gesturing, *Arch. of Neurology, 36,* 144–148 (1979).

RUBIN, H. J. and C. C. HIRT, The falsetto, a high speed cinematographic study, *Laryngoscope, 70,* 1305–1324 (1960).

SAITO, H., T. MATSUI, M. TACHIBANA, H. NISHIMURA, and O. MIZUKOSHI, Experiences with the tracheo-esophageal shunt method for vocal rehabilitation after total laryngectomy, *Arch. Otolaryngol., 28,* 135–142 (1977).

SANDERS, W. H., The larynx, *Ciba Clinical Symposia, 16,* 67–99 (1964).

SANSONE, F. E. and F. W. EMANUEL, Spectral noise levels and roughness severity ratings for normal and simulated rough vowels produced by adult males, *J. Speech Hearing Research, 13,* 489–502 (1970).

SEASHORE, C. E., E. LEWIS, and J. G. SAETVIET, *Manual of Instructions and Interpretations for the Seashore Measures of Musical Talent.* New York: The Psychological Corp. (1960).

SENTURIA, B. H. and F. B. WILSON, Otorhinolaryngic findings in children with voice deviations, *Annals Oto-Rhino-Laryngo, 72,* 1027–1042 (1968).

SHEDD, D. P. and B. WEINBERG, *Surgical & Prosthetic Approaches to Speech Rehabilitation.* Boston: G. K. Hall (1980).

SHELTON, R. L., E. HAHN, and H. L. MORRIS, Diagnosis and therapy, *Cleft Palate and Communication,* eds. D. C. Spriestersbach and D. Sherman. New York: Academic Press (1968).

SHELTON, R. L., A. PAESANI, K. D. McCLELLAND, and S. S. BRADFIELD, Panendoscopic feedback in the study of voluntary velopharyngeal movements, *J. Speech Hearing Disorders, 40,* 232–243 (1975).

SHELTON, R. L. and W. C. TRIER, Issues involved in the evaluation of velopharyngeal closure, *Cleft Palate J., 13,* 127–137 (1976).

SHERMAN, D., The merits of backward playing of connected speech in the scaling of voice quality disorders, *J. Speech Hearing Disorders, 19,* 312–321 (1954).

SHIPP, T., P. MUELLER, and D. ZWITMAN, Letter: intermittent abductory dysphonia, *J. Speech Hearing Disorders, 45,* 283 (1980).

SINGER, M. I. and E. D. BLOM, An endoscopic technique for restoring voice after laryngectomy, *Annals Oto-Rhino-Laryngo., 89,* 529–533 (1980).

SISSON, G. A., F. M. McCONNEL, and J. A. LOGEMANN, Rehabilitation after laryngectomy with a hyopharyngeal voice prosthesis, *Century Conf. on Laryngeal Cancer,* eds. P. Alberti and D. Bryce. New York: Appleton-Century-Crofts (1974).

SKOLNICK, M. L., E. R. GLASER, and B. J. McWILLIAMS, The use and limitations of the barium pharyngogram in the detection of velopharyngeal insufficiency, *Radiology, 135,* 301–304 (1980).

SKOLNICK, M. L., J. SHPRINTZEN, G. McCALL, and S. ROKOFF, Patterns of velopharyngeal closure in subjects with repaired cleft palates and normal speech: a multi-view video-fluoroscopic analysis, *Cleft Palate J., 12,* 369–376 (1975).

SLOANE, H. N. and B. D. MACAULAY, *Operant Procedures in Remedial Speech and Language Training.* Boston: Houghton Mifflin (1968).

SOM, M. L. and L. M. ARNOLD, Hemilaryngectomy, *Otolaryngology, 5,* eds. D. Schenck and M. Miller. Hagerstown, Md.: W. F. Prior, 31–38 (1960).

SOMMERS, R. K. and D. C. BRADY, *A Manual of Speech and Language Training Methods Using the Echorder.* Southampton, Pa.: RIL Electronics Co. (1964).

SONNINEN, A., The external frame function in the control of pitch in the human voice, *Sound Production in Man,* ed. by M. Krauss. New York: New York Academy of Sciences, 68–90 (1968).

SPRIESTERSBACH, D. C., Assessing nasal quality in cleft palate speech of children, *J. Speech Hearing Disorders, 20,* 266–270 (1955).

STETSON, R. H.,   Can all laryngectomized patients be taught esophageal speech? *Transactions of American Laryngological Assoc., 59,* 59–71 (1937).

STEVENS, H.,   Conversion hysteria: a neurologic emergency, *Mayo Clinic Proceedings, 43,* 54–64 (1968).

TAIT, N. A., J. F. MICHEL, and M. A. CARPENTER,   Maximum duration of sustained /s/ and /z/ in children, *J. Speech Hearing Disorders, 45,* 239–246 (1980).

TAKAHASHI, H. and Y. KOIKE,   Some perceptual dimensions and acoustical correlates of pathologic voices, *Acta Oto-Laryngologica, 338,* 1–24 (1975).

TARNEAUD, J.,   The fundamental principles of vocal culturation and therapeutics of the voice, *Logos, 1,* 7–10 (1958).

TAUB, S.,   Air bypass voice prosthesis for vocal rehabilitation of laryngectomees, *Annals Oto-Rhino-Laryngo., 84,* 45–48 (1975).

TAUB, S., and L. H. BERGNER,   Air bypass voice prosthesis for vocal rehabilitation of laryngectomees, *Amer. J. Surgery, 125,* 748–752 (1973).

TEMPLIN, M. C. and F. L. DARLEY, *The Templin-Darley Tests of Articulation.* Iowa City, Ia.: Bureau of Educational Research and Service (1980).

THOMPSON, A. E.,   *Nasal Air Flow During Normal Speech Production.* Unpublished Master's thesis. University of Arizona (1978).

THURMAN, W. L.,   *An Experimental Investigation of Certain Vocal Frequency-Intensity Relationships Concerning Natural Pitch Level.* Unpublished Master's thesis. University of Iowa (1949).

THURMAN, W. L.,   Intensity relationships and optimum pitch level, *J. Speech Hearing Research, 1,* 117–123 (1958).

THURMAN, W. L.,   Restructuring voice concepts and production, *Approaches to Vocal Rehabilitation,* eds. M. Cooper and M. H. Cooper. Springfield, Ill.: Charles C Thomas, 230–255 (1977).

Tokyo Artificial Larynx   (James L. Parkin, M.D., University of Utah College of Medicine, 50 N. Medical Dr., Salt Lake City, Utah 48132.)

Tonar II   (Quan-Tech Division of KMS Industries, 43 So. Jefferson Rd., Whippany, N.J. 07981.)

TOOHILL, R. J.,   The psychosomatic aspects of children with vocal nodules, *Arch. Otolaryngol., 101,* 591–595 (1975).

TUCKER, H. M.,   Reinnervation of the unilaterally paralyzed larynx, *Annals Oto-Rhino-Laryngo, 86,* 789–794 (1977).

TUCKER, H. M., B. G. WOOD, H. LEVINE, and R. KATZ,   Glottic reconstruction after near total laryngectomy, *Laryngoscope, 89,* 609–618 (1979).

Tunemaster III   (Berkshire Instruments, Inc., 170 Chestnut St., Ridgewood, N.J. 07450.)

VAN DEN BERG, J. W.,   Register problems, *Sound Production in Man,* ed. by M. Krauss. New York: New York Academy of Sciences, 129–134 (1968).

VAN RIPER, C. and J. V. IRWIN,   *Voice and Articulation.* Englewood Cliffs, N.J.: Prentice-Hall (1958).

VAUGHAN, P.,   *The Pill on Trial.* New York: Coward-McCann (1970).

Visi-Pitch   (model 6087) (Pinebrook, N.J.: Kay Elemetrics Corp.) (1980).

Vocal Loudness Indicator   (LinguiSystems, Suite 806, 1630 Fifth Avenue, Moline, Ill., 61265) (1980).

Voice Monitor   (Communications Research Unit, Hollins, Virginia: Hollins College) (1977).

WARD, P. H., J. W. SANDERS, R. GOLDMAN, and G. P. MOORE,   Diplophonia, *Annals Oto-Rhino-Laryngo., 78,* 771–777 (1969).

WARREN, D. W.,   PERCI: a method for rating palatal efficiency, *Cleft Palate J., 16,* 279–285 (1979).

WEINBERG, B. and A. RIEKENA,   Speech produced with the Tokyo Artificial Larynx, *J. Speech Hearing Disorders, 38,* 383–389 (1973).

WEISS, D. and H. BEEBE,   *The Chewing Approach in Speech and Voice Therapy.* Basel, Switzerland: S. Karger (1951).

Western Electric Artificial Larynx   (Bell Telephone) (1980).

WHITED, R. E.,   Laryngeal dysfunction following prolonged intubation, *Annals Oto-Rhino-Laryngo, 88,* 474–478 (1979).

WHITLER, L. E.,   One of a Million, *Brotherhood of Locomotive Firemen and Enginemen's Magazine,* 1–6 (April 1961).

WILCOX, K. A. and Y. HORII,   Age and changes in vocal jitter, *J. Gerontol., 35,* 194–198 (1980).

WILLIAMS, R. T.,   Allergic laryngitis, *Annals Oto-Rhino-Laryngo, 81,* 558–565 (1972).

WILLIAMS, R. T., I. M. FARQUHARSON, and J. ANTHONY,   Fiberoptic laryngoscopy in the assessment of laryngeal disorder, *J. Laryngo., 89,* 299–306 (1975).

WILLIAMSON, A. B.,   Diagnosis and treatment of seventy-two cases of hoarse voice, *Quarterly J. Speech, 31,* 189–202 (1945).

WILSON, D. K.,   Children with vocal nodules, *J. Speech Hearing Disorders, 26,* 19–26 (1961).

WILSON, D. K.,   *Voice Problems of Children,* 2nd Edition. Baltimore, Md.: Williams and Wilkins Co. (1979).

WILSON, D. K.,   Voice re-education of adolescents with vocal nodules, *Arch. of Otolaryngol., 76,* 68–73 (1962).

WILSON, F. B., D. J. OLDRING, and J. MUELLER,   Recurrent laryngeal nerve dissection: a case report involving return of spastic dysphonia after initial surgery, *J. Speech Hearing Disorders, 45,* 112–118 (1980).

WILSON, F. B. and M. RICE,   *A Programmed Approach to Voice Therapy.* Austin: Learning Concepts (1977).

WOLPE, J.,   *The Practice of Behavior Therapy,* 2nd Edition. New York: Pergamon Press (1973).

WOODMAN, D. G. and D. POLLACK,   Bilateral abductor paralysis. The post-operative care and speech therapy following arytenoidectomy, *Laryngoscope, 60,* 832–839 (1950).

YANAGIHARA, N. Y. and H. VON LEDEN,   Respiration and phonation, *Folia Phoniatrica, 19,* 153–166 (1967).

ZEMLIN, W. R.,   *Speech and Hearing Science.* Englewood Cliffs, N.J.: Prentice-Hall (1968).

ZEMLIN, W. R.,   *Speech and Hearing Science,* 2nd Edition. Englewood Cliffs, N.J.: Prentice-Hall (1981).

ZWITMAN, D. H.,   Bilateral cord dysfunctions: abductor type spastic dysphonia, *J. Speech Hearing Disorders, 44,* 373–378 (1979).

ZWITMAN, D. H., M. T. GYEPES, and P. H. WARD,   Assessment of velar and lateral wall movement by oral telescope and radiographic examination in patients with velopharyngeal inadequacy and in normal subjects, *J. Speech Hearing Disorders, 41,* 381–389 (1976).

ZWITMAN, D. H., S. G. KNORR, and J. SONDERMAN,   Development and testing of an intraoral electrolarynx for laryngectomy patients, *J. Speech Hearing Disorders, 43,* 263–269 (1978).

ZWITMAN, D. H., J. C. SONDERMAN, and P. H. WARD,   Variations in velopharyngeal closure assessed by endoscopy, *J. Speech Hearing Disorders, 39,* 366–372 (1974).

Index